Critical Essays on
Patrick White

*Critical Essays on
World Literature*

Robert Lecker, General Editor
McGill University

Critical Essays on Patrick White

Peter Wolfe

G. K. Hall & Co. • Boston, Massachusetts

Library of Congress Cataloging-in-Publication Data

Critical essays on Patrick White / [compiled by] Peter Wolfe.
    p.   cm. — (Critical essays on world literature)
    Includes bibliographical references.
    ISBN 0-8161-8846-7
    1. White, Patrick, 1912–   —Criticism and interpretation.
I. Wolfe, Peter, 1933–   . II. Series.
PR9619.3.W5Z6 1990
823—dc20

                                                      89-38924
                                                      CIP

This publication is printed on permanent durable acid-free paper
MANUFACTURED IN THE UNITED STATES OF AMERICA

to Lew Fretz
the Kareem of Kiwiland

CONTENTS

ACKNOWLEDGMENTS

The author wants to thank Costa Haddad and Terry Jones of the University of Missouri-St. Louis College of Arts and Sciences for a grant to cover expenses pertaining to the preparation of the typescript; Marla Schorr for her help with clerical and editorial matters; and Patricia J. Steward of the Interlibrary Loan Division of Thomas Jefferson Library of the University of Missouri-St. Louis for locating important research materials.

INTRODUCTION

Whither the Bunyip Now?

"No formulation of the principal concerns of Patrick White's work comes easily" (131); thus begins the lead essay, by William J. Scheick, in the Summer 1979 special White issue of *Texas Studies in Literature and Language*.[1] In the issue's closing essay, Alan Lawson, probably the sharpest and most thorough student of White criticism, endorses Scheick's verdict: "The history of White criticism," says Lawson, "is full of utterly opposite, mutually exclusive thematic readings" (291). His claim makes us wonder if the confusion he and Scheick refer to stems from a creativity so robust and vital that it resists critical formulations. Or could it be traceable to a cloudy or perverse mind? In either case, it's clear that White criticism in the decade that has passed since Scheick's and Lawson's pronouncements is vast, varied, and illuminating, if not conclusive. Furthermore, this growing body of work abandons the critical trend, deplored by Lawson, to ignore previous studies of White in favor of treating him as if he had never been discussed before. Instead of providing general introductions, recent books and essays have shed fresh, revealing light on particular areas of his mind and art. Don Anderson describes eating as a form of secular and holy communion in White. Using Jungian archetypes, David J. Tacey (1983) finds in *The Solid Mandala* (1966) the key not only to White's artistic crises but to his personal ones as well. Veronica Brady (June 1983), yoking White's sensibility to national themes, reads *A Fringe of Leaves* (1976) as an affirmation of aboriginal values.

The books published on White in the 1980s, besides nullifying Lyndon Harries' 1978 complaint that "separate books on White . . . are still very few in number" (459), also reflect originality, vigor, and precision of focus. A. M. McCulloch's *A Tragic Vision* (1983), an Australian study, argues that the tension between Apollonian and Dionysian elements in White generates a religious tragedy along with a sense of human grandeur rarely attempted by writers today. In a book from Sweden, Mari-Ann Berg, in *Aspects of Time, Ageing and Old Age in the Novels of Patrick White* (1983), connects the passage

1

of time to motifs like childhood, betrayal, water, and clocks. Hilary Heltay's highly detailed analysis, *The Articles and the Novelist* (1983), from Germany, describes White using semantics and syntax to open channels of discourse with the reader. Applying the theories of Wilhelm von Humboldt, Paul Goodman, and Noam Chomsky, Heltay shows how grammatical function can modulate tone, vary perspective, and probe layers of consciousness. In another sharply focused study from Europe, the Swedish critic Karen Hansson, in her *Warped Universe* (1984), recounts the influence of the Bible, Arthurian legend, and individual figures like Blake, Schopenhauer, and Jung upon White's key symbols, like the desert, the garden, the tree, the rose, and the house. Though more general, Britain's John Colmer traces White's growth, explores both his social and moral criticism, and makes some telling artistic judgments in his *Patrick White* (1984). The American Carolyn Bliss leans more heavily upon metaphysics in *Patrick White's Fiction* (1986). Though it should not be indulged, the pain born of failure can transform and redeem; failure often promotes success in White because "its experience both humbles the sufferer and provokes him to further effort" (11).

As impressive as it is, the heightened critical activity of the 1980s has reached no consensus about White's creativity, even though White sometimes seems to be inviting one. There is evidence of a secular optimism and an interest in social bonding in his later work, underscored by his campaigning for both environmental causes and nuclear disarmament since the mid-1970s. The Sydney that is grimy, littered, and morally degraded in *The Tree of Man* (1955) and *Riders in the Chariot* (1961) throbs with warmth and vitality in *The Vivisector* (1970). At the end of *A Fringe of Leaves*, Ellen Roxburgh, following her enslavement by aboriginals, meets a London hardware merchant and widower called Jevons. Her addressing him in her local Cornwall idiom signals her acceptance of him. Though her words are commonplace, her diction lends them special meaning; for years, she never addressed her now-deceased husband in her relaxed cradle tongue. Her comic exchange with Jevons invokes compassion and solidarity. Responding in kind, he also uses regional speech. Brady sees this informality as White's acceptance of personal ties as a way to self-fulfillment. Unlike Theodora Goodman, perhaps White's first visionary, who leaves *The Aunt's Story* (1948) in moral isolation, Ellen appears at the end of *Fringe* alongside a possible intimate. She can help Jevons because, like him, she has lost a spouse. She has also achieved a dignified love with Jack Chance, Jevon's fellow Londoner, the escaped convict who restored her to civilization. "In effect," says Brady of all this, "the novel's center of gravity is closer to that of the traditional novel, being about education in the art of living with others" (1977, 135).

Nor does the endorsement of community start with *Fringe*. Vain and self-acting, Voss wanted no one's approval; he acted to impress nobody. He needed no reason to cross Australia in White's 1957 novel, only a purpose, which, coming from within, ignored outside justifications. Yet his desert trek teaches him that ordeals take on new meanings when shared by others. In weakness lies strength. Here is a truth that defies both reason and vanity. It also helps join him to the human family. Rather than positing an elite of suffering, *Voss* puts self-transcendence within everybody's reach. By failing to cross Australia's dry heart, Voss has created goals for others. Colonel Hugo Hebden, the explorer who twice searches for him after his disappearance, is the first of these others; Voss has inspired him to test his mettle in fresh ways. By such steps, personal development channels into the growth of a national self-awareness. But the Australian future that Voss has helped shape is not exclusively white or European. The aboriginal Jackie, his killer, to whom he is eternally linked, becomes a legend and a prophet. White hints that one of Jackie's dark-skinned hearers will feel vexed enough by his words to discover Voss's place in the aboriginal consciousness.

But such community values fade in White's latest work. Forsaking the social for the personal, Eddie Twyborn of *The Twyborn Affair* (1979), notes, "I would like to think myself morally justified in being true to what I am—if I knew what that is. I must discover" (63). Another who feels responsible to her uniqueness is the fictional memoirist of *Memoirs of Many in One* (1986). Voicing an anxiety more ontological than social, she says to a cabdriver, "I've got to discover . . . the reason for my presence on earth" (157). The crossdressing, role playing, and homosexuality both she and Eddie Twyborn use as means of self-discovery recur in White's 1983 play *Netherwood*. Such transformations justify Thelma Herring's labeling White a poetic novelist. In 1965 Herring said of White, "His affinity is with those who have tried to extend the frontiers of the novel in the direction of poetry" (3). Others have placed his creative core elsewhere. Patricia A. Morley's *The Mystery of Unity* (1972) begins, "The view of man and his world which underlies White's novels is religious in its basic orientation" (1). Morley then calls suffering, salvation, and atonement his leading concerns, arguing from the epigraph, supplied by Gandhi, to his first novel, *Happy Valley* (1939): "the purer the suffering, the greater the progress." Pain leads to spiritual growth. In 1980, Brady concurred with Morley's reading of White as a writer impelled by religion. Calling his tie to Australia "suspicious, if not antagonistic" and citing his relish in presenting those human functions "normally regarded as disgusting," Brady claims Divine Grace to be "the only thing that finally matters in White" (39).

The view that his artistic mainspring is religion finds support in White himself. Implying that necessity joins all things in our divinely ordered universe, he said in 1969, "Religion. Yes. That's behind all my books. . . . I believe God does intervene; I think there's a Divine Power, a Creator, who has influence on human beings if they are willing to be open to him" (McGregor, 220). Rejecting this self-assessment, some of White's critics deny that his warmest loyalties are spiritual. Leonie Kramer, for instance, asks that he be studied as a secular humanist (1973, 10). "Man is the measure of all things" (15) she claims of *Riders*, the novel of White's most heavily freighted with religious materials. Of the chariot that supplies the title of White's 1961 work, she says, disregarding its associations with the book of Ezekiel, Blake, and Jewish mysticism, "It is man-made, not divinely sent" (13). In 1984, Colmer also called White "a secular salvationist" (13). But, like Kramer before him, he slights important evidence. One wonders if White's fascination with the sordid and the brutal in *Vivisector* diverged so far from Colmer's humanist thesis that it prompted Colmer to limit his discussion of the novel to two pages. Other critics have placed White more comfortably in the here and now of everyday. Whereas Peter Beatson's *The Eye in the Mandala* (1976) spells out White's metaphysics, William Walsh, in *Patrick White's Fiction* (1977), stresses the writer's craving for raw experience. Literature for White, Walsh claims, is a form of impacted awareness and participation. Disregarding intellectual figurations and whirligigs, White immerses himself in life's gritty sensuousness, that is, its quantitative aspects.

These aspects acquire resonance from their human associations. Thus Dorothy Green noted in 1974 that White's politics and sociology needed more critical attention (285) and, more expansively, Lawson said of White five years later, "His vision is fundamentally comic" (291). Lawson also said in 1979 that an as yet unwritten article called "Sex and Humor in White's Novels" might explain White's "comprehensive concern with humanity" (284). Such an article would first have to explain the intense self-absorption characterizing White's treatment of sex. In sexual matters, White is always the rapt outsider, torn between attraction and revulsion. He does not rejoice over the human body; sex is not a celebration but a vile animal act with sorry consequences. Lovemakers in *Vivisector* and *Fringe* look like they are trying to hurt each other rather than give tenderness and joy; they couple in an animal's den. "Demanding the ultimate in depravity" (318), two lovers in *Vivisector* become stricken, moaning beasts whose "rooting" assumes "grotesque shapes" (325). The excessive brutality of his portrayals of sex shows the fear, loathing, and envy of a person whose puritanism and sensuality are at odds.

This clash could easily cramp or shrivel a person's sexuality and thus drive him or her to the sidelines (Colmer has referred to "White's extreme solipsism" [1978, 75]). Perhaps White made illuminati like Theodora Goodman of *Aunt's Story* and Mordecai Himmelfarb of *Riders* ugly so that he could accept their spiritual superiority more readily. But the view of White as a bystander goes against the idea, favored by Walsh and others, that he confronts reality so directly and forcibly that he wrests value not only from the ordinary but also from the repellent. White does immerse himself in the why of things to get at the truth. And truth for him always bypasses convenience and comfort. Hurtle Duffield, his artist-hero in *Vivisector*, faces the squalid and the ugly without flinching. His art thrives as a result. His art also supports the notion that White's own art defies the middle-class secularism haunting British fiction. The notion is not new. According to Brady in 1978, White's people are more real when alone than with others. Her argument gains credence from Eddie Twyborn's observation, "Everything important, alas, must be experienced alone" (*TA*, 80). White's true subject for Brady was morality, which she saw as a function, not of personal ties, but of the dialectic born of the tension between a person's body and spirit: "For White, solitude, not society, is the true human milieu, and passivity, not action, the proper mode of being. . . . Characters primarily inhabit their own inner space and draw their strength from it" (111). Identity precedes belonging; a person must be something before he or she can be part of something else. Listening to the private voices of his characters, White records buried experience— the poems we might have written and the lovers we might have embraced. The last sentence of *The Solid Mandala* reads, "Then she [Mrs. Poulter] turned, to do the expected things, before re-entering her actual sphere of life" (309). If the traditional novel in Britain studies social development, Mrs. Poulter's retreat into the opacities of self aligns White with a different literary convention. Perhaps Brady is right to call it "Wisdom literature" (1978, 109).

But she'd also admit that such writing tends to smugness, self-congratulation, and the cultivation of intellectual snobbery. Now White's highly developed and refined art does sneer at Australian middle-class values. But it also records the restiveness and upheaval caused by the loss of cultural continuity. Here is no abdication of social conscience. Though he deplores his countrymen's struggles for goods, land, and cash, his commitment to their souls reveals a sensibility finely tuned to the inner realities structuring their lives. He has tallied the cost of middle-class prosperity. We have already seen how *Voss* describes myth biting into the Australian psyche. *The Tree of Man* also explores the continuities linking people both to each other and to their shared environment. The book's portrayal of an age simpler than ours shows what we have come out of and what we have come through. *Tree* gains legendary grandeur from its common background. The struggles it depicts with flood, fire, and drought could take place almost anywhere. The unconscious unity that the locals display in these crises helps evoke the infancy of our urban culture. Hardship encourages neighbors to join ranks and, by stages, welds them into a community. One family will lighten another's burden, as when the O'Dowds loan Amy Parker their goat to nurse a calf whose mother has contracted milk fever. Many families take part in the novel's next instance of social bonding. Responding to the damage caused by the Willunya floods, local men form volunteer rescue teams while the women dispense bread and soup. The "iron rain" (67) that washes away property and takes life also promotes valor, sacrifice, and a community spirit the area has never before known. With the mayor and the governor cheering them on, the men and women of Durilgai have affirmed the worth of their scrap of sodden turf by risking their health and their lives.

How their heroics fuel a solid sustaining vision in White still needs to be worked out. Perhaps the essays included in this volume will yield some answers and create some approaches to his main themes. You will read the words of yea-sayers and nay-sayers, of Australians and writers from the Northern Hemisphere. These men and women will look at White's plays, short stories, and novels; they will discuss his leading ideas, judge his artistry, and compare him to other creative artists; in some cases, the focus will sharpen to single works, while in others it will open out to survey the forces undergirding his whole career. White's own statements about his work from four decades will show how his amazing career has both developed predictably and branched off into zones of imaginative activity that could not have been forecast.

Overhanging all are White's many bleak thoughts on human nature. So often do these occur that they imply some private sorrow. His practice of making his people look ugly, foolish, or faded has the effect of mocking human purpose itself. No sooner does he show someone acting generously than he belittles the character: "He showed his white teeth, on which a piece of dark fruit had stuck" (*AS*, 265), he says of a man who has just offered a stranger a bed for the night. The presence in his latest work of his drive to denigrate casts further doubt on his ability to dispense simple humanity. *Memoirs of Many in One* (1986) shows rhetorical brilliance serving the dubious end of ridicule: "Reverend Mother is frowning. . . . I am always fascinated by the little black mole at the entrance of her left nostril. Now it is almost jumping off her skin like some demented insect" (110). His most recent work, *Three Uneasy Pieces* (1987), also contains an excess of bile. As in *Vivisector* and *The Eye of the Storm* (1973), the antipodean pseudochic displayed at social gatherings receives more of his malice than is warranted. He degrades party-goers in the story "Dancing with Both Feet on the Ground" by showing them stuffing their pimpled, greasy faces with rich food, wearing gaudy garb, and blundering socially while believing themselves tasteful and elegant.

White scorns Australian consumerism, vulgarity, and superficiality. The smooth, practical suburbanite who covets earthly trophies ignores life's depth and complexity. Those intent on nothing but success and pleasure, White reasons, have perverted what is most human in themselves. But, as his disparagement of the party guests in "Dancing" shows, nowhere does he lash out more angrily at his countrymen as when they aspire to culture and refinement. Is his anger disproportionate? Walsh's reference to "that sense of the nastiness of human life of which Patrick White seems to have had more than his normal share" (1976, 48) draws attention once more to an obsessive preoccupation with people's blemishes and flaws. This preoccupation also calls into question the accuracy of White's instincts about people. In asking how one should live well, White purports to be searching for the best human life. Yet his struggles both to understand and to cope with the problems of being human run afoul of that malaise or maladjustment that Walsh calls nastiness. The duality implied by John Weigel between worldly failure and spiritual triumph slights the resentment gnawing at the discard: "White's eccentrics often turn out to make more sense than the allegedly sane and reasonable people around them. Although their neighbors may shun them, their creator, the novelist, obviously loves them" (43).

And how does he declare his love? Life for White's eccentrics, or visionaries, is a matter of unrelenting travail. Hansson does well to ask, "*Who are the elect?* and *What results do they achieve?*" (215). Though White infers that only the life of the spirit is worth living, he does not link spiritual reality either to love of God or to any social gospel. Sometimes, a character's spirituality even thwarts self-preservation. Illumination in White brings the loss of reason in *Aunt's Story* and the loss of life in *Tree, Vivisector,* and *Fringe.* Stan Parker's theophany in *Tree,* for instance, coincides with the cerebral stroke that kills him. White does not let him savor, let alone share, his vision. By bilking him of the chance to act upon his spiritual breakthrough, White questions both the value of the breakthrough and his own understanding of it. Smiting his visionaries at the moment of vision suggests a failure of either imagination or nerve. This failure informs the confusion Colmer feels when he tries to analyze White's values, loyalties, and preferences. White, grumbles Colmer, divides "his characters into the saved and the damned, but it is not always easy to know what it is that saves and what damns" (1984, 22).

We share Colmer's disquiet. In his elect, White offers no vision of human goodness trapped in moral squalor or degradation. Manfred

Mackenzie calls the four riders of *Riders* "the sides of the soul of a giant Everyman, which is seen here as a divine quaternity" (17). In view of the suffering the riders both absorb and inflict, Mackenzie invites disagreement. How has the pain that occurs in the presence of the riders gained the world a bargain? Have we missed something? White deprives his riders of friends and (with one exception) family, has them commit acts of destruction, and stops them from communicating any vision that may stem from their anguish. Betrayal, guilt, and failure dog them all. Mary Hare accepts the blame for the death of her father as does Ruth Godbold for that of her brother. Haunted because he was seduced by the minister who helped raise him, the aboriginal artist Alf Dubbo goes to Sydney, the city of dreadful night, where he sleeps in a rubbish tip, gets beaten up, and becomes infected with tuberculosis and venereal disease.

The fourth rider, Mordecai Himmelfarb, also knows pain, as Berg has shown: "His road to deeper spiritual insight is so severe that in a sense it destroys his chances of leading a meaningful life. He acquires humility and acceptance but loses something that is so important that he can never really recover from it" (59). This crushing loss comes in several stages. The dangers of being a Jew in Nazi Germany culminated for him in the discovery, after dining with Christian friends, that his wife Reha was arrested and presumably killed by Hitler's storm troopers. To mortify himself, he sheds the privileges and honors he had won as an academic to work as a menial in Australia. His penance proves even harsher than he had expected. Exhausted by traveling across greater Sydney, he is denied the traditional hospitality extended by Jews to each other at Passover; his house burns; he is crucified by some coworkers as an Easter joke.

This last torment shows how White's visionaries often bring out the worst in others. Like Himmelfarb, the other three riders suffer at the hands of those close to them. Mary Hare is mistreated by both her father and her housekeeper-companion; Dubbo is sexually exploited not only by his mentor-minister but also by his landlady; after squandering his paycheck on booze and whores, Ruth Godbold's wife-beating husband dies, leaving her to support herself and her six daughters as a washerwoman.

The illuminati in White's other books also live in a climate of harm. In killing a hawk, Theodora Goodman of *Aunt's Story* kills part of herself, just as his denial of his feminine side leads to Waldo Brown's death in *Mandala*. Called by Colmer "the embodiment of natural goodness and intuitive wisdom" (1984, 32), Doll Quigley of *Tree* murders her retarded brother because she fears that he will not be able to look after himself after she dies. The mercy killing recoils on her: "Doll Quigley was in hell" (484), notes Amy Parker on a visit to her old neighbor and friend in a local asylum. Death also emerges as a function of closeness in *Vivisector*, where Hurtle Duffield drives two lovers to suicide.

As Brady has shown, wreckage like this curbs our approval of White's elect: "Though his heroes and heroines may be 'saints,' they are often also unpleasant people, so that asking the reader to admire them entails a perversion of thought and feeling" (1978, 112). This unpleasantness goes beyond a valid wish on White's part to fend off easy moral judgments. To show a person on both sides of an issue is to show society in action. It also demonstrates that no individual can possess the truth. But White's disparagement of his visionaries is no Brechtian alienation tactic. Except perhaps for Voss and Hurtle, he is not prodding us to think about the impact of his illuminatis' endeavors at the expense of their persons. Rather, he sometimes seems both to relish their woes and to heap on more of them for presuming to probe life's underlying mysteries.

Perhaps the no-win process operates like this: the spiritually gifted person perceives reality more keenly than the rest of us. But his intensity of vision also sets him so far apart from us that he can not come back. Committing oneself to the ineffable causes madness; Sophocles' sphinx, Shakespeare's Fool, and Melville's Pip in *Moby-Dick* all spoke in riddles because they dared not express their visions directly. White's Doll Quigley and Arthur Brown come to grief, having neglected the split between the human and the divine. One must stand close enough to the divine fire to be warmed, but not so close as to be burned. On the other hand, the hearts of those who shrink from the flames stay frozen; the shallow and the complacent can never perceive the truth.

White is not just an important Australian writer; he is also a major international figure. His works bring courage and wisdom to the darkest corners of experience. Yet they also seem to have been written from motives of spite and malice. The spiritual insights won by his elect pale alongside the suffering that brings them about. Theodora Goodman punctures the grandiose and the inflated in order to affirm "the state of simplicity" that in "The Prodigal Son" White called "the only desirable one for artist or man" (1958, 39). When asked if she believes in God, Theodora replies, "I believe in this table" (*AS*, 146). Later she will say, "I believe in a pail of milk" (159), just as her successor, Stan Parker, will say, "I believe in the cracks in the path" (*TM*, 497) leading to his garden. White is not the first major writer to anchor his epistemology in suffering; gain also grows from loss in Goethe, Carlyle, and Henry James. What causes worry in White is the skimpiness of the gain. Is Theodora's belief in a table or a pail of milk enough of an achievement for a woman of forty-five who said as a twelve-year-old when a bolt of lightning slammed her to earth that she wanted to know everything?

Obviously, White thinks so, since he has Hurtle ask in *Vivisector* if anything could be more real than a kitchen table (420).

Nor can we snipe at his belief that the supernal takes root in the ordinary. What puzzles and rankles is how the vision of the supernal runs to waste. "Suffering in White is always teleological" (142), says Beatson, and evidence can be found to support his claim. After great anguish, Voss dies. But his soul is reborn in others as he expands into a legend. And where does Voss fit in the process? Yes, he has enriched the sense of Australianness in those who have responded physically and imaginatively to his struggle. In so doing, he has won a place in both white and aboriginal hearts. But, setting aside the question of whether he would have rather renounced this higher purpose in favor of marrying Laura Trevelyan, we must point out that the novel ends before his vision bears fruit. And *will* it bear fruit? Though Colonel Hebden will search for Voss's remains in the desert, he stands no better chance of success than he did when he came back empty-handed from a similar expedition eighteen years before. Yet Hebden does stand *a* chance. As slim as it is, it surpasses any hopes that might have awaited Theodora, Stan Parker, and Hurtle, all of whose epiphanies vanish before they can induce a new way of being.

Has the pain that brought about their epiphanies been wasted? White's world is rarely gentle and caring, tidy and warm. Perhaps helped by the pieces reprinted in this volume, future critics will show how this harsh world holds, sustains, and inspires White even as it vexes him. The recurring motifs in the work of this moody genius evoke gall and gloom. Rotten eggs appear in his 1939 novel *Happy Valley* and his 1983 play *Netherwood.* A man is run over by a bus in both *The Living and the Dead* (1941) and "A Woman's Hand" (*Australian Letters,* August 1966). A man loses a hand in war in *Tree* and in *Twyborn;* a woman's hair is burned off in *Tree* and hacked off in *Fringe;* characters contract boils in *Fringe* and *Voss* (which also includes a nasty landowner named Boyle). Yet the same writer who can portray his people as weak, selfish, and cowardly will also show them scaling great heights of courage and dedication. The human body that sometimes disgusts him also houses transcendence. In deference to such complexity, he will voice a cherished belief through one of his scurviest characters, as in the following words of Mrs. Jolley, from Chapter 4 of *Riders:* "Everybody is unfortunate, if you can recognize it. . . . But there are usually compensations for misfortune" (71). Some statements of belief will clash with evidence drawn from action and character. Called the source of renewal in *Fringe* (382), women damage their children with their selfishness and cruelty, perhaps irreparably, in *Aunt's Story, Mandala, Vivisector,* and *Eye of the Storm.* For instance, A. M. McCulloch refers to Elizabeth

Hunter of *Eye* as White's "ultimate poet-seer" (109) and his "most complex and dynamic elected character" (128), an assessment that goes against her daughter's condemnation of her as "sensual, mendacious, materialistic, superficial" (*ES*, 589).

Does White encourage such contradictions? In 1978, Ron Shepherd wondered whether some inner demon drove him to withhold from his readers the satisfaction he also denies his stricken characters: "There appears to be a deliberate mystification in White that whenever the author's commitment to some particular idea threatens to become too apparent he will deliberately resort to a rhetoric of uncertainty in order to vitiate any glib conclusion" (32). Glib or satisfying? And does White shift his thinking along with his rhetoric? At times, he claims that ultimate truth not only defies expression; it cannot even be imagined. We never perceive the essence, only the sum of so many parts, and we perceive it from the outside. We lack the vision to penetrate the flaming quick. But if the attainment of divine truth is not given to people, neither is self-knowledge. Carolyn Bliss notes in White's people "the inability to locate, recognize, or permit the true self" (8), and the emptiness of their quests for self-integration supports her claim. Just before his death, Stan Parker intuits a oneness with all of life; he has sensed the grandeur permeating all things. Yet he has also remained ignorant of both the secret places of his heart and the central realities of his life. He and Amy start out as newlyweds, barely acquainted with each other and with the tough, remote area where they have settled. They leave us, and each other, some fifty years later, just as puzzled over their joint existence. Through it all, Stan has toiled in the thickets of ambiguity. He takes his pick, axe, and shovel into the wilderness, where he builds a home, grows crops, and raises livestock. As he acquires ballast and social standing, he makes the land fruitful and orderly. But neither his marriage nor his soul thrives as his farm does. His productiveness and his good name walk together with a growing sense of isolation, puzzlement, and regret he never dispels.

Eddie Twyborn's search for self-being ends in greater frustration. Having lived as a woman for twenty years in between-wars London, he happens upon his mother, perhaps the only person in the world with whom he can risk being himself. Their reunion takes place on a bench adjoining the church where Eadie, now old and widowed, came to pray. She and Eddie/Eadith scribble notes to each other on the flyleaf of her prayer book. After the latter identifies herself as Eadie's daughter, in response to being asked if she's Eadie's son, Eadie says, "I am so glad. I've always wanted a daughter" (*TA*, 423). Eadith takes heart that her mother has seen through her disguise; the recognition proclaims Eadith's existence as solid and abiding.

Moreover, this existence has been welcomed on its own terms. Eadith has finally been accepted for herself.

She can now risk the next step. Buoyed up by her new self-confidence, Eadith becomes Eddie. He puts on men's clothes during the London Blitz. The bomb that kills him en route to his mother seems like a pessimist's practical joke. It also invokes an important question: how can White's people, lacking self-knowledge and self-command, pretend to know God? Logic would decree that the whole cannot be known before the part. But White, ever the intuitionist, said in 1969, "Practically anything I have done of any worth I feel I have done through my intuition, not my mind" (McGregor, 220). The flouting of logic has created new outlets for him. By setting forth themes that he cannot grasp firmly enough to control, he frees himself from the constraints imposed by reason and by time. In *Fringe*, Ellen Roxburgh and Jack Chance dream the same dream simultaneously, and Theodora Goodman wonders in *Aunt's Story* about "the way you can sometimes grasp experience before it's undergone" (80).

But why bother to probe these inner planes of experience? A character in *Netherwood* asks of the truth, "Did that ever bring peace of mind?" (34). The question needs to be asked. As has been seen, people in White who try to know God and to realize their divine potential will meet grief; the task of completing the self ends in self-undoing. But White also believes that self-transcendence is a basic duty; the person who settles for creature comforts and who mouths the stock phrases of whatever creed is in fashion betrays himself. The surrender of ego enriches the ego. Though uniqueness is to be cherished, it can also be enhanced or overcome; loss of self leads to the discovery of hidden aspects of self. Voss's recognition that he is not divine shows him ways to develop his divine potential.

These ways, though, are not everybody's; White offers no prescription for the attainment of freedom and fullness of being. Other than showing how the self must be abandoned before becoming whole, he leaves the drama of self-integration to the individual. "The seed can be sown . . . in many ways" (129), he says in *Riders*. All have pitfalls; all invite danger. None suit everybody. When asked to explain her vision, Ruth Godbold, in the same book, answers, "If I was to tell . . . it doesn't follow that you would see. Everybody sees different. You must only see it for yourself" (285). In each case, though, the quester should be judged on the basis of what he or she attempts, not accomplishes. Theodora Goodman ends her pilgrimage in isolation, Ellen Roxburgh in community. Voss, the most intrepid pilgrim of all, is called both a devil (435) and a saint (438). He also focuses White's 1957 novel because his pride makes his redemption more arduous, intricate, and drawn out than those of his counterparts. But narrative selection does not make him metaphysically preferable to the minor figure, the suburban matron Belle Bonner Radclyffe. "Noted for an opulent and complaisant kindness" (424) and "so constituted that she was always persuaded to see the best in human nature" (426), Belle gains self-being by staying home, raising a family, and socializing. Presumably, she never had to destroy herself prior to becoming solid.

If White's casual treatment of her attainment implies a sadistic relish for the depiction of grief, it also extends the range of behavior through which attainment comes. This range can surge forth triumphantly; the seed can be sown in many ways, indeed. A man in *The Living and the Dead*, White's second novel, intuits "a mystery of juxtaposition" (211). His remark foreshadows one in *Aunt's Story* that calls "true permanence . . . a state of multiplication and division" (278). Permanence also interweaves illusion and reality. Permanence describes the growth and change underlying all existence as a waltz rhythm of melting, converging, splicing, absorbing, branching off, stripping away, and colliding. Both Mrs. Hunter and Theodora achieve revelation through a single overwhelming crisis—Theodora's flattening by a lightning bolt and Mrs. Hunter's being pelted and wrung by a cyclone. Attainment comes to Hurtle and Stan Parker piecemeal rather than all at once. Stan's tour of army duty, his visits to Sydney, and his homesteader's struggles with crops, animals, and weather all hone his vision.

Hurtle's translation involves passing through different phases rather than wheeling in a cycle dictated by the flow of seasons. Though these dramas knit, making a tight cable, they also form discrete units. As a child, Hurtle climbs from the gutter into the gentry. Then he goes to Europe as a soldier, staying on to build and refine both his vision and his craft. After returning to Sydney, he moves "up the line," living rough and painting in the Outback. His second return to Sydney, following this obligatory term of residence alongside his cultural roots, finds him committing himself to others, an effort of the heart that had defeated him earlier. Finally, he overcomes the stroke that paralyzes his painting arm to paint the strange, visionary pictures of his maturity.

Mary Hare, one of White's four riders, follows a different agenda to gain enlightenment. "Eventually I shall discover what is at the center," she says, "if enough of me is peeled away" (57). Peeling away the extraneous, she believes, will disclose her true self. Like Stan and Arthur Brown, she enacts the drama of soul-building close to home, whereas Theodora, Voss, Himmelfarb, and Eddie Twyborn all travel great distances. Their wayfaring calls attention to other differences and similarities. The four wayfarers all seek truth on the edge, not in the middle, like Mary, Arthur, and Stan. But while Stan, as we have seen, has attuned himself to the seasons, Mary and Arthur both seek the truth by nuzzling and burrowing—into shrubs and plants, under the earth, and below the nap of animal fur.

The quest for meaning must also occur within the person. In a 1983 essay, the persevering and perceptive Veronica Brady said, "the dialectical struggle between the two sides of the self [in White] is the fundamental rhythm of existence" (180). The interplay between different sides of a person both confirms the fluidity of existence and promotes self-unity. The self is refreshed and redeemed by encountering the Other. Characters in White who find a neglected, forgotten, or suppressed side of themselves also tap wellsprings of creative energy. The primitive in us not only teaches and delights the sophisticate; it also helps survival. Ellen Roxburgh saves herself by resurrecting the rural values and practices she had suppressed after marrying into the gentry; the dark buried self that comes to life amid her aboriginal captors stirs impulses in her more human than savage. Himmelfarb, Arthur, and Hurtle all heal an internal rift by finding the woman inside them. Conversely, Waldo Brown, Arthur's twin, dies because he tries to suppress his femaleness. Unfortunately, neither his failure nor Arthur's success sets an example for Eddie Twyborn. Androgyny, a fount of strength in *Mandala,* brings shame, denial, and fragmentation in *Twyborn,* Eddie's extended drag act clouding, rather than sharpening, his manhood.

But if White resists giving an agenda for the attainment of clarity and unity, he will show the attainment's effects. The process echoes Keats's ideal in the "Nightingale" ode, where the birdlike singer blends with its songs. Hurtle Duffield knows this harmony, if only fitfully. In his most exalted creativity, he does not know if he is the painter or the thing being painted. The harmony swathing artist and artifact can touch and irradiate personal ties. A woman watching the Brown brothers walking hand in hand observes, "It was difficult to decide which was leading and which was led" (*SM,* 10–11). Finally, the way two women embrace during adversity in *Netherwood* confuses the protector from the protected in an onlooker's eyes.

Now White has always insisted that ultimate truth is out of reach, just like the perfect relationship or the ideal work of art. Yet he has added that God reveals Himself in "inklings" (*FG,* 74). These will release their goodness more easily if approached with a mentality more Eastern than Western. Useful help comes in William Walsh's phrase, "creative tranquility in the midst of turbulence in *The Eye of the Storm*" (1976, 31). By being hurled into the still center of the storm that tore and hammered her fifteen years before the novel's present-tense action, Mrs. Hunter learns the universal parity of existence. This moment of oneness joins her to creation; in both thought and feeling, she identifies with the surrounding wreckage. Later, on her deathbed, she refers to "that state of pure living bliss she was now and then allowed to enter" (*ES*, 24). She is contemplating a level of being where she drifts between being asleep and awake and where distinctions like past and present have disappeared. Besides reordering ontological categories, this semi-consciousness both relaxes her will and lets her blind woman's inner eye take charge. Experienced on the inner planes of perception, things disclose their unity, their stillness flowing into that of the perceiver. Surrendering ego, Mrs. Hunter has transcended judgment and division. Existence itself becomes active, even imperative.

She has merged with the world spirit, having achieved an exalted state where all divisions vanish, even those governing life and death. She no longer needs to impose herself. But by silencing the will, she strengthens and sharpens the will. Her last recorded thought grazes this paradox: "Till I am no longer filling the void with mock substance: myself is this endlessness" (*ES*, 551). Because she cannot imagine the universe apart from her perception of it, she blends with it. But the harmony is short-lived; the finite cannot dwell with the infinite this side of death. Having eclipsed duality, she awaits her final translation. The steps leading to this moment of supremacy recall the dance of Shiva, the Hindu god of destruction, which starts slowly and then speeds till it undoes the work of creation—and the world ends. Like Yeats's interlocking gyres, the collision of the forces of destruction and creation produces a miraculous new order of being, or nonbeing, that defies all description and analysis. This state is called "nirvana," the Sanskrit meaning of which is "extinction," as in the blowing out, or extinguishing, of a candle flame. This eternal silencing of all desires clashes with the Western ideal of the resurrection of the body. In place of everlasting life, nirvana offers eternal union with Brahma; the self, the pampered darling of the West, abandons the fret and insecurity of individual existence to join with the supreme spirit. This blessedness—"the peace that passeth understanding"—eclipses thought and language; White has seen it slip through his rounded locutions, sonorous pronouncements, and epigrammatic flashes. But it can be dramatized and poeticized. The irrational or subreflective modes of interaction he sometimes depicts work as they should—they surmise or glimpse the inexpressible. Concepts that cannot be defined and feelings that cannot be felt touch us at some subliminal level.

Always, there is an insistence that rational discourse will miss this hidden, vital truth, White bemoaning throughout the canon the inadequacies of language. "The truth stops where the words begin" (*Four Plays*, 35), says a character in Act I of *The Ham Funeral* (1947). When asked if a certain conversation told her anything important, a woman in *Voss* replies, "Not in words" (104). "Oh, words, words . . . I do not understand what they mean" (162), complains Mary

Hare of *Riders*, perhaps echoing her author's wish that language could do more than it does. That author puts a different spin on his veiled wish in Elizabeth Hunter's statement, "You can never convey in words the utmost of experience" (*ES*, 414). Yet, in *Mandala* in 1966, seven years before the publication of *Eye*, White seemed content that the most vital, truthful, and accurate expression of reality is wordless. The last—and perhaps key—movement in Arthur Brown's dance of the mandala ends with "his mouth . . . a silent hole, because no sound was needed to explain" (257). We are back in the Hindu sphere. The ultimate revelation defies language.

Readers have noted how stillness and silence in White express wisdom. In *Riders*, Leonie Kramer said in 1973, "the prose seems constantly to suggest more than it states; and there are so many references to the superiority of silence over speech that White seems to be pointing . . . to the notion of a wordless revelation" (9). Brady agrees with Kramer. But she also believes that White seeks meaning through silence in *all* his work (1980, 47). The emphasis White places upon auras, echoes, and intimations has vexed some readers. Dorothy Green claimed in 1974 that his language and ideas often part company. In White, says Green, "too often what sounds profound turns out to be an effect of sonorous tone rather than intellectual substance" (309). Green's disclaimer has merit. Though White's works cry to be written, their power and flow are blocked by a doggedness that tends to solemnity and even inertia. His high artistic aims can result in works more industrious than gripping, more ambitious than realized.

The frustration conveyed by the following passage links both his ponderousness and his bitterness to a failure to perceive the ultimate. The passage comes from his autobiographical *Flaws in the Glass* (1982): "What do I believe? I am accused of not making it explicit. How to be explicit about a grandeur too overwhelming to express, a daily wrestling match with an opponent whose limbs never become material, a struggle from which the sweat and blood are scattered on the pages of anything the serious writer writes?" (70).

White also has a kindly, gentle side. He recognizes that, if God exists outside of human formulas and equations, no human path can lead to Him. The Divine Absence proves that the Divinity is not submissive or passive; He would have left a clearer trail to Himself had He wanted it to be discovered. White accepts God as *Other*. He rejects, in turn, any insolent natural theology that tries to pin Him down. Voss's horrifying ordeals in the desert show him abandoning the path of tradition and subordination in favor of new trackless courses. These courses disclose the complexity of the ordinary world while also intimating its uncanny, nightmarish aspects. What this entails is facing the enduring concerns of humanity—the persistence of the past, including the grip of family, the fight for freedom and self-definition, and the quest for truth in the shadow of death. While White knows no direct route into the heart of the cosmic mystery, he feels a magnetic attraction. His soul awakens. Pondering the groundwork of existence has helped him sense strange, new, acausal ties.

It is fitting that perhaps his most personal novel, *The Twyborn Affair*, should begin with this epigraph from David Malouf: "What else should our lives be but a series of beginnings, of painful settings out into the unknown." White starts with himself. He has thrust himself imaginatively into the center of creation by diving into his own selfhood. One of his goals consists of defining his relation to the world he writes about. He ventures into places few of us have glimpsed, and he makes himself face the worst they have to offer. He is honest, too, in his reactions to this worst. For instance, his view of man both as a beast and as the image of God vexes him. But rather than avoiding the paradox, he faces it. One way he tries to make sense of it is by breaking grammatical rules. He distorts language in order to arrive at truths that can be approached intuitively but not logically. His verbal wrenchings challenge both the actuality of ordinary life and the intangibles governing human conduct.

How effectively does his dense, dark rhetoric redefine connections? No feature of White has stirred so much disagreement as his prose. It has angered readers from the start. A. D. Hope (1956) referred to the style of *Tree* as "pretentious and illiterate verbal sludge" (15). Reviewing *Voss* two years later, Ross Campbell complained of White, "My impression is that he has practically lost the power to write a plain, unaffected English sentence" (18). These attacks have continued. Kramer believes that White's style "subtly undermines his subject" (1973, 18) in *Riders*. Writing five years later, Adrian Mitchell, citing "the notorious difficulties of his style" (6), accuses White of imprecision and sloppiness. Other critics have been friendlier. Walsh appreciates the intent behind the bruising vividness of his prose: "There is an almost Hopkins-like power in the way White outlines the shapes and urgently communicates the intrinsic energy of *things*. The novelist gives the impression of having . . . an almost molecular sense of whatever is going on within objects" (1977, 25). The first critic to call attention to the subtlety and strength of White's style was Harry Heseltine in 1963. His opinion, that White's language is "the very linchpin of what he has to say" (74), has recurred in recent books about White. My own 1983 work, *Laden Choirs*, discusses the beauties and blemishes of White's language (20–27, 67–68), and Carolyn Bliss examines in passing his sentence fragmenting, second-person narrations, and both subjunctive and conditional constructions in her *Patrick White's Fiction* (1986). Perhaps critical works like these two and, especially, Hilary Heltay's *The*

Articles and the Novelist (1983), a meticulous analysis of White's prose, will inspire a descriptive terminology that can decide the importance of style in White.

Without trying to forecast the directions of White criticism, one can assess the benefits to be gained by studying his style. He has an extraordinary sensitivity to natural phenomena—their abundance, heft, and texture. Much of his magic stems from details that evoke emotions rather than simply describing them. Although his prose is sometimes too calculated and literary, its intensity gives the commonplace a freshness, a flow, and a mystery that brings what is being discussed to vivid, thronging life. His writing takes us to Australia. But it also discloses the most opaque and mysterious of all things—the human soul. We can only suggest what it is like to see our way through his inventiveness. We know that we will miss much, that future readings will unearth more, but that even these will not explain everything. Now jagged, now roundly abundant, he speaks in vibrant images. As sometimes happens, though, bad taste will jade the vibrancy. A character in *Memoirs of Many in One,* for instance, dreams of attending a charity ball in Washington, D.C.'s "Adolph Hitler Hotel."

But the daytime logic that invokes moral judgment casts little light on White. The network of values from which he views the world yields no pat answers. In 1978 John Colmer called his fiction "strangely joyless" (53). The passage of six years changed his mind, as can be seen in his 1984 claim that White's major novels "move inexorably towards some grand, positive affirmation about life" (12). The tricky gleams and shadows emitted by White's dark, dissociated vitality may change Colmer's mind again.

Reality as White describes it is more elusive and bizarre than we had thought. Good and evil course through vast tracks of time and space, which may be either empty or congested. We lack both the power and the vision to order this omniform vastness. But we need not quail before it. The recognition that life's meaning often inheres in shadows, depths, and echoes sharpens our minds and souls. It also fosters the heightened receptivity that glimpses the mystery infusing all. Moving and authoritative, Patrick White has enlarged the sphere of human transactions, and he has provided a searching criticism of life. For the brave and the visionary, he has created outlets for spiritual energy and, perhaps, growth.

PETER WOLFE

University of Missouri—St. Louis

Note

    1. All citations in this introduction refer to the bibliography at the end of the volume.

WHITE ON WHITE

The Prodigal Son

Patrick White°

This is by way of being an answer to Alister Kershaw's recent article "The Last Expatriate," but as I cannot hope to equal the slash and dash of Kershaw's journalistic weapons, I shall not attempt to answer him point by point. In any case, the reasons why anybody is an expatriate, or why another chooses to return home, are such personal ones that the question can only be answered in a personal way.

At the age of 46 I have spent just on twenty of those years overseas. During the last ten, I have hardly stirred from the six acres of "Dogwoods," Castle Hill. It sounds odd, and is perhaps worth trying to explain.

Brought up to believe in the maxim, Only the British can be right, I did accept this during the earlier part of my life. Ironed out in an English public school, and finished off at King's, Cambridge, it was not until 1939, after wandering by myself through most of Western Europe, and finally most of the United States, that I began to grow up and think my own thoughts. The War did the rest. What had seemed a brilliant, intellectual, highly desirable existence, became distressingly parasitic and pointless. There is nothing like a rain of bombs to start one trying to assess one's own achievement. Sitting at night in his London bed-sitting room during the first months of the Blitz, this chromium-plated Australian with two fairly successful novels to his credit came to the conclusion that his achievement was practically nil. Perhaps significantly, he was reading at that time Eyre's *Journal*. Perhaps also he had the wind up; certainly he reached rather often for the bottle of Calvados in the wardrobe. Anyway, he experienced those first sensations of rootlessness which Alister Kershaw has deplored and explained as the "desire to nuzzle once more at the benevolent teats of the mother country."

All through the War in the Middle East there persisted a longing

° Reprinted from *Australian Letters* I (April 1958): 37–40; Copyright © Patrick White 1958.

to return to the scenes of childhood, which is, after all, the purest well from which the creative artist draws. Aggravated further by the terrible nostalgia of the desert landscapes, this desire was almost quenched by the year I spent stationed in Greece, where perfection presents itself on every hand, not only the perfection of antiquity, but that of nature, and the warmth of human relationships expressed in daily living. Why didn't I stay in Greece? I was tempted to. Perhaps it was the realisation that even the most genuine resident Hellenophile accepts automatically the vaguely comic role of Levantine beachcomber. He does not belong, the natives seem to say, not without affection; it is sad for him, but he is nothing. While the Hellenophile continues humbly to hope.

So I did not stay in my elective Greece. Demobilisation in England left me with the alternative of remaining in what I then felt to be an actual and spiritual graveyard, with the prospect of ceasing to be an artist and turning instead into that most sterile of beings, a London intellectual, or of returning home, to the stimulus of time remembered. Quite honestly, the thought of a full belly influenced me as well, after toying with the soft, sweet awfulness of horsemeat stew in the London restaurants that I could afford. So I came home. I bought a farm at Castle Hill, and with a Greek friend and partner, Manoly Lasearis, started to grow flowers and vegetables, and to breed Schnauzers and Saanen goats.

The first years I was content with these activities, and to soak myself in landscape. If anybody mentioned Writing, I would reply: "Oh, one day, perhaps." But I had no real intention of giving the matter sufficient thought. *The Aunt's Story*, written immediately after the War, before returning to Australia, had succeeded with overseas critics, failed as usual with the local ones, [and] remained half-read, it was obvious from the state of the pages, in the lending libraries. Nothing seemed important, beyond living and eating, with a roof of one's own over one's head.

Then, suddenly, I began to grow discontented. Perhaps, in spite of Australian critics, writing novels was the only thing I could do with any degree of success; even my half-failures were some justification of an otherwise meaningless life. Returning sentimentally to a country I had left in my youth, what had I really found? Was there anything to prevent me packing my bag and leaving like Alister Kershaw and so many other artists? Bitterly I had to admit, no. In all directions stretched the Great Australian Emptiness, in which the mind is the least of possessions, in which the rich man is the important man, in which the schoolmaster and the journalist rule what intellectual roost there is, in which beautiful youths and girls stare at life through blind blue eyes, in which human teeth fall like autumn leaves, the buttocks of cars grow hourly glassier, food means cake and steak, muscles prevail, and the march of material ugliness does not raise a quiver from the average nerves.

It was the exaltation of the "average" that made me panic most, and in this frame of mind, in spite of myself, I began to conceive another novel. Because the void I had to fill was so immense, I wanted to try to suggest in this book every possible aspect of life, through the lives of an ordinary man and woman. But at the same time I wanted to discover the extraordinary behind the ordinary, the mystery and the poetry which alone could make bearable the lives of such people, and incidentally, my own life since my return.

So I began to write *The Tree of Man*. How it was received by the more important Australian critics is now ancient history. Afterwards I wrote *Voss*, possibly conceived during the early days of the Blitz, when I sat reading Eyre's *Journal* in a London bed-sitting room. Nourished by months spent traipseing backwards and forwards across the Egyptian and Cyrenaican deserts, influenced by the arch-megalomaniac of the day, the idea finally matured after reading contemporary accounts of Leichhardt's expeditions and A.H. Chisholm's *Strange New World* on returning to Australia.

It would be irrelevant to discuss here the literary aspects of the novel. More important are those intentions of the author which have pleased some readers without their knowing exactly why, and helped to increase the rage of those who have found the book meaningless. Always something of a frustrated painter, and a composer manqué, I wanted to give my book the textures of music, the sensuousness of paint, to convey through the theme and characters of *Voss* what Delacroix and Blake might have seen, what Mahler and Liszt might have heard. Above all I was determined to prove that the Australian novel is not necessarily the dreary, dun-coloured offspring of journalistic realism. On the whole, the world has been convinced, only here, at the present moment, the dingoes are howling unmercifully.

What, then, have been the rewards of this returned expatriate? I remember when, in the flush of success after my first novel, an old and wise Australian journalist called Guy Innes came to interview me in my London flat. He asked me whether I wanted to go back. I had just "arrived"; who was I to want to go back? "Ah, but when you do," he persisted, "the colours will come flooding back onto your palette." This gentle criticism of my first novel only occurred to me as such in recent years. But I think perhaps Guy Innes has been right.

So, amongst the rewards, there is the refreshed landscape, which even in its shabbier, remembered versions has always made a background to my life. The worlds of plants and music may never have revealed themselves had I sat talking brilliantly to Alister Kershaw over a Pernod on the Left Bank. Possibly all art flowers more readily in silence. Certainly the state of simplicity and humility is the only desirable one for artist or for man. While to reach it may be impossible, to attempt to do so is imperative. Stripped of almost everything that I had considered desirable and necessary, I began to try. Writing, which had meant the practice of an art by a polished mind in civilised surroundings, became a struggle to create completely fresh forms out of the rocks and sticks of words. I began to see things for the first time. Even the boredom and frustration presented avenues for endless exploration; even the ugliness, the bags and iron of Australian life, acquired a meaning. As for the cat's cradle of human intercourse, this was necessarily simplified, often bungled, sometimes touching. Its very tentativeness can be a reward. There is always the possibility that the book lent, the record played, may lead to communication between human beings. There is the possibility that one may be helping to people a barely inhabited country with a race possessed of understanding.

These, then, are some of the reasons why an expatriate has stayed, in the face of those disappointments which follow inevitably upon his return. Abstract and unconvincing, the Alister Kershaws will probably answer, but such reasons, as I have already suggested, are a personal matter. More concrete, and most rewarding of all, are the many letters I have received from unknown Australians, for whom my writing seems to have opened a window. To me, the letters alone are reason enough for staying.

Patrick White   Patrick White*

Religion. Yes, that's behind all my books. What I am interested in is the relationship between the blundering human being and God. I belong to no church, but I have a religious faith; it's an attempt to express that, among other things, that I try to do. Whether he confesses to being religious or not, everyone has a religious faith of a kind. I myself am a blundering human being with a belief in God who made us and we got out of hand, a kind of Frankenstein monster. Everyone can make mistakes, including God. I believe God does intervene; I think there is a Divine Power, a Creator, who has an influence on human beings if they are willing to be open to him. Yes, I pray. I was brought up an Anglican. Oh, then I gave that away completely. After the war I tried to belong to the Church of England, but I found that so completely unsatisfactory. I wouldn't say I am a

* Reprinted from In the Making, ed. Craig McGregor (Melbourne: Thomas Nelson, 1969), 218–21; Copyright © Craig McGregor 1969.

Christian; I can't aspire so high. I am a very low form of human being; in my next incarnation I shall probably turn up as a dog or a stone. I can't divorce Christianity from other religions. The Jewish, for instance, is a wonderful religion—I had to investigate it very thoroughly for *Riders in the Chariot*. In my books I have lifted bits from various religions in trying to come to a better understanding; I've made use of religious themes and symbols. Now, as the world becomes more pagan, one has to lead people in the same direction in a different way. . . .

I'm really more interested in things urban than things country, in the more sophisticated aspects of Australian life . . . though I come from the country, it's in my blood. The novel I am working on now is set mainly in Sydney. It's about the life of a painter. I've known many painters myself. One of the first I knew was Roy de Maistre: I feel he taught me to write by teaching me to look at paintings and get beneath the surface. I've seen a lot of Nolan on and off, he's a friend of mine; and Lawrence Daws, Rapotec. I like some of Fred Williams's paintings very much; I think he gets closer to the essence of the Australian landscape than most. Why can't a writer use writing as a painter uses paint? I try to. When I wrote *The Tree of Man* I felt I couldn't write about simple, illiterate people in a perfectly literate way; but in my present novel the language is more sophisticated. I think perhaps I have clarified my style quite a lot over the years. I find it a great help to hear the language going on around me; not that what I write, the narrative, is idiomatic Australian, but the whole work has a balance and rhythm which is influenced by what is going on around you. When you first write the narrative it might be unconscious, but when you come to work it over you do it more consciously. It gives what I am writing a greater feeling of reality. When I came back from overseas I felt I had to learn the language again. That is one of the reasons I work in Australia. I write about Australia; you have to do a certain amount of research; and I think it's a good thing to be close to one's roots. It's a good thing, too, to spend some time away from them; it enriches your work. Martin Boyd, Christina Stead—*Cotter's England*, that's a terrific novel. They went away and stayed away. The essence of what you have to say you pick up before you're twenty, really, so it ought to be possible to go away and draw on that. I came back. I work better here because there are no distractions. It would be so boring if I didn't write I would go mad. . . . I have been working on this present novel for three years. Oh, and I've written the first draft of a novella as well. I always like to write three versions of a book. The first is always agony and chaos; no one could understand it. With the second you get the shape, it's more or less all right. I write both of those in longhand. The third draft I type out with two fingers:

it's for refining of meaning, additions and subtractions. I think my novels usually begin with characters; you have them floating about in your head and it may be years before they get together in a situation. Characters interest me more than situations. I don't think any of my books have what you call plots. I used to take notes, once upon a time; and sometimes I begin with a very slight skeleton. But I always think of my novels as being the lives of the characters. They are largely something that rises up out of my unconscious; I draw very little on actual people, though one does put a bow or a frill on from here or there. I find the actual bits, if you do use them, are most unconvincing compared to the fictitious bits. Sometimes characters do enlarge as you write, but within the rough framework of what you had intended. It's fatal to hurry into a book; the book I like least, *The Living and the Dead*, I had to hurry because of the war. *The Tree of Man* took me four years. I rewrite endlessly, sentence by sentence; it's more like oxywelding than writing. Once I used to write at night, from midnight till four o'clock in the morning; but as I got older I decided that was a strain, so now I get up at five and write through the morning and then perhaps from five to seven in the evening. The afternoon is death for anything; I sleep. I have the same idea with all my books: an attempt to come close to the core of reality, the structure of reality, as opposed to the merely superficial. The realistic novel is remote from art. A novel should heighten life, should give one an illuminating experience; it shouldn't set out what you know already. I just muddle away at it. One gets flashes here and there, which help. I am not a philosopher or an intellectual. Practically anything I have done of any worth I feel I have done through my intuition, not my mind—which the intellectuals disapprove of. And that is why I am anathema to certain kinds of Australian intellectual. It irritates me when I think of some of those academic turds, and the great Panjandrum of Canberra who described my writing as pretentious and illiterate verbal sludge. . . . One can't tell in one's own lifetime if what one has written is any good; I feel what I've written is better than some other people's. I like *The Aunt's Story* and *The Solid Mandala* best—the first because for so long nobody would pay any attention to it, and even those who did take any notice didn't read it—I went into Angus & Robertson's library, just twenty-five years ago, and noticed that people had read only the first quarter, they were the only pages which were soiled; and *The Solid Mandala* because it's a very personal kind of book, I suppose, and comes closest to what I've wanted.

I've lost interest in the theatre because you can't get what you want ever. I used to think it would be wonderful to see what you had written come to life. Here in Australia it's very hard to get an adequate performance because of the state of the theatre; but even if you have the best actors in the world it's never what you visualised. One can't say all one wants to say, one can't convey it. Chekov is one of the exceptions who had the kind of subtlety I would like to get into the theatre. I've always been stage-struck. I wanted to become an actor when I was young, but fortunately I became too self-conscious at the English public school I went to. I think it's better to be a writer than an actor. Acting is a very untidy kind of life, it's all very ephemeral; your novel might last, but your performance won't. And I'm not really interested in happenings and all that kind of rubbish. Not so long ago I thought of writing an opera; I had this idea that I thought would have made a good opera. But it didn't work out. A waste of time, really. I'd better keep on writing novels. Short stories? I don't really like writing them so much—though I have nearly got enough for another volume. All my effects are cumulative, and one doesn't really have the time to get the effects you want. The novella is more satisfactory; you can put more into it. Sometimes if I become very depressed while writing a novel and I get an idea for a short story I get that down, and afterwards I feel as though I have been liberated somehow.

I am not writing for an audience; I am writing, and if I have an audience I am very glad. I shocked some people the other night by saying writing is really like shitting; and then, reading the letters of Pushkin a little later, I found he said exactly the same thing! It's something you have to get out of you. I didn't write for a long time at one stage, and built up such an accumulation of shit that I wrote *The Tree of Man*. I wouldn't call myself a humanist; I am indifferent to people in general. But I have always been gregarious. This myth that I'm not has been put about by bitches that I wouldn't have in my house. I like people, but I like to choose my people. I'm not isolated; I know quite a lot of people in the theatre, in the art world. When we first came back to Australia we lived at Castle Hill because we wanted to live in the bush, and yet be close to the city. Then it became just another suburb; we were surrounded by little boxes. So we moved closer in. It makes it easier to have people to dinner, go to the theatre, films. Harry Miller took an option on *Voss* to make it into a film, but we could never agree on a director. Which writers have influenced me? Joyce and Lawrence, certainly. Lawrence I liked so much in my youth I'd be afraid to read him now. The nineteenth century Russians, too. Then at Cambridge I did a degree in French and German literature, so I got to know something about that. Proust influenced everybody. I seem to do less and less reading, especially fiction, though I reread *Madame Bovary* not so long ago when I was having a pause from writing—it really knocked me right over, it was so wonderful. When I was in Dublin I reread Joyce's *Dubliners* and realised I'd missed out on half of it before. Of the American novelists the people I like are Bellow and Updike, who are fairly detached. They owe their quality to their detachment.

I am interested in detail. I enjoy decoration. By accumulating this mass of detail you throw light on things in a longer sense: in the long run it all adds up. It creates a texture—how shall I put it— a background, a period, which makes everything you write that [much] more convincing. Of course, all artists are terrible egoists. Unconsciously you are largely writing about yourself. I could never write anything factual; I only have confidence in myself when I am another character. All the characters in my books are myself, but they are a kind of disguise.

A Conversation with Patrick White   Thelma Herring and G. A. Wilkes°

Q. Some of the published statements about your life seem vague; would you care to clarify them? Your early education, for example?
A. It's difficult to put dates to some of the events in my early life, though there are isolated episodes which remain very vivid. I know that after I was born in London (1912) my parents brought me back to Australia aged six months. Until I was three we had a flat in a block called "Cromer" in Phillip Street where the Wentworth Hotel now stands. In 1915 we moved to "Lulworth," Rushcutters Bay (out of which grew the Bonners' house in Voss and the Courtneys' house in The Vivisector). When I was five (1917) I started going to a kindergarten, "Sandtoft," in Ocean Street, Woollahra, and later on to Cranbrook. How long I spent at each is difficult to say. Perhaps two years at each, or three at "Sandtoft" and only one at Cranbrook. I was sent to Cranbrook because my father was one of the founders and one of my great-uncles built the original house—so there was this link. But I didn't stay there long because I suffered increasingly from asthma in Sydney. I went to Tudor House, Moss Vale when I was nine (1921) and stayed till 1925. (Moss Vale became Sorrel Vale in The Aunt's Story, and Mount Ashby which you can see from the school, the volcanic hill near the Goodmans' farm "Meroë." In 1925 I was taken by my parents to England. We must have left about the beginning of April because the sea voyage from Sydney to England took about two months in those days. We arrived in London on 28

° This interview was conducted on 29 March 1973 and first appeared in Southerly 33 (June 1973): 132–43. The questions were asked by Miss Thelma Herring and Professor G.A. Wilkes, who express their thanks to Mr. White for giving so generously of his time, and especially for checking and revising the rough transcript of the talk.

May, on my thirteenth birthday, and stayed in a hotel in Knightsbridge opposite the block of flats where I was born. I started school at Cheltenham the winter of that year, but before that spent some months at a tutor's at Portishead near Bristol. My school years were pretty dreary. I hated Cheltenham, its regimentation. But there was always the possibility of going to the theatre in London during the holidays. I was taken to Paris for the first time when I was fourteen, and remember seeing a play by Sasha Guitry in which his wife Yvonne Printemps played the boy Mozart on his first visit to Paris. I can still remember Mozart's blue eyelids and the smell of that red-plush theatre.

I left school and returned to Australia in 1929, working for a year as a jackeroo near Adaminaby, and a second year near Walgett. A third year I spent getting ready to pass the entrance exam to King's College, Cambridge. I was supposed to read History at Cambridge and was coached in that subject by Fred Wood, then at Sydney University, and later Professor of History at Wellington, N.Z. He was very shocked by my style, as other Australian academics have been since. The Woods had a house at Blackheath to which they used to go in the holidays, and I would be driven over from Mount Wilson, where we had a house for many years, to more History sessions with F.W. (Actually, the day I arrived in Cambridge I felt I couldn't face any more History, and decided to read Modern Languages (French and German) instead. It was a lucky decision. Because I had to go as often as possible to France and Germany to improve myself linguistically.)

My life at Cambridge (1932–35) was rather uneventful. I met none of the great. But I used to hang around A.E. Housman's rooms hoping I might see him come out. I never did. But I heard him give the Leslie Stephen Lecture in which he shocked people by telling them all his best poetry had been written while he was either ill or drunk. I don't think I knew Wittgenstein and Moore existed while I was at Cambridge. I've certainly never read them although I've been asked whether I've been influenced by them. Probably I couldn't understand them if I tried. I did read a great deal at that time, mostly in French and German, and that was a great eye-opener. If I didn't make the most of Cambridge in other ways, it was because I was far too shy to approach those who would have interested me.

Q. What did you do after leaving Cambridge?
A. I lived in London, first in a bed-sitter in Ebury Street, later in a flat opposite, then in one round the corner in Eccleston Street, in a house which belonged to Roy de Maistre the painter. I suppose I was drawn to Ebury Street in the first place because of a youthful admiration for George Moore the novelist. There was also a house

farther up the street in which Mozart is said to have composed his first symphony while on a visit to London as a boy. Later on I discovered de Maistre, of whom I'd always known because my god-mother's sister was married to one of his brothers. I owe an awful lot to Roy. He introduced me to painting and music, and through that I think I learned to write. I started writing in Ebury Street— several bad plays, which nobody wanted to produce. I even tried to get into the theatre. I went down to the Westminster where Rupert Doone had begun producing Auden's *Dog Beneath the Skin,* and asked him whether he would give me a job. Nothing came of it. He wanted somebody who could "do things with his hands," and I had to confess I was completely useless in that respect. But I was always hanging round theatres. Most of my friends in those days were actors. In Roy's studio I met Henry Moore and Graham Sutherland on one occasion. I can't remember what anybody said, and I was certainly far too shy to utter a word. Sometimes I used to see Francis Bacon. In those days he was a young man with a beautiful pansy-shaped face and rather too much lipstick. He lived in a house at the Chelsea end of Ebury Street, not far from the Mozart house, with an old Nanny who used to shoplift when they were hard up. Francis designed a magnificent desk for me which I was mad enough to get rid of along with most of my worldly possessions when I burnt my bridges and came back to live in Australia after the War. At that stage Bacon was destroying almost everything he painted. He had an obsession for false teeth. He was always painting those. I can remember him going into a trance over lines scribbled on a hoarding—he was overcome with admiration for the perfection of these random arabesques.

I also wandered over a lot of Europe during the years between Cambridge and the War. I wrote *Happy Valley* in the flat in Ebury Street, and revised it at Ciboure, across the river from St. Jean de Luz, where Roy de Maistre advised me to go. I went to New York for the first time in the spring of 1939 to try my luck with *Happy Valley*. I travelled over a lot of the States, but was particularly infatuated with New York. I might have remained there and taken American nationality if war hadn't broken out. Before that I began *The Living and the Dead.* I returned to London after the outbreak of war, but during that long Maginot Line period when nothing was happening, I decided to wangle back to the States to finish my book at least. I finished the book, and returned to London for the second time about August 1940. I can remember lying on the pavement at the corner of Ebury and Eccleston Streets the night the first bombs fell, and thinking this surely can't be happening. Those first nights of the Blitz I spent in the house of my old Italian-Swiss landlady. We used to go down to the cellar at first, but after a bit one couldn't be bothered, lying on the floor, listening to the other lodgers fart. I stayed in my room with a bottle of Calvados for courage, reading the *Journals* of Eyre.

Then I went into the RAF. I was stationed for a bit outside London before being posted to the Middle East.

Q. And after the War?

A. On V.J. Day I was in Greece. After Christmas I was posted back to England for demobilization. I just can't put dates to the next few moves. I know that while in London I lived at that same lodging-house, which no longer functioned as one, but my landlady took me in for the sake of old times. There I wrote the first part of *The Aunt's Story.* But London at this period was like a graveyard filled with memories of the Blitz. I also felt terribly hungry as there was so little to eat. To fill my belly may have been the chief and ignoble reason why I decided to re-visit Australia to see whether I could settle there. On the way I stopped off in Alexandria to see my friend Manoly Lascaris, and while there I wrote the second part of *The Aunt's Story.* The third part I wrote on the deck of the *Strathmore* on my way back to Australia, and revised the whole book while staying with my mother in Sydney. This time I only spent a few months in Australia, and decided I might as well settle down somewhere here.

Q. When did you write *The Ham Funeral?*

A. I wrote it in London after this first preliminary visit to Australia, when I met Dobell the painter and he told me the story of the actual funeral with which he had been involved. Again in London I was living in the house of my old landlady Mrs. Imhof. The house in the play is more like one of those farther down in Pimlico than Mrs. Imhof's, and there is nothing of Mrs. Imhof herself (God rest her soul) in Mrs. Lusty. The play was revised only slightly before it was performed in Australia years later.

Q. You began to write at a very early age?

A. Oh, I think I was ten when I first wrote a play—in three acts—called *Love's Awakening,* about a man who went out to "buy" a divorce, had supper with the Other Woman, but eventually decided to stay married. There was another play about this time, in blank verse—I think it was called *The Bird of Prey*—about a *femme fatale* in Florence who had a cellarful of lovers in chains. (You see, I started reading very early, the whole of Shakespeare for the plots and the blood, the kind of magazines maids used to love, and particularly *The News of the World,* [which] an English married couple working for some cousins used to have sent out to them.)

Q. There were also some early novels?

A. While I was a jackeroo I used to shut myself up at night with a kerosene lamp and write. The first novel was called *The Immigrants*, about English people who settle in the Monaro and have a hard time. There was another called *Finding Heaven* (a quotation from the Gilbert Murray translation of I forget which Euripides play), written partly at Mount Wilson, partly at Walgett, about the depression in Sydney. A third was called *The Sullen Moon*, which was beginning to get somewhere. It had the germ of *The Aunt's Story*. After *Happy Valley* I wrote another novel called *Nightside* which never got published. It was about a French cabaret dancer, really an Australian, Lily from Mosman, who becomes Lys in Paris, and who is murdered by a German kink. It wasn't as bad as that makes it sound. It might have found a publisher if I had persisted. But I didn't like it enough. I burnt it in the pit before we left Castle Hill.

Q. Looking back over your novels, would you be conscious of certain preoccupations recurring, or of particular things you have tried to do?

A. Life in Australia seems to be for many people pretty deadly dull. I have tried to convey a splendour, a transcendence, which is also there, above human realities. From *The Tree of Man* onward (that started under the title *A Life Sentence on Earth*) I wanted to suggest my own faith in these superhuman realities. But of course it is very difficult to try to convey a religious faith through symbols and situations which can be accepted by people today.

Q. Are you then conscious of changes in yourself as a novelist as you've gone on?

A. Of course. A man changes all the time. If I say I had no religious tendencies between adolescence and *The Tree of Man*, it's because I was sufficiently vain and egotistical to feel one can ignore certain realities. (I think the turning-point came during a season of unending rain at Castle Hill when I fell flat on my back one day in the mud and started cursing a God I had convinced myself didn't exist. My personal scheme of things till then at once seemed too foolish to continue holding.)

Q. Would you make a dividing line between *The Aunt's Story* and *The Tree of Man*?

A. Perhaps the conclusion I came to was already developing in my unconscious.

Q. Could not an idea like 1 Corinthians 1.27 be applicable to *The Aunt's Story*: "God hath chosen the foolish things of the world to confound the wise; and God hath chosen the weak things of the world to confound the things which are mighty"?

A. It could be applicable, but it was not in my mind when I wrote.

Q. What then is the difference between *The Aunt's Story* and the later novels?

A. *The Aunt's Story* is a work which celebrates the human spirit, but I had not yet begun to accept (except perhaps unconsciously) that I believe in a God.

Q. When in *Riders in the Chariot* Miss Hare is offered a Bible to read, she prefers Anthony Hordern's catalogue. This suggests that you are not interested in institutionalized religion.

A. I can't associate my own faith with Churches. Nor can Miss Hare. In any case, the Bible would have been a bit difficult for her. She is slightly subnormal. And Hordern's catalogue was a "good read." I used to find it fascinating myself.

Q. Then a person living as she does without contact with scriptures or church could be living a religious life?

A. Oh, yes. She worshipped while crawling on all fours through her jungle of a shrubbery. All four main characters in *Riders in the Chariot* lead religious lives, Himmelfarb and Mrs. Goldbold consciously; Alf Dubbo's attempts at painting are worshipful acts. (I develop this of course through a more sophisticated character in *The Vivisector*.)

Q. There's a tendency in criticism nowadays to be suspicious of the heroic, the visionary, the intuitive: the critic seems to require that such themes be presented ironically, or else be somehow criticized while they're being presented.

A. I am myself suspicious of the heroic. I don't think any of my novels is heroic. All are certainly ironic—the fact that one is alive at all is an irony. Voss was a monomaniac, rather than a hero, and like almost all human beings flawed and fallible.

Q. But some would say that the visionaries in *Riders in the Chariot* are being presented ironically. Is that a misreading?

A. As visionaries they are not treated ironically. But as human beings, in the details of their daily lives, it is impossible to avoid irony.

Q. What of the presentation of Stan Parker's experience in the storm in *The Tree of Man*?

A. That is not ironical, except on a human level. (When I fell on my back in the rain and mud and started cursing God, there was plenty of irony around, though the event itself was a serious matter.)

Q. In all your work you show a willingness to "chance your arm" (as the saying is). How important in a novel are principles like plausibility and verisimilitude? For example in the "telepathic" communication of Laura and Voss?

A. ESP research in recent years has surely proved that telepathic communication does exist. I'm continually receiving evidence of it myself. I'm convinced that life is built on coincidence and strange happenings. But in all this, and in spite of not writing what could be called naturalistic novels, you have to keep in touch with fact, which I feel I do.

Q. Are the analogies you have made with painting and music part of this?

A. It is difficult to express what I have to express in a naturalistic medium in the age in which I live. I feel you can do far more with paint and music; I am hobbled by words.

Q. But words surely can be more expressive. For a moralist. . . .

A. I am not. I don't want to be a moralist. I don't think I have preached sermons in any of my books. I say what I have to say through the juxtaposition of images and situations and the emotional exchanges of human beings. Not everybody seems able to grasp this, but a certain type of mind can—from all social levels, from the most sophisticated to the semi-literate. But of course it sticks in the guts of those who are rigidly rational—what some Australians proudly refer to as "a trained mind."

Q. In reading your novels I don't really feel that you are being limited by the novel form. I am not conscious of these constraints.

A. Oh yes, the constraints are there. I find words frustrating as I sit year in year out reeling out an endless deadly grey. I try to splurge a bit of colour—perhaps to get a sudden impact—as a painter squeezes a tube. But there isn't the physical relief a painter experiences in the act of painting. I wish I had been a painter or composer. Or I might have been able to solve my problems as a poet. . . . No, I had no acquaintance with Eliot's *Four Quartets* until I heard Robert Speaight's recording of them a few years ago. I realize anybody *could* be influenced by such magnificence.

Q. Is the novel, or the medium of prose, perhaps too explicit?

A. In one sense; in another, I enjoy that explicitness—the accumulation of down-to-earth detail. All my novels are an accumulation of detail. I'm a bit of a bower-bird.

Q. There is a good deal of treatment in your work of experience that goes beyond the trajectory of what is familiar and traditional in the novel?

A. I feel that my novels are quite old-fashioned and traditional— almost Nineteenth Century. I've never thought of myself as an innovator.

Q. Where would you find the tradition?

A. In the Nineteenth-Century Russians, certainly; in Stendhal, Flaubert (not the Romantic Flaubert of *Salammbo*) and Balzac. Sometimes in Dickens.

Q. I don't mean the down-to-earthness, but the treatment of areas of experience outside the normal range?

A. That would be more particularly in the Russians. Alain Fournier's *Le Grand Meaulnes* must have influenced me in my youth. I expect I could think of others, but it's difficult when asked pointblank.

Q. It worries me that in valuing intuition, you seem to reject reason.

A. I don't reject it but I think intuition is more important, creatively, in the beginning. Perhaps not for everybody. But everything I write has to be dredged up from the unconscious—which is what makes it such an exhausting and perhaps finally, destructive, process. I suppose all my characters are fragments of my own somewhat fragmented character. My first draft of a novel is the work of intuition, and it is a chaos nobody but myself could resolve. Working it up after that—the oxywelding—is more a process of reason. The last version is your last chance—and you hope it won't be suicide. . . . No. I haven't read Plotinus or the neo-Platonists on the intuitive powers of the mind.

Q. Could I ask about symbolism in the novels? Do you begin with a planned system of symbols?

A. This awful symbol business! I suppose I begin in some cases with a central symbol—the Chariot or the Mandala, for instance. But anything else crops up as I go along, more often than not, unconsciously. (Two examples: in *The Eye of the Storm*, the novel I have just finished, Elizabeth Hunter, the central character, encounters some black swans while she is reprieved from death by the eye of an actual storm on an island off the Queensland coast; the swans recur again in her mind when she is an old, bed-ridden, partly senile woman, and gather her in the moment before death. It is only since writing the book that I have discovered the swan is a symbol of death. My other example of the unconscious use of symbols is connected with the maiden name of this same Elizabeth Hunter. I called her "Salkeld," because I met someone of this name while I was writing the book, and it had something pleasing and apt about it. Elizabeth Salkeld grows up on a farm, on the edge of a river fringed with willows which play a certain part in her life. Not long ago I was glancing through a dictionary of surnames and came across the name Salkeld: Old English for "sallow-/willow-wood." I am glad to make these two true confessions before some symbol-spotter pounces on my swans and willows.) In their pursuit of symbols many academic critics don't seem to realize that writers and painters often make use of images and situations from real life because they have appealed to them as being beautiful or comic or bizarre. Hence the bear in Buñuel's *Exterminating Angel:* its significance once came up during an intellectual discussion, when the son, answering for the father, explained that Buñuel had been at a party in New York at which a live bear was introduced, and forever after wanted to use a bear in a party scene in one of his films.

Q. There are some colours that recur in the novels as though with more than naturalistic significance. Purple, for example, when Stan and Amy are under the mulberry tree, or when Theodora and Pearl Brawne go into the pub in *The Aunt's Story*.

A. Colours, like symbols, are made too much of by those indefatigable unravellers. Can't we use a colour because it *is*, or because we happen to like it? If purple crops up under the mulberry tree, aren't mulberries purple? And when Pearl and Theodora drink port in the pub, it's because ladies like Pearl used to order port because it was their tipple. ("Mine's a port-'n'-splash, love"). Though purple in some contexts does have transcendence, as does gold. I don't know about zinc, which you say recurs in association with inhumanity. The frustrated painter in me is fascinated by zinc-coloured light, particularly off metallic waves. I probably also associate it with bitter mornings over milk pails and separators and wash-tubs.

Q. Towards the end of *The Tree of Man* Mrs. Fisher talks to Stan about bees: "such lovely, dark, living gold."

A. A swarm of bees is a lovely sight, a kind of live mesh. Perhaps this was intended to establish something slightly special and sensual between them, but it's too long ago for me to remember exactly.

Q. Are the names of characters sometimes symbolically expressive?

A. Some—Himmelfarb and Mrs. Godbold, obviously, and Miss Hare (a sacrificial creature in several mythologies) and Dubbo, the name an aborigine from those parts might have been given. I've already explained how I hit on Elizabeth Hunter's maiden name (Salkeld) and that it has a symbolic significance by pure accident. No, "Laura" has nothing to do with Petrarch, I chose it as an appropriate name for a woman of the time. "Arthur" in *The Solid Mandala* seemed to me a simple, blameless name. (I hadn't read *The Faerie Queene*.) "Tiarks" in *The Living and the Dead* is a clumsy name for a clumsy person. I knew a man called Holstius (*The Aunt's Story*) and I suppose I liked the suggestion of "Holz" (wood) for a sturdy, though non-existent character.

Q. In *The Vivisector* there are some characters who are "stroked by God," and this recalls the episode in *Riders in the Chariot* where Ruth Joyner's brother has his head crushed like a melon under the hay-wagon, and "for the first time, life, that ordinarily slack and harmless coil, became a fist, which was aiming at her personally." Is this element of inexplicable violence in the world an issue in the novels?

A. Yes. It won't leave you alone. Violence can be explained (man is like Frankenstein's monster who periodically gets out of control) but natural violence—acts of God—are difficult to understand, and the sufferings of innocent people. However, at the same time you can't *explain* the genius of Bach and Mozart, or a rather squalid old man like Turner—none of the great artists—or saints. So one has to accept the depths along with the heights.

Q. The epigraph from Blake in *The Vivisector* speaks of cruelty, and some characters project this on to God, e.g., Hero says, "God is cruel! We are his bagful of cats."

A. There are times when most of us will drown a bagful of metaphoric cats. That Hero's husband has drowned a bagful of actual cats is particularly shattering, because her husband is also her God in spite of her lust for Duffield. Hero is Greek Orthodox and I don't think any Greek Orthodox ever rejects God whatever the more sophisticated ones may tell you.

Q. Duffield himself doesn't know what he believes in, "beyond his own powers, the unalterable landscape of childhood, and the revelations of light." After Hero returns disillusioned from the chapel on Perialos, he can only point to the golden hen pecking at the crumbs round the café table, in consolation. Can his celebration of the world in painting be seen as a mode of worship?

A. To begin with, that fussy, industrious little Greek hen, if you have seen one, is in herself a "revelation of light." That is why I introduced what may seem irrelevant to some readers. I do it through Duffield, whose "celebration of the world in painting" is of course a "mode of worship." I think Duffield realized this from the beginning, though only unconsciously. Finally it emerges, as I try to show. Only at the end will he admit it. (I believe that most people, if they are honest with themselves, have in them the germ of a religious faith, but they are either too lazy, or too frightened, or too ashamed intellectually to accept the fact.)

Q. *The Vivisector* seems to be concerned a good deal with the artist's struggle to be honest with himself, as in Duffield's work on his self-portrait?

A.Yes, he eventually smears it with shit and throws it down the gully after Nance Lightfoot has, possibly, been driven to suicide.

Q. There is a puzzling passage in which Olivia sees the "Pythoness at Tripod" painting and accuses Duffield of bringing Rhoda and Muriel together to suit his own purposes. She asks, "Is it honest?" This points to a literal realism one wouldn't expect you to uphold. Why should it be *dis*honest unless one expects a photographic likeness? Duffield very properly replies, "Only the painting can answer that," but he goes on to talk of the painter's being only human, as if he feels guilty. Why should Olivia say this—why is it dishonest?

A. Olivia is thinking about it in human terms, not as an artist, in spite of her passion for art, because Rhoda is a hunchback dwarf and Muriel a hysteric. In his painting Duffield is combining the weaknesses of both, which doesn't seem to her fair. Duffield, though an artist, also experiences moments of guilt as a human being.

Q. May we ask about your new novel *The Eye of the Storm?*
A. I don't really want to talk about it. In a few months it will be out, and anyone interested can satisfy their curiosity.

Factual Writing and Fiction   Patrick White*

What I'm going to try to talk about is how the pursuit of truth differs in factual writing and fiction, according to my own experience.

As a writer of fiction it's a difference I've only recently had to face up to. I've never wanted to write an autobiography, trundling over a long life introducing the celebrities one meets for five minutes and most of whom aren't at all interesting anyway. Instead I decided to do a self-portrait to try to show what I *think* I am and how it came about. It's the kind of writing which survives only if it is the quintessence of truthfulness. I should say the most difficult kind of factual writing. As one goes along one wonders: is the novelist in me taking over? Shall I perhaps overdo the flaws in my anxiety to portray the real person? At the period when I was growing up we tended to regard reality as predominantly sordid. Certainly it is easier and more dramatic to record, say, the cry of horror as a cockroach flies into the open mouth than to convey the strength of spirit in Aya Sophia, Constantinople, after centuries of humiliation under Islam.

A couple of years ago I had a conversation with the English painter Bridget Reilly, who confirmed some of my doubts. "You run the risk of painting White blacker than he is." I remember another of her remarks during that same conversation: "I started a house and studio in the South of France thinking I could paint there in detachment and ideal surroundings. But you can't. Even abstract painters can't afford to sever their roots." This is what I think I sensed before returning to live in Australia after Hitler's war. Australian expatriate writers, and artists in general, eventually starve in the absence of their natural sustenance. Journalists are a different breed. Their roots are air roots. I often envy them their freedom as I sit endlessly at my desk, my bronchial tubes filling up as I work. Anyway, I came

* This is the text of the address given by Patrick White for the National Book Council Awards 1980, and printed in the *Age*, the *Sydney Morning Herald*, 11 October 1980, and *Australian Literary Studies* 10 (1981): 99–101.

back, and wrote novel after novel. Whether it's been a waste of time, or whether they convey the truth I was searching for, only time, not Professor Kramer, will show.

And now towards the end of my life I am doing this dangerous thing, the self-portrait. Recently I read a potted, one-volume version of George Sand's *Ma Vie*. As a fundamentally sincere woman she couldn't help telling the truth. But a lot is left out—anyway in the abridgement—perhaps the rest is scattered through the 20 volumes I haven't read. The impression one gets is of a watercolour of the kind of woman Courbet might have painted in oils—one of those *demoiselles* stretched dreaming on a river bank, her necklaces of Venus fully exposed. In his biography of George Sand, drawing on the opinions and experiences of those who knew her, André Maurois probably gives us the actual woman—a great force and sounding board at the time when she lived—like most of us full of obsessions and delusions.

A lot of her strength came from devotion to her native province of Berry. She was the greatest advocate for roots.

This is not intended as a vulgar joke at George's expense, but as a plea to artists to cling to the soil from which they grew—even if it is the grit of Melbourne's pavements—or the garbage of Sydney gutters. Actually George, in spite of her reputation as a female Don Juan, was not so hot where sexuality entered in. She was less the passionate lover than an earth mother in search of the Absolute in love and faith—which she never found. But in the course of her turbulent life, as woman, man, lover, novelist and pamphleteer, political and social revolutionary, descended from royal bastards and plebeian birdsellers, she attracted many dedicated friends and equally dedicated enemies who all contribute to her portrait. Another emancipated woman of the day, Marie d'Agoult, Liszt's aristocratic mistress, said of George, "She used her lovers like the chalk you write with on the blackboard, and then ground them to dust under foot." George, though a noble soul, realised that friendship is in many ways a game of hurt for hurt. She said of Marie, "Everything about her is artificial— teeth, breasts, aristocracy. Her financier family bought the title under the Regency." Sounds a bit like the Colonies.

Which brings me back to what I should be talking about: fact and fiction in Australia. It has always troubled me that so many Australian novelists are content to explore an autobiographical vein instead of launching into that admittedly disturbing marriage between life and imagination—like many actual marriages in fact—all the risks, the recurring despair, and rewards if you are lucky. Certainly most of the novels George wrote are autobiographical. But this is not what I want of our Australian novelists—writing so diligently about their Catholic youth, their Catholic lapse. Why it recurs, I suppose, is because Australians are taught to revere the pragmatic, the documentary approach. I have a 94-year-old aunt who used to tell her aspiring novelist nephew, "I always feel guilty if I read a novel—because it isn't true." (Actually what she read was mainly Ruby M. Ayres, self-confessed Queen of the Tripewriters.) But I do think my aunt's was one of the prevailing attitudes in the past— which didn't depress or influence me because I had the good fortune to escape and spend several years of my earlier life in other parts of the world.

If George Sand has helped me out in this talk tonight, there is a book by another writer which will carry me further into what I want to say about the difference between truth in factual writing and fiction. It is Axel Clark's biography of the poet Christopher Brennan. To me Brennan is a painfully mediocre poet who lived at a time when Australia was desperately in need of poetry, and culture generally. He was probably a considerable scholar—I'm not in a position to judge. As I see him his importance lay in his nonconformity, in a surreal element he added to a smug colonial society badly in need of a purge. Clark makes this clear after shovelling his way through mountains of turgid poetry. His book seems to one who is in no way a scholar a model of dogged scholarship. But what I find most exciting about this biography is that it lights the way to fiction. It astonishes me that some novelist of Roman Catholic background, instead of writing up his own Catholic boyhood and lapse, did not seize on Brennan, a figure of doom and high tragedy—such a grand lapse from the Austral-Irish-puritan faith, into the depths of physical and spiritual squalor, and finally the almost operatic return into the bosom of his Church. Well, there it all is—still waiting for somebody.

In suggesting this I don't advocate a documentary or historical novel. Axel Clark could not have done the factual version better. Personally I tend to dislike historical novels, and have avoided writing them because of the strictures they impose on the imagination. Instead, on a couple of occasions, I have taken a historic character or moment, as starting point. I feel this is permissible if you preserve psychological credibility and respect your aesthetic principles—the fiction need not decline into romance. If, instead of writing *Voss*, I had written a novel about Leichhardt, in whose life there was no woman his obsessive equal, or if in *A Fringe of Leaves* I hadn't substituted Ellen Roxburgh for Eliza Fraser, little more than a hard-bitten shrew from the Orkneys, neither novel would have had the psychological complexities, the sensibility, and the passion I was able to explore.

But I've gone on long enough about myself. The night belongs to the prize-winners, each of whom has pursued truth and shone a light on what till now we have accepted as the forms of reality and the motives for human behaviour. If I ask you to put up with me just a moment longer, it's because I'm tempted to end on a slightly political note, though some of my friends may again accuse me of humourlessness. So many Australians are made uneasy if one feels intensely—whether in writing, life, politics. And when it comes to politics, I can't help being intensely aware of the hypocrisy, side-stepping, and arrogant disregard for truth in recent years. The voice of the Fuhrer can be heard in the land, and unless we have in us enough passionate concern to alter course radically from the one we have been pursuing—I feel Australia could be lost.

REVIEWS

Happy and Unhappy
[*Happy Valley*]
Seaforth [Kenneth] Mackenzie°

Patrick White, the Australian-born author of this first novel, *Happy Valley*, records a saying of Mahatma Gandhi's: "It is impossible to do away with the law of suffering, which is the one indispensable condition of our being. Progress is to be measured by the amount of suffering undergone. . . ."

He is, by this, treating his reader fairly, from the beginning. Happy Valley is a township of which, in the end, the most you know is that there it is very cold in winter, very hot in summer. Mr. White's intention has been to show, with differing degrees of irony, that one must not judge the contents by the label. The Gandhi quotation is, in fact, a warning, not unlike that which Dante saw written over the gate. Happy Valley was not a happy place.

But Happy Valley itself does not matter: the township, the summer heat, the winter cold, have little to do with the author's preoccupation, which is with several men and women and children who lived in the town. His theme is suffering, that "indispensable condition of our being," out of which joy—or death—may come. Everyone in Happy Valley is, in some degree, unhappy.

This sounds unpromising enough material for an author whose experience, in terms of time at least, is not large. It not only sounds so, but it is so; and, if for that reason only, Patrick White's novel should be acclaimed as it deserves. It is good.

The author makes no compromise with his reader, nor with any one of his characters. For a long while not one of these is sympathetic: only when, almost unexpectedly, first one and then a second love is revealed, do four people shed the cobwebs of secret and intractable despair and so escape from Happy Valley. The others remain there: two die.

The novel is good for the one and good reason that the author is honest. Looking into it closely, I find he has built it on three seasons—winter, summer, and another winter. This, whether it was

° Reprinted from *Desiderata* (Adelaide) 40 (May 1939): 19–20.

intended or not, has controlled the structure of the "plot": the first winter is of discontent, the summer is of joy (for some people), and the second winter is of, shall we say, wisdom, and for some of escape.

In this way the story has a shape which otherwise it might have lacked, since it has a "plot" which is chiefly of the mind and the emotions. Those who came, and those who were there in the beginning, are suspended always between a past and a future, and always you are asking of yourself as you read, not "What will they do?" but, "What will become of them?"

Of the people of the story there is not much to be said, since the author has said most of it. Except perhaps for Hagan and the schoolmaster's wife, I never saw any of them very clearly, although they were always to be felt; but I can give a reason for this sort of myopia.

It is that the characters, except for those two, have been handled subjectively. You share or overhear their thought, and thus look through, not into, their eyes. By doing this you often catch bright glimpses of other people, but seldom at first-hand.

Whether this is right or wrong no one should dare to say. It is the author's own affair, and if he does it well he has justified his method. Someone, speaking of Happy Valley, mentioned Joyce; but— even supposing this method of assessing a work were strictly fair— the work made me think more often of Faulkner than of the Irish writer.

And it made me think more often of Patrick White than either of those others. Some people find it hard to criticise a book they have liked and approved of, and Happy Valley is such a book.

Leave the author's future alone. Refrain from saying: Here is a new writer who should do great things. Mr. White has "done" something which, while it is not great, is good.

You need not approve of the too-even graph of that "progress" of Gandhi's, nor of the carefully written hysterias of people's thought, nor of the minor key of the writing itself. These do not signify, when set in the balance against the honesty and strength and clear insight of the man who wrote the work. It is the first time such a work has been written by an Australian about Australia—but I do not think that should matter, either!

The Bunyip Stages a Comeback
[*The Tree of Man*]   A. D. Hope°

From time to time that mythical Australian monster, the Bunyip, stirs in his swamps or mountain gullies. For a few weeks some little township is terrified by mysterious bellowings at night, by the tracks of some large beast discovered by day. Dogs howl. Cattle disappear. Men carry shotguns and women lock their bedroom doors. Then it is discovered that the Bunyip was just an outside wild dog, a mad bull or, in one case, a sea-going crocodile that had strayed too far south. The scare is over. But the legend of the Bunyip persists. Some day he really will appear and ravage Reedy Creek or Upper Coolangabooloo.

The Bunyip of Australian literature is the mythical Great Australian Novel. From time to time we hear that it has appeared at last. Publishers hold a special corroboree. Rival novelists lock their doors and say their prayers. Critics reach for their shotguns. Very soon the excitement dies down as it is perceived that this is, after all, just another novel.

Mr. Patrick White's publishers are therefore naturally cautious. *The Tree of Man*, they say, has many of the qualities of the great novel. But the word has got around that Mr. White's book is, in fact, the genuine Bunyip. For one thing it is very big. And at first sight it has all the earmarks which traditionally distinguish The Great Australian Novel. The pattern is all too familiar. It is a story of pioneering. It is a family saga. It contains a flood, a drought and a bushfire. It describes for our enjoyment the humours of life and character in a little bush community, with the conventional sympathetic treatment of the battlers on the land and the unsympathetic treatment of those who are rich enough not to have to battle. There is, of course, a comic Irishman. There is even the rescue of a beautiful girl from a burning homestead and there is the lonely woman in the bush at the mercy of the chance wayfarer—only he is a commercial traveller, this time, instead of the swaggie or bushranger of fifty years ago. All it lacks is the tale of the child lost in the bush. He is there, of course, but he has changed into a boy lost in the floods.

As a matter of fact none of these things is of any importance and the book is not about them. I cannot tell why Mr. White should have chosen to disguise his novel in the old Bunyip skin. What he is writing about has nothing essentially to do with Australia, or with pioneering, or with the pattern of country life. It is the story of the

° Reprinted from *Sydney Morning Herald*, 16 June 1956, 15; courtesy *Sydney Morning Herald*.

simple lives of a simple man and woman such as you could find anywhere in the world, in any walk of life and perhaps in any grade of society. Nothing much happens to them. They take up land in the bush not many miles from Sydney and establish a reasonably prosperous dairy farm. A little settlement grows up around them. They have two children. The boy turns out badly. The girl moves to the city, marries a solicitor and rises in the world. There are grandchildren. The man and his wife grow old and die. There is in fact no story, no plot in the ordinary sense. It is simply the portrait of two lives, the random pattern of life itself observed and imagined with passionate and tender concern and touched with a sense of the mystery of all living. It is this which redeems and explains Mr. White's massive depiction of the commonplace. In spite of some serious defects of manner, he really has, as his publishers claim, one essential of the great novelist: the ability to create real people and a real world for them to live in. He has what the Australian novel largely lacks, the power to present people who are important to us in themselves, chief characters who impress us by something out of the common order— in this case, integrity. Integrity is as rare and exciting a quality as genius or beauty and Mr. White can both depict it and show its secret cause with that touch of the tragic which must always attend the depiction of what is rare and great in human life. The book is hardly a novel, for it has no action in the Aristotelian sense. It is none the worse for that, for it shows something more fundamental than mere plot is capable of revealing.

For all that it is not a successful book. Mr. White has three disastrous faults as a novelist: he knows too much, he tells too much and he talks too much. A novelist who knows too much about his characters, who gives the impression that every detail of their lives and thoughts is an open book to him, is in danger of making them seem contrived. If he tells all he knows he is in danger of being tedious. It is the fallacy of the modern psychological novel that people become more real and vivid by being turned inside out. Mr. White has fallen right into this trap and, if his principal characters succeed at all, it is in spite of his irritating and persistent omniscience. But worse than this, he is the victim of his own ingenuity and loquacity. The novelist needs a plain style, a clear easy stride, a good open texture of language to carry him to the end of his path. Sometimes, when Mr. White forgets his darling artifices, he achieves this; but for the most part he tries to write a novel as though he were writing poetry, and lyric poetry at that. It is one of the delusions of our time that novels can be written in this way. The imagery, the devices of poetry are effective because they are wedded to metre. Practised in prose they look absurd and pretentious. It is also very tedious to have to read a prose lyric of five hundred pages, in which the sharp edge of poetic phrase, the flicker of verbal fancy demands our constant and exquisite awareness. However delightful at first, it produces in time irritation, then torture and finally a numbness of the brain. Mr. White cannot describe a character drinking a cup of tea without making a poetic image of it. "Down through him wound the long ribbon of warm tea. He felt glad." He cannot simply say that a man was thirsty. It has to be: ". . . his ordinarily moist and thoughtful mouth, fixed in the white scales of thirst."

As one might expect, all his golden words are spent long before he comes to passages of intenser feeling and, trying to go one better, he achieves this sort of thing: "But his body was flooding her with tolerance. They flowed together in the darkness. The coasts of tenderness opened to admit their craft. Sleep swam out to meet them, from under the trees." It makes one pine for the old-fashioned row of asterisks.

A great deal of the book is written in what I believe was once called "experimental prose." The sentence is abandoned as a unit: instead we have detached phrases masquerading as sentences or even as paragraphs. Most of the book has a jerky, staccato movement reminiscent of Hemingway, but even more of Hemingway's master and original, the immortal Mr. Alfred Jingle. And when the author condescends to write an ordinary sentence it often turns out like this: "She was, after all, pretty or feverish, holding her neck high, which was too thin certainly, as she sat gathering crumbs with correct fingers." Or like this: "It was fortunate for Mrs. O'Dowd that life itself is hugger-mugger. And transient. Breaking into small pieces, of which her eyes were forever taking stock, and never seeing enough, most likely, they were restless and black."

Well, I still hope to see the Bunyip before I die. It might even be Mr. Patrick White who produces it; but not till he learns that, whatever life may be like, the English language is neither hugger-mugger, nor transient, and that it is never safe to break it into small pieces as a means of writing a novel. When so few Australian novelists can write prose at all, it is a great pity to see Mr. White, who shows on every page some touch of the born writer, deliberately choose as his medium this pretentious and illiterate verbal sludge.

Poetic Symbolism in Novel by Patrick White [Voss]

Kylie Tennant[*]

If you can imagine the "Rime of the Ancient Mariner" as a Victorian romance, you will have an approximate idea of the effect of *Voss*, the Book of the Month in America, the Book of the Month in England, which appears at last in Australia, the praises of the literary world dripping off its long serpentine form.

Books about Colonial Sydney, worthy in their way, there have been enough to surfeit us; but *Voss* has an El Greco thunderstorm light about it. The book is weird, macabre, cruel and of a nightmare strength. It fixes you with its glittering eye.

In *The Tree of Man*, Patrick White gave us a broad, sunlit landscape with one simple heroic figure standing, a mountain around which rolled great clouds of poetry. *Voss* is the hellish undershadow cast by *The Tree of Man*.

Voss, a shabby, irritable German adventurer, with frayed cuffs and an obsession, with his demoniac vanity, his fussy meticulousness and vitality, his pale eyes, his uncanny perceptiveness and callousness, is a complex and civilised man who plunges into the desert that is partly the interior of Australia crossed by the explorer Leichhardt, but on another level is the hell of the human mind.

Voss is the sacrificial god-man; and with him go into the desert the adoring simple boy, the poet, the devout scientist, the ex-convict rapt in survival, the aristocratic young landowner, the scoundrel and two aborigines. They are discovering new country and they are discovering themselves.

"Human behaviour," the author comments, "is a series of lunges, of which, it is sometimes sensed, the direction is inevitable."

The formal setting is Colonial Sydney from which Voss leads his expedition.

The book begins with a series of domestic scenes: the young girl, Laura, receiving the alien adventurer awkward in the parlour, while her family are at church; the picnic, with the businessmen sitting on the wave-lapped rocks with their wives and children; the evening party at which Laura offers to pray for Voss, and he rejects her prayers.

In Sydney, Voss collects his followers, his supplies. Through tense, discordant scenes, the wind, known as the "brick-fielder," blows like the personality of the man who has disturbed the cosy parties.

[*] Reprinted from *Sydney Morning Herald*, 8 February 1958, 12; courtesy *Sydney Morning Herald*.

One of the finest passages of descriptive writing in the book is the scene when the expedition sets out from Circular Quay.

"What kind of man is he? wondered the public who would never know. If he was already more than a man they really did not care. . . . They did, moreover, prefer to cast him in bronze than to investigate his soul because all dark things made them uneasy, and even on a morning of historic adventure, in bright primary colours, the shadow was sewn to the ends of his trousers where the heels of his boots had frayed them."

There is only one link with life that Voss cannot snap, the thread of understanding that binds him to Laura, the niece of the merchant, Bonner, who finances his venture.

However far Voss goes, the girl, on the dark occult level of his imagination, goes with him. She is the feminine alter-ego whom he cannot reject or deny.

He plunges out into the unknown, and Brendan Boyle, the corrupt aristocrat living in squalor with his tribe of blacks and his rum, sees him go, farewells him.

"To peel down to the last layer," Boyle yawned. "There is always another and another of yet more exquisite subtlety. Of course, every man has his own obsession. Yours would seem to be to overcome distance, but in much the same way of deeper layers of irretrievable disasters. I can guarantee that you will be given every opportunity of indulging yourself to the west of here. In stones and thorns. Why, anyone so disposed can celebrate a high old Mass, I do promise, with the skull of a blackfeller and his own blood in Central Australia."

Whether you read *Voss* as a narrative of adventure, as a psychic love story, or as a re-creation of a period of history, the tension rising to a horrifying and gruesome climax will hold you.

But Patrick White is essentially interested in personality, in character and the spiritual struggle of these men, as much as their tortures of thirst and hunger. Voss, he indicates, has a greater breaking strength than any of his companions, and because of this enormous endurance, he undergoes, in some mystical sense, an apotheosis.

This, from some Philistine quality in myself, I found the most unbelievable part of the book. Voss was such a dislikeable individual; Patrick White had been at such pains to make him an insufferable egotist, and the breakdown of his demoniac vanity was nothing I cared to contemplate.

The potentiality to endure torture, the author infers, is a virtue. Courage, apart from the character of the man who possesses it, is a good thing in itself.

Voss was transmuted by suffering. This should be exalted, but I found it rather depressing.

The pace of the book, the strength and power of the prose, the tension and dramatic force, were all there, but when the book strikes off into the deserts of mysticism, I am one of those people who would sooner slink off home.

Patrick White obtains his most striking effects by contrasting the formal surface of Sydney's constricted society with the reality of emotional suffering, the "torment of the spirit."

There is, for example, the dependable Dr. Badgery, the ship's surgeon, who loves Laura and knows that on the night of the dance she is suffering for the lost explorer: "So the surgeon returned presently to his ship, and had soon restored the shape of his orderly life, except that on occasion the dark waters would seep between the timbers. Then he would welcome them, he would be drowning with her, their transparent fears would be flickering in and out of their skulls, trailing long fins of mutual colour."

The dance provides another example: " 'I could hint,' Mrs. Bonner says, 'to one or two of the more responsible girls that it is almost morning.' O reason, Mrs. Bonner, speak to the roses and the mignonette. They will be trampled, rather, or float up and down in the silver seas of morning, together with the programs and the used napkins."

And in the desert: "A skeleton of a gelding, of which the eyes had gone milky with blight, and the crimson sores were the only sign of life, stumbled and fell with a thin scream into the gully, where he lay, and lunged, and continued to scream."

One of Voss's followers recognises him in this book as "the ugly rock on which truth must batter itself to survive." It is certainly a jolt to the humdrum of our surface literature.

White's Triumphal Chariot
[*Riders in the Chariot*]   Geoffrey Dutton*

Patrick White's latest novel, *Riders in the Chariot*, is his most comprehensive achievement. In scope it overflows countries as did *The Aunt's Story;* it digs deep as *The Tree of Man* into a local ground; it gives the imagination a vision of transcendent love, as did *Voss*, but in this case with considerably more impact on the inward eye. This book should win White many new readers, and reassure a lot of old ones. The style, often found difficult in the earlier books, is just as individual but more perfectly modulated to experience, and

* Reprinted from *Australian Book Review* 1 (November 1961): 1,3; courtesy Geoffrey Dutton.

the dialogue is much closer to contemporary idiom, especially when those cadences have been masterfully twisted to satirical ends. White has allowed his great gifts as a comic writer more room in this novel than ever before; at the same time, on the deepest levels, he continues to explore that same no-man's land between tragedy and comedy that has fascinated him in all his books. As for the symbolic elements in this novel, the critics will be out with their nets and tweezers to catch them, but White's chariot will elude them as it thunders across the sky in the fiery wake of those other chariots of Ezekiel, Apollo, Plato and Blake. That is to say, the symbols in this novel operate where they should, on an imaginative rather than an intellectual level, and a vision is all the more powerful when it comes to you through someone whose quality of response you cannot doubt. White's primary achievement here is on a human level; he has loved those characters he can, and all too clearly understood those whom he has hated.

White's novels have all had a firm structural design. In this case it resembles the spokes of a wheel, whose axle grinds dustily in the shabby heart of Sarsaparilla, a small town, if not a suburb, on the outskirts of Sydney. Converging on this centre are four main characters: Miss Hare, the cracked old spinster who lives in the ruinous magnificence of the great house at Xanadu; Mordecai Himmelfarb, the Jew who has been a professor in Germany and is now a bloody reffo boring holes through steel plates in a factory; Alf Dubbo, the half-caste who is also an artist; and Mrs. Godbold, the ex-maid who lives with her brood and her brutal husband in a shed. Though all four are exiles from red brick subtopia, Mrs. Godbold is triumphantly at home in life. The earth-offering White made in *The Tree of Man* has borne marvellous fruit in Mrs. Godbold; she lives on through the tortures and deaths of the others, a convincing proof that the human race will still bake bread on the day the world ends.

Radiating out from these characters are their past lives, incorporated with great technical skill into a sequential narrative. Miss Hare introduces the action, with a moth-holed movement of ill-organized skirts. Yet although she cannot cope with those aspects of life commonly thought necessary, and although her huge house of Xanadu is the pleasure-dome of a discredited past, she is nevertheless alarmingly sane in her perceptions, as true to nature as the insects and grasses she is most at home with. She reminds one of the epigraph from Olive Schreiner to the last part of *The Aunt's Story:* "When your life is most real, to me you are mad." As in the earlier novel, White's sympathy with such a creature is unfaltering, and he laughs at her also, as one can at somebody one really cares for. The house itself, and the account of Miss Hare's parents and upbringing, is a grand satirical swipe at the buffeting that civilization has taken in its efforts to transplant in Australian soil. With ironical detachment White sets Xanadu between the over-refinement of its builder, Norbert Hare, and the vulgarity of its eventual destroyer, Sarsaparilla. Mrs. Jolley, the housekeeper engaged by Miss Hare, is a genteel but deadly emissary of that destructive process.

All White's novels have been concerned, in varying degrees, with the workings of disintegration, but until *Riders in the Chariot* these workings have been chiefly internal. Here he is much more openly concerned with the forces of evil, from the scale of a village to that of a nation. In Sarsaparilla Mrs. Jolley and her friend Mrs. Flack are the local manifestations of the faceless monster that attacks Himmelfarb, his wife and friends in Germany, and from which he is the sole if not the lucky survivor. The Himmelfarb section is an extraordinary work of re-creation. Those who on reading *Voss* were busy turning White into a Catholic mystic will now find that all along he must have been an Orthodox Jew. Himmelfarb escapes from Europe with only his religion left him; even his glasses are gone. As he says himself, on arrival at Sydney, "The intellect has failed us." As for Miss Hare, the intellect had never particularly supported her, so she and Himmelfarb get along together very well. In another sense, they are both refugees from collapsing cultures.

Mrs. Godbold is the next character to be shown in the perspective of her history. She also has come a long way, from the flat fen country in England, through service amidst the *longueurs* of an upper middle class Australian household, to her shed at Sarsaparilla. The Tom Godbold who had tumbled her on the beach at Bondi and had been oppressed by her honest talk of sin and marriage is pursued by her terrifying goodness even into Mrs. Khalil's brothel at Sarsaparilla. This hilarious but desperately sad episode is one of the finest in the book, a blend of White's deadpan humour and unsentimental pity. It also leads into the realising of the fourth major character, the half-caste Alf Dubbo, when "that bloody abo" erupts into Mrs. Khalil's quiet well-run establishment, bursting into song and dance.

"Go easy!" interrupted Mrs. Khalil. "I don't allow language in my place. Not from clients. If I'm forced ter use a word meself, it's because I got nowhere else ter go."

"Why don't they lock 'im up?" Mr. Hoggett complained.

"Why?" asked Mrs. Khalil, and answered it easy. "Cos the constable 'imself is in the front room, as always, with my Lurleen. . . ."

So he sang, and stamped, and stamped on a cat or two, which yowled in their turn. Baskets fell, of lingerie, which the sun had hardened into slabs of salt fish. As the abo jumped and raised hell, Mollie Khalil appeared to have started jumping too, or at least her breasts were boiling inside the floral gown.

"Catch 'old of 'im, willya, please! Someone! Mr. Hoggett, be a gentleman!"

She had revived herself somewhat, with something, to cope with a situation, and now was holding her side hair, so that the sleeves had fallen back, from rather moister, black-and-whitest armpits.

"Not me!" said her client, though. "I came 'ere for a purpose. Not for a bloody rough-'ouse."

"But the constable!" she had to plead. "He will disturb the constable."

Alf Dubbo works as a sweeper at the factory where Himmelfarb is employed. He has been reared as a Great Experiment by a parson and his sister. The parson builds up his character with Latin verbs and then seduces him; Mrs. Pask, the sister, teaches him the rudiments of painting. This, later on, like Himmelfarb's religion, is the one asset that is left Dubbo.

In Miss Hare and Dubbo, White indicates the extremes of Australian, or any other, life. There are a number of brilliant characters in between, such as Rosetree, the apostate Jew who runs the factory, and his wife Shirl; the foreman, Ernie Theobalds; Bob Tanner and his girlfriend, Else Godbold; the loathsome Blue.

It is ironical that Himmelfarb, who escaped the holocaust of Europe, should be destroyed in peaceful Sarsaparilla. But one of White's major themes has always been that we start destroying each other right here at home, and, as Tom Godbold finds out, one has to be strong to suffer not only the full force of hate but also that of love. And worst of all, perhaps, is casual destruction. Miss Hare understands this very well. As she says to Himmelfarb: "Men usually decide to destroy for very feeble reasons. Oh, I know from experience! It can be the weather, or boredom after lunch. They will torture almost to death someone who has seen into them. Even their own dogs." All that Himmelfarb can console her with is his conviction that "the simple acts we have learnt to perform daily are the best protection against evil." But she sees that the ultimate evil will come through the agency of women like Mrs. Jolley and Mrs. Flack, that "the most devilish ideas will enter the heads of some women as they sit together in a house at dusk and listen to their stomachs rumble."

White sees the Australian casualness as giving an extra twist to that old knot tied of cruelty and humour. No deep convictions animate Himmelfarb's fellow factory-worker Blue who, egged on by Mrs. Flack, recrucifies Jesus in the person of Himmelfarb on Good Friday. The horror of this tragedy is that it is all good clean fun, no harm meant. "Because Blue the vindicator was also Blue the mate. It was possible to practise all manner of cruelties provided the majority might laugh them off as practical jokes. And there is almost no tragedy which cannot be given a red nose." *Riders in the Chariot* reminds one that the most convincing agents of evil have always been good blokes; Iago, for instance.

There is nothing like a sense of humour for the avoidance of awkward issues. This is succinctly put in the vernacular to Himmelfarb by Ernie Theobalds: "Remember, we have a sense of humour, and when the boys start to horse around, it is that that is gettin' the better of 'em. They can't resist a joke. Even when a man is full of beer, you will find the old sense of humour hard at work underneath. It has to play a joke. See? No offence can be taken where a joke is intended." But half the reason that Himmelfarb has been destroyed is that he never had any intention of taking offence.

Although *Riders in the Chariot* deals with evil to a greater extent than any other of White's books, it offers also a compelling vision of redemption. All four major characters have seen the Chariot; there is no particular need to ask precisely what it is. As Himmelfarb answers his wife, whom he loves: "Just when I think I have understood, I discover some fresh form—so many—streaming with implications." The capacity to see it is enough, it is an indication of compassion and humility as well as of imagination and faith, and the vision of it is authentic in the character, not foisted on to the action by the author. This is an advance on *Voss*, where the transcendent dialogue between Voss and Laura sometimes became hard for a mortal reader to approach. In this book, to use Blake's terms, White has presented a vision of eternity by first showing clearly a grain of sand.

White has always made language work hard, but his efforts are completely vindicated in this book. De Quincey's words on style could be taken as completely relevant to White, that here "there arises a case entirely different, where style cannot be regarded as a dress or alien covering, but where style becomes the incarnation of the thoughts." In a way, White is doing nothing more than obeying the ancient principle of decorum; his language is always the incarnation of the matter in hand. Its simplicities are full of meaning, as when Mrs. Jolley and Mrs. Flack come to spy on Himmelfarb's shabby house and non-existent garden: " 'Not even a geranium,' said Mrs. Flack, with bitter satisfaction." At the other extreme, its complexities are relevant to character or occasion, and should not be detached; an example is the near-surrealist description of the train-ride through Sydney which is seen through the eyes of Himmelfarb when he is drunk. The only faults are certain obsessive details, such as the frequent mention of pores of skin.

This novel, as *The Tree of Man*, ends with the arrival of the bulldozers and the erection of the brick villas of suburbia where once had been the fantastic excesses of Xanadu. But, in *Riders in the Chariot*, Mrs. Godbold walks past the villas, under a vision of splendour, her feet firmly on the earth. White has a mind comprehensive and mature enough to go beyond bitterness, to give us the vision and the earth. This is a superb achievement by a novelist we knew to be great but now find to be even greater.

Mysteries of Sensual Identity
[*The Twyborn Affair*]
Nancy Schapiro°

A new novel by a Nobel Laureate is always an occasion and this one by Patrick White is no exception. I'm having difficulty, however, defining exactly what kind of occasion it is. The story is strange, haunting, full of surprises. It's a beautifully written book with fascinating characters. Altogether an interesting occasion, and a cause for celebration, but there is more to the book than the story, more to the characters than their words and actions imply. This "more" is what gives ambiguity to the occasion and great significance to the work.

The first part of this tripartite novel is set in France in the early months of 1914. Rumors of war have begun to intrude into the idle world of vacationing Australians Joanie and Curly Golson. Curly is restless and eager to return to the business of Golson's Emporium and Sewells' Sweatfree Felt Hats, in Sydney. Joanie, however, is wallowing in culture, and in the midst of an infatuation with a young woman, Eudoxia Vatatzes, who is living with, and allegedly married to, an elderly Greek.

There is a mystery about Eudoxia which intrigues Joanie. She is very young and very beautiful and yet seems to be passionately in love with her increasingly feeble and senile husband. Joanie flirts with Eudoxia, who seems to return the interest. In writing a letter to an old friend in Australia, Eadie Twyborn, Joanie reveals her past lesbian involvement with Eadie, and hints of a suspicion about Eudoxia's identity which concerns Eadie "more than anyone." The letter is never finished, the suspicion never revealed, because Curly interrupts. The Vatatzes have disappeared, war is rumbling, and the Golsons catch the next ship home to Australia.

Part Two is set on a ranch in the Outback of Australia. Young Eddie Twyborn has returned from the war and has hired out as a ranch hand in order to live simply and strenuously, and to find himself. He slowly adjusts to the rough life and becomes intimate with the simple working people with whom he lives. He also becomes the lover of the ranch owner's wife. He attempts to patch up relations with his mother (the aforementioned Eadie Twyborn) and with his

° Reprinted from *St. Louis Post-Dispatch*, 30 March 1980, 4C; courtesy Nancy Schapiro.

father. These relations had been ruptured a few years previously when Eddie had disappeared abruptly on the eve of his marriage engagement. Part Two ends with a homosexual rape and Eddie's decision to leave Australia once again.

Part Three takes place in London in a bawdy house run by one Mrs. Eadith Trist. Her house is patronized and supported by Lord Gravenor, who is in love with Eadith and introduces her to London society. She is accepted and, in fact, courted, as a stylishly outlandish, eccentric and witty addition to salons and country houseparties. She loves Lord Gravenor but refuses to allow the relationship to progress beyond friendship, and for good reason. As you may have guessed, Eddie, Eadith and Eudoxia are one. Eadie Twyborn, widowed and piteous, turns up in London, is reunited with her child, and the book ends as the first bombs fall on London and catch former Lieutenant Eddie Twyborn on his way to visit his mother.

The three parts of the novel are unified by continuity of character. Joanie Golson turns up "down under" and in London, and Eadie Twyborn is also present in all three sections. Above all, Eudoxia, Eddie Twyborn and Mrs. Eadith Trist share a past, and an identity, which constitute the underlying unity of the whole. As for the ambiguity, the "something more" which adds significance and depth to a beautifully moving story, that is indicated by a number of elements. The names given the characters are representative. Twyborn can be read as twice born; the theme of rebirth is certainly central. Eddie, Eadie and Eadith share most of the letters and sounds of the word "head" and represent the centrality of consciousness in the flux of physical appearances. Mrs. Trist represents the ultimate sadness of a confused sexual identity, as well as the final tryst with human destiny.

The setting and structure of the novel also point to wider significance. The center section is set in Australia and the Australian characters are dominant in all segments. They try to force themselves into the effete forms of pre-World War I decadence in Europe, they harden and toughen into the macho mold of Australian outbackers, they fall into final disarray as the hangers-on of London society.

The Twyborn Affair, then, seems to be an affair of greater magnitude than a first reading may divulge. It is more than just an affair of the Twyborns; it is an exploration of sexual, national and human identities. It is an occasion for all of us.

The Anguished Quest for Self-Discovery [*The Twyborn Affair*]

Peter Wolfe°

The theme of Patrick White's remarkable new novel is conveyed by one of the novel's epigraphs, from White's fellow Australian David Malouf: "What else should our lives be but a series of beginnings, of painful settings out into the unknown, pushing off from the edge of consciousness into the mystery of what we have not yet become." As the book's main character, Eddie Twyborn, knows, a person needs a fixed, stable reference from which to push off into the unknown. Twyborn frets that he doesn't know himself well enough to test himself. At age 25, he says inwardly, "I would like to think myself morally justified in being true to what I am—if I knew what that is. I must discover."

The rest of the novel treats his anguished quest. A person who doesn't know whether he'd rather be a man or a woman can serve as the subject of comedy. In White's hands, this basic question of identity has tragic reverberations. Never has White, winner of the Nobel Prize for Literature in 1973, challenged himself so deeply; never has he written with such compassion. Twyborn's search for identity is prompted less by lust, cash, and titles than by need. White emphasizes his private turmoil by aligning it with a public disaster—war between nations.

Part One of *The Twyborn Affair* takes place in spring 1914, when the European powers were mobilizing for World War I; at the outset of the second part, Twyborn has just been discharged from the Australian army, where he served as a lieutenant and won a DSO. The action ends during the London Blitz some 20 years later.

Other dangers, doubts, and insecurities help convey Twyborn's hauntedness, White referring often to homosexuality, sex between generations, cross-dressing, ocean crossings, and disguises. Everybody feels either homeless, disoriented, or trapped. Twyborn's "I arrive everywhere too early, or too late" describes a torn psyche in a conflict-ridden world. Struggle dogs him. In his search for madder music, he forfeits the consolations of the here-and-now. He is never where he wants to be. His rating the refinements of sex higher than simple lust ironically divides him both from his deepest needs and those he loves.

At the same time White claims, through him, that the unwillingness to try new ideas serves stagnancy, discourages diversity, and bridles independence. Progress doesn't come from the sane, reason-

° Reprinted from *St. Louis Globe-Democrat*, 29–30 March 1980, 10D.

able person. Only the outcast presses for change, even if he suffers for it later.

The struggle between Eddie Twyborn's wish to belong and his discontent with established sexual norms invokes White's best novelistic gifts. In Part One, for instance, White practices the art of misdirection with all the cunning of a detective writer. Playing fair all the way, he plants enough clues to overcome our fear of being deceived or mocked. Only after Part Two is under way do we see that we have been reading about a major development in the Twyborn family drama and that White has given us enough evidence to make the connections.

Another turnabout shapes Part Three. Although set mostly in a London brothel, the action is chaste, formalized, and confining. Because abandon without controls is destructive, the drive to self-fulfillment often ends in self-denial. *The Twyborn Affair* stands as White's answer to those who have complained about his neglect of plot development. A breakthrough from the standpoint of both technique and vision, his eleventh novel sets a standard of excellence that other fictional works of the 1980s will have a hard time meeting.

Patrick White: The End of Genius [*Memoirs of Many in One*]

David J. Tacey°

It is sad to see genius in decay. It is even more disconcerting to see the products of that decay hailed as artistic triumphs. *Memoirs of Many in One*, a thin, insubstantial novel, full of contrivance and wilful theatricality, is said to be "vintage White" (David English, *The Age*, 5 April, 1986), "a great game" (David Malouf, *The Weekend Australian Magazine*, 5–6 April, 1986), "a great comic novel" (Thomas Shapcott, *The Sydney Morning Herald*, 5 April, 1986). Deterioration and loss of creative genius so clearly mark this novel that it is bizarre, to say the least, that critics and reviewers are unable to acknowledge it and face it squarely. The same can be said of *The Twyborn Affair* (1979), which is strained, mechanical, and hollow inside, yet which received virtually unqualified acclaim: "Literary master in full cry"; "White has not yet begun to write." Many readers find these rich helpings of praise alarming and offensive, and are unable to reconcile their own readings of these texts with the "official" views. White

° Reprinted from *Meridian* (La Trobe University English Review) 5 (May 1986): 89–91; courtesy David J. Tacey.

clearly enjoys a cult following in Australia, and it is as a result of this pseudo-religious adherence that his admirers, imitators, and devotees keep informing us of the "greatness" of his latest effort. Has the awarding of the Nobel Prize in 1973 so shocked our provincial faculties that we are unable to be objective about our "world-class" novelist? Or are we overcompensating for the apparently cool, critical response to White's early works? In our anxiety to avoid being classified as academic philistines or reactionaries, are we passing every new White text with inflated praise? Does criticism have a guilty conscience—are we all atoning for A. D. Hope's notorious review of *The Tree of Man?* There are a number of ways in which our current critical impotence can be approached and analysed—but never finally justified.

A major factor in all of this is the tyrannical stand of Patrick White himself. He has been playing bully to the critical establishment since the 1950s, and we are all so terrified of his frequent attacks and smarting words that critical judgement has been silenced. And White keeps pounding away at our straw-heads, which have long since lost the capacity to put things in perspective or to disagree with him. Much of his late-Romantic resentment for society as the Great Antagonist gets transferred to the academic world, and many Australian academics have such low self-esteem and inbuilt inferiority that they accept White's outlandish attacks as natural and inevitable. White's fictional characters are prone to blame their own internal sufferings upon a mythical "THEM," and White himself invariably locates "THEM" in educational institutions and newspaper editorial rooms. His attack upon critics attains its most extreme, literal expression in *Memoirs,* when Alex Xenophon Demirjian Gray opens fire upon an audience during a theatrical performance, hoping to shoot "the Critic"—"King Vampire Harry"—from *The Sydney Morning Herald.*

Critical judgement is frequently eclipsed by cults, fads, and fashions, which make themselves respectable by posing as ideologies. The ideology to which White makes his appeal is that of homosexuality and gayness. White can do virtually anything, write the most appalling trash, and somehow it is all justified under the wondrous banner of gayness. *Memoirs* is a wonderful dragshow, says David Malouf; it's about display, revelation of surfaces, letting it all hang out. No need to worry about the slipshod sentences, the barely discernible structure, the shoddy design, because White is parading the gay banner and that is in itself a worthy thing to do. The same happens when Marxist critics acclaim weak novels because they happen to demonstrate some simplistic Marxist formula. The ideology is more important than the work of art itself, which exists merely to flatter a certain point of view. White's reviewers find *Memoirs* so terribly daring, so wonderfully explicit: "There is no debate about White's gayness, no mileage to be got from coyly wondering if maybe that little allusion to so and so really means such and such" (English). We are all chuckling hysterically, naughtily, so pleased that the old aunt has finally come out of the closet. And for as long as Australian intellectuals find gay ideology rewarding, fascinating, entrancing, critical judgement will be held in abeyance, and we will be overvaluing all the ephemeral pieces of personal indulgence which White is foisting upon us. The last stage of White's career is tedious, unremarkable, boring, yet some are saying that the new-look White, the dazzling, daring, night-club entertainer "may rival in time his great namesake, the Nobel prizewinner—the mystic . . . of Centennial Park" (Malouf).

The recent novels, apparently, reveal the real person behind the literary facade, the high camp behind the high seriousness, the play-fulness behind the once-stern metaphysics. Because depth and reli-giosity is unfashionable nowadays, this is felt to be a movement toward honesty, reality, post-modern sensibility. Those of us who failed to understand *Riders in the Chariot* or *The Solid Mandala* are already breathing sighs of relief. Now there is no need to come to terms with those heady works, because all we need to know about is the gayness which underlay them all, and which is now exposed for all to see. The major works are already being read as old-fashioned monuments of modernism, museum-pieces, which served as a polite mask for the real feelings and attitudes of the author. If White had been starting his career now, this argument runs, there would be no Chariots or Mandalas, no "modernist trappings" (English), just plenty of good, honest homosexuality and polymorphous perversity. White's career can now be read as a simple Freudian cycle: early repression of homosexual desires; the sublimation of these into spiritual and symbolic structures; the return of the repressed in the late stages of his career. It's much simpler than we had thought; Freud triumphs after all, despite apparent Jungian complexity.

There is something characteristically Australian in this collapse into bodily desires and Freudianism. We love it when high-mindedness hits the ground, when religiosity falls into shallowness, trivia, and excrementalism. But there is no need to lop this tall poppy with the Australian scythe, for White is keen to do it for us. The man who has despised Australians for most of his career has become the classic Australian: knocking over cultural values, hitting out at established authorities, destroying anything sacred. White is determined to de-stroy his own image while we look on, to strip himself naked, as does Alex Xenophon Demirjian Gray, in full view of the paying audience. There is something wild and anarchic in his recent dem-onstrations, a desire not only to shock the audience, but also to abuse his own reputation. We are reminded of Hurtle Duffield in *The*

Vivisector, smearing his own shit upon his newly completed "Self-Portrait." In a sense White's last two novels, as well as his own *Self-Portrait,* have attempted to smear dirt and shit upon his own religious edifice, his literary *oeuvre,* and his past. He seems to delight in his own self-levelling, to relish his own collapse, and to enjoy the stench of his own decay.

Alex Gray is a desperate and pathetic figure. She spends most of her time storming the gates of self-knowledge, for although she makes many attempts to discover "something more positive than life" (p. 144), she is never given access to the inner world of the self. She remains on the profane, external side of her own experience and imitates the Inner Way. Alex goes through all the motions, acts out the drama of individuation, adopts various masks and guises, but everything is phoney and contrived. Her life could be described as a psychopathic parody of individuation, in the sense that her acting out of the psychic drama leads her to criminality, vandalism, delusion, and death. The desire to integrate her spiritual side leads her to seize a drunken derelict from Centennial Park (whom she supposes is a mystic in disguise) and to lock him up in the "priest's hole" in the attic. The desire for spontaneity and self-expression leads her to shop-lifting, prowling and poaching, exhibitionism, and indiscriminate attacks on the public. And all the while she keeps telling herself (and White keeps telling us) that this psychopathic parody means something, that it is leading her to salvation. Her task is to play-act for all she is worth, to cajole herself and others into a sense of her higher status, and to bluff her way to enlightenment.

Some readers will say that I am missing all the fun, that "Patrick" (who is also a character in this novel) is playing games, that the novel is "an extraordinarily good parody-pastiche" (Kerryn Goldsworthy, *The National Times,* 4 April, 1986). David English reports that "Those of us who can share a joke are already cackling." Yes, it's about as funny as a guerrilla attack on the centre of Sydney, or a car-bomb attack on the Art Gallery. The humour is violent, strained, hysterical; there is a sense of letting loose which can only seem funny to the infant who shits his pants in a concert hall. And as to this work being a conscious self-parody, I would say that while there is partial evidence of this, the overriding impression is that Alex Gray herself is stuck in the parodic mode. There is more darkness and despair in this text than the frivolous "drag-show" reading would allow. Alex desperately imitates the patterns and postures of Elizabeth Hunter, Hero Pavloussi, Mary de Santis, but nothing works: every one of her imagined or actual excursions leads to disaster.

Alex Gray constructs an entire world of values, ideas, and attitudes, with a citizenship of one. She believes herself to be genuinely inspired, and chastises her daughter for not appreciating her genius.

Inevitably, she feels her position threatened and becomes paranoid and defensive. People seem to be wanting to snatch her memoirs, to destroy her secret world, and to deny her the "creative" outlet she seeks in spontaneous, bizarre-violent enactments. It is to her advantage, of course, to see her psychopathic behaviour as "creative" and to imagine that society is trying to steal creativity from her. Increasingly society becomes linked with repression, sadism, brutality, and is personified in the police (who frequently arrest her and carry her away) and in psychiatrists (who strive, she thinks, to make her insane like them). Ultimately, society becomes identical with the straitjacket, and when fears of social consequences arise during one of her freakish episodes she has a vision of Professor Falkenberg "holding out the seamless canvas jacket, its blind sleeves, its dangling tapes" (p. 101). " 'Just you try to create, my girl' " warns the psychiatric nurse, " 'and you'll be back in this before tea's up' " (p. 172). This is the psychopath's view of the world: society is seen as a nightmare of repression and restriction, whereas "to create," to express the personal self, is identical with a lunatic eccentricity which invariably invokes social reprimand. Life is a choice between two kinds of madness, one which has social support, and one which releases the id and personal desires.

A major problem with this novel is that we are asked to believe Alex's delusive system, to adopt it as our own. For the novel to work, the reader must identify with the central character and look out upon the world through her crazed eyes. Unhappily, most reviewers succumb to her own inflated reading of her experience: "Alex Gray is the most endearingly eccentric of all White's female characters. Whatever she tackles, and it is always disastrous, she plunges into it with the sort of recklessness and energy we can only admire. . . . The book is a celebration of the will to celebrate, to pummel out some necessary space for the wonderful and zany in a wretched and constricting world" (Shapcott). Alex would be happy with this assessment of her memoirs; we'd be her pal for life. We have mistaken her madness for genius, her violence for creativity, and see the world, along with terrorists, derros, and revolutionaries, as an oppressive straitjacket inside which we have to "pummel out" space for the psyche. In effect, we have taken a pew next to her in the asylum, and become one of the "Happy Few Who Know Better," hating the world, dreaming in our constriction of the pleasures of dereliction and abandonment.

Crusades Against Hoopla and
Pain [*Three Uneasy Pieces*]   Carolyn Bliss°

Patrick White's *Three Uneasy Pieces* is a slender, 10,000-word short story collection, which makes a sharp and caustic statement in its timing, an intriguingly antiphonal suggestion in its prose. Published in December of 1987, it was rushed into production before 1988 in order to avoid any appearance on White's part of having validated Australia's Bicentennial by issuing a celebratory volume. So anxious was White to disassociate himself from the Bicentennial hoopla that he snatched the manuscript from its original Melbourne publisher, when that house was unable to meet his December 31 deadline, and handed it over to astonished and delighted Pascoe Publishing, a small firm whose head man, Bruce Pascoe, admits that the book's acquisition is "more of a windfall than a coup." Taking full advantage of its windfall, Pascoe had the book typeset in a matter of days, took White's corrections on the proofs by telephone, and reportedly "camped" at the printer's until the first run of bound copies was delivered. The volume's triumphant copyright date is 1987.

Judgmental, preemptory, irascible: White's censure of the Bicentennial seems of a piece with his recent public persona. But his book collects "uneasy pieces," works which shed a very different light on Australia's only Nobel Laureate in literature, an indisputable master of his art and one of the twentieth century's greatest novelists. This new light is a gentle and subdued one: mellow, conciliatory, finally almost serene. All three of the volume's pieces are written in the first person and adopt a voice which begins in reflection and moves toward confession. Thus, while the book sounds again the note of penitential self-exposure that has counterpointed White's fiction at least since *The Vivisector*, it settles at last for a kind of shriven self-acceptance that expands in the direction of a wider reconciliation.

The first "uneasy piece," entitled "The Screaming Potato," is a scant two pages long. Within this meager space, however, it manages to develop an image of excised potato eyes into a comment on the inevitably cruel and murderous exigencies of living. Like Heriot in Randolph Stow's *To the Islands*, the elderly narrator of "The Screaming Potato" is forced to equate life itself with preying and to offer up the prayer to be either absolved or disabused of his deep sense of guilt. In this story, even lettuce, parsnips, and potatoes whimper or scream as we prepare them for our nourishment, and all our acts

° Reprinted from *Antipodes: A North American Journal of Australian Literature* (Spring 1988): 3; courtesy Robert Ross, editor.

are marked and marred by "a fair bit of gouging" and "the chopping to be done."

The narrator of "Dancing with Both Feet on the Ground" is also an old man, one who has learned that life must be celebrated only "cautiously." In its opening image of careful, arthritic dancing in a kitchen—"Over spilt milk. through lettuce leaves and potato peelings. Bloodstains too . . ."—"Dancing" echoes the volume's opening piece, as it also does in the rest of the story's prevalent food imagery, which pictures sustenance as always inadequate, saccharine, or accusatory. The story's other controlling image is that of dancing, whether in a solitary moment of unreason and abandon which "M" might term "senility," or in the ballroom of a winter-locked European hotel remembered from the days of youth. As the story not so much unfolds as dilates, the act of dancing begins to suggest the teleological nature of time, which drives over those it fells or will fell. These include the pretentious, widowed Contessa whose feet of Australian clay paddle the air when she slips on the hotel dance floor, and the still upright narrator who shuffles toward an uncertain future and shares with the sham Contessa a need for faith aroused by the icy draughts of approaching mortality. As in White's novel *Voss*, life in this story is like a river which runs over "upturned faces," but also a river whose light and motion mirror "figures of the timeless dance."

The center of the book's interlocking pieces is the last and longest story, "The Age of a Wart." Here we find again the White who notes the extramundane dimensions inherent in the humblest, most disgusting physicalities. In *A Fringe of Leaves*, a boil became "spiritual matter"; here it's a wart. Wart and boil are put to similar thematic purposes: to link characters of spiritual affinity, in this case the narrator and his afflicted schoolmate Bluey Platt. As youngsters, both the boys grow matching warts on their right hands, and the narrator is sure he caught his from his classmate. Bluey, whose real name is Tancred, after the Christian Crusader of history and Rossini's opera, resembles the narrator in other ways as well. Both will be artists, one working in lives and substances and the other in words; both could be mystics; and they are, as Bluey claims and the narrator later acknowledges, "twins." Yet the latter initially chafes at this identification with someone of indifferent academic achievement and an address on the "Wrong Side." Accordingly, he cures himself of his emblematic wart through, as it eventuates, an act of deliberate will. Soon he also loses proximity to his friend, as Bluey's sojourn with western Aboriginals and the narrator's schooling in England separate them.

Following his formal education, the narrator and his bad chest sit out the subsequent War in a Scottish hotel, where he begins to write the novels which will bring him fame, honors, degrees, and self-contempt. He describes them as works which only "pretended to search for truth, reality, in carefully chosen words and the studied sentences of literature." Suspecting that Bluey, whose wart must have survived to "praise . . . the ugliness of life," could admit him to a reality he circles unsteadily and desperately craves, the narrator mounts an instinctive crusade to reclaim him.

Tancred, meanwhile, carries his own crusade against suffering through the worst of the War and its aftermath, leaving signs to surface everywhere for the narrator. Still, he remains beyond reach of his friend. The search for Tancred thus becomes a pilgrimage whose stages are signaled by relics and testimony, but only inter-mittent and unsatisfactory epiphany. True revelation must await the reappearance of the wart, which seems to the now dying narrator a melanoma whose darkness may engulf the world. His extremity sum-mons twin Tancred, who rejoins him in a reconciling vision in which evil dies, a brotherhood of suffering and survival is affirmed, man's potency is proclaimed, and the story closes.

The "three uneasy pieces" of White's latest book thus ultimately yield the ease of resolution. Yet a caveat is called for. White could be tempting us to make too much of this resolution, something the style may be warning us against. These stories lack the convincing density and scope of the major novels and even of much of White's short fiction. Instead of proceeding by means of a rich proliferation of ambiguous, evocative, but finally consonant detail, they merely gesture toward implication through a shorthand predicated on sugges-tive imagery.

Nonetheless, transcribed in the reader's heart or soul, which, as always in White, receive more credence than the intellect, the signs of this shorthand constitute a prayer much like that of Le Mesurier in *Voss:* a petition that the spirit come to rest "in true love of all men and in you, O God, at last." It is a wrenching prayer to raise, one founded in a humility which White's fiction insists must be forever and painfully repossessed. These stories, too, trace that repetitive process. But they also hint that if White shuns the chauvinism of the Bicentennial, the volume which heralds this renunciation simulta-neously reaches toward the family of man. As a member of the family, I welcome him amongst us.

ARTICLES AND ESSAYS

Odyssey of a Spinster: A Study of *The Aunt's Story*

Thelma Herring°

"But old Mrs. Goodman did die at last." The first eight words of a novel have seldom told so much as the arresting opening of *The Aunt's Story*. Introducing the name of the woman whose domination of her family determines much that happens in the early chapters, it establishes the fact of her death before the story moves back into the past: the unconventional conjunction at the beginning, giving a sense of continuity, plunges us into the flux of events, and, complemented by "old" and "at last," hints at the long period of frustration for at any rate one survivor which has preceded. It is a warning that we are entering upon a novel in which style is important, in which we need to pay more than the usual amount of attention to words.

As Australia's most experimental novelist Patrick White owes nothing to local literary tradition. His affinity is with those who have tried to extend the frontiers of the novel in the direction of poetry. One imagines he would assent to the view expressed by Virginia Woolf in 1927 that the future of the novel lay in a compromise between prose fiction and poetry, the taking on by fiction of "something of the exaltation of poetry, but much of the ordinariness of prose."[1] From the beginning this trend has been discernible in his work.

The Aunt's Story (1948), the third of White's novels to be published, is the first which fully reveals him as an artist of powerful and original vision. Although it may have been overshadowed in critical attention and popular esteem by the three novels of larger scope written since his return to Australia, on its smaller scale it sets out to do something no less difficult and, I would argue, achieves its end more successfully. True, it has not the tortured intensity of *Voss*, nothing perhaps quite so continuously impressive and moving as the account of Himmelfarb's life in Europe in *Riders in the Chariot*: but

° This article first appeared in *Southerly* 25 (1965): 6–22; reprinted from *Ten Essays on Patrick White from* Southerly, edited by G. A. Wilkes (Sydney: Angus and Robertson, 1970), 3–20.

neither has it the disconcerting inequalities of these novels and *The Tree of Man.*

Tentative though they are in many ways, White's first two novels show him already grappling with themes which were to engage him at a deeper level in *The Aunt's Story,* and seeking to adapt the techniques of Joyce and Virginia Woolf (not yet fully assimilated) to present what is to him the basic human problem: "the ultimate separateness of soul."[2] *Happy Valley* (1939), though it is his least characteristic novel, is typical in concerning itself with "a world of allegory, of which the dominating motif was pain" (p. 77), and the epigraph from Mahatma Gandhi on the law of suffering, which ends: "the purer the suffering, the greater is the progress," is even more applicable to some of the later books, including *The Aunt's Story,* than to *Happy Valley* itself, which does not explore the theme fully. It anticipates *The Aunt's Story* in showing that the sensitive human being can hope for happiness only in rare moments of illumination: through art, as when Oliver Halliday listens to Bach played in a French church; through the beauty of some object such as the shell which Rodney gives Margaret; or through a momentary recognition of affinity with another human being, as when the two lonely children exchange glances in the schoolroom. Only insensitive characters get what they want—and it is doubtful whether it is worth having. Hilda Halliday gets her dreary security by hanging on to a husband who doesn't want her; Sidney Furlow perjures herself in order to blackmail Hagan into marrying her—a very poor bargain; Amy Quong, one of whose three passions is for possession, after causing the deaths of both Vic and Ernest Moriarty by her anonymous letter, acquires Vic's lustre bowl which she has coveted. The character who emerges as the most highly developed human being is the outsider Margaret Quong, half-Chinese, half-Australian, who at the age of thirteen accepts the loneliness of her destiny with a silent, touching dignity and fortitude, having learnt to expect nothing from others and to endure without useless protest.

Belief in the law of learning through suffering goes back at least to Aeschylus,[3] and several references show that Greek tragedy was indeed in White's thoughts.[4] The most substantial recalls it, however, only to draw a bitter contrast: "There is something relentless about the hatred induced by human contacts in a small town. At times it seems to have a kind of superhuman organization, like the passions in a Greek tragedy, but there is seldom any nobility about the passions of a small town . . ." (p. 191). Hatred for the meanness of the herd, its incapacity to suffer and to learn, balances White's compassion for the fear and pain and loneliness of the individual; *Happy Valley* is an early study of the ignoble small community of which Sarsaparilla later becomes the symbol.

But, although the point of view is characteristic, there is something unsatisfactory about the presentation of the theme. Despite various references to the search for significance, a design, in what happens, the design seems to be imposed by the author rather than discovered. The plot is very carefully patterned so that the violent climax of the story of the Moriartys provides the resolution of the other main entanglements: but one is convinced neither of the inevitability of Oliver's renunciation of Alys (he speaks of not willingly destroying, but takes no account of the probable destruction of *her* happiness), nor of the reality of the progress to which their suffering has led. Too little has been seen of Oliver and Alys *together* for us properly to judge the value of their experience, and the final impression is that they are too negative and ineffectual to make much spiritual progress.

The Living and the Dead (1941) is distinguished from White's other work by its setting, the London of the brittle 1920s and bewildered 1930s; and far from justifying the glib assumption that as an expatriate he cannot possibly write as well about another country as about Australia, it seems to me rather to support Jack Lindsay's view that "[White's] roots lie in English culture and society."[5] It is arguable that he understands (though he may dislike them equally) Bayswater or Pimlico as a social milieu much better than Sarsaparilla; and certainly as a *place* London is much more vividly realized (and I don't refer merely to the accumulation of physical details) than, say, the Durilgai of *The Tree of Man*. The limitations of *The Living and the Dead* are not due to the choice of an English setting, but are the natural limitations of a young novelist still struggling towards maturity as an artist.

The atmosphere of this novel is one of decay, aridity, nullity, death; and the sense of stifling enclosure is intensified by the imagery—the recurring cocoon metaphor and such phrases as "an eiderdown of sleep," "the anaesthesia of snow," "the grey pall of words." London is the brown sad city of *The Waste Land*, to which spring brings no ecstasy. Even music, usually a source of beauty in White's novels, is part of the decadence: "the spun caramel of violins, a drawn-out Massenet," "a rheumaticky *pizzicato* that was Grieg" in a Lyons' Corner House. It does not need the repetition of the phrase "the marble wasteland" to recall the world of Eliot's early poems; and it is difficult not to attach significance to the choice of a name for the hero. Elyot Standish (a forerunner of the Poet in *The Ham Funeral*) is a younger Prufrock, always standing on the shore looking on, afraid of getting his feet wet, afraid of being alive.

It is through the experience of Elyot that White endeavours to work out his theme of the opposition between the spiritually dead and those who are truly alive, using several times the metaphor (also used by Virginia Woolf) of the envelope enclosing each personality, ensuring its separateness. Elyot in his fear of involving himself cherishes separateness till he perceives that he must make the crucial choice, which is complicated by the fate of the "living" characters, his sister Eden and Joe Barnett, who choose spiritual "life" at the cost of death in the Spanish Civil War; but it may be objected that in preferring to "the protest of self-destruction" "an intenser form of living" (p. 331) he reaches a very vague solution.

It is misleading to say as Marjorie Barnard does that the novel "ends where it began."[6] True, the *story* returns to its beginning after showing in retrospect (like the first part of *The Aunt's Story*) the events which have culminated, just before the novel opens, in the death of the protagonist's mother. This is emphasized by the repetition at the beginning of the final chapter of the paragraph at the end of the first in which Elyot in the drawing-room of his mother's house thinks of those who have been within its walls and others with whom he has had contact outside: "Alone, he was yet not alone, uniting as he did the themes of so many other lives" (pp. 20, 333). But this recapitulation is not quite the end. Whereas he had reflected before the first occurrence of the passage that "there was never any means of communication with the faces in the street," after the second he goes out and finds the faces in the night buses "potentially communicative": having boarded a bus, "He felt like someone who had been asleep, and had only just woken."

Elyot, it is implied, genuinely chooses life—a form of intensification through imaginatively entering into the lives of other people. Here, surely, is a hint of the theme taken up and given very surprising development in Part Two of *The Aunt's Story*. The trouble is that Elyot's choice is stated rather than demonstrated; we don't see him *experiencing* this intenser form of living, and nothing in the novel leads us to believe him capable of it. Moreover, hatred in this case almost overwhelms compassion; White responds imaginatively far more to the boredom and horror of the dead than to the glory of the living, and the simple carpenter Joe Barnett, a character built according to Lawrentian formula rather than comprehended from within, is inadequate to suggest the "ecstasy" that should balance the "sickness."

There is nothing factitious about *The Aunt's Story*, however, no suggestion of contrivance in reaching a neat resolution. A new discipline in style matches the inner certainty of the writer as he examines the relation between wisdom and suffering, and the full weight of his theme is carried by Theodora Goodman, who is one of White's most finely and fully realized characters.

In Part One, "Meroë," we see the child whose vision would not exclude the grub in the heart of the rose become the middle-aged spinster too honest to marry Huntly Clarkson, the loved aunt and unloved daughter who "came when the voice called" (p. 9). Since she is denied the joys of a creative artist her intelligence and sensibility are a source of anguish to her except in "moments of insight" shared chiefly with her father, but also with people like the Man who was Given his Dinner and the Greek cellist Moraïtis, with whom she experiences affinity in a brief moment of contact. The happiness she enjoys in her father's company and her love for her home are beautifully implied by the account of their riding together:

> She listened to the clinking of the stirrups, and the horses blowing out their nostrils, and the heavy, slow, lazy streams of sound that fell from the coarse hair of their swishing tails. Theodora looked at the land that was theirs. There was peace of mind enough on Meroë. You could feel it, whatever it was, and you were not certain, but in your bones. It was in the clothes-line on which the sheets drooped, in the big pink and yellow cows cooling their heels in creek mud, in magpie's speckled egg, and the disappearing snake. It was even in the fences, grey with age and yellow with lichen, that tumbled down and lay round Meroë. The fences were the last word in peace of mind. (pp. 23–24)

—a passage which illuminates her later statement of faith to Sokol-nikov: "I believe in a pail of milk . . ." (p. 159).

Her father's death, described with a moving brevity and restraint, is the beginning of Theodora's alienation from the world: other relationships, with Frank Parrott and Huntly Clarkson, the men she might have married, she terminates herself by the shooting of the hawk and the clay ducks, acts which emphasize her separateness. After the shooting of the hawk, with which she had identified herself, "I was wrong, she said, but I shall continue to destroy myself, right down to the last of my several lives" (pp. 73–74). Even with her niece Lou, Theodora is conscious of "the distance that separates" (p. 137), though with Lou, who is so like her in various ways but has "no obvious connexion" with either of her parents, she has a special relationship which is adroitly suggested by juxtaposition rather than stated. The paragraph in which Fanny's pregnancy is announced immediately follows one describing Theodora's sensations after Mo-raïtis's concert:

> . . . the music which Moraïtis had played was more tactile than the hot words of lovers spoken on a wild nasturtium bed, the violins had arms. This thing which had happened between Moraïtis and herself she held close, like a woman holding her belly. She smiled. If I were an artist, she said, I would create something that would answer him. Or if I were meant to be a mother, it would soon smile in my face. But although she was neither of these, her contentment filled the morning . . . (p. 117)

Here in germ is the idea of the relation of the spiritual lovers Voss and Laura to Rose Portion's child, but much more discreetly handled than the elaboration of the idea in physical terms in *Voss*.

The other characters in this first part of the novel are outlined with clarity and precision, and White's wit in presenting the alien, commonplace world outside Theodora's secret life has a poise and certainty of touch lacking in some of his later satirical passages: of Fanny, for instance: "You remembered the flesh of early roses, but under the skin you could read arithmetic" (p. 86). And how well he places the destructive Mrs. Goodman in the early pages—the woman born as Theodora suggests with an axe in her hand, whose great tragedy was "that she had never done a murder. Her husband had escaped into the ground, and Theodora into silences" (p. 99), who could however kill happiness in a breath:

> Once there were the new dresses that were put on for Mother's sake.
> "Oh," she cried, "Fanny, my roses, my roses, you are very pretty."
> Because Fanny was as pink and white as roses in the new dress.
> "And Theo," she said, "all dressed up. Well, well. But I don't think we'll let you wear yellow again, because it doesn't suit, even in a sash. It turns you sallow," Mother said. (pp. 26–27)

In White's later novels and short stories there is increasing evidence of an unresolved conflict between the points of view of the visionary and the connoisseur: if all that matters is qualifying for a seat in the chariot, why care, it may be asked, whether people know the difference between an Aubusson carpet and Wilton wall-to-wall, or prefer texture-brick to stone? Yet in *Riders in the Chariot* it almost seems as though Mrs. Jolley is evil *because* she likes pastel shades. Mrs. Goodman's evil qualities are much more solidly based.

Unlike her sister Fanny, of whom their father says that "Fanny would always ask the questions that have answers" (p. 40), Theodora reaches out for deeper experience. At the end of this section she makes a great advance in self-knowledge in recognizing the "core of evil" in her from which springs her hostility to her mother and the necessity of destroying "the great monster Self," but she also realizes that she has not yet the humility needed. The rest of the book shows the process by which she attains that humility.

When Theodora goes to Europe after her mother's death and enriches her mental experience by entering in imagination into the lives of the amusing and pathetic eccentrics at her Riviera hotel, where in the symbolic *jardin exotique* "the soul, left with little to hide behind, must . . . come out into the open" (p. 146), she experiences "the great fragmentation of maturity"[7] of which the epigraph from Henry Miller speaks, discovering, as Holstius points out later, that these "created lives" are interchangeable, "the faces . . . only slightly different aspects of the same state" (p. 188). They take on aspects of people she has known—Katina of Lou, for instance—but also of Theodora herself: if Katina shares her more attractive qualities, Lieselotte possesses her destructive impulses. In this bubble world of unreason, both sinister and comic, the inconsequential dialogue has a kind of wild sense: as when Mrs. Rapallo bids the General after the breaking of the nautilus: "Go, hang out your soul to dry. You Russians were always damp" (p. 225). Her confession that her daughter the Principessa does not exist, and General Sokolnikov's that he is only a major, undermine this life of illusion by letting in a measure of reality; and it is finally terminated by the destructive and purgatorial fire, in which the acquisitive Demoiselles Bloch lose their possessions and those subject to consuming passions their lives.

The epigraph to Part Three ("When your life is most real, to me you are mad") points to the hazard of talking, as most critics do, of Theodora's madness in the latter part of the novel. White avoids such simple labels.[8] "Who's crazy and who isn't? Can you tell me that?" the Man who was Given his Dinner had asked (p. 45). (The doctor who takes charge of Theodora pointedly refers to her condition as *"lucidity."*) As Marjorie Barnard has said: "The world is arraigned, not Theodora."[9]

Walking with Sokolnikov between the sea and the houses, Theodora had perceived in the landscape that there was "no break in the continuity of being" (p. 188). By the beginning of Part Three, when as she writes to Fanny "I have seen and done," her awareness of the difference between doing and being enables her to recognize, as she journeys across America, an "integrity of purpose and of being" in "the full golden theme of corn" and the "counter-point of houses," whereas she herself is a discord: there is "no safeguard against the violence of personality" (p. 274). Her decision is announced abruptly: "Then, in a gust, Theodora knew that her abstraction also did not fit"—so she gets off the train and finally takes refuge in the empty house. Must she mortify herself to the very end? the reader who is neither saint nor mystic may be tempted to ask. But from the first, compromise has been shown to be unnatural to Theodora; the sudden decision, implicit in what we already know of her, commands assent.

To strip oneself of inessentials is a necessary preliminary for illumination. Theodora when she reached the Hôtel du Midi took out objects of her own (few and simple though they were) "to give the room her identity" (p. 144), but now when she abandons the train she throws away her tickets and even gives herself a false name: "This way perhaps she came a little closer to humility, to anonymity, to pureness of being" (p. 284). And so she is prepared for the "ultimate moment of clear vision," when Holstius, that imaginary composite of the men from whom she has learned wisdom, tells her she must accept the two irreconcilable halves, joy and sorrow, flesh and marble, illusion and reality, life and death: "And you have already found that . . . there is sometimes little to choose between the reality of illusion and the illusion of reality" (p. 293). Though she has to defer to those who prescribe the reasonable life and insist on taking her into custody, Theodora wins the game for her soul.

This search for "pureness of being"—which is ultimately to prove, in the words of *"Little Gidding,"* "A condition of complete simplicity (Costing not less than everything)"—is a recurring theme in White's work, from the early short story "The Twitching Colonel" to *Riders in the Chariot.* Colonel Trevellick, a retired Indian Army officer, affirms that "only in dissolution is salvation from illusion": "I shall strip myself, the onion-folds of prejudice, till standing naked though conscious I see myself complete or else consumed like the Hindu conjuror who is translated into space," whereas Maud, his wife, had been, he reflects, "attached to her self beyond escaping."[10] And a similar image is used by Miss Hare: "Eventually I shall discover what is at the centre, if enough of me is peeled away."[11]

Theodora, then, like Voss, goes forth on a journey which is also a journey of spiritual discovery; but whereas Voss is the explorer, Theodora is the traveller wandering in the Old and New Worlds. And this points to the significance of White's use of the *Odyssey* motif.

The landscape of Part One of *The Aunt's Story* is said to have been suggested by the country round Moss Vale,[12] though, characteristically, White does not obtrude local references; it is also a symbolic landscape associating Meroë, the Goodman home, with both Ethiopia and the Greek islands, by means of the skeleton trees, described as "the abstractions of trees, with their roots in Ethiopia," and the live trees, "a solid majority of soughing pines" (p. 20), later associated with the stunted pines of Greece. (It is relevant to recall that *The Aunt's Story* was written shortly after Patrick White had spent a year in Greece; during the war he had been stationed for a time in Northern Africa.) In a passage referring to the foreign books which Theodora's father used to read (p. 22), two authors are named: Herodotus and Homer, and there is mention of the story of the crocodile and the trochilus which Herodotus tells in his second volume, dealing with Egypt. In an earlier chapter of that volume, just after discussing the mystery of the sources of the Nile, Herodotus speaks of the Ethiopian capital, a great city called Meroë, on an island of the same name, though he does not describe it in detail. At first Theodora rejects the thought of the second Meroë, but in time it becomes "a dim and accepted apprehension lying quietly at the back of the mind" (p. 23). Later through Moraïtis she perceives an analogy between Meroë and Greece, each being a country of bones. This association is stressed by the image of the pines, the emotional value of which is made explicit in the reference in *Riders in the Chariot* to "a scent of pine needles, the waves of which, at the best of times, will float their victims back into the intolerable caverns of nostalgia" (p. 201). In *The Aunt's Story*, they suggest Ithaca, the goal of Odysseus' journey; it is also relevant, since Ithaca is as it were an aspect of Meroë, that Milton's Mount Amara,[13] "by som suppos'd Tru Paradis,"[14] is situated in Abyssinia ("where *Abassin* Kings thir issue Guard . . . under the *Ethiop* Line by *Nilus* head")?

From the days of the early commentators on Homer the *Odyssey* has been frequently interpreted allegorically, for example, by the Neoplatonists, and George Chapman, working out his own interpretation of Ulysses reaching spiritual greatness through the endurance of adversity, wrote in his commentary on his translation: "The information or fashion of an absolute man, and necessarie (or fatal) passage through many afflictions (according with the most sacred Letter) to his natural haven and countrey, is the whole argument and scope of this inimitable and miraculous Poeme."

The example of Joyce in describing a spiritual quest within a Homeric framework inevitably springs to mind, since he is certainly one of the major shaping influences on White's early work, as seen for instance in the experiments in stream of consciousness from "The Twitching Colonel" onwards and perhaps in the theme of *The Living and the Dead*. (It is surely not mere coincidence that the words of that title are also the concluding words of Joyce's story "The Dead"?) The use of recurrent imagery and symbolic colours[15] in *The Aunt's Story* itself probably owes something to his example. Even if it were *Ulysses*, however, and not simply the Greek landscape which prompted White's use of the *Odyssey* motif, his method is individual. He does not attempt anything like the elaborate structural parallels of *Ulysses*, but by allusion and image uses the *Odyssey* as a means of indirectly defining character and theme and as a kind of short-cut to emotional intensity. It may not be fanciful to detect occasional echoes in the story itself: in Part Three Theodora stripping herself of all her possessions recalls Odysseus returning to Ithaca in the disguise of a beggarman, the greeting given her by the Johnson's scruffy red dog suggests Odysseus' welcome from his old dog Argus; when Mrs. Johnson brings Theodora water to wash herself, just before she gives herself a false name, we may remember Odysseus' old nurse washing his feet and recognizing him. But what White is concerned with is pointing up his theme by a very free method of allusion; the significance often lies in the variations and reversals.

The motif is introduced in relation to Theodora's father, who reads in a room on the side of the house where the pines are: ". . . the perpetual odyssey on which George Goodman was embarked, on which the purple water swelled beneath the keel, rising and falling like the wind in pines on the blue shore of Ithaca" (p. 68). A romantic dreamer, he talks to Theodora of Nausicaä, a name "as smooth and straight and tough as an arrow," then suddenly realizes that he has a daughter of his own: "she has grown, he said, straight as a brown arrow" (p. 69). The allusions, while, in the second case, conferring a grace on Theodora, reveal George Goodman as very unlike Odysseus, the clear-eyed man of action. His tragedy is that although he travels he never sees Greece, he cannot escape from his Penelope, whereas Mrs. Goodman's world "had always been enclosed, her Ithaca, and here she would have kept the suitors at bay, not through love and patience, but with suitable conversation and a stick" (p. 93).

Theodora herself, as well as being at one point Nausicaä, at others is connected both with Telemachus and with Odysseus. In the early scenes with her father, sharing his life on their estate, she plays Telemachus to his Odysseus, and mourns the dwindling of Meroë as Telemachus mourns the wasting of his substance by the suitors—but here, ironically, it is Odysseus himself who is responsible for the decay, and at the end of the story, when she finds a father-figure in Holstius, the reminders of George Goodman[16] add greatly to the poignancy of these final scenes. When Theodora has to leave Meroë after her father's death it becomes identified in her mind with Ithaca. At her meeting with their former servant, Pearl Brawne, who reminds her of her father and the past, the imagery, drawn from Odysseus' encounter with the Sirens, suggests the irresistible power of her memories: "Theodora would have blocked her ears with wax. She could not bear to face the islands from which Pearl sang" (p. 133).

Having embarked on her odyssey, Theodora hopes when she reaches the Hôtel du Midi that the garden will be "the goal of a journey," for hitherto she has been disappointed in her travels through "the gothic shell of Europe . . . in which the ghosts of Homer and St. Paul and Tolstoy waited for the crash" (pp. 145, 146); but the hotel itself is part of the "gothic shell." The atmosphere of decadence recalls the world of *The Living and the Dead;* it is not until she reaches the New World that Theodora attains her final vision. Homer, St. Paul and Tolstoy are, I suppose, associated as each representing a type of spiritual quest; they contribute to the pattern of this section, Homer through the *Odyssey* theme, St. Paul through Theodora's reading of the *Acts,* Tolstoy because parts of it are like a parody of the Platonic Idea of a Russian novel (and this perhaps is the point of the rather surprising information that Mrs. Goodman could read Russian).

At the end of Part Two the Nostos theme is sounded. Theodora, purged by fire, decides to go home, but it is not now the blue shore of Ithaca but the black volcanic hills of Ethiopia which summon her: Fanny is startled to receive a letter saying "the time has come at last to return to Abyssinia" (p. 271). The final and most radical manipulation of the *Odyssey* theme is still to come, however: having travelled far and learnt much, this wanderer does not return home after all. The end of Theodora's quest is to make her independent of places as of people. Soon after her father's death she wrote to her friend Violet Adams: "At first I thought I could not live anywhere but at Meroë, and that Meroë was my bones and breath, but now I begin to suspect that any place is habitable, depending, of course, on the unimportance of one's life" (p. 90). Finally, as people become interchangeable in her mind, so do places. When she goes off on her own up the mountain road she finds herself "walking between pines, or firs, anyway some kind of small coniferous tree, stunted and dark" (p. 277); and the lonely house in which she takes refuge is described in terms ("a thin house, with elongated windows, like a lantern" [p. 289]) recalling the madman's folly near Meroë, "a narrow lantern" near the summit of a hill, "the black cone of Ethiopia that had once flowed fire" (p. 61).

It will be clear from my discussion of the *Odyssey* theme that the use of recurring images is an important feature of *The Aunt's Story*—one which James McAuley[17] and Marjorie Barnard[18] have briefly noted. Throughout White constructs an extraordinary reticulation of images—roses, bones, the clock, tables and chairs, fire, zinc—which by repetition, juxtaposition and contrast acquire symbolic value.[19] Thus the wooden images, commented on by McAuley, which are used to suggest the physical appearance of Theodora, her angular honesty, and the wooden box of her personality which encloses her except in rare moments of spiritual exaltation, are frequently contrasted with images of flowing and of fire. The knife, which first appears unobtrusively as the little silver paper knife which Mrs. Goodman mislays at the time when Theodora has Frank Parrott at her mercy and which is found again after his engagement to Fanny, figures again as the meat-knife with which Jack Frost cut the throats of his wife and children—an incident, apparently irrelevant, introduced proleptically for its thematic value before the culminating appearance of the knife which Theodora picks up when tempted to kill her mother.

White clearly wants his symbols to work by poetic suggestion rather than the rigid consistency of allegory; the risks involved are ambiguity and obscurity. In the Odyssean context Theodora's large and timeless hats might suggest a traveller, but they may simply signify identity, as when she deliberately leaves behind the hat with the black gauze rose which Mrs. Johnson uncomprehendingly returns to her. Again, there is a danger of ambiguity when the symbols acquire different moral connotations in different contexts. When Lou, "as unpredictable as water," is contrasted with her brothers, whom "you could have piled into two heaps of stones" (p. 15), it is clear that Lou's spiritual potentialities are much greater, and there is no question that fluidity is preferable to rigidity. But when Theodora, wearing "a long, an oblong dress," goes to the Agricultural Show with two fashionable women, and her attitudes are "those of carved wood" whereas "the powdered, silky, instinctively insinuating bodies of the other women flowed" (p. 122), the moral values implicit in the contrast are reversed.

Even if abundance occasionally becomes excess, the images are of great value in linking the parts of the novel and tracing a significant pattern. The symbol of the rose, for instance, expands through its use in different contexts, gathering accretions of meaning. It is first used in the description of Meroë, in association with the skeleton trees and the pines: the *artificial* rose garden situated (oddly for Australia?) on the south side of the house and made at the behest of Mrs. Goodman in clay carted specially from a great distance. Theodora sees the reflection of the roses in bed and for her they become a symbol of beauty. She remembers her happy childhood at Meroë as "an epoch of roselight" (p. 21), and later contrasts herself unfavourably with Fanny and Pearl Brawne, both of whom resemble roses: but the exquisite Fanny's appearance is deceptive and Pearl is soon overblown. At the Hôtel du Midi the maroon paper roses in her bedroom are associated with lust and meretriciousness: finally Theodora wears the hat with the black gauze rose, also artificial, "more a sop to convention than an attempt at beauty" (p. 274), but black like Theodora herself.[20]

The way in which White by juxtaposing images can enrich their meaning and draw his themes together is well illustrated in the description of Huntly Clarkson's dinner party for Moraïtis:

> Huntly's table was smouldering with red roses, the roselight that Theodora remembered now, of Meroë. She swam through the sea of roses towards that other Ithaca. On that side there were the pines, and on this side Moraïtis. (p. 111)

The imagery alone tells much about the state of Theodora's feelings and the significance for her of this encounter with Moraïtis.

An interesting example of the metamorphosis of an image in different contexts occurs first in the description of Theodora carrying her baby niece, "beautiful as stone, in her stone arms the gothic child," and, a moment later after Fanny claims the child, "ugly as stone, awkwardness in her empty hands" (p. 119). A few pages later this scene is recalled when Theodora tells her mother that she won a kewpie in a feather skirt at the Show, and Mrs. Goodman imagines her carrying it through the crowd: "In her hate she would have hewn down this great wooden idol with the grotesque doll in its arms" (p. 126). Occurring so soon after the image of Theodora as a Madonna with Child, it carries the suggestion that in winning the kewpie she has in effect ended her own chance of maternity, since the episode virtually ends her relationship with Huntly Clarkson.

Adverse criticism of *The Aunt's Story* has tended to concentrate on Part Two; Vincent Buckley for instance has applied the phrase "a soft cocoon of imprecision"[21] to the prose here. That there should be a change to a more fluid style as we pass from reality to illusion is however appropriate; and as Theodora lives her fantasy life her vision naturally assumes a dreamlike quality. For instance, Pearl Brawne in Part One is described in images which suggest what she looked like to Theodora, but one feels that she sees what any sensitive observer might see:

. . . . you looked up through Pearl, and it was like looking through a golden forest in which the sun shone. Pearl was beautiful. Pearl was big and gold. Her hair was thick heavy stuff, as coarse as a mare's plaited tail. It hung and swung, golden and heavy, when she let it down. (p. 34)

Whereas we see Sokolnikov through the eyes of a woman whose vision is peculiar to herself:

The General sighed as deeply and as endlessly as cotton wool, but when he smacked his lips, or sucked from his fingers whatever it was, the suction of rubber sprang into the room, out of his face, for this was rubber in the manner of the faces of most Russians. His lips would fan out into a rubber trumpet down which poured the rounded stream of words . . . (p. 156)

Part Two is certainly difficult, a bold experiment in rendering the mental life of Theodora by a more dramatic method of blending past and present, illusion and reality than ordinary interior monologue. On a chance remark Theodora will build a fantasy of the past involving herself, as when Katina's reference to an earthquake prompts her to imagine herself as the governess of the child Katina, experiencing that earthquake; or memories of her own past will attach themselves to present happenings, as when Katina proposes a picnic: " 'I dare say it will be made,' Theodora Goodman said wryly, remembering another stiff group beside the church" (p. 232)—that is, her disappointment as a schoolgirl when Frank Parrott after church one day proposed a picnic which he promptly forgot. When the General speaks of his mannish sister Ludmilla, Theodora smiles "because her boots rang hollow on the cold yellow grass, and in her armpit she felt the firmness of her little rifle" (p. 156), which implies without any authorial intrusion that Theodora not only identifies herself with Ludmilla but also associates the General with her father. A still stranger transformation occurs when after she reads her Testament she and the General figure as Lukich and his younger brother Pavel in an adventure with some Russians, one of whom is called Petya, to whom the General, discoursing on the Russian Revolution, proclaims that "a movement requires a rock" (p. 216). When she speculates whether the walls of the round tower enclose "the smell of nettles, and possibly a dead bird, some personal exaltation or despair" (p. 251), the images recall the emotions associated with the discovery of Pearl and Tom among the nettles and of the dead crow beneath the pew, and with the shooting of the little hawk.

The Aunt's Story is the work in which White has advanced furthest towards the frontiers of poetry. It is perhaps true that a novel cannot well bear the strain of such a complex pattern of symbolic imagery; in the larger novels that have followed there has necessarily been a loosening of texture in the prose, which in Riders in the Chariot has become a more flexible narrative medium, though there has also been an increase in syntactical eccentricities from which The Aunt's Story is relatively free. It is also true, however, that the kind of vision which White is trying to embody in this book demands the subtlest and richest use of language for its realization. The Aunt's Story asks careful reading; that it deserves it is the proof of its quality.

Notes

1. "The Narrow Bridge of Art," in Granite and Rainbow (Hogarth Press, 1958), p. 18.

2. The Living and the Dead, p. 136. References are to the following editions of the early novels: Happy Valley (Harrap, 1939); The Living and the Dead (Eyre and Spottiswoode, 1952); The Aunt's Story (Eyre and Spottiswoode, 1958).

3. Cf. Agamemnon, pp. 173ff.

4. Cf. ". . . the old woman [the midwife], standing there as leisurely as a chorus from Euripedes" (p. 14); Mrs. Furlow announcing Moriarty's death "with the clarity of a Greek messenger" (p. 284).

5. "The Alienated Australian Intellectual," Meanjin XXII (1963), p. 58.

6. "The Four Novels of Patrick White," Meanjin XV (1956), p. 160.

7. Cf. the comment on the Parkers in The Tree of Man: "It was obvious that these lives had never shattered into coloured fragments" (p. 95).

8. Cf. Blake: "as I was walking among the fires of hell, delighted with the enjoyments of Genius, which to Angels look like torment and insanity . . ."(The Marriage of Heaven and Hell).

9. "Theodora Again," Southerly XX (1959), p. 54.

10. "The Twitching Colonel," The London Mercury (April 1937), pp. 606, 607.

11. *Riders in the Chariot* (1961), p. 57.

12. Peter Hastings, "The Writing Business" (Sydney *Observer*, 21 March 1959).

13. This is discussed by J. L. Lowes in *The Road to Xanadu*, immediately after his reference on pp. 373–4 to Bruce's account of the island of Meroë.

14. *Paradise Lost*, IV, pp. 280–3.

15. The colour symbolism was first pointed out by Marjorie Barnard in her review in *Southerly* XX (1959), pp. 51–55.

16. For instance, on his second appearance Holstius wears a Panama hat.

17. See his review in *Quadrant* 12 (1959), p. 91.

18. "The Four Novels of Patrick White," *Meanjin* XV (1956), p. 165. See also H. P. Heseltine, "Patrick White's Style," *Quadrant* 7 (1963), pp. 61–74.

19. White is reported to have said: "Music helps me with the structure of a book" (Ian Moffitt, "Talk with Patrick White," *New York Times Book Review*, 18 August 1957). This use of images like musical themes is obviously an example.

20. Cf. the roses "as brown as paper bags" of the Ethiopian Meroë (p. 23).

21. "Patrick White and His Epic," *Twentieth Century* XII (1958), p. 246, an article reprinted in *Australian Literary Criticism*, ed. Grahame Johnston, O.U.P. (1962).

The Tree of Man: An Essay in Scepticism

Leonie Kramer[*]

Since critics of *The Tree of Man* agree that the novel is about Stan Parker's metaphysical quest and dying illumination, it might seem unnecessary to retrace the steps of his journey towards enlightenment. But, while agreeing that Stan Parker is engaged in a search for the grounds of his belief, I dissent from the general judgment as to the nature of his discovery. Further, though critics have attended to the form of the novel,[1] and to the implications of White's symbolism,[2] I think there is need for an exploration of the connection between Parker's spiritual quest, and the form in which White expresses it. All White's novels are characterised by a very rigorous formal structure. In each, one is made aware of his strict supervision of the progress of the narrative, the disposition of the characters, and the stylised sequences of their dialogue. The apparently spontaneous overflow of life that is so characteristic of Dickens and Dostoyevsky, for example, is notably absent from White, as indeed it is from most modern novelists. There is a deliberation which suggests that each step is carefully planned, and that the whole action is moving towards a predetermined end. Curiously, that end, when it comes, might not seem so inevitable as one would expect, nor as

[*] Reprinted from *The Australian Experience: Critical Essays on Australian Novels* edited by W. S. Ramson (Canberra: Australian National University Press, 1974), pp. 269–83.

appropriate as that of the more conventionally plotted, yet also more casually narrated novel.

In the structuring of *The Tree of Man* White has sought no simple correspondence between meaning and form. The chronological sequence of events, covering three generations, and leading from the opening up of a tract of land to the drift to the cities and the encroachment of suburbia, defines the literal level of the novel. A linear structure of this kind permits surprises and minor ironies, but does not reinforce them by deliberate reference or comment. Had White been content with a simple chronological organisation of his novel, he would have produced a work much nearer the social realism of a chronicle of pioneering such as Miles Franklin's *All That Swagger.* When A. D. Hope, in his review of *The Tree of Man,*[3] complained that White had introduced all the old Australian clichés—flood, fire and drought—he evidently failed to observe that White uses these episodes to take the novel away from purely literal considerations. Flood, fire and drought *are* great Australian commonplaces, but in *The Tree of Man* they become structural principles, and have a quasi-symbolic relationship to the literal events. Objects and characters are also given a non-literal role. The silver nutmeg grater, the white rosebush, Madeleine, the struggling ants, recur as signals of thematic emphases in the novel. In addition, certain areas of literary reference, especially those to the Bible, *Laocoön* and *Hamlet* point to a meaning which cannot be derived from the contemplation of the literal facts.

The author's guiding hand is also clearly steering the reader's responses. Often his presence is much more definite than in later novels. In *Voss, Riders in the Chariot, The Solid Mandala* and more particularly *The Vivisector,* White shifts, often subtly and almost imperceptibly, from presenting the consciousness of his character, to directing the reader's attention firmly to a particular attitude. The result is confusion or ambiguity, and it is not always easy to decide whether to protest at the one, or applaud the other. Perhaps the best example of White's appearance in *The Tree of Man* is the sentence "One, and no other figure, is the answer to all sums" (p. 497).[4] I would argue that White's assertion at this point shows up a weakness in the handling of Stan's dying revelation. The only way in which White can make the point about wholeness and oneness is by stating it himself; he cannot, though, validate it in terms of Stan's actual experience. (Why the point needs to be made at all is a question of some interest).

There are, however, other instances in the novel of White's firm direction of the meaning, often in relation to character. Some of these authorial comments are necessary because in Stan Parker White has chosen an uncommunicative protagonist. So he must inform us that Stan "would long to express himself by some formal act of recognition, give a shape to his knowledge, or express the great simplicities in simple, luminous words for people to see" (p. 225). Or again, "She had grown fond of this boy, which he had allowed, for sentimental attachments are easier to maintain than relationships which demand love" (p. 244). Adumbration of future possibilities (also a habit of White's) is expressed in "He accepted the sharp and melancholy pain as something that his flesh must in the end suffer" (p. 248). Sometimes White extends his investigation of character by such comments as "And as she watched this erect and honourable man she realized with blinding clarity that she had never been worthy of him. This illumination of her soul left her weary, but indifferent. . . . In time the knowledge that some mystery was withheld from her ceased to make her angry, or miserable for her own void" (p. 326). Sometimes, more tentatively, White reaches out to general experience, as in "The moons of milk were in themselves complete. Everyone sensed this, perhaps, and bowed the head" (p. 229). By central structural episodes, recurrent motifs, and direct invasion of the narrative, White underpins the chronological sequence in such a way as to focus attention upon the stages of Stan Parker's metaphysical quest.

This quest has its own form. Over the course of his life within the novel, Stan accepts various explanations of his world. His persistent attempts to make sense of it lead him to entertain possibilities such as pantheism and Christianity. But one by one these possibilities are discarded. White presents Stan's journey towards understanding in the form of an essay in scepticism, which proceeds by examining and then rejecting certain positions. Some of the most significant events of Stan's life provide him with experiences likely to deny rather than affirm a belief in any God, let alone in a benevolent one. His final revelation is the result of an emptying out. It is a fulfilment, then, in a somewhat ironic sense. The novel adopts the standard sceptical precedure of moving towards a positive assertion through a series of proposals which are overthrown. Yet curiously Stan, unlike Amy, seems from the outset to be self-sufficient. Amy "waited for the warmth, the completeness, the safety of religion" (p. 28). But Stan "did not feel the necessity to translate his own life into brave words. His life as lived was enough" (p. 29). He "had not yet needed God" (p. 30). In so far as he has been able to think, it is to conclude that "he was a prisoner in his human mind, as in the mystery of the natural world" (p. 46).

The first explicit reference to Stan's adult contemplation of religion is brief. In the local church he is confused and awkward; only the sounds and sights of the world outside make an impression upon him. These he thinks, "could perhaps have been the grace of God" (p. 64). At the end of the flood, a broken piece of stained glass, which casts a temporary glow of crimson and "disintegrating gold" over ordinary objects, is a relic of "dead prayers in the drowning church" (p. 95). It is obvious, comments the author, that the lives of Stan and Amy, "each closed in himself . . . had never shattered into coloured fragments" (p. 95). By the end of Part I of the novel White has established Stan's contentment with his daily life, his inability to communicate his insights, and "the goodness of their common life" (p. 97). This section ends with a scene of silent, but deep communion between the Parkers and their world. "For that moment they were limitless" (p. 97).

It is not until Part II that Stan becomes preoccupied with the problem of certainty. He begins to need a guarantee of the truth of his own observations. He seeks for signs of reality, certainty and permanence, of which he once had no doubt (p. 17). In this section he is seen, for the first time, at the centre of his man-made world. "All was ranged round him, radiating out from him in the burning afternoon" (p. 109). Stan's pleasure in his creation, though, is qualified by the further insight that he and Amy are "the centre, but precariously, and he wanted to be certain" (p. 111). A "warm belief in some presence" (p. 111) is the best he can manage. During the christening of his first child Stan is soon "wandering quite frankly beyond the confines of the crude church, unashamed by a sudden nakedness that had fallen upon him" (p. 124). At the same time the words of the service and "the flesh of relationships, were becoming secondary to a light of knowledge" (p. 124). At this point Stan's quest begins to take on apocalyptic tones. "Events of immense importance would take place if only the moment of lightning could occur" (p. 150). When the storm comes it turns into "an ecstasy of fulfilment" (p. 151). Stan Parker seems to be sitting "right at the centre of it" (p. 151), as earlier he had sat at the centre of his created world. But as the storm goes on "his flesh had doubts and he began to experience humility" (p. 152). In this state "weakness and acceptance had become virtues" (p. 152). In his confusion he prays to God "for the sake of company," and at the end of the storm he is "in love with rightness of the world" (p. 152).

It is clear that at this point White is plotting an important stage of Stan's progress towards spiritual enlightenment. Yet, in spite of his eloquent assertion of Stan's discovery of humility and the rightness of the world, the evidence upon which the discovery rests is slender. White tries to make words do duty for experience, and the result is that while he certainly communicates Stan's experience intellectually, its emotional impact is small. The problem is partly that of trying to bring together the literal and non-literal levels of the novel at this point. The storm is to do duty as an image of the state of Stan's soul, without adequate preparation in terms of Stan's own character. In particular, Stan's need for certainty is in some respects at odds with the attitude to experience that he has demonstrated up to this moment.

The next stage of his progress is beset by even greater difficulties. After the storm comes the fire at Glastonbury, and an immediate problem is how far to press the legendary associations that the name Glastonbury evokes. Stan's experience in the fire is prefaced by an authorial comment to the effect that the approach of fire makes men aware of details of the natural world, and that they discover "an austere beauty that they now loved with a sad love, that comes when it is already too late" (p. 166). The fire is required to do double duty as punitive destroyer of the Armstrongs' selfish world of materialism, and as purifying refiner of Stan Parker. But at the heart of this episode White leaves a mystery. Its challenge to Madeleine's way of life is clear enough, and her confrontation with Stan at the height of the fire is a recognition of their common humanity. For Madeleine the fire means the acknowledgment of weakness and dependence; for Stan the illusion that Glastonbury contains "all that he had never done, all that he had never seen" (p. 178) is shattered. But White's language in this scene is both elevated and curiously evasive. "Is it, possibly, better to burn?" (p. 178) is asked before Stan enters the burning house. Once inside, he remembers *Hamlet.* "All things in the house were eternal on that night, if you could forget the fire" (p. 179). Stan mounts the stairs on a mission "of some mystery" (p. 180), "approaching some climax, the birth of the saviour or sacrifice, it was not clear which, came quicker" (p. 180). Later, after their mutual recognition, Stan and Madeleine enter "a phase of pain and contained consciousness" (p. 183). Finally, Stan's burns are described as "the superficial wounds of the flesh. If he was trembling, it was because he had come out of the fire weak as a little child . . ." (p. 185).

After the fire, as before it, revelation is possible. Those people who return to their farms feel full of new resolve. "Because they had looked into the fire, and seen what you do see, they could rearrange their lives" (p. 186). But what do you see, and what, in particular, does Stan see? Stan, in contrast to Amy, has "experienced exaltation by fire" (p. 187). But there is no evident aftermath of the fire in Stan's development. He has "moments of true knowledge . . . telling him of the presence of God" (p. 190). In these moments too he will see the relationship between all things—leaf, sun and his own burned hand. But there is nothing to connect these moments with the fire. Neither can his sense of his own impermanence as against the permanence of the natural world (p. 191) be traced back to the earlier experience. His search for certainty finds him, at this point, regarding his wife as "about all the certainty he had." So, having survived flood and fire, with only occasional insights to comfort him, Stan enters the war.

So far, Stan has given no definite shape to his notion of "the presence of God." Part III is preoccupied with the nature of Stan's belief, and the consequences of his rejection of it. In the mud of the war he thinks "with increased longing of a God that reached down, supposedly, and lifted up" (p. 204). But he cannot pray. After he returns from the war he does not reveal to Amy that "he no longer believed anything can be effected by human intervention" (p. 214). He is also, however, described as making his observations of the world around him "from the dream state of the sleeper" (p. 216), and it is suggested that he is slowly waking from his dream. He is still reluctant to accept anything as permanent, and must prove permanence for himself. Doll Quigley seems to be able to ignore "the stronger, muddier currents of time" (p. 218), and Stan speculates about the purposes of God being made clear to "some old women and nuns, and idiots" (p. 218). His uneasy relationship with his son makes him feel that acts of terror (such as floods) "did begin to illuminate the opposite goodness and serenity of the many faces of God" (p. 253). After Ray's disappearance, Stan's belief in God is for the first time positively affirmed.

> Although he had acquired the habit of saying simple prayers, and did sincerely believe in God, he was not yet sufficiently confident in himself to believe in the efficacy of the one or the extent of the other. His simplicity had not yet received that final clarity and strength which can acknowledge the immensity of belief. (p. 282)

But, later, it is revealed that Stan believes because "he had been told for so long that he believed" (p. 302). He has periods of doubt. He prays, and tries to fit "those stern and rather wooden prayers to his own troubled and elusive soul" (p. 303). The season of drought gives emphasis to the dryness and separateness of his relationship with Amy. It is at this point that Amy's adultery occurs, and that, on her husband's behalf, she acknowledges to her casual lover the belief in God that Stan has not acknowledged himself.

White links this episode with Stan's spiritual quest by a phrase. Amy feels that, in committing adultery, she has spat "into the mystery of her husband's God" (p. 310). The phrase reappears when Stan, suspecting his wife's infidelity, drives crazily into the city, gets drunk, and sees a "Godless" sky. "He spat *at* [my italics] the absent God then. . . ." (p. 333) and his "soothing saviour" is not God, but the anonymous stranger who helps him up from the gutter. He returns home to "a fresh phase of life" (p. 342), but more significantly, to freedom from "the opposition of God. . . . Once he had been bowed down by belief" (p. 351). This section of the novel ends with Stan's

establishment of freedom from belief, though it is a qualified resignation to his new state. He is "more or less resigned to that state
of godlessness he had chosen when he vomited God out of his system
and choked off any regurgitative craving for forgiveness . . ." (p.
356). (It is interesting that in this sentence White has added to and
thus changed the sense of the original scene of Stan's drunkeness.).
By this point in the novel, Stan has passed through several distinct
phases—his initial conviction of the worth of life as he lives it leads
to a search for proof of permanence, which, in retrospect, does not
seem to have been provided by experience of flood, fire, or drought.
The experience of war and its aftermath consolidates the habit of
belief. This, however, is destroyed by his discovery of his wife's
infidelity. His relationship with God is, then, analogous to his relationship with Amy. Both habits collapse together. By the end of Part
III of the novel Stan has found a way of returning to his domestic
life; he has not yet found a conviction to replace what, as a young
man, he took for granted. He has not yet learnt to do without God.

It is left to Amy and her grandson to glimpse the truth, and it
is significant that at this point, White again takes clear control of the
narrative, by insisting that "there is a mysticism of objects, of which
some people are initiates, as this old woman and boy" (p. 398).
Through the same piece of broken stained glass which before had
coloured the ordinary world crimson and gold, the Parkers' grandson
sees *his* mandala—the wholeness of cumquats (p. 399). In his senile
sickness, Stan still expresses his pain by calling on God, and in his
convalescence, while appearing aimless, he in fact is in a state of
spiritual activity, in which the landscape moves in on him "with
increased passion and intensity" making him aware of "the ruthless-
ness of divine logic" (pp. 411–12). This experience, together with a
visit to *Hamlet*, brings to his understanding the imminence of death
and his ignorance of his own destiny. Again White intervenes at this
crucial point, to remark that "it is not natural that emptiness shall
prevail" (p. 422). Stan goes to a communion service, and hopes for
God, though he later confesses that he does not know much about
him, but hopes in the end to. "What else is there that would be any
use to learn?" (p. 457). Stan does not find the answer to his question
until the day of his death. He is crippled by a stroke "with the
connivance of God" (p. 492), but it is the instrusion of an evangelist
offering him salvation by faith which leads Stan to his final revelation.
The "large, triumphal scheme" finds him once more at the centre
of his created world, but his illumination comes only with his spitting
out the "heaviness of phlegm" which he calls God. Only then does
he discover the faith founded on fact—on the "incredible objects of
the earth" (p. 497), the cracks in the path, and the struggling ants.

The vacuum left by belief in God has been filled by belief in his own perceptions. Man, not God, is the measure of all things.

Much attention has been paid to the meaning of this penultimate chapter of *The Tree of Man*. The consensus of critical opinion is that by placing Stan Parker at the centre of his garden, on the day of his death, White has created a mandalic symbol, and that Parker's perception that his jewel-like gob of spittle is God, represents his recognition that divinity is immanent.[5] Whether it is also transcendent seems, for some critics, to be debatable.[6] That Stan, the instant before his death, is granted a spiritual illumination, is unquestioned, and I think it would generally be agreed by critics that, in G. A. Wilkes's words, "fulfilment for Stan lies not within life as normally lived, but beyond it."[7] My analysis of the chapter, and the events which precede it, though accepting the notion of revelation, departs substantially from the general view of the meaning of the novel.

It is certainly true that Stan defines his own notion of the truth by reacting against the unwelcome doctrine of the visiting evangelist, who offers him salvation through "the steam roller of faith" (p. 495). Stan discovers, however, neither the immanence nor the transcendence of God, but God's irrelevance. Only after spitting out God is he able to see that "One, and no other figure, is the answer to all sums," though his leap to this conclusion is, it seems to me, imposed upon him by the author's voice, and does not convincingly follow the logic of his struggle for enlightenment. His expulsion of God on the last day of his life is unlike his earlier experience in the city. His loss of belief then was brought about by an emotional crisis; his expulsion of God at the end is a rational act, backed by his full realisation of his human powers. It may also be noted that Stan's progress through life has at last brought him back to his starting point. It has taken him a lifetime to be able to believe what he knew all along—that the natural world is "true." The Stan of the end of the novel is different from the man at the beginning in that knowledge and belief have joined forces. He no longer needs a supernatural support.

Stan's illumination leaves many questions unanswered. While the general outline of his progression to understanding is clear—from unthinking acceptance, through desire for permanence, to belief in God, loss of faith, hope for renewal of faith and final rejection of God and acceptance of a world without God—the steps in this spiritual journey are by no means always validated by the experience the novel offers. The major weakness of the book is White's failure to make credible connections between Stan's actual life as a small farmer, and his role as discoverer of a doctrine of the unity of human life and material objects. The stages of Stan's daily experience run parallel to assertions about what life means. The chief symptom of White's failure is his persistent recourse to verbal expansion of the meaning beyond what the events themselves permit.

The world of *The Tree of Man* is a world of dwindling belief in God and a divinely established order. Berkeley's guarantee of the existence of the material world is no longer credible. The moment before his death Stan Parker takes up a position not unlike Johnson's famous refutation of Berkeley. If man is to believe, the argument runs, he can believe only in the evidence of his own experience. Stan's instinct tells him that the stones and ants he knows so well are real; to ask for a divine guarantor of their reality is to see them as contingent. Once he rids himself of God, the obstacle to his faith in the primary reality of objects, he is able to see the world truly, and to believe in it. To have reached this point, however, is not to have solved either the problem of permanence or the problem of meaning. It leaves open the possibilities that the world will end, and that it is, in any case, no more than a random collection of single objects, fragmented and incoherent.[8]

It is clear quite early in the novel that Stan Parker sees himself at the centre of a pattern—all paths radiate out from the place he has established. The mandalic image of Stan's garden in which "all was circumference to the centre" (p. 493) insists, however, upon the absence of premeditated patterning. "There was little of design in the garden originally, though one had formed out of the wilderness" (p. 493). In the human dimension the creation of design is casual and accidental. The God of Genesis created his world according to an ordered, purposeful plan, and saw that it was good. The improvised garden of the Parkers grows into a form of its own. In his first reference to himself as the centre of his cleared earth and enlarged house, Stan appears to recognize his centrality, so that, like the God of Genesis, he can take pleasure in his creation. On his final afternoon in the garden, however, it is the author, not Stan, who sees him at the heart of the circles which radiate out even to the penultimate one "enclosing all that was visible and material" (p. 494). No doubt White intends Stan's realisation that the answer to all sums is one to be a recognition both of the wholeness of the world (imaged forth in the mandalic garden scene) and of man's power to understand its wholeness. But Stan's convincing *experience* is, even at the end, of the individual objects of the natural world, not of its wholeness. The Nietzschean image of ants struggling joyfully upwards has a concrete actuality lacking in his abstract philosophical sum.

Even the somewhat perfunctory move from what Stan observes to what he apprehends does not alter the fact that in *The Tree of Man* what man perceives as design is in fact the aggregation of accidents. Pattern emerges from the unforeseen. It is not imposed form without (as by a divine architect), but grows casually from within, not by human plan but by improvisation and accident. When Stan goes to the city in search of Ray, he has no plan. As a young man, White reminds the reader at this point, "he had hewn at trees with no exact plan in his head" (p. 275). But White also remarks that "In the end he had hewn a shape and order out of the chaos that he had found. He was also an improvisor of honest objects in wood and iron, which, if crude in design, had survived to that day" (p. 275). Improvisation creates the Parkers' garden. "It was a haphazard sort of garden" (p. 371), yet it takes on the shape and significance of a mandala. The shrubs that Amy Parker has "stuck in," and her passionate planting followed by forgetfulness of what she has planted, produce the microcosmic model at the centre of which Stan spends his last hours. Improvisation, then, not planning, produces human order; and the pattern created in this way will disclose itself to a clear-sighted *human* consciousness. God the creator-planner is not merely unnecessary as an aid to the discovery of human design; he actually inhibits that discovery.

In establishing his version of a creation myth White offers no simple relationship between human perception of design, and the form in which the novel expresses this perception. Both language and structure need to be considered at this point. H. P. Heseltine's very interesting analysis of some aspects of White's style opens up several important critical issues, but no critic has yet fully tackled the relationship of White's style to his meaning.[9] A. D. Hope's original criticism of White's prose in *The Tree of Man* was extravagantly expressed and inadequately documented. But his strictures pointed to a very real problem. The cows and the cabbages, for example, are described in a prose which seems excessive to the needs of descriptive background, as well as self-indulgent:

> The young cabbages that were soon a prospect of veined leaves, melted in the mornings of thawing frost. Their blue and purple flesh ran together with the silver of water, the jewels of light, in the smell of the warning earth. But always tensing. Already in the hard, later light the young cabbages were resistant balls of muscle, until in time they were the big, placid cabbages, all heart and limp panniers, and in the middle of the day there was the glandular stench of cabbages. (p. 27)

If White is trying to display an order and unity in nature by moving between the human, animal and vegetable worlds and showing their common vitality, then this description makes sense. But more important, perhaps, is his need to establish the independent existence of the natural world, since this is to become the grounds of Stan's final belief in the here-and-now. A belief in the validity of objects is a necessary part of his recognition that God is dispensable. Therefore, the solid presence of the natural world, and its independence of any supernatural support, needs to be demonstrated. White attempts, I believe, to create that sense of solid, independent completeness, by constant insistence on the strength and "truth" of sense-perceptions—the touch of skin, the smells of the earth in all its moods, the taste of experience, the sounds of the natural forces of thunder, wind, fire and water. His words, it might be said, do not so much render the material world, as create Stan's experience of it. The landscape has the general features of an actual world, but it lacks fine detail. White constructs a landscape of sensations, and of large allegorical significances. The stringy barks stand above the bush "with the simplicity of true grandeur"; "Birds looked from twigs, and the eyes of animals were drawn to what was happening" (p. 3). It is a formal landscape, an artist's abstraction from the real. White uses it to register the immediacy of the Parkers' sensual experience, to assert the consonance between the recurrent natural cycle of the seasons and human experience, and to link the four elements, and their periodic appearance as dominant natural forces, with crises in human emotion. Throughout the novel White provides, through language, metaphor and structure, the evidence that Stan Parker's world is real, and that he is at one with it, and understands its most delicate changes of mood and meaning. (It is still reasonable to argue, however, that on this point the novel needs less evidence than the author actually adduces.) Stan is all along, like Mary Hare in *Riders in the Chariot*, in possession of the truth and the certainties he believes are yet to be disclosed. His revelation shows him the validity of his own experiences. He is illuminated because he discovers that he is able to believe in what he has always known.

The structural principles upon which the novel rests—the cycle of seasons, and their correspondence with youth, maturity, and old age, and the continuity of experience, represented by recurrent verbal patterns, are in distinct opposition to the thesis of the novel. Here is no "fallacy of imitative form." The nature of the design is clear to the reader long before it is revealed to Stan. That his senses bring him individual experiences which are true and related—he is the guarantor of their reality in much the way that Berkeley's God is the guarantor of the material world—is made plain from the beginning. The reader knows that Stan's God is dispensable long before the evangelist cures him of religion by offering him salvation. The novel demonstrates that human design is the aggregation of accidents, but it does so by strict adherence to an order of events, and by a highly formal patterning of its subject matter. There is, then, a sharp contrast between the kind of statement the novel makes, and the way in which the statement is presented.

I do not regard this observation as a criticism of the novel, but rather as a very interesting pointer to a position which is more fully developed in *Riders in the Chariot* and *The Vivisector*. It is that the artist transforms ordinary human experience and enables it to be seen as significant, by imposing a strict formal structure upon it. Stan Parker has the insights of an artist but lacks his skills. Much can be made of his inarticulateness, but his is not the inarticulateness of a man who is sceptical of the value of words. On the contrary, his silent gestures are a substitute for "the poem that was locked inside him and that would never otherwise be released" (p. 25). His "desire that had never been fulfilled" is "to express himself in substance or words" (p. 110). There are in him veins of "wisdom and poetry" (p. 24). But he is not the artist, and because he cannot give shape and expression to his wisdom, he must have an exponent.

The poem that Stan Parker cannot write will, it is clear, be written by his grandson, whom it is tempting to see as White's version of himself. The small boy has become owner of the fragment of broken stained glass (once the property of the child of the flood), and through it he sees "the crimson mystery of the world" (p. 498). His poem is to be about "life, all life" (p. 499), and its ingredients, as listed by the child, are immediate and vivid sense impressions. As yet they are unshaped, no more than "little bits of coloured thought." This last chapter of the novel discloses that all that has preceded it is in fact the poem about Stan Parker's life. The last words of the novel "so that, in the end, there was no end" refer not to the succession of generations but to the fact that Stan Parker's death is the point of departure of the artistic recreation of his life.

If, then, one is able to accept Stan's vision of the world as One, it is because the artist has recreated it as One. If the God of Genesis can no longer be seen as the architect of design, the artist can take his place by discerning and communicating the shape of human experience. The guarantor of Parker's permanence and meaning is not God, but the artist. The fact that Stan Parker has his revelation only minutes before his death might, in itself, seem to suggest a pessimistic view of the ability of the ordinary man to make sense of his life. But it also confers a special importance upon the artist, by making him the creator of a form which gives expression to the random, unspoken and incomplete insights of his protagonist.

One is left with the paradox that a novel which dwells on the reality of sense impressions is nevertheless abstract and generalising. Stan Parker is not permitted to be merely an ordinary man, prohibited by his natural taciturnity from telling his own story. He is also required to be a large, representative figure, who might, in an earlier age, have been labelled Everyman. The mode of the novel is allegorical, and so far from exploring character and experience, it makes assertions about them to which, by the force of his intervention as narrator,

White seeks the reader's assent. The difficulty is that the evidence upon which agreement might be reached is not always supplied. Nothing that has been said about Stan Parker, either directly or indirectly, can lead one to assent to his discovery that "One . . . is the answer to all sums." At such a point (as in the Glastonbury section), it becomes clear that White wants to carry the novel beyond its own terms of reference. But the additional meaning comes from without, not from within the events and characters. It is a creation of the controlling intelligence of the artist, and it is a revelation of the artist's search for form.

It might be heretical to suggest that *The Tree of Man* is less impressive as a novel about a metaphysical quest, than as a commentary upon an important aspect of Australian experience. It mythologises the struggle to create order out of a hostile country, and to learn the language of an austere and often grudging environment. It also dramatises aspects of the class structure and intellectual attitudes. It is true that, as White intended it should, it represents an attack upon that "dun-coloured off-spring of journalistic realism" that he thought at the time (not entirely correctly) to be a representative Australian novel. Nevertheless it stands in the centre of the preoccupations of writers of Australian fiction from the nineteenth century onwards, not least in its sceptical attitude towards metaphysical speculation, its attention to the common objects of the natural world, and its endorsement of secular humanism.

Notes

1. Manfred Mackenzie, "Apocalypse in Patrick White's *The Tree of Man*," *Meanjin Quarterly* XXV, 4 (1966), pp. 405–16.

2. A. P. Riemer, "Visions of the Mandala in *The Tree of Man*," *Southerly* XXVII, 1 (1967), pp. 3–19, reprinted in *Ten Essays on Patrick White*, ed. G. A. Wilkes (Sydney, Angus and Robertson, 1970), pp. 109–26.

3. *Sydney Morning Herald* (16 June 1956).

4. All page references are to *The Tree of Man* (London, Eyre and Spottiswoode, 1956).

5. See, for example, B. Kiernan, "Patrick White," *Images of Society and Nature: seven essays on Australian novels* (Melbourne, Oxford University Press, 1971), pp. 95–147; J. F. Burrows, "Stan Parker's Tree of Man," *Southerly* XXIX, 4 (1969); pp. 257–79; P. A. Morley, The Quest for Permanence," *The Mystery of Unity* (St. Lucia: University of Queensland Press, 1972), pp. 97–115.

6. Riemer, "Visions of the Mandala in *The Tree of Man.*"

7. G. A. Wilkes, "Patrick White's *The Tree of Man*," *Southerly* XXV, 1 (1965), pp. 23–33, reprinted in *Ten Essays on Patrick White*, pp. 21–33.

8. White may seem to be extending Ivan Karamazov's argument about a world without God, where everything is permitted. Unlike Dostoyevsky, however, White

does not consider the consequences of atheism for human morality. His concern here, as in *Riders in the Chariot*, is with aesthetics, not morals.

9. H. P. Heseltine, "Patrick White's Style," *Quadrant* 7 (1963), pp. 61–74.

Voss and Others   William Walsh°

So far in this study I have concentrated on the text, its structure and significance, and paid scant attention to other critics. In this section I want briefly to present other views of *Voss*. This will have the double advantage of allowing the reader to decide among various and sometimes opposed responses to the novel, and of bringing together material otherwise scattered, sometimes in inaccessible places.

Patrick White appears in 1961 in the bleached officialese of *A History of Australian Literature* as one of a number of rampantly unknown new writers. The historian acknowledges the presence in him of a considerable talent but finds him self-consciously sophisticated, affected, conscientiously unpleasant, and tiresomely reminiscent of Joyce. In sum, he is taken to be a considerable but spoilt talent. When *Voss* appeared in England in 1957 it was given an almost lyrical reception by the reviewers. The same was generally true of the Americans. Only the Australians themselves were dubious. Penelope Mortimer, as one can see from the back of the Pelican edition of *Voss*, was even moved in the *Sunday Times* to invoke the name of Tolstoy. While this erred on the side of hysteria, it was probably nearer the mark than the reaction of the Australian Ian Turner, who disliked the style in which *Voss* was written—"a parodist's pushover"—on the grounds that "Australians are brought up to prefer the plain weaves of their own writers to the Gothic embroidery which is characteristic of *Voss*" (Turner, p. 74). The same writer sees *Voss* as a parable and Voss as an allegory for the historical Christ: "Voss has his disciples, his persecutors and his betrayer; his agony and his reconciliation; his stigmata and his crucifixion. He is the divinity who humbles himself before the least of his servants. And he troubles the minds of men, and they record his legend" (Turner, p. 71). While Turner rejects the manner of *Voss* on account of its Gothic quality, he condemns the substance of *Voss* for its un-Australian note. The qualities which conquered the Australian continent, he explains, were human skill, hard grafting and a fair measure of luck. "A rational realism is much more characteristic of our way of thinking than is the contemplation of infinite mysteries. For us, there is more trag-

° Reprinted from *Patrick White:* Voss, Studies in English Literature 62 (London: Edward Arnold, 1976), 40–49.

edy—our sort of tragedy—in Rory O'Halloran, who lost his child in
Such is Life, or in Tom Hopkins, who lost his youth in Lawson's
Settling on the Land, than there is in Johann Ulrich Voss, whose will
was humbled in the Australian desert" (Turner, pp. 74–5). *Voss* must
be rejected on this view because "he is exploring, in an Australian
environment, a mind, a way of thinking, that is foreign territory to
most Australians" (Turner, p. 75).

Those who are not Australians, and no doubt some who are, will
wonder what is the nature of this peculiarly Australian tragedy and
regret that the mind manifested in *Voss* should appear to an Australian
to be so uncompromisingly alien. White himself among his ambitions
for this novel had placed precisely the opposite of what Ian Turner
desired high on the list. "Above all I was determined to prove that
the Australian novel is not necessarily a dreary, dun-coloured offspring
of journalistic realism. On the whole," he said in 1958, "the world
has been convinced, only here, at the present moment, the dingoes
are howling unmercifully. . . ." *(Australian Letters).* It was in pursuit
of this aim that White, who describes himself as something of a
frustrated painter and a composer *manqué,* attempted to give to *Voss*
"the textures of music, the sensuousness of paint," and "to convey
through the theme and characters of *Voss* what Delacroix and Blake
might have seen, what Mahler and Liszt might have heard."

Robert Fry, another Australian critic, was offended not so much
by the absence of the Australian spirit as by the presence of the
Christian one. He finds the novel suffused by the more morbid aspects
of Catholic mysticism, which project an unacceptably undignified
conception of man. "It conceives of man in isolation from man,
selfishly working out his own salvation, giving nothing in human
relationship except humility, and taking all in acts of penance" (Fry,
p. 41). Remarks of this kind, and they are representative of certain
Australian reactions, treat the novel in a savagely abstract way. Meanings torn out like this from the dense and figured body of the novel
are so general, so detached, that they have little relationship to the
concrete and realized work present before us.

On the other hand, it cannot be denied that White does fall into
the error, intermittently, or perhaps only rarely, of pressing the
symbolic sense too hard. An Australian critic, A. A. Phillips, calls this
the algebraic use of symbolism, in which one has to state to oneself
the equation $X = Y$, a process which disturbs the kind of response
fiction demands. He finds this algebraic symbolism most apparent in
Voss: "Many readers—if those whom I have encountered are typical—
seem to find some pedantic element in the book's structure softens
the impact of the imaginative conception. In particular, that ghostly
love-affair won't get off the page, won't acquire the flavour of an
experience. . . . He here seems to be content if his reader intel-

lectually receives the meaning he has set out to convey" (Phillips, p. 457).

As I have indicated in my own treatment, White's tendency towards algebraic symbolism is the consequence of a failure in creative and critical alertness and not an inevitable result of his method. Certainly his art, which is nearer the norm of the poetic than that of many contemporary novelists, is sometimes marred by this hankering after symbolic symmetry. But it is a fault of the moment rather than of the technique. Nor do I think A. A. Phillips at all right in arguing that White's characters have lost their freedom to grow since they are pushed and pummelled into predetermined positions. Voss himself is profoundly transformed in the course of the novel and so is Laura. And I cannot agree that White's method implies the existence of a long series of detailed correspondences between episodes in *Voss* and the life of Christ. The parallelism is subtler and less quantitative than this.

Symbols, myths and archetypal patterns are terms that appear frequently in the current critical account of White. No doubt this is in part the effect of the contemporary standing of this kind of critical habit, in part of White's gift, particularly evident in *Voss*, for dealing with profound and universal themes in an epic mode. Patricia Morley, trained in the school of Northrop Frye where criticism is primarily concerned with the system of ideas implicit in a work of art, and secondly with the images and archetypes which sustain it, finds that White's work relies not only on such writers as Dostoevsky and Tolstoy, Blake and Bunyan, but even more on the older traditions on which these artists drew, the Judeo-Christian-Classical heritage. "Through the use of archetypes and images common to Western literature, White's novels obtain a richness of association, a cumulative power and an impersonal dignity" (Morley, preface, p. vii). She sees *Voss* as a modern version of the *Divina Commedia*: "As in Dante's great epic, Voss's literal journey is both an allegory of the progress of the individual soul towards God, and a vision of the absolute towards which it strives" (Morley, p. 118). Patricia Morley's book, *The Mystery of Unity*, demonstrates clearly that if you begin with the idea that *Voss* is a modern version of the *Divine Comedy*, you will undoubtedly be able to prove it. If in the course of your demonstration the body of the novel itself grows more and more invisible, so much the worse. Not that Patricia Morley's treatment is by any means the most extreme example of this method of approach. Her work exhibits a certain sense of proportion and some feeling for the texture of the novel. John Beston has quite transformed the novel in his treatment into a contemporary *Imitation of Christ* or a doctrine of spiritual progression. He quotes Laura's remark to Dr. Kilwinning at the height of her sickness, "How important it is to understand the three stages.

Of God into man. Man. And man returning into God" (p. 386). This is important because, in Beston's view, Laura's statement about the three stages of man's spiritual progression, although he acknowledges it to be somewhat cryptic, enunciates the central theme of *Voss*. One can say of this, as one can say of Morley's view, that there is undoubtedly some notion of this sort implicit in *Voss*. But to abstract it in this abrupt and summary form distorts the shape and blurs the complex experience embodied in the novel.

A more modest version of the spiritual theme in *Voss* is given by G. A. Wilkes in his *Australian Literature: A Conspectus:* "Voss leads an expedition across the Australian continent in order to mortify and exalt himself by suffering, as though in rivalry with Christ, to prove that man may become God. . . . Voss seeks transcendence through a supreme egotism. What makes him so compelling a figure, however, is rather his vulnerability in this attempt. He must try to extinguish all human feeling in himself, not only by welcoming the privations of the journey, but also by repelling all emotions of fellowship—the suspicion that he may be thought to love his dog, Gyp, compels him to execute her forthwith" (Wilkes, p. 92). This plain statement has much to recommend it in its temperance and straightforwardness. It is developed in a more metaphysical way in an impressive essay by the distinguished Australian poet James McAuley in his essay "The Gothic Splendours" (*Ten Essays on Patrick White* edited by G. A. Wilkes). He shows that *Voss* aims to produce effects more commonly found or attempted in poetry. He even suggests that *Voss* fulfils this aim with greater depth and more sustained intensity than most Australian poetry. McAuley sees *Voss* as a story organized around the contrast between the urban society of Sydney and the unexplored Bush: provincial gentility, commercialism, conventional piety, on the one side; on the other, the world of extremes in which concealment and compromises are torn away. Not that *Voss* relies on this too-simple contrast. The world of Sydney, for example, *is* the Bush, "the country of the mind," for Laura. The Bush pictures an inner world that the urban man may enter also "if he has the courage and metaphysical depth to explore his selfhood and his relation to God" (McAuley, p. 36). The conquest of a continent is the outward aspect of Voss's inward expedition. "What Voss is dedicated to is the self-deification of man, to be achieved in his own person, through boundless will and pride and daring" (McAuley, p. 38). To be a self-subsistent, self-sufficient God requires one to abhor humility and to need no one. According to McAuley, White's novel is not simply the realization of a purely fantastic eccentric theme, the megalomania of an individual, but the use of this view to interpret imaginatively a tension within modern civilization. McAuley's reservation about *Voss* has to do with the "wary evasiveness" with which this issue is finally handled. "The Christian framework is assumed in the book for the purpose of stating the issues, and up to a point for resolving them. But in the last part the framework of interpretation seems itself to slip and become unclear" (McAuley, p. 45). McAuley's essay, which is one of the best accounts of the religious and metaphysical reading of *Voss*, finally blames Patrick White, it appears, for using the Christian framework instead of believing it. But this seems to me to misunderstand the nature of the artist's possibly unscrupulous use of whatever lies to hand in the way of means for helping him to realize his perception. I see nothing improper in White's use of the Christian myth. The only question is whether it is successful, whether his use of it is adequate for his artistic purpose.

It may well be that the reader will turn with some relief from these metaphysical readings of the novel, from literary criticism as philosophic tract or theological commentary, to something firmer and more specifiable. Systems of ideas and their accompanying sets of images and archetypes have a strongly volatilizing influence on any novel. Of course, ideas, philosophic and theological, do influence the form and tone of fiction but they are present in a more oblique and incidental way than the commentaries I have adduced would suggest. That the idea "deeply lurks in any vision prompted by life" was the way Henry James thought of the existence of the idea in the novel. Let me therefore turn to a harder kind of notion about the novel advanced, for example, in a sensitive essay by the American critic George Core. He notes White's capacity to make the far reaches of the Australian landscape come palpably to life. In his view the country in *Voss* has a character as definite and individual as Hardy's Wessex. "The author not only incorporates the thickness of detail in common life . . . but he can also render the feeling that the vast landscape of Australia inevitably makes on the the most casual observer. It is the same dimension of vastness that one encounters in nineteenth-century Russian and American fiction—in Tolstoy, Turgenev, Lermontov; in Cooper, Melville, Norris. This sense of spaciousness and desolation is central to *Voss*" (Core, pp. 3–4).

I should like at this point to refer the reader to some less enthusiastic responses to White's work. Such a powerful and singular literary personality is bound to intrude, sometimes harshly to intrude, into the universe his fiction evokes. (We cannot make about White's work those calm, formal distinctions which Eliot favoured between man and theme, artist and suffering.) All of his novels, *Voss* no less than the others, bear the indelible stamp of his personality, and comments made about other novels may frequently be appropriate to *Voss*. George Steiner, for example, writes:

> The reciprocities of minute material detail and vast time sweeps, the thread of hysteria underneath the dreary crust, the play of

European densities against the gross vacancy of the Australian setting, are the constant motifs of White's fiction. . . . (Steiner, p. 109)

He notes that in almost every one of White's novels and short stories there is what he calls "an eruption of savagery." In *Voss* this eruption of savagery is very much more restrained. If it exists at all it is in the deaths of Voss and his party. But that is a development which issues coherently and naturally from the situation. Other critics take the view that the domination of White over his material becomes a form of cheating. Christopher Ricks says of White:

> What was once the glory of the novel—its specificity, its knowledgeability, its being in possession of and putting you in possession of so much of the evidence (all of it?) on which you could judge for yourself—is at present the stunting impoverishment of the novel, since it is a permanent and well-nigh irresistible invitation to irresponsibility, to cheating, to the crucial immorality of the artist which Lawrence stigmatized as putting the thumb on the scale. (Ricks, pp. 19–20)

While Ricks castigates the intrusion of White into his work as the putting of a thumb onto the scale, other critics react in a more favourable manner to that personality, particularly as it is shown in the prose. "[There] are few contemporary novelists," writes Peter Ackroyd, "who have the fastidious eye and ear of Patrick White. His prose is instantly recognizable: it has a South American sonority and plumpness" (Ackroyd, p. 771). John Barnes, on the other hand, finds *Voss* one of the most dramatically effective of White's novels, but spoiled by mannerism, lushness and portentous mysticism (Barnes, p. 100). The dislocated syntax which many find intolerable in White, and which a famous Australian poet A. D. Hope once called "pretentious and illiterate sludge," has by other critics been felt to be an individual and functional skill. Harry Heseltine in *Quadrant* (1963) maintains that from the time of his earliest work White has established a large fund of recurring interests which force their way into his prose as characters, situations and images, and that these are the spring of his style and the peculiar voice of his sensibility. People's hands, their skin, their breathing—the reader will remember Rose at the very beginning of *Voss*—are sensitive indicators of their natures. White refines, that is, from the grossness of a condition the subtlety of a mental state, a gift that has the fullest scope in *Voss*. White's presence in his novels and the language of their expression—the two topics which engage the interest of so many critics—are spoken of in a highly idiosyncratic but also enlightening way by the distinguished Australian writer Hal Porter. He speaks of the style as composed of "razor-bright sentences, glassy clauses, vitreous jig-saw slices of par-

adox and poetry, the fastidious gluing on of sharp-edged fragments."
But beneath the glaze there are "startling flashes, alert shadows,
movement" (Porter, p. 1347). As to presence he says: "Although
perilously involved with his characters' wilful doings . . . he looms
most, and mysteriously, on the outskirts of their curdled imaginations,
a sky-line silhouette, blurred and ambiguous, yet immovably always
there, creator and destroyer in one" (Porter, p. 1348).

Several critics have noticed White's stylistic adaptation to the
matter in hand. For example, Barry Argyle, in an admirable critique
of the novel, observes how White chooses two styles to convey the
differences of intention and circumstances of the members of the
expedition on the one hand and of Sydney society on the other. For
those in the desert "the language is filled with metaphor and the
analysis metaphor presumes, to which is added some of the resources
of the obsessed and humourless Voss's native German" (Argyle, p.
42). The language in which the Bonner group is described is much
less poetic and self-revealing and more ironically dissecting. "As they
are without an ideal to which their lives can approximate, the author's
commentary must provide one by which their limitations may at least
be gauged and perhaps understood" (Argyle, p. 44). Laura, a member
of the Sydney group, is with them but not of them. Her relationships,
particularly those with Rose, are expressed in an idiom closer to that
used for Voss and his company. The quality of the Voss dialect,
spiritual and Teutonic simultaneously, is peculiarly German, as Barry
Argyle comments. It is German in its mysticism, in its Nietzschean
pretensions, and perhaps German too in a more repulsive, Hitlerian
way. Barry Argyle's estimation of the novel is balanced and discrim-
inating. On the whole he judges it to be a success. Another critic,
Vincent Buckley, finds it ultimately a failure. He finds the concept
magnificent but Voss himself grotesque: "Voss's inner being is too
nearly stifled by the weight of the analogies he is forced to carry"
(Buckley, p. 422). Voss's spiritual state is brilliantly exhibited in the
observed detail but White's persistent allegorizing finally dehumanizes
him. The emptiness of the Bonner-Sydney connection serves to demonstrate the stature of Voss but in the end, in Buckley's view, "it is
the stature of a mission, a destiny, rather than of a man" (Buckley,
p. 423). Buckley is profoundly impressed by White's capacity to bring
such diverse kinds of human beings as Voss and Laura, and the lives
they stand for, into a mutually enlivening relationship, but he is also
convinced that "there is something tainted about a creative habit
which insists on an allegorical reading and then blurs the meaning
it points to" (Buckley, p. 424). John B. Beston, in a decidedly more
persuasive essay (*Quadrant*, 1972) than the other I have referred to
(though not I think a wholly convincing one), analyses this essential
Voss-Laura relationship in the novel. He finds it complex and confusing

since in their meetings they show antagonism and rivalry but in their separation a mystical closeness. White, in order to show their isolation from the rest of mankind, glorifies their spiritual pretensions. They pass as mystics and fail as human beings.

One of those who finds the balance of allegory and actuality beautifully poised in *Voss* is R. F. Brissenden, whose brief note on *Voss* can be recommended on several counts. He stresses more than most the achievement of *Voss* as a historical novel when men, "particularly artists, intellectuals or explorers (and Voss is all three), seem, more often than not, to have seen their actions either in a religious light or in a light conditioned by the absence of religion" (Brissenden, p. 30). The imaginative truth with which Voss is realized as an explorer is matched with the skill in which the tone and manners of colonial society in nineteenth century Sydney are evoked. Nor does Brissenden accept, as so many critics do, that Voss is simply and brutally a "Christ figure." As Brissenden sees it, the Christian legend is an element, and a functional one, in the tale, and "*Voss* always remains a novel, that is a convincing fictional representation of credible human beings, and . . . never hardens into the abstract over-simplifications of pure allegory" (Brissenden, p. 33).

Voss is also remarkable in showing much less grimly than White's later novels that sense of the nastiness of human life of which Patrick White seems to have more than his normal share, and which produces in a good deal of his work a flinching distaste towards the common and the raw in human life. John Barnes, in the essay already alluded to, makes this fact the principal ground on which he judges White. His impressive talent is thwarted, according to this critic, by a distaste for the subject matter of the novelist, namely human living. White's work reminds Barnes of Lawrence's complaint about Flaubert, that he stood away from life as from leprosy. Undoubtedly there are passages in White's later work which make it easy to see what Barnes means, and perhaps I may quote here what I wrote on this topic some years ago (*A Manifold Voice*, pp. 124–5):

> We see in his work not only a positive but also a negative revelation. No matter how gifted a writer in Western society, even in so fresh and vital a form of it as the Australian, he cannot, it seems, help reproducing in his sensibility a certain failure of sureness or grasp in the contemporary experience of human nature. A neurotic twist or distortion, the reflection of a defect in our civilisation, forces itself into the work, even when, as with Patrick White, the writer is disposed by temperament and belief to a central and steadily traditional vision of man. . . . The statement of the artist can never be merely a comment; it is always in part the response of a participant. A sensibility so quick and inclusive as Patrick White's, however much it may be spiritually detached from the assumptions ruling contem-

porary society, is nevertheless bound, as it realises itself in art, to reflect not only the artist's individual vision but the radical disorder of the society it is turned upon.

In *Voss*, however, we are more conscious of the powerful treatment of the central theme, the human will and its transformation by grace, and other Whitean qualities. There is, for example, the unerring depiction of the quivering lesser characters. There is the sad, sour wit which brings decisively to heel colonial airs and graces. There is the strange empathic sense for physical objects and vegetable life. There is a gift for luminous generalization. And finally, one may note, White's predilection for the odd, the extreme, and the extraordinary— in this case for Voss and Laura—and his attribution to them, as a gift or grace, the possession of a special non-discursive mode of consciousness through which, in conditions of simplicity and suffering, the ultimate realities may be attained. And while one must not neglect to observe the features which mar *Voss*—the syntax bowled disconcertingly on the wrong foot, the passages which are too worked, too thick, too opaque—one cannot but feel, certainly I feel, that we are in the presence of a significant, peremptory talent. What makes Patrick White extraordinary is his power to discover and present Wordsworthian depths and distances. How reviving it is, at a time when the death of the novel as well as of literature itself is daily signalled, to find a major figure working with such confidence and power on a theme so large and so inclusive.

Works Cited

Ackroyd, Peter, review of *The Cockatoos*, *Spectator* (22 June 1974): 37–40.

Argyle, Barry, *Patrick White* (Edinburgh and London: Oliver and Boyd, 1967).

Barnes, John, "A Note on Patrick White's Novels," *Literary Criterion* VI (Winter 1964): 93–101.

Beston, John, "The Struggle for Dominance in *Voss*," *Quadrant* XVI (July/August 1972): 24–30.

Brissenden, R. F., *Patrick White* (London: Longmans, Green, 1966).

Core, George, "A Terrible Majesty: The Novels of Patrick White," *Hollins Critic* XI (February 1974): 1–16.

Fry, Robert, "Voss," *Australian Letters* I (1958): 40–41.

McAuley, James, "The Gothic Splendours: Patrick White's *Voss*," in *Ten Essays on Patrick White*, ed. G. A. Wilkes (Sydney: Angus and Robertson, 1970), 34–46.

Morley, Patricia A., *The Mystery of Unity: Theme and Technique in the Novels of Patrick White* (Montreal and London: McGill-Queens University Press, 1972).

Phillips, A. A., "Patrick White and the Algebraic Symbol," *Meanjin* XXIV, 103 (1965): 455–61.

Ricks, Christopher, "Gigantis," *New York Review of Books* (4 April 1974): 19–20.

Steiner, George, "Carnal Knowledge," *New Yorker* (4 March 1974): 109–13.

Turner, Ian, "The Parable of Voss," in *An Overland Muster*, ed. Stephen Murray-Smith (Brisbane: Jacaranda, 1965), 71–75.

The Mandala Design of Patrick White's *Riders in the Chariot*   Edgar L. Chapman°

The epigraph to Patrick White's *Riders in the Chariot*, from William Blake's *The Marriage of Heaven and Hell*, emphasizes the "prophetic" and religious character of the novel. The epigraph is the famous passage in which Blake records a meeting with Isaiah and Ezekiel, and thus aligns his work with the mission of those majestic Old Testament prophets. White, by the choice of this epigraph, boldly places himself in the line both of biblical prophets and of secular visionaries like Blake who have sought to create in man "a perception of the infinite."[1]

The chief symbol which unites White with the tradition of Old Testament prophets, the New Testament Apocalypse, and Blake's visionary poetry is the chariot with its four riders, which is also an archetypal symbol of deity in Jewish Cabbalistic tradition, as Patricia Morley, among others, points out.[2] The chariot consolidates the symbols of these traditions with the influence of Jungian thought, which plays a major role in White's personal mythology.[3] For the chariot with its four riders can be identified as a cosmic mandala, Jung's symbol of unity, deity, and transcendence, that Jung claimed to find throughout world culture as a universal symbol.[4] As Peter Beatson indicates, the mandala is a central symbol in the later White novels, from *The Solid Mandala* on.[5] And Morley finds instances of the mandala in *Riders in the Chariot* itself; but, like Beatson, she stops short of identifying the chariot as a mandala symbol, describing it simply as a "quaternity."[6] However, mandalas are not only circular in structure, but often fourfold in nature, like White's chariot with its four human riders, who become transfigured into images of divinity in Alf Dubbo's painting in the novel.[7] White's four visionary figures are mystics who travel diverse and individual roads toward transcendence. The nature of these mysticisms and the implications of White's chariot as a Jungian fourfold mandala for the design of the novel have not been fully explored by prior criticism. In what follows, I shall attempt to trace the design more fully, and thus join earlier scholars in a confirmation

° Reprinted from *Texas Studies in Literature and Language* 21, no. 2 (Summer 1979): 186–202; by permission of the author and the publisher; © 1979 by the University of Texas Press.

of William Walsh's assertion that White is, in the largest sense of the word, a "religious" novelist.[8]

1

It is worthwhile to examine C. G. Jung's concept of the quaternity archetype, and the variety of fourfold patterns it may assume. In *Psychology and Religion* Jung describes quaternity symbols as being older than the Greeks, as existing in the symbolism of non-Western peoples, and thus being primary and apparently universal expressions of Jung's theoretical collective unconscious.[9] Such symbols, Jung explains, are "always associated with the idea of a world-creating deity," except for, usually, "those moderns in whom it occurs." Since quaternity symbols take the shape of fourfold or "squared" circles, or mandalas, it is easy to identify Ezekiel's chariot with the mandala and quaternity archetype.[10] Mandala symbolism is elaborated in the ancient notion of the four elements, the four seasons, the four faculties of the mind, the Christian idea of the four evangelists, Ezekiel's four creatures, and so on.[11]

The fourfold symbolism suggests an integration into unity and wholeness, and for Jung—as is true for Blake, according to his modern critics—the fourfold character of mandala symbolism describes ultimately a unity of God and man. Because modern men tend to live either by a rationalist theism which defines God as wholly "outside man"—a theism of dead formalism for Jung, as for Nietzsche—or in agnosticism, modern men have failed to see the true implications of such quaternity symbols. In Jung's view, "they insist, as do certain Christian mystics, on the essential identity of God and man, either in the form of an *a priori* identity or of a goal to be attained by certain practices or imitations, as known to us, for instance, from the metamorphoses of Apuleius, not to speak of certain yoga methods."

"The use of comparative method shows without a doubt that the quaternity is a more or less direct representation of the God who is manifest in his creation."[12] Jung goes on to argue that one can discover God through the dream visions projected by the subconscious mind, however mystical and unorthodox they are. Typically, Jung then disclaims objective knowledge of God's existence: the modern split between faith and knowledge is preserved. As a scientist, Jung can only observe that he has objective evidence of the "existence of an archetypal God-image, which to my mind is the most we can assert about God psychologically."[13]

An interesting comment on Jung's concept of the mandala is provided by one of his most articulate expositors, Edward F. Edinger. Edinger remarks that Jung sees the mandala as a basic archetype of the self, and for Jung, "all images that emphasize a circle with a center and usually with the additional feature of a square, a cross, or some other representation of quaternity, fall into this category."[14]

A recent book containing many artists' conceptions of mandalas includes several that are divided into quaternities.[15] The conception of the quaternity is virtually interchangeable with the mandala, or is a completed form of it. Another quaternal mandala uniting White with Blake and Ezekiel is Blake's symbol of the four zoas. Like Ezekiel's chariot, and White's chariot, it is a quaternal unity which may be "regarded as four aspects of one Cosmic Man," as Beatson has observed.[16]

When the fourfold scheme of *Riders in the Chariot* is examined, it is obvious, even superficially, that White has sought to make his quaternal mandala represent a unity of diverse types and conditions of humanity. White's four visionaries are two men and two women, two native Australians and two emigrants. One has no formal religion, one is a rational Jewish intellectual, one is a working-class evangelical Christian, and one is an aboriginal with a "primitive" religious consciousness. On the level of "realism" one "rider" represents an Australian "aristocracy" in decay, one represents the homeless person displaced by World War II, one represents the working class, and one represents the despised "blacks" of Australia. (Technically, aboriginals are "white," but their status in Australia combines some of the worst deprivations of American blacks and American Indians.)

But in addition to these obvious religious, social, and ethnic diversities, White has made his four riders embodiments of some less apparent symbolic qualities. Each represents a major mystical tradition. Each is associated with one of the four traditional elements of air, earth, fire, and water, one of the systems of symbolism used by White, according to Beatson.[17] Each rider represents one of the four Jungian faculties of the mind in his visionary quest and apprehension of the numinous or transcendental world.[18] And each rider is identified with an appropriate sense relating to his or her role in White's symbolic scheme. Specifically, Mary Hare, the nature mystic of White's quaternity, is associated with the element of air, the Jungian faculty of sensation, and the sense of touch. Mordecai Himmelfarb, the German Jewish scholar and rationalist who becomes an initiate of Cabbalistic mysteries, is associated with the element of fire. Himmelfarb represents the Jungian faculty of reason and is associated with the sense of smell. Mrs. Godbold, the working-class evangelical mother, is identified with the element of earth; she represents the Jungian faculty of feeling and is associated with hearing. Finally, Alf Dubbo, the aboriginal painter, is associated with the element of water. Dubbo represents the Jungian faculty of intuition (or imagination) and is associated with sight (or, metaphorically, vision).

This patterning of the characters is more than an abstract scheme.

Rather, it is dramatized in the characters' actions, particularly in the "memory" sections devoted to each of the "riders." The foils White uses for each character represent oppositions to their visionary quests enacted by characters who live on the "finite" level. These assertions may be illustrated by a brief study of each of the four riders, particularly the retrospective or "memory" sections devoted to each.

2

The first of the riders in the chariot is Mary Hare, the eccentric heiress living in her father's deteriorating dream mansion, Xanadu. Mary represents the approach, by nature mysticism, to the transcendent world imaged in the chariot. Her "perception of the infinite" is developed and affirmed through an innocent and childlike acceptance of finite nature. The reader first meets Mary on a walk, where "an early pearliness of light, a lamb's-wool of morning promised the millenium" (RC, p. 3). Yet despite her loving involvement in nature, her acceptance of the natural phenomenon in what Martin Buber has taught us to call an "I-Thou" relationship, Mary Hare does not quite achieve her desire for mystic identification with the world of nature until late in the novel, when she comforts the human in the immolated Himmelfarb.

But Mary strives for a sympathetic identification with animals, plants, and the soil that would overcome the subject-object relationship. Her mysticism resembles that of affirming natural images found in the American poets Emerson and Whitman.[19] She has even tried, in her innocence, to tame the snake in the garden of Xanadu. In this childlike acceptance, Mary has rebelled against her father, Norbert Hare, the gentlemanly romantic who "required perfection in horses, as in everything, and usually got it, except in human beings" (p. 21). Her indifference to ordinary standards of comfort makes her the target of sneers from commonplace minds like Mrs. Jolley.

Her kind of mysticism helps to define her role in the mandala pattern of the novel. As a lover of nature, Miss Hare is frequently in the out-of-doors; her element is air. When Dubbo paints her as in his Deposition painting, near the novel's end, he presents Mary Hare "at the center of a whorl of faintly perceptible wind" (p. 490).[20] In her spontaneous response to the phenomenal world, her lack of calculation and reflection, she embodies the Jungian faculty of sensation, expressed especially in the sense of touch.

Associated with air, Mary is often outside during her appearances in the novel. She is frequently presented walking through the neighborhood from the post office to Xanadu. Generally, she meets the other riders or visionaries in the outside world, under the plum tree, for instance; by contrast, her difficulties with Mrs. Jolley usually take place inside the mansion, and one of her most horrifying childhood experiences was hiding in a closet with her mother during her father's "false suicide." It was also outdoors, in an encounter with nature, that Mary first confronted the vision of the chariot. She and her father had been watching the evening sky, in a rare moment of communion and understanding. Her father had even, uncharacteristically, condescended to caress Mary. The sunset had become a vision of the chariot, and Norbert Hare was moved to be philosophical:

> Her father said: "Who are the riders in the Chariot, eh, Mary? Who is ever going to know?"
> Who, indeed? Certainly *she* would not be expected to understand. Nor did she think she wanted to, just then. But they continued there, the sunset backed up against the sky, as they stood beneath the great swinging trace-chains of its light. (pp. 20–21)

Since each of White's four visionaries apprehends the vision of the chariot in a different way, the means of revelation is symbolic of the mystical road each will travel. Hence Mary's discovery of the chariot mandala comes in an epiphany of natural beauty.

Mary's embodiment of the faculty of sensation and the special importance of her sense of touch can be illustrated by instances both from "the present" of the novel and from the "memory" section in Part One. Mary's participation in the natural world is often expressed by a reveling in the sensation of touch: "But the way developed over good, soft loam, and velvet patches of leaf mould, lovely if the knees were allowed to sink for a moment into a surface from which rise the scent of fungus and future growth" (p. 8). At times this sheer physical ecstasy from the sensations created by nature becomes a ritual of worship:

> At one stage she fell upon the knees of her earth-coloured practical stockings, not because she was discouraged, or ill—she had reached the time of life where acquaintances and neighbours were always on the lookout for strokes—but because it was natural to adopt a kneeling position in the act of worship, and because intense conviction will sometimes best express itself through the ungainliness of spontaneity.
> So she rested a little upon her knees, under the great targe of her protective hat, and dug her blunt, freckled fingers into the receptive earth. (p. 9)

Touch is the means for Mary's most intense acts of communication. Her dependence on touch is shown repeatedly in the memory section of Part One, as in the sunset epiphany she shared with her father. One of the best examples of Mary's communication through touch occurs when she experiences a moment of sympathy with Cousin

Eustace, whose visit had seemed to be such a painful failure in the eyes of her parents.

The imagery of tactile sensation is pervasive throughout Part One, where Mary's viewpoint is dominant. But in contrast to Mary's acceptance of sensation and nature are the characters of her father and Mrs. Jolley. Norbert Hare, as the memory section shows, is a failed romantic, and the crumbling house of Xanadu is a monument to his hopeless dream of perfection. Norbert had tried to shape the Australian landscape to his desire, but had been defeated by the sheer intractability and perversity of nature, its resistance to the perfection of design that the human mind would impose on it. Mrs. Jolley, the housekeeper who becomes Mary's tormentor in the novel's present and who serves figuratively as the snake in the garden at Xanadu, embodies a limited commonsense vision that is another dramatic contrast to Mary's childlike love of nature. Her mentality accepts the finite world as it is and refuses to risk any pursuit of a mystical quest, if indeed it would acknowledge the possibility of one.

Despite such opposition, Mary finds a moment of nearly complete fulfillment, toward the end of the novel, when she comforts the dying Himmelfarb. In warming Himmelfarb's feet in his last agony, Mary presses her face and body against the bedclothes, achieving the physical and mystical ecstasy she has longed for: "Miss Hare had, in fact, entered that state of complete union which her nature had never yet achieved. The softest matter her memory could muster—the fallen breast-feathers, tufts of fur torn in courtship, the downy, brown crooks of bracken—was what she now willed upon the spirit of her love" (p. 471).[21] After Himmelfarb's death, she stumbles homeward through the familiar natural landscape, still transfigured by her emotions: "Her instinct suggested, rather, that she was being dispersed, but that in so experiencing, she was entering the final ecstasy. . . . She was all but identified" (pp. 472–73).[22] In short, Mary Hare has come as close to identity with nature, transcending the dichotomy of subject and object, as White can imagine is humanly possible.

3

Whereas Mary Hare is a mystic of nature, Himmelfarb, White's archetypal wandering Jew, follows—and sometimes deviates from—the mystical tradition of the Cabbala and esoteric Judaism. Within the quaternal mandala pattern, Himmelfarb represents the faculty of reason and is associated with the element of fire. The sense of smell has a special importance for him, although as a thinker who follows inner vision, his sensory experience is less vivid than that of the other riders.

Is it not paradoxical that Himmelfarb embodies the faculty of

reason, yet follows a path of mysticism? The explanation is provided
by a brief study of Himmelfarb's experience. In childhood and youth,
Himmelfarb is torn between the secular rationalism of his father and
the devout Jewish piety of his mother. For a time in his youth, the
rationalism seems to win, as Himmelfarb pursues a career of secular
scholarship. But Himmelfarb is disillusioned by his father's pragmatic
"conversion" to Christianity, and after taking his post at Bienenstadt's
university, he begins his return to his Jewish roots, first by marrying
into the Jewish community there, and then by discovering Cabbalistic
mystical works. Thus Himmelfarb represents reason enlightened by
the inner vision of Judaism, reason enlightened by the Cabbalistic
seekers' quest for God.

Himmelfarb contrasts the "inner way" of Jewish mysticism with
the nature mysticism of Mary Hare when he converses with her: " 'It
is still difficult for us to appreciate, except in theory,' said the man.
'Until so very recently, we were confined within ghettoes. Trees and
flowers grew the other side of walls, the other side of our experience,
in fact.' " And he adds, " 'I am a Jew, and centuries of history have
accustomed one to look inward instead of outwards' " (p. 96).

The motif of fire is associated with Himmelfarb's long search. At
first Himmelfarb seems at home with the candles of Jewish tradition,
but, as more than one critic has noted, his effort to avoid a destiny
as a symbolic Jewish shaman, a *zaddik*, leads him to wander. The
inner fire of boyhood devotion becomes the tormenting fire of youthful
sexuality, followed by the fire of scholarly and intellectual zeal. The
two memorable passages from mystical treatises that Himmelfarb
discovers at Bienenstadt emphasize the metaphors of light and fire,
symbolizing mystic illumination and the mystic's passionate journey
toward God. The first of these, from a disciple of Abulafila (although
it has not been generally noted), describes a light that is supernatural,
that lingers after the extinction of the seeker's candle (p. 140).[23] The
second passage, from the mystic Eleazar of Worms (again the source
is not generally noted), speaks of the "flame of heart-felt love" of
God that devours the seeker, until "all his thoughts burn with the
fire of love for Him" (p. 141).[24]

Opposed to this inner fire is the outer fire of history, which
Himmelfarb experiences in the "holocaust" against the Jews during
Nazism and World War II. Even Himmelfarb's liberation from the
prison camp comes during the fire of a bombing raid, during which
he is pummeled into unconsciousness. After the war, Himmelfarb,
after a brief visit to Israel, emigrates to Australia, where he eventually
enters the "infernal pit" of the bicycle factory at Barranugli. He
shares Ezekiel's vision, with its fire imagery, with Dubbo, the Abo
(p. 333). Finally, he experiences his personal passion in the Good
Friday reenactment of the Crucifixion, and his life comes to an end

following two fires: the outer fire of persecution that finally takes tangible form in the flames that burn his shack; and the inner fire of mystic consummation that inflames his vision (his physical vision as well as his spiritual eye) at the moment of death (p. 471).[25]

The imagery of scent has a particular felicity for Himmelfarb, whose weak eyesight is underscored by his need for glasses, and whose sensory responses in general are subordinated to his inner vision. In the memory section, Himmelfarb's olfactory sense is stimulated by the "spices of tradition," and Himmelfarb is particularly sensitive to the smells that are pleasant, such as the scent of evergreens in the forest outside the Friedensdorf death camp, which seems to mock the Jews about to enter it (p. 121).[26] In Himmelfarb's final vision of himself as the archetypal man of Cabbalistic vision, there is an important emphasis on scent:

> Again, he was the Man Kadmon, descending from the Tree of Light to take the Bride. Trembling with white, holding the cup in her chapped hands, she advanced to stand beneath the *chuppah*. So they were brought together in the smell of all primordial velvets. (p. 462)

In dramatic contrast to Himmelfarb are not only the German bigots and the Australian chauvinists, but also his father, whose rationalism finally evolved into a "conversion" of convenience, and Harry Rosetree, who in the present of the novel accommodated his identity as a Jew to the prevailing Gentile culture of Australia. Both are Jews who betrayed their heritage, whereas Himmelfarb fulfilled his destiny as wandering and suffering Jewish scapegoat and Adam Kadmon.

4

Mrs. Godbold, the third rider in the chariot, embodies the mystical fervor of evangelical Christianity, although she is not portrayed as a regular attendant at any church. Since her vision of the chariot originates in Christian piety, it is a more familiar kind of mysticism for most readers than Miss Hare's or Himmelfarb's, yet there is nothing stereotyped about Mrs. Godbold's faith. In the mandala pattern of the novel, Mrs. Godbold embodies Christian faith and charity. She is associated with the element of earth and the Jungian faculty of feeling, and her special sense is hearing.

Auditory imagery has great significance throughout Part Four, where Mrs. Godbold's present and past are rendered from her point of view. The memory section reveals that her awareness of the chariot vision had come from a nonconformist hymn (p. 245). One of the most stirring moments of her childhood was the ecstasy she felt from hearing the organ in the cathedral (pp. 252–54). In the turbulence of her unhappy marriage to Tom Godbold, she comforts herself by singing hymns at the ironing board, while eking out a meager income to support her family. At Mrs. Khalil's bordello, Mrs. Godbold is attracted to Alf Dubbo not just from compassion, but by his lusty singing.

Mrs. Godbold's association with the element of earth is equally apparent. A ponderous woman, surrounded by a brood of children, she has the qualities of an earth-mother archetype. A recurrent action throughout Part Four and the passages where her point of view is dominant is her bending to comfort the fallen. In her memory section, her first important act as comforter comes when, at haymaking, she picks up her stricken brother, whose head had been crushed by a wagon wheel, and carries his body to her father in town. Later, as Mrs. Chalmers-Robinson's maid, Ruth stoops to lift up her mistress, who has fainted at one of her fashionable luncheons on learning of her husband's business failure. Again, Ruth's marriage to Tom Godbold originates from the evening when Godbold drops to his knees, on the beach at Bondi, to confess his dependence. (Ironically, Tom's physical strength disguises his spiritual weakness, his fear of being alone and adrift in the world.) Although it is Mrs. Godbold who is knocked to earth by her husband at the beginning of Part Four, it is Mrs. Godbold who goes to Mrs. Khalil's brothel to rescue her husband from his figuratively fallen position of dissipation. At Khalil's however, it is not Tom Godbold whom Mrs. Godbold lowers herself to help—for Tom is now beyond help—but Alf Dubbo, the half-caste "blackfellow." When the drunken Dubbo collapses from an attack and spits up blood, it is Mrs. Godbold who "stooped, and wiped the blood away" (p. 302). All these acts of compassion lead to Mrs. Godbold's climactic deed of succoring the fallen when, near the end of the novel, she takes the "crucified" and dying Himmelfarb to her shed to care for him in his final hours.

White's narrative sharply contrasts Mrs. Godbold with her husband and, in the memory section, with her mistress, Mrs. Chalmers-Robinson, in the days when Mrs. Godbold was Ruth Joyner, a lady's maid. An earthy man, Godbold resents his wife's psychological and spiritual strength, and tries to hide from his despair caused by his poverty, large family, and poor prospects by plunging himself into drink and sexual excess.[27] And Mrs. Chalmers-Robinson is an upper-class lady who tries to keep as much distance as possible from the earth and its unpleasant facts (much like the young Elizabeth Hunter in *The Eye of the Storm*). Ruth Joyner represents everything that is socially (and metaphysically) beneath her.

Ruth Godbold's life is an embodiment of love, pity, and Christian charity for those around her, the faculty of feeling elevated to the heights of saintliness. At one point, she becomes almost an allegory of pity. At the end of Part Four, where the narrative moves ahead into the future, Mrs. Godbold is shown weeping on the street corner after viewing her husband's body at the hospital. She seems momentarily transfigured into an archetypal *mater dolorosa*:

> She cried, rather, for the condition of men, for all those she had loved, burningly, or at a respectful distance, from her father, seated at his bench in his prison of flesh, and her own brood of puzzled little girls, for her former mistress, always clutching at the hem and finding it come away in her hand, for her fellow initiates, the madwoman and the Jew of Sarsaparilla, even for the blackfellow she had met at Mrs. Khalil's, and then never again, unless by common agreement in her thoughts and dreams. (p. 307)

5

The fourth rider in the chariot, Alf Dubbo, apprehends his vision of the chariot through sight, from his encounter with a painting, and later he transforms the vision imaginatively in his own final obsessed work. Dubbo represents the artist's way to the world of transcendence. The most Blakean figure of the riders, Dubbo is associated with the element of water; he embodies the Jungian faculty of intuition (or imagination), and his sense is sight or vision.

Even a casual reading reveals that Dubbo's dominant sense is sight. The sections of Part Five and Part Six where action is presented from Dubbo's point of view are rich in color imagery, with ten references to colors appearing in the paragraph describing the town where Dubbo was reared (p. 336). Dubbo's sensitivity to visual imagery is stressed repeatedly in his painting and in his response to people: Miss Hare, for instance, is the "fox-coloured woman," when Dubbo sees her warming Himmelfarb's feet (p. 469).

Dubbo's association with the element of water is stressed in the opening lines of his memory section:

> Alf Dubbo was reared in a small town on the banks of a river which never wholly dried up, and which, in wet seasons, would overflow its steep banks and flood the houses in the lower town. The river played an important part in the boy's early life, and even after he left his birthplace, his thoughts would frequently return to the dark banks of the brown river. (p. 336)

The river as a symbol of Dubbo's boyhood innocence perhaps alludes to Coleridge's "Alph, the sacred river," that evocation of Edenic innocence in "Kubla Khan." Dubbo was born by a river, lives by a river with Mrs. Pask and the Reverend Tim Calderon, and dwells by another river with an aging prostitute, Mrs. Spice. After his fall from innocence is complete, Dubbo is separated from rivers, but his association with water continues in a less obvious way, through his painting and through the imagery of polluted blood that he discharges in his illness. In his last burst of creativity, while painting the Deposition of Himmelfarb, Dubbo dreams again of his childhood and of walking by the riverbank beside the Reverend Calderon, his mentor and foster father. After the completion of the painting, Dubbo feels that his blood has turned to water, until, ironically, he hemorrhages again. In the last chariot painting, Dubbo achieves an illusion in which the total effect seems "as though the banks of a river were to begin to flow alongside its stationary waters" (p. 493). This final river image is set in ironic contrast with the massive hemorrhage that ends his life at the completion of the painting.

As an artist who apprehends the "perception of the infinite" in his Deposition and Chariot paintings, Dubbo is a Blakean figure. Certain Blakean themes are developed in Dubbo's painting. For Blake, as for Ezekiel, the purpose of art was to create a vision of transcendence showing an identity between God and man. By recreating the image of the Crucifixion with Himmelfarb as Christ and Miss Hare and Mrs. Godbold as the two Marys, and by creating his vision of the chariot with the four riders, Dubbo uses art to renew religious myth. The vision of the chariot is essentially an apocalyptic one, portraying the four riders as bearers of the divine within them, and this apocalyptic painting is reminiscent of Blake's obsession with creating the image of imaginative apocalypse.[28]

As a visionary of the divinity within ordinary men and women, Dubbo stands in sharp contrast to the Reverend Calderon, for whom Christianity was an Anglo-Saxon sentimentality, and to Mrs. Pask, for whom art is essentially a genteel diversion. In his indifference to the monetary value of his paintings, Dubbo is ironically contrasted with Hannah, the prostitute who sells his earlier paintings, and Humphrey Mortimer, the collector, representatives of the materialism of Australian society. The indifference of Dubbo to the fate of his paintings is ironically underscored, not only by his death but by their obscure fate after they are sold at auction. For Dubbo it was sufficient reward to have completed his painting and unified his vision of the chariot with the world of his experience. Just as Miss Hare is the nature mystic, Himmelfarb the scholarly and Cabbalistic mystic, and Mrs. Godbold the mystic of Christian piety, Dubbo is the artist visionary who achieves his mystic quest.

6

White's *Riders in the Chariot* is constructed around the mandala quaternity of the four characters who are eventually transformed into the riders in the divine chariot. The chariot symbol, a Jungian mandala image, attempts to consolidate symbolism from Ezekiel, the New Testament, Cabbalistic tradition, the evangelical Christian tradition, the prophetic spirit of William Blake, and the myth created in the psychology of C.G. Jung. In this vast synthesis, White dramatizes the theme that diverse mystical "ways" all ultimately become one way, part of one pattern in the attempt of human seekers to find a union in the spirit with transcendence.

White's four seekers represent diverse mystical traditions. Miss Hare is a mystic of nature, affirming the phenomenal world so completely by loving participation in it that she ultimately affirms the numinous world. Himmelfarb follows the inner way of the spirit, seeking to transcend images to find union with God, but finally reaching fulfillment in the suffering of his role as archetypal wandering Jewish scapegoat and Adam Kadmon. Mrs. Godbold follows the road of evangelical piety, finding her fulfillment in her acts of love and her acceptance of the suffering world around her. Dubbo achieves his perception of divinity through creating in his painting a vision of the spiritual seekers in his life, thereby renewing the vision of Christianity by an art which overcomes conventional boundaries. A Blakean artist, Dubbo uses the imagery of the world about him to recreate the visionary tradition of Christian art.

In dramatizing the theme of the ultimate identity of diverse mystic roads, White's novel justifies Hyatt Waggoner's assertion that it demonstrates "artistically, how 'the way up' and 'the way down' could be thought of concretely as 'the same,' not just because they arrive by different routes at the same 'end' but because the routes themselves so often run parallel."[29] "The way up" in Waggoner's terminology is the *via affirmativa*, the mystic's way of affirming the images of the phenomenal world with the purpose of ultimately transcending it: this is the road of Miss Hare and Alf Dubbo.[30] "The way down" is the *via negativa*, the mystic way as more traditionally defined by such writers as Evelyn Underhill: it may be called the denial of self and the images of the phenomenal world in the effort to reach deity and transcendence; in short, it is the way of Himmelfarb's Jewish mysticism and, to a lesser degree, Mrs. Godbold's Christian piety.[31]

In addition to describing the unity in diversity of his four visionaries and their separate quests for the chariot mandala, White has employed a rich pattern of symbolism in portraying the experience of his major characters. Each of the four riders is associated with one of the traditional elements, with a particular sense, and with a special Jungian psychological faculty. By using this pattern to dramatize the experience of his seekers, White enriches and unifies the texture and narrative of the novel, which at times seems sprawling.

Not only is *Riders in the Chariot* White's own massive Jungian mandala, but the action actually describes the creation of this quaternal mandala symbolizing an identity of humanity and divinity. The novel is both carefully patterned and richly dramatic. Although William Walsh has commented that *Riders in the Chariot* seems somewhat too schematic in its design, one may argue that the converse is true.[32] In dramatizing the creation of his chariot mandala, White sets his major characters in sharp conflict with the cultural and spiritual wasteland of Australia. The contrast between those who lack the "perception of the infinite" and the mystics is stark and vivid. White seems to envision an apocalyptic division between the spiritually illuminated and the spiritually obtuse sunk in mundane experience. In these apocalyptic contrasts, the massive synthesis of symbolism attempted, the unity forged from diverse mystical traditions, and the frequent prophetic tone of the novel, *Riders in the Chariot* earns its epigraph from Blake. It is an act of imagination that may be favorably compared with the ambitious imaginative syntheses of Blake and Jung.

Notes

1. The epigraph to *Riders in the Chariot* quotes three paragraphs of *The Marriage of Heaven and Hell* from the dialogue between Blake and the prophets Isaiah and Ezekiel. The prophets are established as predecessors of Blake in the prophetic role of heightening human consciousness of the divine, which is defined in rather broad terms as seeing "the infinite in everything" by Isaiah. The quotation from Blake not only calls attention to the source of the chariot symbol, but aligns White with Blake.

2. Patricia Morley, *The Mystery of Unity* (Montreal: McGill-Queens Univ. Press, 1972), pp. 153–57. A more hostile reading of the novel which also discusses Cabbalistic and biblical sources for the work is J. F. Burrows' "Archetypes and Stereotypes in *Riders in the Chariot,*" *Southerly*, 25 (1965), 46–68. Burrows, however, is uncertain of White's intentions and achievement. An attack on White's use of symbolism is J. D. Heydon's "Patrick White," *The Oxford Review* (Spring 1966), 33–46. Heydon regards White's use of symbolism and creation of a myth to be a grandiose mistake.

Two early book-length studies also evade or express qualified views about White's symbolism, particularly in *Riders in the Chariot*. Barry Argyle, in *Patrick White* (Edinburgh: Oliver and Boyd, 1967), gives a readable account of the fiction through the middle sixties, treating White primarily as a realist and avoiding discussion of the sources and meaning of much of the symbolism. R. F. Brissenden, *Patrick White*, rev. ed. (London: F. Mildner and Sons; and Longmans, Green, 1969), offers some sensitive commentary on White's symbolism, but is skeptical about White's more ambitious symbolic narratives, including *Riders in the Chariot*. Brissenden is particularly concerned about the equation—as he sees it—of Nazism with Australian chauvinism and good fellowship. On pp. 30–35, Brissenden characterizes *Riders* as an ambitious failure, a ruined mansion like Miss Hare's Xanadu in the novel.

3. Morley, pp. 164–83, notes various mandala images in the novel. Manfred Mackenzie, in "Patrick White's Later Novels: A Generic Reading," *Southern Review*, 1 (1965), also treats some Jungian motifs in White's *Riders*, and a valuable article on Jungian motifs in *The Tree of Man* is A. P. Riemer's "Visions of the Mandala in *The Tree of Man,*" *Southerly*, 27 (1967), 3–19.

4. J. E. Cirlot, *A Dictionary of Symbols*, trans. Jack Sage (New York: Philosophical Library, 1962), pp. 190–94. Many of Jung's writings on mandalas are collected in C. G. Jung, *Mandala Symbolism* (Princeton, N. J.: Princeton Univ. Press, Bollingen

Paperback Edition, 1972). This paperback monograph is an extract from *The Archetypes and the Collective Unconscious*, vol. 9, part I, of *The Collected Works of C. G. Jung*.

5. Peter Beatson, *The Eye in the Mandala* (New York: Barnes and Noble, 1976), pp. 163–65.

6. Morley, pp. 153–54.

7. See, for instance, Cirlot, p. 193. *Mandala Symbolism* provides some illustrations of mandalas divided into four parts, as for instance, figure 33 and figure 45.

8. William Walsh, *Patrick White's Fiction* (Totawa, N.J.: Rowman and Littlefield, 1977), p. 129.

9. Violet S. deLaszlo, ed., *The Basic Writings of C. G. Jung* (New York: Modern Library, Random House, 1959), pp. 501–02.

10. *Basic Writings of Jung*, p. 319, identifies mandalas with certain biblical symbols such as the Garden of Eden and the Heavenly City of the *Apocalypse;* quaternities are also identified with the Heavenly City and the four evangelists (pp. 521–22). *Mandala Symbolism*, p. 62, has an explicit identification of a quaternity mandala with Ezekiel's vision (in a footnote).

11. *Basic Writings of Jung*, pp. 520–22.

12. Ibid., p. 523. Jung is somewhat like William Blake in finding God within man, although Jung uses a myth of the collective unconscious, while Blake constructed a myth of the redeemed human imagination as divine; there is some overlapping, but the two are not quite the same.

13. *Basic Writings of Jung*, p. 523. Jung is aware that he is building a myth and makes frequent disclaimers as a scientist of any claims to absolute truth.

14. Edward F. Edinger, *Ego and Archetype* (Baltimore: Pelican Books, 1973), p. 4.

15. Jose and Miriam Arguelles, *Mandala* (Berkeley: Shambala Books, 1972), p. 62 and p. 114, for instance.

16. Beatson, pp. 91–92.

17. Beatson, pp. 138–49, in a chapter on the presence of the four elements in White's work; but Beatson ranges over the entire canon of White's novels without analyzing the presence of the four elements in any one novel. The discussion of fire, pp. 141–43, does treat Himmelfarb's relationship to fire briefly.

18. Jung's four faculties of mind are sensation, reason (or thought), feeling, and intuition (or imagination). There is, of course, some overlapping of functions in the different faculties. See *Basic Writings of Jung*, p. 253, for a definition of the four faculties or functions. June Singer, in an excellent exposition of Jungian theory, in *The Boundaries of the Soul* (Garden City, N.Y.: Doubleday Anchor Books, 1973), discusses Jung's four faculties in detail on pp. 209–27. It should be noted that development of each faculty may aid another—for instance, the development of sensation may aid intuition or imagination—and it should be noted that in White's symbolism of the senses, the fifth, taste, is considered an aspect of touch.

19. Miss Hare's relationship to the part of nature she has made her own is clearly defined in *Riders*, p. 14, where White writes, "All that land, stick and stone, belonged to her, over and above actual rights," and continues to describe Mary's identification with the objects of her territory.

The nature mysticism of Emerson is expressed more in his essays than in his poetry, especially in such works as "Nature." For Whitman's nature mysticism, the main text is "Song of Myself," and a valuable exposition is James E. Miller, Jr., *A Critical Guide to Leaves of Grass* (Chicago: Univ. of Chicago Press, 1957).

In English literature the closest analogue to Mary's mysticism is probably Wordsworth's poetry, especially *The Prelude;* but Mary does not proceed to an abstract conception of God as Wordsworth attains in his Mt. Snowden experience.

20. There are three references to wind in the description of this painting. There are many more instances than those I cite associating Miss Hare with the element of air.

21. It is not until she commits her being to warming Himmelfarb's feet that Miss Hare goes beyond her earlier level of communion with nature to a surrender and absorption of the self with the other that is nearly as complete as can be achieved within the normal physical limits of human life.

22. The word "identified" suggests self-transcendence, her near union with the landscape, and her sensory impressions seem to be identical with objects.

23. Beatson (p. 112) notes that "readers interested in the background of the Chariot" should consult Gershom Scholem's *Major Trends in Jewish Mysticism* (1941; 3d rev. ed. rpt. New York: Schocken Books, 1961); but Beatson does not cite the sources of the quotations from Cabbalistic tradition. The passage about the light remaining after the candle's extinction is to be found on page 150 of Scholem, as part of a long quotation from Abulafia's disciple; Scholem dates the treatise at about 1295 and suggests that it was written in Palestine (p. 146). Although White may have used Scholem as a source, his version of the quotation in *Riders in the Chariot* is slightly different, indicating a different translation.

24. This quotation from Eleazar of Worms is found in a slightly different version in Scholem, p. 95. Eleazar of Worms was one of three influential German medieval masters of Hasidism; he died, according to Scholem (p. 82), between 1223 and 1232.

25. *Riders in the Chariot,* p. 471. In the paragraph describing Himmelfarb's death, apparently a final stroke, he seems to see fire everywhere, a sacred, transforming fire, it should be noted.

26. *Riders in the Chariot,* p. 121, refers to the spices of tradition. On p. 189, there is the reference to the scent of pines as the prisoners descend at Friedensdorf. There are a great many olfactory images in this section, although Himmelfarb as a realized character in fiction also has other senses. The Himmelfarb memory section is very vivid, despite the limitations imposed by White's conception of Himmelfarb as a man with weak eyesight.

27. Beatson, p. 37, notes a pattern whereby innocent characters in White's fiction sometimes drive other characters to a paradoxical self-destructiveness. Tom Godbold is one of the examples given.

28. This view of Blake is now commonplace since the revolution in studies in romanticism in the last thirty years. The book which began the stress on Blake and his hope for an imaginative apocalypse, and which emphasized the apocalyptic character of the prophetic works, is Northrop Frye's *Fearful Symmetry* (Princeton, N.J.: Princeton Univ. Press, 1947). It is possible that White was influenced by this book.

29. Hyatt Waggoner, *American Poets: From the Puritans to the Present* (Boston: Houghton Mifflin, 1968), p. 648. Waggoner's comment is part of an interesting discussion of Emersonian and Whitman mysticism, and the inadequacy of many conventional discussions of mysticism, which appear to focus primarily on one or another orthodox tradition. "The way up" and "the way down" are phrases originating probably in a famous paradox of Heraclitus ("the way up and the way down are the same way") quoted by T. S. Eliot as the epigraph to "Burnt Norton," the first of the *Four Quartets.*

30. Waggoner, pp. 638–39.

31. Evelyn Underhill, *Mysticism* (1910; rpt. Cleveland: Meridian Books Reprint, 1955) is a famous study of mysticism that tends to focus strongly on the negative way of medieval mystics, the mysticism that begins by denial of self and images, in order

for the seeker to reach a union with a transcendent God. Underhill has little of value to say about a mysticism affirming nature or images of the phenomenal world leading to a final confirmation both of the world and of a transcendent divinity.

32. Walsh, p. 66.

Patrick White: The Great Mother and Her Son [The Solid Mandala]

David J. Tacey°

WHITE AND JUNG

Many critics of the Australian novelist Patrick White have claimed that the writer has made conscious use of Jung's ideas and archetypes. A. P. Riemer has been the most vocal in espousing this view. He argues that both *The Tree of Man* (1956) and *Riders in the Chariot* (1961) rely heavily upon Jungian material and that the recognition of this is important for the comprehension of White's intentions. He even goes so far as to add that "a novelist's use of such arcane material will inevitably involve questions of propriety: but I prefer this problem of artistic licence to be fought out elsewhere, as I have no doubt it will be" (Riemer 7, p. 116). This line of thought is entirely misdirected. White's novels seem Jungian because the writer has in his own way drawn upon the deep unconscious and its archetypes. It is precisely this fact that makes the novels so powerful and accounts for their genuine visionary quality. They are not products of his conscious mind but spring up, as it were, from the creative unconscious. A writer does not have to read Jung to formulate archetypal configurations—he has rather to turn within and enter into his own dialogue with the imagination. This, surely, is the mark of all great imaginative or visionary art.

Far from basing his work on Jung, White claims not even to have read him before the mid 1960s, after all his most "Jungian" novels had been written. In a letter to the writer of 14 February, 1976, he says: "I did not read Jung until about the time of *The Solid Mandala*, when somebody gave me *Psychology and Alchemy*." And again in a letter dated 28 September, 1975, he writes: "I did not know of Jung's work at the time of writing *The Aunt's Story*. I don't think I had even heard of him, though I may have as I had read some Freud."

° Reprinted from *Journal of Analytical Psychology* 28 (1983): 165–83; by permission of *Journal of Analytical Psychology*; © 1983 The Society of Analytical Psychology.

Jungian influence is evident in *The Solid Mandala* (1966). The title itself betrays some knowledge of Jung, and the text reproduces passages from his work. Yet even here it is wrong to be deterministic about the relationship, to argue that the psychologist provided "source materials." White's vision of the circular form was in evidence long before his reading of Jung. It appears in every work from *The Living and the Dead* (1941) to *Riders in the Chariot* (1961). It seems to me that White's reading of Jung had no real impact upon his literary vision. All it did was to allow him to name—or rather to misname— the image which had been central to his work. I say "misname" because White's symbol was never a true mandala, a symbol of the integration of personality, but rather a representation of the uroboros, the womb-like image of unconsciousness (Neumann 6). The crucial distinction between the uroboros (circle-as-beginning) and the mandala (circle-as-end) is not recognised by the novelist, for whom each and every circle-image is indiscriminately regarded as a "mandala." White's characters merge into the oceanic oneness of the uroboros and, by a systematic misapplication of the individuation paradigm, the author translates this movement toward disintegration into terms of self-realisation and wholeness. The end result is that White—and his critics—talk about psychological and spiritual triumphs which bear no relation to the actual *regressions* which take place in the fiction. Thus I do not believe that White's contact with Jung's work was profitable; instead, it engendered confusion and presented a false lead to the critics. If anything it suggested that the author did not really understand his work, that the literary vision was autonomous and independent of his conscious intentions.

THE MYTH AND THE COMPLEX

Each White book is a variation upon a single myth relating to the figures of the great mother and her eternal youth. In every novel the same movement is established: the *puer aeternus* enters and is devoured by the mother-image. The term *puer aeternus* is used in the matriarchal context established by Jung and von Franz, not in the sense adopted by James Hillman—*senex-et-puer*. The fatal marriage of mother and son is one of the earliest mythologems in Western culture. The Oedipus myth is itself a late derivation of the incestuous drama, which can be traced back to the neolithic and upper paleolithic eras (James 3). It depicts a world where nature is omniscient, where the masculine spirit constantly succumbs to her strength. Thus in the myth—as in White's stories—the son does not mature psychologically beyond adolescence; he remains vernal, phallic, supporting the goddess in her natural cycle and finally yielding to her in death.

In psychology we speak of a "mother-complex" whenever the unconscious as matrix or source appears to have the upper hand, when it attracts more libido to itself than that which is readily available for conscious development. The son does not escape the primal situation, but is always held fast by the maternal earth. In White's *The Tree of Man* there is a crucial section during the Wullunya flood sequence where we find the image of an old, dead man hanging upside down in a tree (White II, p. 74). This image disturbs Stan Parker when he first encounters it, and it continues to plague him throughout the story. He never realises the symbolic meaning of the image, but of course it aptly sums up his own inner situation. Like the "Hanged Man" in the Tarot, he lives life in an inverted way. His career is a long, downward slide into the world of the earth mother, finally recaptured by her at his death. The *puer* is fixed upon the maternal tree and unable to wrest an individual existence from the pull of the earth and the tremendous inertia of the unconscious. Himmelfarb in *Riders in the Chariot* ends up literally bound to the disfigured jacaranda tree at the back of Rosetree's factory. All through his life he is assimilated to the maternal world and manipulated by a group of powerful mother figures. At the beginning of the story we find him "imprisoned" beneath an enormous flowering tree at Xanadu, and at the end he is found dying helplessly upon the Tree of Death. His life follows the pattern of Attis-Adonis, the pagan sacrificial god who was co-ordinated to fulfil the mythic and seasonal cycle of the mother goddess.

MISREADING THE MYTH

Now White himself presents the mother myth in a wholly positive light; in fact he (mis)presents it as Christianity. Just as the maternal round is viewed as a "mandala," so the *puer's* longing to return to the mother is seen in the context of man's desire for unity with God. The protagonist is extinguished in the source-situation and the author assumes he is becoming "at one" with the divine. It appears that the ecstasy of dissolution (i.e., loss of ego and its limitations) is confused with the heightened feeling of religious integration and spiritual endeavour. White chooses to ignore completely the nihilistic and regressive character of uroboric regression.

But while the teller focuses upon the ecstatic aspect of dissolution, the tale itself tends to emphasise the destructive and devouring nature of the process. It does this by constantly creating images of the "terrible mother" whenever a dissolution-striving character approaches the matrix, as in these passages:

> . . . Sometimes, and tonight, Theodora went and sat beneath the apricot tree. She took a book that she would not read. She marked

her page with a dock and sat. And as she sat, there seemed to be no beginning or end. Meroë was eternity, and she was the keeper of it.

Before Mother broke in, "Theodora, Theodora, where is my little silver paper-knife?"

Mother's voice made the hot air quiver. (White 10, p. 79)

. . . At this point, Theodora sometimes said, I should begin to read Gibbon, or find religion, instead of speaking to myself in my own room. But words, whether spoken or written, were at most frail slat bridges over chasms, and Mrs. Goodman had never encouraged religion, as she herself was God. So it will not be by these means, Theodora said, that the great monster Self will be destroyed, and that desirable state achieved, which resembles, one would imagine, nothing more than air or water. She did not doubt that the years would contribute, rubbing and extracting, but never enough. Her body still clanged and rang when the voice struck.

"Theo-*dor*-a!"

I have not the humility, Theodora said. (p. 128)

In both sections of *The Aunt's Story* (1948) the demanding and abrasive voice of the mother follows hard upon the protagonist's longing for self-dissolution. In the first, we find Theodora about to merge into an uroboric eternity, with "no beginning or end," when suddenly the mother's voice breaks into the scene and destroys the vision of paradise. In the second we find her musing about how best she might destroy the ego-personality, here referred to as "the great monster Self," when again the voice interrupts her pursuit of ecstasy and forces her to attend to its demands. Thus, while the character feels she is surrendering herself to the matrix, she is actually being "seized" by the mother-image and devoured by an aggressive force. The longing for dissolution is—in the symbolic language of the inner world—a submission to the witch-like power of the unconscious, a giving in to its demands.

It is my belief that the tale acts compensatorily here not merely to the attitude of the central character, but to that of the author himself. In every novel he presents the same longing for dissolution and in each case the tale responds by throwing up images of snarling, devouring, and sometimes teeth-sucking, mothers. The "unconscious" of the teller responds as only it can—by creating symbolic images of the unacknowledged negative side of the longing. But the meaning of these images is never realised—the "mothers" are treated as external phenomena, and never as psychic figures pointing to internal reality. Consequently, White's work is plagued with some dozens of terrible mothers, each of whom is treated literally as the "enemy" of the protagonist. Jung provides a vivid account of the situation: Always he imagines his worst enemy in front of him yet he carries the enemy within himself—a deadly longing for the abyss, a longing to drown in his own source, to be sucked down to the realm of the Mothers. (Jung 4, p. 355) There is a peculiar irony in the fact that although White is a self-confessed writer of phantasy ("My characters are not based on real people, they simply well up from the unconscious . . ." (White 8)) he does not treat his characters as phantasy figures. The stuff of the psyche is taken concretely, though it is metaphorical in origin and intent.

There is only one point in White's fiction where there is a near realisation of the inward nature of the devouring mother:

> "Mother, must you destroy?"
>
> "Destroy?" asked Mrs. Goodman.
>
> "Yes," said Theodora. "I believe you were born with an axe in your hand."
>
> "I do not understand what you mean. Axes? I have sat here all the afternoon. I am suffering from heartburn."
>
> At night Theodora Goodman would bring her mother cups of hot milk, which she drank with little soft complaining noises, and the milk skin hung from her lower lip. She was old and soft. Then it is I, said Theodora, I have a core of evil in me that is altogether hateful. But she could not overcome her repugnance for the skin that swung from her mother's lip, giving her the appearance of an old white goat. (White 10, p. 121)

Here we find that the highly-charged projection is simply not fitting the reality of the old, ailing woman with dyspepsia. The psychic image "bounces back," as it were, so that the character is forced to admit to the possibility of her own "core of evil." But the realisation is merely intellectual, or situational. Almost immediately the projection returns with the same intensity as before. This is confirmed soon after by the fact that Theodora contemplates murdering her mother. As she takes up the little silver paper-knife she wonders whether cutting Mrs. Goodman's throat might "cut the knot" that binds her (p. 123). But the regressive tie to the mother is psychic; it cannot be severed by an act of violence. After carefully weighing up the pros and cons, Theodora decides against actual matricide: "She threw back the thin knife, which fell and clattered on the zinc . . . and went on to her room, away from the act she had not committed" (p. 123).

Often in White the characters contemplate killing or actually attempt to kill the terrible mother. In *The Tree of Man* Mick O'Dowd tries to shoot his domineering wife, and at odd points is seen chasing her around the house with an axe. In a fit of despair Stan Parker wrestles with an old hag on a beach near Sydney. Even Alf Dubbo, the quiet and reclusive artist in *Riders in the Chariot*, makes a murderous attack upon a prostitute who has him caught in her sphere of power. At a symbolic level it is right that the *pueri* should feel impelled to destroy the dragon-mother. Yet the dragon to be slain is within themselves—in their own longing for the matrix, their desire to be dissolved in eternity. They cannot "see" the dragon because it is too close to them. They cannot "kill" it because that would mean conquering their own yearning for anonymity—the thing they value above all else. So the primordial figure remains their perpetual, if dreaded, companion: the uroboros mystic and the dragon-mother are an inseparable pair, they constellate each other.

THE CALL FOR CONSCIOUSNESS

In *Voss* (1957) and *Riders in the Chariot* White's Christian misinterpretation of his central theme reaches its most systematic and advanced stage. Voss's craving for self-annihilation and his eventual reduction at the hands of an archaic goddess are wrongly interpreted in terms of Christian sacrifice and the redemptive mystery of "man returning into God" (White 12, p. 386). Himmelfarb's subservience to the Great Mother and his ritualised, Attis-like existence are falsely conceived in the context of Christ's suffering and crucifixion. Not only does this misapplication distort (and greatly overvalue) the content of the work, but it also damages Christianity itself, in so far as it is identified with the pathological obsessions of the mother's son.

But all this changes with the publication of *The Solid Mandala* (1966). In this work the unconscious itself rises up in reaction to the author's misreading of the myth. Here the inner life takes on personified form in the figure of Arthur Brown, the "retarded" shadow-brother who rejects the Christian frame (cf. " 'All this Christ stuff . . . doesn't seem to work. But we have each other,' Arthur said" [p. 200]) and who urges his "conscious" twin to see exactly what is taking place in the inner world. Arthur attempts to show Waldo that he is caught up in a psychic complex (the "knot" at the centre of the glass marble) and that he must extricate himself from it before any spiritual maturity can be achieved. *The Solid Mandala* is a very desperate novel, which reflects the urgency of the inner self, its longing to be freed from its present infantile condition, and to be met and understood by ego-consciousness. Arthur senses that if Waldo does not achieve realisation, he will not either; that salvation is a dialogical process requiring the participation of conscious and unconscious.

Waldo, however, does not appear to possess a personality which is capable of positive involvement with the inner world. Whenever the unconscious makes its approach he either puts up an acute resistance, clinging to his sterile and completely rational ego-position, or he loses himself altogether in the uprising content. This ambivalence is strongly evident in his relationship with Arthur. Intellectually, Waldo demonstrates a profound resentment toward his twin. He views Arthur as an ever-present threat to his freedom and civilised consciousness: "Waldo would have liked to go permanently proud and immaculate, but his twin brother dragged him back repeatedly behind the line where knowledge didn't protect" (White 14, p. 46). Yet deep within there is an irrational urge to give in to Arthur, to abandon his identity in his brother's maternal embrace:

> That night Arthur tried to drag him back behind the almost visible line beyond which knowledge could not help.
>
> Arthur was taking, had taken him in his arms, was overwhelming him with some need.
>
> Waldo should have struggled, but couldn't any more. The most he could do was pinch the wick, squeeze out the flickery candleflame.
>
> The stench of pinched-out candle was cauterizing Waldo's nostrils. But he did not mind all that much. He was dragged back into what he knew for best and certain. Their flesh was flickering quivering together in that other darkness, which resisted all demands and judgements. (pp. 47–48)

Waldo is here depicted as a helpless, exhausted child-ego in the embrace of his shadow-brother. This is one of the rare moments where conflict between the brothers comes to an end. But this state of surrender is to be sharply differentiated from the ideal state of creative co-existence. It simply marks the temporary collapse of the ego-personality, its resignation to "Arthur," to darkness (Waldo himself snuffs out the candle), and to unconsciousness. "He was dragged back into what he knew for best and certain," i.e., he returns to where he "belongs," to his own uroboric personality. But at first light Waldo resumes his rational ego-position far above the threshold of the inner world. Then his brother becomes once more the antagonist and Waldo attempts to defend his rationality, until "night" takes him back into Arthur's arms. This is the relentless course of the infantile ego: it oscillates wildly between flight and resignation, between rigid resistance and nihilistic surrender.

Marie-Louise von Franz has suggested that this problem is typical of the *puer aeternus*. The *puer's* longing for self-extinction is so strong that it makes all contact with the unconscious difficult and problematical. There is little strength in the ego-structure itself, so that whenever contact with the inner life is made, it falls over into it. In this situation consciousness cannot be broadened or deepened—it either remains as a defensive barricade against the unconscious, or it is swept away entirely (Franz I). The *puer* must learn to encounter the irrational mother-world without succumbing to its absorptive attraction. Ironically, the strength Waldo needs to defeat the mother-complex is forthcoming from the unconscious itself. Arthur says: ". . . if you should feel yourself falling, I shall hold you up, I'll have you by the hand, as I am the stronger of the two" (White 14, p. 210). But Waldo does not allow Arthur's positive aspect to emerge. If he would attempt a dialogue with Arthur—not merely to surrender blindly to him, or to fight him off—the infantile brother could become the instrument of wholeness and integration.

The same is true of Arthur's glass marble, his "solid mandala." Throughout the novel this image functions mainly as an uroboros, a symbol of the maternal round, and of psychological infantilism. For Waldo it is a mere boy's toy which is best left in the playground where it belongs. But it is clear from the text that the marble could *become* a mandala (i.e., a conscious totality) if Waldo would learn to accept it. The marble itself, with the "knot" at its centre, is suggestive of an archaic mandala, whose opposites are as yet undifferentiated and confused. But Waldo refuses to take on the burden of realisation, to unravel the tangled complex:

> Arthur had turned, and was towering, flaming above him, the wick smoking through the glass chimney.
> But his skin, remaining white and porous, attempted to soothe. Arthur put out one of the hands which disgusted Waldo. . . .
> Arthur said: "If it would help I'd give it to you, Waldo, to keep."
> Holding in his great velvety hand the glass marble with the knot inside.
> "No!" Waldo shouted. "Go!"
> "Where?"
> There was, in fact, nowhere. (p. 169)

And in a later section we read:

> "If it would help I would give it to you, Waldo, to keep," Arthur said.
> Offering the knotted mandala.
> While half sensing Waldo would never untie the knot.
> Even before Waldo gave one of his looks, which, when interpreted, meant: By offering me a glass marble you are trying to make me look a fool, I am not, and never shall be a fool, though I am your twin brother, so my reply, Arthur, is not shit, but shit!
> As he shouted: "No, Arthur! Go, Arthur!" (p. 273)

Waldo sees only the infantile, ridiculous aspects of Arthur's sacred talisman. For him the inner world and its contents are completely negative and shadowy. And so because he is not prepared to dialogue with the symbolic dimension in any way, the cloak of infantilism is never removed, the archaism remains intact.

Arthur himself becomes increasingly impatient with his brother's inadequacy. As we see from the above quotation, he already fears that Waldo "would never untie the knot." Towards the end of his career Arthur considers that he might be able to carry out the work of realisation himself. By way of *The Brothers Karamazov, The Upanishads,* Japanese Zen, and Jung, Arthur hopes "to storm his way, however late, however dark the obscurer corners of his mind" (p. 280). But he is not at all suited to intellectual pursuits. His lumbering mind cannot deal with abstract thought: "As for the Indian lotus, he crushed it just by thinking on it" (p. 281). The shadow-brother is trying to do the work that should be done by the ego-personality. Arthur makes very little progress in his mission of understanding—in a sense it is a foregone conclusion that he will not succeed. For the inner self cannot reach its goal alone; it requires a partner in ego-consciousness. It can guide, facilitate, even force the ego into recognition, but it cannot complete the process itself.

Poor Arthur becomes obsessed by "the Books" and makes regular visits to the public library, where he is the cause of amusement among the library staff. It is here that Waldo—an officer at the library—catches his brother reading at a desk, and where he reveals his paranoid stand against Arthur's work of realisation:

> "What will it do for you? To understand?"
>
> "I could be able to help people," Arthur said, beginning to devour the words. "Mrs. Poulter. You. Mrs. Allwright. Though Mrs. Allwright's Christian Science, and shouldn't be in need of help. But you, Waldo."
>
> Arthur's face was in such a state of upheaval, Waldo hoped he wasn't going to have a fit, though he had never had one up till now. . . .
>
> "Everybody's got to concentrate on something. Whether it's a dog. Or," he babbled, "or a glass marble. Or a brother, for instance."
>
> Waldo was afraid the sweat he could feel on his forehead, the sweat he could see streaming shining round his eyes, was going to attract more attention than Arthur's hysteria.
>
> "Afraid." Arthur was swaying in his chair. "That is why our father was afraid. . . . He was afraid to worship some thing. Or body."
>
> Suddenly Arthur burst into tears.
>
> "That's something you and I need never be, Waldo. Afraid. We learned too late about all this Christ stuff. From what we read it doesn't seem to work, anyway. But we have each other."
>
> He leaned over across the table and appeared about to take Waldo's hands. Waldo removed his property just in time.
>
> "You'd better get out," he shouted. "This is a reading room. You can't shout in here. . . ."

"Please," he repeated, and added very loudly: "sir!" (pp. 199–200)

Arthur has sensed the urgency of their situation, and now puts it nakedly before Waldo for the first time. He has arrived at the crucial point: fear. It is Waldo's fear of the depths, of the unknown in himself, which prevents him from embarking on a spiritually mature and responsible existence. And it is because Arthur's diagnosis is so accurate that Waldo is forced to order him out. But before he goes Arthur insists that Waldo need not be afraid, because they "have each other." In other words—or so I read it—Arthur assures Waldo that he would not fail him if he should decide to turn within, to uncover meaning and spiritual value. Arthur accurately supposes that the orthodox religious way is not for them—they must seek redemption through the inner, psychological path. Arthur boldly proposes a new *religio* involving a "careful consideration" of the glass marble and of internal symbolic facts. Still, Waldo fails to separate the essence of Arthur's discourse from its infantile and fragmented presentation: it remains absolute nonsense to him.

THE COLLAPSE OF THE EGO-PERSONALITY

The final and almost epic event in the life of the twins is the walk down Barranugli Road—an event which is woven throughout the scenes of the first half of the novel, to provide a thread of continuity as well as to act as an allegory of their life's journey. The walk appears to summarise the agonising relation between the brothers—for while Waldo sees the walk as his attempt to destroy Arthur, to drive him to a heart attack, Arthur views the walk as his final attempt to get Waldo to turn toward the urgent and pressing psychic realities. The ironic twist is that it is Waldo who dies at the end of the walk—for Arthur's dramatic exposure of the contents of the unconscious proves fatal for Waldo's defective ego-personality. The walk therefore encapsulates the contradictory strivings of the brothers, and its outcome points to the fate of the rational self which continues to resist individuation when it is being demanded by the brother within.

Arthur's first move is to draw Waldo's attention to his negative mother-fixation. He does this by referring to Mrs. Poulter, the figure who acts in the story as a personification of the maternal principle, and by goading Waldo into a recognition of his hatred for her:

"I wonder why Mrs. Poulter is so awful?"

Arthur, puffing, threatened to topple, but saved himself on Waldo's oilskin.

"I don't say she's *awful!*"

> "If you don't say, it's likely to fester," said Arthur, and sniggered. . . .
> "It's splinters that fester," Waldo answered facetiously.
> "Perhaps," said Arthur, and sniggered again. (p. 28)

Waldo cannot articulate his hatred of the maternal principle because it is an irrational, psychic problem—but Arthur warns that what cannot be expressed is likely to fester. Here Arthur displays his psychological insight and his awareness that Waldo is refusing to admit to an important inward factor. In this instance Arthur functions in his paradoxical capacity: he is the divine child with a profound awareness of symbolic reality, and his is the infantile shadow who goads his brother and who "sniggers" at Waldo's inability to face up to the maternal world.

Arthur's next step is to turn to the problem of Waldo's writing. Waldo is the classic would-be artist throughout the story, but he produces nothing substantial because inspiration does not come, or he refuses to allow it to emerge. Arthur realises that his brother's creativity is "festering" in his inner world and tries to urge Waldo to write about simple things. He invites him to write about "Mr. Saporta and the carpets, and all the fennel down the side roads," because, he says, simple things "are somehow more transparent—you can see right into them, right into the part that matters" (p. 30). Waldo is shocked and disgusted by his brother's advice: "He could have thrown away the fat parcel of his imbecile brother's hand." Waldo cannot believe that the shadow-brother could be anything other than a source of annoyance. He retorts: " 'What do *you* know?' " indicating that Arthur, his handicap, his burden, could never help him in his work, much less provide genuine inspiration.

But Arthur remains persistent:

> "You know when you are ill, really ill, not diphtheria, which we haven't had, but anything, pneumonia—you can't say we haven't had pneumonia—you can get, you can get much farther in."
> "Into what?"
> It tired Waldo.
> "Into anything."
> The wind coming round the corner, out of Plant Street and heading for Ada Avenue, gave Waldo Brown the staggers. Arthur, on the other hand, seemed to have been steadied by thoughtfulness.
> He said: "One day perhaps I'll be able to explain—not explain, because it's difficult for me, isn't it, to put into words—but to make you *see*. Words are not what make you see." (p. 57)

Arthur again directs Waldo inward, into the centre of things, the essence of experience. But the realm beyond words, the path to the silent matrix, is for Waldo a journey into disintegration and night.

His rational ego could not cope with the archetypal descent, whether through illness (as Arthur suggests) or through acceptance of the irrational dimensions of experience. Although he would find poetry enough to fill his notebooks and fulfil his creative dreams, he is not willing to risk the descent and be rejuvenated by the source.

At this point Arthur directs the discussion toward his own need, his desire to become conscious and achieve self-awareness:

> "I dunno," Arthur said. . . . If he stumbled at that point it was because he had turned his right toe in.
> "Mrs. Poulter said," said Arthur.
> "Mrs. Poulter!"
> Waldo yanked at the oblivious hand. Mrs. Poulter was one of the fifty-seven things and persons Waldo hated.
> "She said not to bother and I would understand in my own way. But I don't, not always, to be honest. Not some things." (p. 58)

By implication, Arthur links his own quest for understanding with his urgent beckoning of his brother toward the inner world. Arthur needs his brother to turn inward so that he too might see. The reference to Mrs. Poulter is most intriguing: she tells Arthur "not to bother" with his work of realisation. Here Mrs. Poulter acts as the Great Mother who is antagonistic to knowledge and *logos*, and Arthur's differentiation from her suggests that he is moving away from the uroboric and maternal image.

But again Waldo refuses to become involved, "he would not listen any more," though Arthur himself was "tired of telling" (p. 58). Both parties are exhausted: Waldo by demands he cannot or will not meet, and Arthur by rejection and disappointment. At this stage Waldo recalls the purpose of the long walk: to induce a heart attack in Arthur's big, old-man's body. Waldo increases the pace of the walk, while Arthur, "trotting like a dog" (p. 63) behind him, tries desperately to keep up. And as they turn a corner at great speed Waldo is almost collected by a passing vehicle, which causes them to steady themselves and finally to turn home. This gives further dimension to the central theme: although Waldo is trying to abuse Arthur he merely endangers himself by his course of action. The truck slams into the flap of his oilskin as he attempts to drive Arthur to his death. Denial of the shadow-brother is ultimately a denial of self; the desire to "kill" the unconscious is a form of self-murder.

And it is to self-destruction that his thoughts now turn:

> But he would arrive, and after they had struggled with the gate, and pushed the grass aside with their chests . . . he would go . . . and collect the box from on top of the wardrobe, that old David Jones dress box in which Mother had kept the little broken fan and some important blue dress. . . . Now he would make it actually

his, all those warm thrilled and still thrilling words falling from their creator's hands into the pit at the bottom of the orchard into ash smouldering brittly palpitating with private thoughts. (p. 118)

This is a familiar pattern: if he cannot defeat Arthur, or resist him successfully, he gives in to the unconscious and turns self-destructive. This is apparent in his desire at this point to enter the "devouring" female womb, to have sex with "some lovely lousy girl," and "get the pox and not do anything about it" (p. 116). This shows that the downward drag of the mother-complex is finally defeating his pathetic masculinity and his resistance to the lower world. Also, the image associated with the anticipated destruction of his writing is chthonic-maternal: he would push aside the grass with his chest and destroy his papers in the earth-pit at the bottom of the orchard. This denotes a sacrificial ritual in the likeness of the *puer*-god: a journey into Nature and a surrendering of his creative essence to the earth. In reality, his masculine spirit has always dwelt in the depths of the matrix—just as his writings have long been stored in mother's dress box—but here he contemplates consigning his *logos* aspect even deeper into the uroboros.

And as the twins return to their house in Terminus Road we find Waldo unable to resist Arthur's demands for love and unity. However, the "unity" achieved here, as before, is not mandalic but psychologically incestuous and uroboric:

> . . . Arthur was waiting to trap him, Waldo suspected, in love-talk. So that he broke down crying on the kitchen step, and Arthur . . . led him in, and opened his arms. At once Waldo was engulfed in the most intolerable longing. . . . He could not stop crying.
>
> Arthur led him in and they lay together in the bed which had been their parents', that is, Waldo lay in Arthur's vastly engulfing arms, which at the same time was the gothic embrace of Anne Quantrell [that is, Anne Brown (née Quantrell), his mother] soothing her renegade Baptist. All the bread and milk in the world flowed out of Arthur's mouth onto Waldo's lips. He felt vaguely he should resist. . . . But Arthur was determined Waldo should receive. By this stage their smeary faces were melted together. (p. 208)

Here the uroboric fusion of the brothers is stated as never before: Arthur is identified with Anne Brown, the mother, Waldo becomes her son-husband and the resultant psychological image is the incestuous union of mother and *puer*. That is to say, the positive mandalic aspect which Arthur brings to bear on the situation is overwhelmed by Waldo's "intolerable longing," his secret desire for self-extinction in the uroboros. When Waldo gives in to Arthur he surrenders to his own mother-complex, not to Arthur's mandalic vision. Thus while Arthur works to the benefit of the ego-personality, the ego works to its own demise. It is pitifully unaware of what the shadow-brother requires it to do, or of what it means to attempt the true union of opposites.

From here Waldo's course is a steady decline into the matrix. Arthur's demands become greater as he makes a last bid for individuation. He recovers the blue dress, which Waldo had thrown into the laundry after his grotesque transvestite ritual, and now holds it up before him, "so that Waldo might see his reflexion in it" (p. 212). Waldo protests vehemently—" 'Put it away!'' he shouted. "Where it was!' ''—but this dreadful image of his maternal fixation has already reawakened his guilt and anxiety. Here Arthur acts, as always, as the psychopomp who digs up the past and thrusts its images before the ego-personality. And now there is the discovery of Arthur's so-called blood-poem, which appears in the story as a kind of "extension" of the dress:

> Arthur threw away the dress.
> Which turned into the sheet of paper Waldo discovered in a corner. . . . On smoothing out the electric paper at once he began quivering.
> Then Waldo read aloud, not so menacingly as he would have liked, because he was, in fact, menaced:

> > " 'my heart is bleeding for the Viviseckshunist
> > Cordelia is bleeding for her father's life
> > all Marys in the end bleed
> > but do not complane because they know
> > they cannot have it any other way' ''

> This was the lowest, finally. The paper hung from Waldo's hand. (p. 212)

All the contents of the unconscious have at last burst forth in a spectacular procession of images. And these images appear to be interchangeable: the dress "turned into" the blood-poem. In the psychic complex everything is intermingled and interrelated, so that its contents sometimes merge into a symbolic continuum. The poem evokes the image of the teeming maternal womb, the "cycle of blood" in which life is bathed. It is a kind of hymn to the *magna mater*, evoking her destructive aspect (as Vivisectionist), her life-sustaining aspect (the Madonna), and her perpetually mourning character (Cordelia). Arthur says that the poem was written to "celebrate their common pain" (p. 294)—and we can only assume that he was trying to come to grips with the meaning of the mother figure, to bring to awareness this potent image from the depths of their shared psyche.

Waldo is enraged by the poem, not merely because it activates his psychic complex, but because it is a literary form (however inadequate) which threatens his own rôle as the secret poet of the

Brown family. After he turns away from Arthur to examine his own writings, Waldo is forced to admit that his poems are "lustreless" and that "time had dried . . . his papers," whereas "Arthur's drop of unnatural blood continued to glitter, like suspicion of an incurable disease" (p. 212). At this Waldo is moved to destroy his writings in the manner already elucidated in his waking phantasy. And after he "scatters his seed" (p. 213) he turns his rage toward Arthur. In desperation Arthur offers the glass marble, but by this stage all is lost. Waldo launches an attack upon Arthur, but in so doing he kills himself—dying in a paroxysm.

Arthur runs out of the house and imagines, in his confused simplemindedness, that he has murdered his brother. Of course, in one sense this is true. As the shadow-figure who forced the ego-personality to an encounter with the archetypal forces he is partly responsible for Waldo's death. But Waldo's disintegration is ultimately wrought by himself. If the ego refuses to accept responsibility for the life within, that life must eventually turn malignant and destroy the ego. The personality undermines itself by neglecting to attend to the soul's urgent need for transformation.

THE MOTHER'S TRIUMPH

Waldo's death signifies the dissolution of ego-consciousness into the mother-world. Arthur is now alone, and his own rationality and orientation appear to disintegrate with the death of his brother. He too descends into the matrix, not in death, but in madness, a kind of psychological death.

After fleeing from the scene of Waldo's death he embarks on a psycho-physical journey into the underworld. He becomes an idiot-child blubbering on street corners. He sleeps in dark alleys, under towering grass, and is urinated on by wandering drunks (one of whom mistakes him for a corpse). He contemplates appealing to friends for help, but realises that his tragedy is too great for others to bear; he must journey alone through his desolation, and through the desolated streets of a nightmare suburbia. It is during this phase that he is engulfed in a wave of self-pity, sentimentality, and infantilism. He is now a helpless *puer*, wrecked by experience.

But in White's fiction a peculiar thing happens when the masculine ego is destroyed: the mother goddess becomes triumphant and ec-static. Symbolically, the "mother" as matrix is rejuvenated by the descending libido. The ego's loss is her gain; its death is experienced as a homecoming to the unconscious. This is strongly evident in *Voss*, where the aboriginal mothers shriek in ecstasy as the German explorer begins to dissolve physically into the barren earth. In *Riders in the Chariot* Mrs. Flack bursts into hysterical, self-satisfied laughter when she learns that Himmelfarb has been subdued, and Mrs. Godbold, the self-styled "good" mother, is delighted when she receives the ruined body of her *puer aeternus* after his crucifixion upon the tree. And so it is here: Mrs. Poulter becomes exultant and overwhelmingly "maternal" after Arthur descends into the matrix: ". . . it was necessary to take him in her arms, all the men she had never loved, the children she had never had" (White 14, p. 311). Prior to Arthur's catastrophe Mrs. Poulter was a relatively minor presence in the novel, but suddenly she assumes archetypal proportions and emerges as a formidable earth goddess. This transformation has puzzled many readers, but it has to be understood as mythic realism, in the light of internal symbolic changes within the fictional psyche.

Mrs. Poulter celebrates Arthur as her "saint" and pledges her eternal devotion to him: "She would carry him for ever under her heart, this child too tender to be born" (p. 311). As he is led away to a mental asylum Mrs. Poulter promises to visit him regularly, and to bring his favourite sweets, the orange ju-jubes. Thus Arthur leaves the fictional stage as a pitiful, defeated *puer,* who is both nurtured and overshadowed by the mother goddess.

A crucial moment in the final scene is where Arthur and Mrs. Poulter contemplate one of the glass marbles and see their faces reflected upon its shiny surface: ". . . she saw their two faces becoming one, at the centre of that glass eye, which Arthur sat holding in his hand" (p. 312). This indicates that Arthur's talisman has irrevocably become an uroboros, mirroring the primordial unity of the maternal world, the conjunction of the mother and her unborn child. The "mandalic" aspect of the marble was a mere possibility, something never realised because consciousness refused to participate in the emergent vision.

White criticism goes astray at this point. Seemingly unaware of the regressive—and markedly pathological—context in which this *coniunctio* occurs, critics have found in this scene a consummation of the mandalic vision. A. P. Riemer asserts that Mrs. Poulter becomes at the end "the custodian of this symbol of perfection"; "she is the anima," he says, "capable of mandalic experience" (Riemer 7). Thelma Herring argues that the novel demonstrates the "fulfilment" of the "quest for totality" (Herring 2). This is an example of the misuse of Jungian ideas, of a critic's failure to grasp the archetypal context of the narrative. True, the title of the book and White's ambiguous presentation of the final scenes contribute to this confusion. And the mother figure's experience of "fulfilment" at the end may have prompted readers to think in terms of resolution and achievement. But surely the processes of decay and degeneration are obvious enough. If the mother triumphs it is only because Arthur, Waldo and the mandalic vision have failed.

THE MOTHER IN SEARCH OF HERSELF

With the collapse of the ego-structure in *The Solid Mandala* development of the masculine personality comes to an end in White's fictional world. The male figures from here on are caught up in the matrix and exist in a state of permanent psychological incest. Hurtle Duffield, Basil Hunter, and Eddie Twyborn have an easy access to the maternal womb, yet each is overwhelmed by that same ecstatic source. Duffield senses that he has spent his entire career inside a "padded dome, or quilted egg, or womb. . . . He continued dragging round the spiral, always without arriving" (White 15, p. 165). Basil Hunter is described as being "womb-happy" (White 16, p. 263) and lives in a perpetual incestuous phantasy. He is held fast in the mother-womb and unable to develop a separate identity: "He [saw] himself in the belly of a spiritual whale: unlike Jonah's, his would not spew him out till she died, and perhaps not even then" (p. 501). Eddie Twyborn languishes in an orgy of autoeroticism and infantilism, but he has no real personality of his own—he takes on the character of the mother-image and lives as a female figure (as Empress Eudoxia and eventually as Mrs. Eadith Trist). Everywhere the fictional ego is swamped by forces over which it has no control—it is assimilated to the mother-world.

But while the male consciousness sinks into oblivion the maternal archetype pursues a vigorous and extraordinarily productive course of self-development. This is hardly surprising in view of what we have already seen. When the libido is no longer used to support the ego-structure it is quickly absorbed by the archetypal complex. In the novels of the 1970s (*The Vivisector, The Eye of the Storm, A Fringe of Leaves,* and *The Twyborn Affair*) the mother goddess embarks on an epic journey of self-discovery, assuming a number of different guises but always with the same goal of integration before her. The life that the conscious personality could not live is seized by the autonomous figure and used to promote *her* individuation.

Nowhere is this more apparent than in *The Eye of the Storm* (1973), the work which occasioned White's Nobel Prize award (White 16). Here Mrs. Elizabeth Hunter attempts a thorough exploration of her psychological being, and achieves a remarkable synthesis at the end of the story. The fact that Mrs. Hunter reflects an archetypal presence, not a "real" character in any sense, is suggested in her rather mythic, fluid characterisation. In the novel she is an ancient, dying woman who spends more of her time in the night-world than in the conscious state. She is always sleeping, dozing, half-waking, and involved in countless excursions into memory and dream. She appears to be all things to all people, and her masks are as incongruous as they are numerous: bed-ridden geriatric, lustful mistress, domineering mother, "old witch" (p. 83), "mummy" (p. 45), "barbaric idol" (p. 116), "chrysalis" (p. 9). But only in this changing, dynamic form can the archetypal presence be made manifest. Only a vastly inclusive figure such as Mrs. Hunter is large enough to allow the Goddess to "incarnate" into fictional reality.

Mrs. Hunter is the *dynamis* and centre of all that takes place in the novel. The story appears to emanate from her, as though it were a product of her dreaming. All the other characters—male and female alike—appear as mere extensions of her being. None has autonomy or freewill, but each is subjected to the mother and acts as a catalyst to her process of growth. The characters embody particular attributes of her nature, and are urged to undergo various ordeals so that she, in the end, can attain greater wholeness. Sisters de Santis and Manhood embody her spiritual and instinctual selves, which are at first opposed, but which, through conflict and realisation, achieve a working relationship with each other. Dorothy de Lascabanes is the power-seeking daughter who is forced to learn the limitations of power, and the housekeeper Lotte Lippmann is the all-providing, all-nourishing mother who must attempt to sharpen and control her undifferentiated personality. The novel traces several "minor" individuations, none of which amounts to anything truly significant in itself, but which together form part of a tremendously cohesive integration inaugurated by the central figure.

In the climactic scene of the novel—the haunting sequence dealing with Mrs. Hunter's experiences at the eye of the storm—no reader would wish to deny the mother's achievement of a fully integrated selfhood. At the point of death all the polarities of her being, having undergone extensive differentiation throughout her lifetime, are brought into an ideal and almost incomprehensible totality. Her death is a supremely apocalyptic experience, not a denial of her existence, but an affirmation of all that she has been and of everything she has become.

But what is of immediate concern to us is that the mother should attain all this after the collapse of the son and the dissolution of ego-consciousness. This shows that the individuating impulse is an autonomous factor, and that if the ego is unwilling to co-operate with it, individuation goes on anyway, but now works against the personality. A process of growth must begin, and it can either occur positively in the light of consciousness, or in the darkness of the underworld, where it develops the archetypal figure at the ego's expense.

A NOTE ON THE MOTHER IN AUSTRALIAN CULTURE

White's work, though perhaps the most chilling and awesome expression of the great mother *mytheme* in Australian art, is by no means atypical of the cultural productions of this country. One can detect the presence of this deity in the poetry of the early colonists, in Adam Lindsay Gordon, Christopher Brennan, John Shaw Neilson, Ian Mudie, and the Jindyworobaks. The mother also dominates the mythic background of novelists such as Brian Penton, Joan Lindsay (*Picnic at Hanging Rock*), Rolf Boldrewood, D. H. Lawrence (*Kangaroo*), Martin Boyd, and David Malouf. She is also evident in the life and work of Percy Grainger, Arthur Boyd, Fred Williams, and Russell Drysdale. Barry Humphries, whose alter-ego "Edna Everage" seems more powerful than the masculine personality itself, is a clear example of the predominance of this archetype in Australian life. Perhaps this country, this "Down Under," or Antipodes, really is the underside of conscious Western civilisation, where the ego is at the mercy of matriarchal forces and where individuation appears to take place in reverse.

The mother rules the interior life of this country—she ruled here for 40,000 years as the aboriginal earth goddess and she continues to hold sway in the cultural and psychological life of modern Australia. In "Mind and Earth" Jung quotes Australian aboriginal tribesmen as saying: "[men] cannot conquer foreign soil, because in it there dwell strange ancestor-spirits who reincarnate themselves in the new-born" (Jung 5, p. 49). Be that as it may, it is certain that the psychology of Australians has been profoundly influenced by the archetypal dominants of this land. The problem is that we have yet to evolve ways of working with the forces that we encounter here. For the most part, the imported European persona carries on oblivious to the powers that rule in the depths. But artists and sensitive Australians have made initial, if inadequate, attempts to penetrate to the inner world. Patrick White is a pioneer who, like Theseus in Greek mythology, journeyed into the lower realm and grew fast to the rocks. He risked the descent and was strangely absorbed into the archetypal field of the mother goddess. One can only hope that future writers and artists will learn from White's example, and discover positive and affirmative ways of dealing with our presiding mythic deity.

References

1. Franz, M.-L. Von. (1970). *The Problem of the Puer Aeternus*. Zürich. Spring Publications.

2. Herring, T. (1970). "Self and shadow: the quest for totality in *The Solid Mandala*," in *Ten Essays on Patrick White*, ed. G. A. Wilkes. Sydney. Angus & Robertson.

3. James, E. O. (1959). *The Cult of the Mother Goddess*. London. Thames & Hudson.

4. Jung, C. G. (1912). *Symbols of Transformation: Collected Works* 5, 355.

5. ———(1927). "Mind and earth." *Collected Works* 10, 49.

6. Neumann, E. (1954). "The Uroboros," in *The Origins and History of Consciousness*. London. Routledge & Kegan Paul.

7. Riemer, A. P. (1970). "Visions of the mandala in *The Tree of Man*," in *Ten Essays on Patrick White*, ed. G. A. Wilkes. Sydney. Angus & Robertson.

8. White, P. (1973). Radio interview on Canadian Broadcasting Corporation (unpublished). Quoted by courtesy of Professor R. Wilson, University of Alberta, Canada.

9. ———(1941). *The Living and the Dead*. Harmondsworth. Penguin.

10. ———(1948). *The Aunt's Story*. Harmondsworth. Penguin.

11. ———(1956). *The Tree of Man*. Harmondsworth. Penguin.

12. ———(1957). *Voss*. Harmondsworth. Penguin.

13. ———(1961). *Riders in the Chariot*. Harmondsworth. Penguin.

14. ———(1966). *The Solid Mandala*. Harmondsworth. Penguin.

15. ———(1970). *The Vivisector*. Harmondsworth. Penguin.

16. ———(1973). *The Eye of the Storm*. Harmondsworth. Penguin.

17. ———(1976). *A Fringe of Leaves*. Harmondsworth. Penguin.

18. ———(1979). *The Twyborn Affair*. London. Jonathan Cape.

Jaws [*The Eye of the Storm*]   Peter Wolfe°

Nothing before *The Eye of the Storm* (1973) could have prepared us for the book's new maturity in subject, approach, and procedure. Here White demonstrates his appreciation of the incongruity of experience, and especially of unlooked-for turns in social behavior. A morsel of unchewed pear that shoots out of a distraught mouth can incite a little drama of its own. Relying more on accurate observation than on technical virtuosity, White adopts a rich, supple Jamesian idiom. The touch that seems quicker and lighter than before chimes with artistic intent. *Eye* is a long, complicated novel written in long, complicated sentences. Like James, White at his best doesn't wag a finger to make his points, instead letting them emerge incidentally from the action. His allusive, polyphonic style displays the splendor of brilliant, socially accomplished people; one woman says to another, while pinning an expensive jewel on her dress, "See? I haven't altered you. . . . Only heightened a mystery which was there already, and which is too valuable not to respect" (p. 167). Such diction permeates both dialogue and narrative. The cadence and word choice in the following formulation of male elegance depend on a carefully developed Jamesian precision: "Freshly shaven cheeks giving off gusts of an aggressive, though not disagreeably pungent lotion; hair cleverly

° Reprinted from *Laden Choirs: The Fiction of Patrick White* (Lexington: University Press of Kentucky, 1983): 175–196. © 1983 by the University Press of Kentucky.

trimmed to within an inch of Romantic excess; clothes pressed or laundered to a degree that the man of the world demands, then ignores" (p. 410). That this grooming, though carefully noted, isn't mentioned by those witnessing it helps give the book a sense of subtext that sometimes enforces and sometimes undermines the action. An event will often count less than the feelings of its participants. Moreover, these feelings may disclose a surprising aspect of what is being said and done, as an apparently minor concern leaps to the foreground. White's controlling vision lends consistency to the drama of minute discriminations. Updating James's international theme, *Eye* features the pursuit of money and power by two Australians, both of whom can boast European titles. But the novel does more than study upper-class manners. The Australia that forms the bedrock of *Eye* prizes equality over authority and hierarchy. White contrasts early-century rural Australia with the affluent, urbanized Australia of the 1960s, and he records the impact of working-class energy upon this change. Beaky, wiry, uneducated speech helps convey the pervasiveness of the impact. Rather than aping the Jamesian idiom, White tunes it to a contemporary register. He may even ridicule it. Of a jammed toilet, someone notes inwardly, "It was nothing and everything" (p. 303).

Jokes can backfire, and, as the paradox implies, the White of *Eye* sometimes labors small points to the detriment of narrative flow. He subordinates life to literature most often in his descriptions of working-class characters. Neither the minor figure nor the action he undertakes in the following passage deserves such rhetorical flourishes. Despite his admiration for simplicity, White refuses to let the farmer Rory Macrory take another slice of mutton because Macrory likes the taste or because he (whose thick eyelashes typify White's Irish Australians) is hungry: "Cocking his head, lowering his eyelids, his lashes so thick they looked as if they were gummed together, or fringed with flies, he agreed delicately to accept another helping of mutton" (pp. 410–11). *Eye* manifests its literary self-image in other ways. White affects elegance by using the word *masticate* instead of *chew* and saying *cleanly* instead of *clean;* he could also be reflecting the aesthete's disdain for physical science in his erroneous reference to sciatica (a disorder of the sciatic nerve, one of the largest and longest in the human body) as a "superficial pain" (p. 578). Happily, such flaws rarely pit the richly marbled surface of *Eye*, perhaps White's best-controlled and sustained work.

Besides helping us know and judge White's characters without authorial intervention, this well-tempered abundance moderates the negativity fretting the book. Doggedly unsentimental, *Eye* belongs to the hard-headed, militant branch of modern fiction of which malice forms the underpinning. The beached black carcass of a dead dog in chapter 7 symbolizes the absent deity, or loss of faith, as in the "Proteus" section of *Ulysses*. This horrible portent climaxes a series of sordid images accompanying an outdoor luncheon taken at Watson's Bay. A businessman falls through a chair amid gales of boozy laughter; the restaurant then degenerates into a shambles of "disordered tables, crumpled napkins, lipstuck glasses, the skeletons and shells of fish" (p. 351). Squalor soon dominates the once-festive area: "Scum, and condoms, and rotting fruit, and rusted tins, and excrement" (p. 352) litter the beach adjoining the restaurant where the dead dog appears. This ugliness tallies with the Hunter children's visit to Sydney, which culminates in incest, death, and isolation. Its force is felt elsewhere as well. On her way out of the restaurant, the book's most saintly character, a nurse, trips and falls. Her dining companion falls several times during the action. Earlier his sister had hissed (p. 268) while opening an envelope containing a large check. Supporting both this primitive imagery and the idea of depravity the imagery puts out is the recurrence of worms in the action. White consistently juxtaposes worms with something delicate and fragrant. As the nurse's fall at the end of chapter 7 showed, ancient evil threatens all; it has already engulfed the Hunter family. A worm invades a peach at the end of an elaborate dinner party in chapter 2; "lashing themselves into a frenzy of pink exposure" (p. 209), worms defile a rose garden. Dorothy Hunter, the Princesse de Lascabanes, worries that her mother will "worm out" (p. 216) a secret she has been harboring. Finally, one of the book's most dramatic scenes, in which Elizabeth Hunter tries to pry some sleeping pills from a nurse, contrary to doctor's orders, takes place with Mrs. Hunter sitting on the same toilet where she will later die.

The moral decay symbolized by the toilet and the worm attains dramatic expression in the book's scathing descriptions of Australians socializing. Blanket judgments in White are usually carping. Because man can best know and save himself while alone, people in groups vex him. Dinner parties and other social gatherings bring out their vanity, pretensions, and affectations. The worm in the peach served to Mrs. Hunter at a fancy dress dinner prefigures the adultery she will commit only hours later. The coincidence of her rut with her son's fall from a tree hundreds of miles away shows the worm burrowing deeply into Australia's homes and gardens. So pervasive is it that once it shows its pink, featureless face, it can work its way on family members miles and a generation apart. Evil reverberates, even when White's purpose seems more satirical than metaphysical. Dinner parties don't succeed because the men fart and talk shop, ignoring their overdressed, heavily made-up wives, who pass the time in malicious gossip. Australian *haute monde* suburbia lacks the civilized graces needed to throw a proper dinner party. Substituting ostentation for breeding, a suburban family in *Eye* serves too much food and drink, fogging the conversation of the diners: the hostess, already about to pass out, offers a guest "a brandy balloon, more than half filled" (p. 295). Her conduct typifies White's recent work, which often makes vacuity and nastiness a function of bad table manners. Characters who misbehave around food will commit worse gaffes elsewhere. A luncheon guest in *Vivisector* refuses to go home until he has filled a manila envelope with lobster salad. During a dinner party in *Twyborn Affair*, food falls on the floor, champagne bottles overturn and spill, and a socialite tries to undo the trousers of a younger man while talking to him on a couch.

If White ridicules his bit players, he magnifies and intensifies their foibles in his leading figures. None of the characters in *Eye* likes each other, and all feel ill used. All *are* ill used. Elizabeth Hunter doesn't want to have sex with the marine ecologist Edvard Pehl on Brumby Island, off the Queensland coast; she only flirts with him to score a point off her daughter, Dorothy. Fifteen years later Dorothy and Basil unite to reduce their dying mother's retinue. Money lust has created this partnership of a brother and a sister who haven't seen each other for years. Each needs the other for support, yet each despises the other both for mistreating their mother and for being so blatantly mercenary. Each, too, sees his/her faults reflected in the other. Because they have taught each other that the grubbiness of self is inescapable, they try to enlist a third party to do their bidding. They hope the family solicitor, Arnold Wyburd, will move their mother into a nursing home where she can die at moderate cost. Exploitation has been thriving to the side of this plot. Mrs. Hunter and her housekeeper, Lottie Lippmann, have been using each other to whet their respective appetites for cruelty and masochism, and one of Mrs. Hunter's nurses, Flora Manhood, uses Basil as an unsuspecting stud.

1

White's metaphor for the destructive woman is the loveless mother. A stranger to compassion and charity, she will damage her children by devouring or suffocating them, as did Amy Parker and Alfreda Courtney; to compensate for Maman, Harry Courtney took up the maternal office by providing masculine gentleness. She can bully them (Austin Roxburgh's mother in *Fringe*), favor one of them over the other (Julia Goodman), neglect them (Shirl Rosetree), compete with them (Doris Bannister of "The Night the Prowler"), or exploit them (Mumma Duffield). Eadie Twyborn gainsays maternal love by becoming a lesbian and a drunk. Characters like Theodora Goodman, Mrs. Poulter, and Ellen Gluyas Roxburgh imply that sympathetic women in White are sympathetic only because they have been spared the burdens of motherhood; mothers in White's fiction inflict damage. Bypassing only the vagaries of Eadie Twyborn, Mrs. Hunter denies her children in each of the ways indulged by her counterparts. It is plausible that Dorothy and Basil have left Australia, that they avoid their mother during their time in Sydney, and that they prefer staying in hotels rather than in their childhood home. They deny her the satisfaction of playing the caring, sheltering mother; nor do they want to stop one of her barbs should she revert to her former destructiveness. Their resentment over her dying so expensively also makes sense. Dorothy's solitary life in genteel semi-poverty and her actor-brother's rejection of life in favor of a theatrical image of it describe pathetic shadow existences alongside the fierce splendor of their mother's brilliance, age-wrecked as it is.

This brilliance cows Dorothy more than it does Basil, and it could cow her even more if she were to know all it has done. Her mother did in fact what Dorothy only does in fantasy—have sex with the family solicitor, Arnold Wyburd. Moreover, she embraced Wyburd when he was young and vital, whereas Dorothy's fantasies only begin when he is elderly. Even though Mrs. Hunter didn't seduce Edvard Pehl on Brumby Island, she kept him out of a willing Dorothy's bed. So assured is she of her dominance over Dorothy that, fifteen years later, as she lies on her deathbed withered and blind, she reminds Dorothy of the Brumby Island incident at the precise moment Dorothy has come with Basil to talk her into a nursing home. Not only has she intuited the purpose of her children's visit; her reference to Brumby Island also serves notice that, feeble as she is, she welcomes the worst they can throw at her. The comparison between her and Shakespeare's Cleopatra, inferred by a description of a dress she wore at age seventy-one, captures her magic: "Age had not tarnished its splendor, nor blunted its fluting" (p. 420). Obviously, the wearer's virtues have brought out the virtues of the dress.

These, bound up as they are with her faults, are less easily assessed. Like Alma Jugg Lusty in *The Ham Funeral*, she both creates and destroys. Thanks to her beauty, her riches, her subtlety, and her nonsense, she moves at a grander level. Elizabeth Hunter is as paradoxical, unpredictable, and full of meaning as a piece of holy writ. Her age (eighty-six) has made her both frail and, because of her strong will, frightening. White stresses her decrepitude not to belittle her but to contrast it with her inner strength. The description of her drinking—"The lips suggested some lower form of life, a sea creature perhaps, extracting more than water from water" (pp. 22–23)— suggests both a ghoulishness and a wisdom that has set her apart from the other characters. Like his sister, Basil feels intimidated by this primordial energy; he wouldn't have dared to broach the subject of a nursing home without Dorothy alongside him. Also like her, he wants Mrs. Hunter to die so he can have her money. His survival, he claims, depends on her death. Nor can she complain of mistreatment, since she has used people her whole life. In trying to hasten her death, Basil is merely applying a morality learned from her. Besides, turnabout is fair play. Referred to as "a great baby" and "an almost chrysalis" (p. 9), Mrs. Hunter regresses to infantilism before she can be a parent. Having denied her children the maternal benefits of love, tenderness, and protection, she can only offer them money. She withdraws her will to live in order to give Dorothy and Basil her only remaining treasure. Everything tallies. If money is her only bequest, it is all her children want from her. Again, she can't complain. Dorothy and Basil don't know how to love because she has never taught them how.

The single-mindedness of their fortune-hunting shows Dorothy and Basil living up to their last name (which is also the name of the valley in New South Wales where White's family has owned land for four generations).[1] The name Hunter applies even more vividly to their mother, whose spotless white dresses and elusive personality suggest Diana, or Artemis, the moon goddess and huntress of classical mythology. Mrs. Hunter's arrows, like Diana's, hit their mark, as is shown by her verbal accuracy; both her humor and her malice have wounded many. What is more, she searches out her quarry with skill, like any other good hunter. As a young socialite she rode horses, a hobby indulged in by other proud, destructive beauties like Sidney Furlow of *Happy Valley* and Madeleine of *Tree of Man*. People still fear her, yielding to her demands for obedience and worship. These demands take many forms, as befits her strong will. If permitted, she would disturb an off-duty nurse for a trifle. Such an imposition fits with her practice of demanding good value from her retainers. Besides doing their assigned jobs, her cook dances, her cleaning woman tells stories, one nurse, a trained cosmetician, applies her makeup, and another gives spiritual instruction. In the first chapter three nurses, her cook, a doctor, and a lawyer flock to her bedside to do her bidding. She has become the still center of a moiling, racketing world during a time of upheaval. Her having instigated great activity in others while remaining motionless herself defines her as a spiritual force. In addition to meeting Eliot's definition of God in *Four Quartets*, she suits the Zen philosopher D. T. Suzuki's qualifications for the attainment of enlightenment: "The center of life-gravity remains immobile, and . . . when this has successfully taken hold of all the life activities . . . whether in a life of quietude and learning or in one of intense action, a state of self-realization obtains, which expresses itself in a most exquisite manner in the life and acts of the person."[2]

Most of Mrs. Hunter's acts refer to herself. She is enlightened, irradiated by an inner gleam that gives her mastery over the young, the mobile, and the sighted. Hers is a case of the blind leading the blind in this work about degrees of blindness. White demythologizes her internal strength at the same time that he raises it to the religious dimension; she is to be seen as a person, rather than as a goddess. Her sumptuous material surroundings bespeak vanity and selfishness. The many mirrors hanging in her Moreton Drive home aggravate these traits, as does a comparison between the pictures of her and her husband adorning the dining room. The picture of decent, simple Bill Hunter is smaller than that of his widow; Bill's ego was smaller, too. He died quietly on his farm, where he would least distress those who loved him. From the large, elaborately carved bed where she lies, his widow attracts retainers and relatives; those buzzing around her all serve vanity, which naturally both blinds and confines.

What helps give her vanity a metaphysical *frisson* is her having endured a cyclone on Brumby Island by herself. Eschewing simplified moralities, White portrays the storm both as Mrs. Hunter's punishment for betraying Dorothy, who had flown from France to be with her after her marriage broke up, and her honor, because she emerges from it renewed. The big storm frees her inner self, negating the ego and opening new inlets of perception. She calls her pelting by the storm "the utmost in experience" (p. 414) and "the highest pitch of awfulness the human spirit can endure" (p. 424). This terror flattens and trivializes everything else that has happened to her. It releases her spirit from her body. Torn, hammered, and recast, a new self comes to life amid the smashed, soaked furnishings of her hosts' cabin. Being whipped into the still center of the wild storm has taught her the universal parity of existence. In this moment of oneness she merges with nature, identifying both in her thoughts and her feelings with the surrounding wreckage. Her identification defies reason. As always happens to White's characters at the moment of revelation, the tempering of her spirit is a function of her physical battering. She is soothed by her belief in her oneness with the shambles of dead fish, horsehair, and iron as "the most natural conclusion" (p. 425) of the storm. The contingent has grazed the absolute. If her mighty ordeal won't improve her ethics, it will nonetheless steel her for all future trials. Surviving the cyclone helps her fend off the voracity of her children, White interrupting the visit in which Dorothy and Basil rehearse the alleged virtues of a nursing home (in chapter 8) with a long flashback to Brumby Island. Mrs. Hunter connects these two events, and so should we. The self-presence that carried her through the cyclone will help her weather the gusts set in motion by her children's greed. Her strong will, her trial by storm, and her queenly first name all put her as close to Shakespeare's Lear, a role that obsesses Basil, as their greed puts her children to Goneril and Regan.

Lest we make too much of the equation, we must recall that the inwardness of White's vision blurs the objectivity of factual experience. Mrs. Hunter's past and present, her memories and feelings, all exist on a par. Her life can't be judged objectively; the quality of life depends upon how a person sees it. Because a person's life is what he/she makes of it, Voss expands into the greatness he intuits within himself, and Hurtle Duffield grows artistically at a time when a stroke, the infirmities of age, and a retrospective exhibit of his work all tell him to slow down. Given her venom and her vanity, Mrs. Hunter's deathbed thoughts occasion a more complex self-inventory. Her great years, her thunderclap experience on Brumby Island, and the wavering of her mind have not put her beyond self-justification or self-blame. She needs the deep reservoir of self-knowledge the years have created if she is to sink the strong sense of guilt which keeps surfacing. This guilt is a byproduct of success. After a life of winning and owning, she suspects that she has nothing. She is right. Riches impoverish, and success divides. Her beauty, her social rank, and her cunning have won her many prizes, but they have also made her fatally selfish. She has lived fully, and she hasn't lived at all. Specifically, she has never learned how to give. What is more, her insight into this failing is sharpened by the belief that no one in her circle merits her generosity or self-sacrifice, and by the suspicion that she has crushed any worthiness capable of being crushed. Human debris surrounds her. The skiapod, a legendary sea beast with whom she identifies and whose jaws open so wide that it can swallow larger fish, has devoured or dismembered everyone.

This rapacity has tarnished all her trophies. She might well ask, on the day of her death, "Haven't I been sleeping all my life?" (p. 442). Despite her many triumphs, she fears that reality has escaped her. Her never having touched her husband's penis, her vivid recollections of her two adulteries, and her inability to breast-feed her children explain her problem as a failure to love. Her heart is strong but insensitive. Bullying and manipulating people has drained the vitality from her. How to restore it? She expects no love from her children; their wrecked marriages, their avoidance of her, and their enthusiasm for her money as opposed to her welfare all show that they have no love to give. For this lovelessness she feels responsible, if not guilty. She doesn't need to receive love so much as to extend it. She nursed her husband in his last sad days out of duty, not out of love; she never saw Basil act professionally, even though he was performing in a play while she was in London; she tormented Dorothy when she came to Brumby Island for motherly comfort. This ex-socialite who charmed, fascinated, and thrilled hearts over a long and brilliant career has never opened her own heart to another. Instead, she has worn herself out reaching for hollow, trivial prizes. Having imposed her iron will, she has blocked the flow of spontaneous life. Her refusal to let life happen to her constitutes a lack of faith. Ironically, the strong will of this dilapidated queen has brought about her undoing, not her fulfillment. Lying on her deathbed, she clutches greedily at her few remaining scraps of life, a Hunter stalking new game. As her remarkably strong pulse indicates, she wants to grace her life with love before it ends.

A difficult job: the power she has gained over a lifetime of getting what she wants impedes the selfless outgoing of love. It also hides her vulnerability. One of her favorite cover mechanisms consists of brewing trouble. Whereas more prudent souls shrink from embarrassing or painful subjects, she welcomes them. She seems to relish the discomfort of others. One of her cook's song-and-dance routines ends when she, Mrs. Hunter, opens her rheum-gorged eyes as wide as she can and stares at the onlookers. Earlier she had stunned her solicitor and onetime lover, Arnold Wyburd, by referring playfully to Basil as "our son" (p. 280). But the main target for her malicious mirth must be Wyburd's prim, retiring wife. Envying Lal Wyburd's sane, orderly routine, Elizabeth Hunter has been shocking and torturing her for years. Not content merely to seduce her straitlaced husband, she constantly snipes at Lal's unstylishness and her freckles. One of the book's funniest scenes shows Lal visiting her on the day of her death and being reduced to flatfooted dismay by her flashing wit. Looking in another direction as Lal enters her room, Mrs. Hunter accuses her of neglecting the possibly cancerous freckles mottling her hands; she denies Lal food and makes the denial sound like Lal's idea; she taunts her by referring knowingly to Arnold. But even then she hasn't finished scoring off her visitor. After grazing the most intimate realities of Lal's life with her non sequiturs, half-truths, and manufactured solicitude, she gives Lal a turquoise chain. The reason for the gift emerges only after Mrs. Hunter dies. Wyburd notes on his return from the funeral that the chain has made Lal's neck look red, shriveled, and heavily freckled. Blind Betty's last joke on Lal was to give her the chain because she saw with her inner eye that it would accent Lal's worst features. In mitigation, she pays for the joke that her blindness and her death stop her from relishing first hand, bequeathing Lal $5,000 as back wages for being tormented, precisely the same amount she presented to both of her children upon their arrival in Sydney. The equality she bestows upon her victims signals an acceptance of responsibility for her misdeeds.

If her wrongs to Dorothy on Brumby Island and elsewhere are righted at all, the righting comes at the moment of Mrs. Hunter's death. The mother withdraws her will to live while sitting on the toilet; she literally prefers to die than to be stowed in a nursing home. She will give her children what they want and deserve, but in her own way. The style of her death mocks them, expressing her disdain for both them and their greed. Does White approve of this parting shot? He judges his brilliant heroine shrewdly but also sympathetically. Her last recorded conscious thought is a prayer to her husband which acknowledges his goodness, her love for him, and her sorrow over having failed him. It may be her greatest, because her most selfless, moment. Her death, which follows shortly, is described as a union of two infinities, her spirit drifting into the spirit world. Also central to White's judgment of her is her dying in a sitting position. Whereas her children fall from grace by violating both the Fifth Commandment and one of the Western world's strongest taboos, incest, she dies without falling. Even in death she needs no foreign titles or honors to prop her up. That she dies on the same night, perhaps at the same moment, when Dorothy and Basil are committing incest makes her death the grisly fruit of their rut. Any such connection made by her children between the two events might have made her smile ruefully.

Beyond help or hurt, this bringer and destroyer of life outshines all her counterparts. She wets and soils her bed; her bones creak; her mind wanders. Like Hurtle Duffield, though, she withers and blossoms at the same time, having cultivated other senses to offset her blindness. She notes the "fatty laugh" (p. 74) of her doctor, and she says inwardly of Wyburd, "He smelled old. He sounded dry" (p. 25). Her amazing mind, though unsteady, remains sharp "on its better days" (p. 85). She speaks Flora Manhood's innermost thoughts as Flora is thinking them; she upstages Basil when he plays his grand homecoming scene; the intuition, or second sight, she has cultivated to make up for her loss of eyesight helps her score at will upon both Dorothy and Lal Wyburd. Though she may confuse present events, claiming to have just heard a doorbell that rang hours before, she accurately recalls events from long ago. Though fixated on the past, she won't romanticize it: "They were walking . . . beside this great river. No, it wasn't: it was the shallow and often drought-stricken stream which meandered through everybody's place" (p. 23). White's entering her stream of consciousness to select events from her long, colorful life nearly puts her beyond blame and guilt; yet it also deepens blame and guilt in the way that only first-rate psychological realism can. The conniving Betty Hunter would rage, pout, or coyly produce a dimple to get what she wanted. She would also destroy. Reared in a broken-down farmhouse, she wrecked both her own cheap dolls and the prettier, more numerous ones of her little friend Kate Nutley. Because dolls meant more to her than anything, they had to be destroyed. The knowledge that her own poor assortment of dolls could never equal Kate's fine collection sparked her hatred of all dolls everywhere. Other recollections of the past maintain a consistency between her many acts of spite and envy. In old age she is still, intriguingly, very much herself. *Eye* sets her past and present lives before us simultaneously. She sees in her mind's eye (and we see, too) her younger incarnations doing things that will form her character. In a passage that prefigures her dying attempts to redeem herself, she seduces Wyburd the same day the nervous young solicitor brings her will to sign. Being faced with her mortality has whetted her greed for life. Besides signing her will, she works her will—as she'll do many times in the future. In retaliation, Wyburd steals a sapphire from her just before her death; she owes him that much after decades of having manipulated and bullied him.

White's time-shifting within the stream of her consciousness brings her before us as a legend and a person, a great beauty and a haggard husk. At all phases of her life she discloses the same capacity for good and evil. She may wince while being tended to by a nurse, but the cause is the pain brought about by a recollection, rather than the nurse's touch. This polyvalence rests on White's nonlinear portrayal of her. She refers to "that state of pure living bliss she was now and then allowed to enter" (p. 24), a level of being where she neither sleeps nor wakes and where distinctions like past and present disappear. In this semi-consciousness she reorders time, her will relaxes, and her inner eye takes charge. Experienced on the inward planes of perception, things reveal their unity, their stillness flowing into that of their perceiver. Elizabeth Hunter's blindness, frailty, and guilty self-knowledge lose their sting. She has transcended judgment and division. Existence itself has become active, even imperative. To partake of this miracle suffices for her. The spiritual equilibrium she attains is mirrored by her supine immobility. She comes even closer to perfect union with the indigodd than did Hurtle, who was also more demonic than angelic. The difference between the two characters is attributive. Whereas Hurtle's divine intimations came from his inventiveness, those of Mrs. Hunter bespeak her whole self.

2

Both of Mrs. Hunter's children have titles; both live in glamorous European capitals. La Princesse de Lascabanes and Sir Basil Hunter embody an important feature of the middle-class push to get ahead. They have inherited both the drive and the dream from their mother, a poor farm girl who acquired money, property, and social rank. So triumphant was she that her children aimed even higher and succeeded more wildly. But outdoing their mother in the scramble for earthly prizes has undone them. With their European establishments, they have scored high in Australian terms. Seen as people rather than romantic exile-aristocrats, they look futile and empty. Their inner fears, longings, and frustrations, so out of keeping with their shiny public images, surface quickly. Having been denied maternal protection, support, and nourishment (as has been mentioned, Mrs. Hunter couldn't breast-feed her children), they bring a heavy charge of anger with them to Moreton Drive. Their anger they unload. It has already been seen how neither one of them spends much time with her, stays at her home, or disguises his/her disapproval of the cost required to maintain her. Dorothy even pinches her nose while cleaning it, the memory of Brumby Island still rankling her. After serving notice that they plan to move her into a nursing home, they never see her again. Nor do they attend her funeral. Her request for sleeping pills, which she doesn't need, coincided with their arrival. Aware of their long-standing resentment, she prefers death from an overdose to the neglect and cruelty they have learned from her.

They don't need to see their mother after telling her that she is to be moved from Moreton Drive. They have said the final word on the topic that brought them to Sydney, to begin with. Wasting no time, they interview the director of the local nursing home into which they want to book their mother as soon as the death of a present occupant creates a vacancy. They try to heal freshly opened psychological wounds in the interim. Smarting with guilt and feeling fragmented by denying their mother, they go to their childhood home in the back country to trace other ancestral roots. These roots drive more deeply than they had imagined. Seeing "Kudjeri," their father's property, makes them feel as if living in Europe has severed them from their vital sources. But Europe has also infiltrated their blood-streams; observing psychological accuracy, White assures that the Hunter children bring post-childhood conditioning with them to Kudjeri. Basil, for instance, declaims a speech from *The Merchant of Venice* and thinks of acting the role of Richard II, another exile who returns to his homeland to find himself dispossessed. Dorothy, whose European tenure has sagged after its brilliant start, harks back to the mother she has just denied as a role model. Dorothy imitates Mrs. Hunter, wearing the white dresses that were once her mother's hallmark and flirting with the Macrory children in the same way that her mother did with the Warming children fifteen years before. But the self-renewal she attains is wholly her own. For the first time she feels at home. She sews, cooks, peels potatoes, and arranges cupboards "as though she had taken possession of the house" (p. 487). The solidness that comes from immersing herself in the routine of the Macrorys, the present owners of Kudjeri, affirms itself quickly. She feels strong and useful. Anne Macrory says that the family can't manage without her. Basil's references to her as Dorothy Sansverina

(p. 484; after a character in Stendhal's *Charterhouse of Parma*) and Dorothy Cahoots (p. 592) pay further tribute to her growth.

The visit to Kudjeri affects Basil differently because he undertakes it in a different spirit. Unlike the strident, priggish Dorothy, he can let himself go, and he looks hopefully to the future. What he wants most is wholeness. The job of separating what he is from what he does presents obstacles, though. He feels out of place amid the rural simplicity and traditional family values of Kudjeri. The career that has elevated him professionally, even winning him a knighthood, has dwarfed him emotionally, and the smoothness of his rehearsed responses sometimes appalls him. Yet the trip to Kudjeri was his idea, and it touches a sensitive nerve. Like Dorothy, he responds in ways that he never does elsewhere; he savors the sensation of mud curling around his toes, while the scents exuded by the local flora give crisp new meaning to long-dormant memories.

Some of these memories refer to Dorothy. All along he, Dorothy, and their mother have been denying the importance of their bond. In fact, Mrs. Hunter is so excited to see her daughter for the first time in fifteen years that she wets herself; Basil she won't even receive in bed, insisting that she be propped in a chair wearing full makeup and a lilac-colored wig. Dorothy's Parisian veneer cracks at the sight of the mother toward whom she claims indifference. Basil's nonchalance in stating that he hasn't seen either his sister or his mother in half a lifetime is refuted by his failing at sex and then vomiting from drink during his stopover in Bangkok. Despite his breezy tone, the prospect of a family reunion has jarred him.

The only Hunter who accepts the meaning of the family is decent, kindly Bill. An outdoorsman whom White treats more gently than his earlier incarnation, Harry Courtney of *Vivisector*, Bill sees his son act on the London stage. The same simple dignity that later silences any complaints about the liver cancer that is destroying him keeps him from both asking his wife to join him at the play and visiting Basil backstage. A man of quiet purpose, he needs no fanfares to advertise his comings and goings. His dying with the onset of winter on the acreage he loves attests to his harmonious nature. He deserves the statue put up in his honor in the town of Gogong, near Kudjeri. That his widow misses the unveiling of the statue also rings true. Ashamed of having dismissed his tenderness and generosity, she has buried her guilt under a glittering cosmopolitan facade. Her children would have suffered no such qualms had they bothered to learn of the unveiling. Bill Hunter's decency always bored them; neither of them budged from Europe either to console him in his last days or to attend his funeral. Adopting a tone of self-congratulation, Dorothy cites important obligations in Paris, even though others with the same obligations (like her truant husband) have been neglecting them;

Basil's letter of regret carries the same claim of martyrdom. So mean-spirited are the Hunter children that their very neglect of Bill (Basil says that he doesn't think about his father for years at a stretch) supports White's indirect request that this local hero be viewed as a moral exemplar.

Their stay at Kudjeri makes this mean-spirited pair sharply aware of their pain. Fear, need, and the iron grip of the past drive them into bed naked. Dorothy's chittering words uttered weeks before, upon her arrival at Kudjeri, "I've never felt more frightened . . . not even on my wedding night" (p. 473), have taken on a prophetic ring. They also sound the note of ambiguity that peals through all of White. Dorothy's coupling with her brother shows a willingness to defy one of society's strongest taboos for his sake. At the same time they are declaring their faith in each other, she and Basil are getting closer to their own feelings and thus to themselves. Their incest is an act of mutual self-acceptance, clearing a path to self-being they couldn't find in Europe. Yet both lack the patience, the goodness of heart, and the self-respect to profit from their act. Each has always seen in the other a reflection of his/her greed, ineffectuality, and treachery. From the outset they have joined forces reluctantly. These uneasy allies-to-be meet for the first time in the book in a solicitor's office. The "steel and concrete cell" (p. 258) where the meeting occurs symbolizes the lovelessness of their union, the resurrection of which both delay by coming late. This reluctance lingers. Though their union brings them closer than either party had wanted or thought possible, it creates no permanent healing. Basil and Dorothy have sex in the same bed in which they were conceived because, in usurping their parents' roles, they believe they can wipe out the past and start anew. Their act backfires. They can't negate their parents, the most vital part of a common past that has been saturating their spirits for the past weeks, without negating themselves. Lear's infamous proposition, "Nothing will come from nothing" (I, i, 92), has done its work on them. The offspring of their sexuality is death, their mother dying at perhaps the exact time they are coupling.

More will come to grief than Mrs. Hunter. The damage her children incite begins to surface immediately. Having just shown them abed, chapter 10 ends in darkness; unwarmed and uneasy, Dorothy and Basil lie awake amid the "frozen ridges" (p. 527) of their parents' bed, the full moon fixing them in its stark, sterile glow. The opening words of the next chapter, spoken by their mother, "Is it cold, sister?" (p. 528), could easily have come from Basil, given the chill surrounding him at the end of the previous chapter. Only in the next sentence does White let on that the scene has shifted. But Mrs. Hunter's death later in the chapter and her dream about

Dorothy and Basil as unborn twins both show that the shift is only spatial. The action of chapters 10 and 11 is continuous, as were the Australian and European interludes of the Hunter children. The mystery of unity swathes all. Upheavals jolt whole families in White's fiction, as the death of Waldo Brown in *Solid Mandala* and Hurtle's rediscovery of Rhoda Courtney in *Vivisector* showed. Manfred Mackenzie describes the incest at Kudjeri as "suicidal": "It is as if Basil and Dorothy would accelerate their mother's death by black magic,"[3] he says of their self-defeating exorcism. The death rattle set in motion by her children's bedsprings reverberates in Mrs. Hunter's dream, as the cold weather that gripped Kudjeri forces the summer athletes in the park fronting Moreton Drive to dress in warm clothing. This same chill marks her children's response to her death. In prepared-sounding cadences, Basil refers to her vanity and (twice) to her materialistic values, probably to hide his lack of feeling. An equally ungrieving Dorothy cries briefly, but only for the bereavement of her hostess, Anne Macrory, who loved Mrs. Hunter after meeting her but once. Dorothy has never loved anyone enough to bewail a particular death. Embarrassed by their hypocrisy, she and Basil avoid each other's eyes during their mourning session with Anne.

The split between them widens. Ironically, the mother whose death they craved had been holding them together by giving them a common cause. They reject her gift. Their last encounter begins in the same solicitor's office where they first met, brought there once more by money rather than love. They will never meet again. Their final separation squares with skipping their mother's funeral. By passing up this last goodbye, they fail to put closure on the most vital and most rankling relationship of their lives. They have learned nothing. Avarice has whittled them down to nothing. And nothing will come from nothing.

The Hunter sib drawn more deeply into the abyss is Dorothy. A dry stick who worries about cancer, she neither fits nor belongs anywhere: "Dorothy Hunter's misfortune was to feel at her most French in Australia, her most Australian in France" (p. 49), White says of her after she laboriously clears customs at Sydney International Airport. Alienation and displacement have been dogging her. After marrying a foreigner from a different generation, nationality, and social class, she found herself abandoned. The old-world patina on her French prince had tarnished and chipped. Hubert de Lascabanes, a sham aristocrat, presumably ended a long career of dalliance (which included a Venetian gondolier) by discarding Dorothy for a Cincinnati margarine heiress. The Catholicism Dorothy had adopted in order to marry Hubert has stopped her from divorcing him. Her pride, still smarting from the Brumby Island incident, stops her from returning to Australia, even though Paris offers her only a doubtful claim on a smudged title and a leaking gas stove in an underfurnished flat. Her reversals have soured her and left her nowhere to turn. She doesn't even know *how* to turn. Whereas her husband censured her for controlling her feelings too well, her mother censures her for indulging them. She has become so emotionally knotted that she won't dent the $5,000 check her mother gives her to buy a good dress. As mean with others as with herself, she also roots in the garbage bin of her mother's kitchen to see how much food the servants have wasted, listens in on telephone conversations, and stands just outside open doors in order to eavesdrop.

Some hundred years after Christina Light, the future Princess Casamassima, appeared in Henry James's *Roderick Hudson* (1875), this heiress of all the ages has descended to eavesdropping and garbage-mongering. Everything ennobling is wasted on her. She is too brittle and stingy to profit from her revelation on the flight out. She lacks the simple warmth to accept Basil's luncheon invitation after seeing him for the first time in decades; her moral cowardice moves her to spurn his overtures of love after their mother's death. Her booking a flight to Paris without telling him typifies this devious, sly Regan figure. Although she introduces the subject of nursing homes to her mother, she speaks vaguely and briefly, leaving the details to Basil. Then there is her habit of defecting without giving notice. She left Brumby Island in a pique and without saying goodbye. Her exit from Sydney, again undertaken at the earliest possible moment, constitutes a denial of her tie with Basil. Joining forces with him to get their mother's money and then sealing their union incestuously has hardened the shell encasing her. But problems can't be solved by bouncing them off a shell or by running away from them. The meaning of what she and Basil did will continue to bedevil her. She couldn't need him any more than she already does, even if she were his embryonic twin of their mother's dream.

Veronica Brady has called her sagging peacock of a brother "the hollow man of artifice whose life is a tissue of insincerities and lies and whose main concern is to escape the truth of himself."[4] She is partly right. The similarities between Basil and Dorothy do make him his sister's spiritual twin; he is Dorothy writ large. He spends less time than Dorothy with their mother, and he tries just as hard as Dorothy to convince himself of their mother's unfitness, emphasizing her materialistic ways so that he can fleece her with impunity. Also like Dorothy, he worries about not belonging. His legal daughter was probably sired by another man. (He and Dorothy could both be sterile—their mother's joke and legacy.) His sleeping on Mitty Jacka's couch in London, in Janie Carson's hotel room in Bangkok, and in a Sydney hotel point up the homelessness of this man. About his living arrangements in London nothing is said. He lives among shadows. The artifice of the stage has dulled his responses to the outside world, including himself; his four-hour delay in Bangkok makes him aware of his inability to provide himself good company. His clumsiness is another sign of his being out of step with reality. Acting more like a clown or a slapstick comic (which could be his true calling) than a tragedian, he trips, flops, and stumbles through the action. This "victim of knobs and corners and low-hung lintels" (p. 477) fell from a tree and broke his arm as a boy; he slid on a banana peel that a playgoer had thrown onto a Glasgow stage; he almost overturns a bar stool in Bangkok. Nor does returning to Australia improve his bearings—he trips on the steps outside his mother's home after having been in the country only a few hours. At Kudjeri, where he goes to find a foothold on life, he cuts one foot while padding in mud, and he catches the other in a moldy old boot.

Before Basil can walk with practical feet, he must first acquire moral balance. He knows that he has no time to waste. Having been knighted by the Queen for playing the title roles in *Richard II*, *Hamlet*, *Lear*, and *Macbeth*, he has seen his career start to flag. His theatrical airs have also started to irk him. Lacking simple conviction, he turns everything he does into a bravura performance. The letter in which he tells his dying father that he can't come to Kudjeri shows him at his most theatrical-contemptible. Despite his joviality, he tries to give the impression that Bill Hunter is lucky to get so much as a letter, given his son's busy schedule and the superficiality of their relationship ("We scarcely ever spoke to each other, did we?" [p. 202]). During his father's decline he is rehearsing *Macbeth*, a play that treats the denial of basic human values. Ironically, the vanity-ridden Basil will play his most important role unconsciously, when his mother's nurse, Flora Manhood, singles him out to sire her baby. Performance becomes reality, as both her acting and her sense of mission outpace his.

His punishment for denying basic human values follows as remorselessly as Macbeth's. Judged on his own terms, those of the theater, he has failed. Greatness in acting often consists of an actor's ability to step outside of himself in order to become another person. Having inherited his mother's ego, he can't let himself go. His great private sorrow inheres in his having failed at King Lear, a role he deems nearly unplayable but within his artistic ken. To play Lear he would have to depersonalize himself with the utmost severity, given his belief, at age fifty, that the role can only be acted by an old man with the build of a young one. But while he dreams of playing Lear, he comes across an even greater artistic challenge—Mitty Jacka's Drama of the Unplayed I. Life grows knottier but perhaps also more rewarding with age, as Stan Parker and Hurtle Duffield learned. An independent London producer, Jacka wants Basil to play himself in her nonplay. Rather than working from a script, he will use material from his own life. He will present his own feelings, not those of a character created by someone else. Because his identity won't be caged by a role, he will enact his whole self, rather than just a part of it. Basil fears this challenge, having long ago substituted dramatic technique for sincerity. Better to fail as a performer, he reasons, than as a person. But the news of his mother's stroke fuels his waning resolve. After visiting Jacka in London's Beulah Hill (Beulah is the land of peace and rest visited near journey's end in the Bible), he goes to Australia to raise money for the nonplay. He soon finds that both his life and his livelihood depend on his mother's death. In view of his desperation and the warmth connoted by his many overtures to Dorothy, he bids well to succeed. If he fails to make it in his prescribed terms, he will do so in a way consistent with his dramatic flair and newfound honesty. Revisiting the countryside where he grew up has strengthened him. Furthermore, his ability to shake off Dorothy's many rejections shows that he's not stopped by setbacks. Unlike his sister, he'll gamble on his feelings.

But perhaps Flora Manhood, the nurse of twenty-five who finds Mrs. Hunter dead, garners the most from the drawn-out deathbed ordeal. Brady judges well to fault this hoyden who carries a gaudy plastic handbag, cadges free lunches, and prefers artificial over natural flowers: "Sister Manhood . . . lives by an ideology, the religion of a hollow, materially-oriented culture. Vulgar and ignorant, she is terrified of pain and of everything she cannot control for her own pleasure."[5] This pleasure Manhood rates highly but defines narrowly. She resents her lover, Colin Pardoe, a pharmacist who reads Unamuno and listens to Mahler, because his self-improvement program stands as a reproach to her laziness. Easily bored, she speaks often of quitting her job at Moreton Drive, where she despises everybody but Mrs. Hunter. This unmoving mover has sparked a bonfire of activity in Flora: "I don't seem to have control over myself" (p. 278), the nurse whines; so powerful is her patient that she has robbed Flora of her ability to act on her own. Flora's disparaging references to "the old witch" (p. 86) and "a geriatric nut" (p. 304) express her resentment of the older woman's grip upon her interior life. But even though she resents Mrs. Hunter, she cannot deny her, as did Dorothy and Basil. In fact, she admires her so much that she connives (unsuccessfully, it turns out) to have Basil's baby; she wants to play a vital role in her dying patient's rebirth. Yet she is also the only member of the Moreton Drive retinue who defies Mrs. Hunter. She knows she can risk surliness and defiance because she applies Mrs. Hunter's makeup and thus preens her ego; vain and selfish herself, she knows how much her cosmetic skill means to her patient. She refuses Mrs. Hunter's gift of a pink sapphire because of the conditions that accompany it, and, immediately detecting her patient's purpose, she turns down her request for free access to her sleeping pills.

Mrs. Hunter's death changes Flora more than it does anyone else, this common flower blossoming psychically if not physically. Flora acts as if Mrs. Hunter's spirit passes into her at the moment of death. Inspired by her patient, who, like her, grew up on a poor farm, she responds with perfect tact to the sexual overture of the attending physician: "Dr. Gidley . . . if you've forgotten your wife, I haven't forgotten my patient. I'd like to treat her respectfully" (p. 565). Respect and tenderness continue to rule her, as devotion replaces duty in her hierarchy of values. Usually anxious to bolt Moreton Drive the moment her shift ends, she works long past her time to expedite final details with appropriate reverence. The hours following her departure from Mrs. Hunter's house reveal her as whipped and weary. She has no job; her scheme to become pregnant has failed; she walks away from her cousin, her only living relative, after the latter suggests that they live together. According to her last recorded words in the novel, "I'm nothing" (p. 573), she is like a hollow vessel. But she can be filled. Going against Lear's claim that nothing will come from nothing, her hollowness constitutes the state most friendly to spiritual activity in White.

Mary de Santis, the night nurse or "the archpriestess" (p. 19) of Mrs. Hunter's sickroom, needs no such hollowing out. She sets no store by the self. Asking nothing, she has always lived to serve others. What was drudgery to Flora sustains her. The humbler the job the better, she believes. Mrs. Hunter's statement that Mary is complete comes close to being true. She will invent jobs both to test her faith and to keep herself in that bare, unaccommodated state where she is most sensitive to a patient's needs. After Mrs. Hunter's death she prepares to nurse an even more difficult patient, whom White introduces six pages from the end to affirm the strength of Mary's goodness. White also lets Mary hold the stage alone at book's end, showing that self-negation may be the best instrument for survival.

3

On duty, significantly, in the book's opening scene, Mary closes the action by feeding the birds on Mrs. Hunter's dawn-lit lawn. This symbolic reference to St. Francis of Assisi (Dorothy visited Assisi with her husband) gives her devotion a religious coloring that sets her apart from the other characters. Australia's industrial middle class is puzzled by its own comfort. Though it has inherited the egalitarianism and independence of the frontier, it also enjoys the ease and privilege that upward mobility brings. *Eye* accounts for this unsettling change. Others besides Mrs. Hunter and her children improve their material lot but droop in other ways. Rory Macrory marries above his station; Flora Manhood goes from a banana farm to Sydney, where she trains as a nurse. Yet each retains a stubborn charge of working-class truculence. Flora resents Col Pardoe's efforts to improve himself, and she stands up to Mrs. Hunter. Macrory, the gruff, up-country farmer, refuses to be impressed with Dorothy and Basil's titles and honors when they visit him at Kudjeri. Moreover, he outdoes them in tact and breeding by turning them down when they offer to pay for his hospitality. Like Bill Hunter, Kudjeri's former owner, Macrory helps spell out White's moral preference for the country. Again, the infusion of rural values into his cosmopolitanism becomes Basil's best hope for rebirth. This indirect criticism of the urban inferno adds to the novel's persuasiveness. Timely references to women in Mia Farrow haircuts, pantsuits, and miniskirts, to Vietnam, and even to the silent majority (p. 331) reveal *Eye* to be keenly sensitive to contemporary language, styles, and attitudes. This sensitivity is thematic. A work in which two people fly 12,000 miles within two days *should* describe the world in which such rapid, wholesale change occurs.

Continuity, though, exerts as much force as does change, lending both dialectical rhythm and historical depth to the book's stylish intelligence. The country-born Elizabeth Hunter, who spent her ad-olescence and early youth in the nineteenth century, evokes Australia's frontier tradition—as does her junior, Arnold Wyburd, to a lesser degree. Then there are the literary references which evoke Australia's European heritage. (Australia's aboriginal heritage will be featured in *A Fringe of Leaves,* White's next book.) The most outstanding of these references is to *King Lear.* Brian Kiernan noted some tie-ins between Shakespeare's play and *Eye:* "Basil's ambition to play the most difficult of tragic roles, and his and Dorothy's ingratitude to their mother, the centrality of the storm incident all suggest that we are invited to consider a parallel with Lear."[6] His running parallel is richly thematic. If Dorothy's sly treachery invokes Regan and if the more flamboyant Basil's comparisons between himself and Goneril make sense, then the cook's reference to the Hunter children as murderers (p. 488) invites another issue: the absence of a Cordelia surrogate. Our vain search for Cordelia amid this band of Hunters calls forth both the disrepair of the Hunter family and the menace building around Elizabeth, an octogenarian preparing to divide her spoils while clinging to life. Wyburd's popping a button from his shirt and Basil's fondness for quoting Lear's request that his shirt button be undone help make Cordelia an imaginative presence; only when stripped of all does Lear appreciate Cordelia's goodness. Mrs. Hunter's granddaughter, Imogen, is named for a Shakespearean her-oine as virtuous as Cordelia, but she lives in distant England and has never met Mrs. Hunter. That her namesake appears in *Cymbeline*—

a work, like *Lear*, centering on an early English king—makes her inability to soothe her grandmother all the more regrettable.

But Mrs. Hunter rarely needs to be soothed. Her first name (which is also that of England's most illustrious monarch), her long life, and her magnanimity, all echoing Lear, suggest the means by which she defeats her enemies. Further parallels with Lear focus her remarkable powers still more sharply. Although Basil covets the role of Lear, he sees his mother as Lear's true-life counterpart. Her dying on the commode, which she calls her "throne," conveys her strength and wisdom. She rules to the last with a serenity that can ennoble something as improbable as a toilet. In a drunken reverie which takes place while Basil is flying back to England, members of his circle fuse and overlap with Shakespeare's people. His mother is always the king; such power does she wield that the audience must help the whole cast stamp her into her coffin at play's end. Such wit has she exerted over the years that he feels foolish and deprived of a role to play. Her fusions of wisdom, humor, and senile nonsense make her a better choice for the role of Fool than Basil, to whom she even materializes as Edgar, a good son, in a parody of the Dover scene (*"Poor Mum's acold"* [p. 493]) he enacts near Kudjeri. Finally, her blindness invites a parallel with Gloucester, loyal parent and servant to the king. This dominance explains Basil's wish that his mother die. Her material existence, marginal as it is, robs him of space in which to grow and to be.

The wish to overthrow and supplant the mother also resonates with the Freudian overtones sent out by the generational conflict. The Eye of the novel's title teases out Oedipal associations amply justified by the action. Corresponding to Mrs. Hunter's physical blindness is the moral blindness of her children. As in Sophocles, blindness in *Eye* refers most pointedly to family trouble; problems outside the home in both Sydney and Thebes stem from problems within. The family touches all. Dorothy marries a man old enough to be her father; she fantasizes about having sex with Wyburd, her Australian father surrogate; after looking incestuously at Basil the first time she sees him in the novel, she sleeps with him. Basil already knows the Oedipal orbit. In Bangkok he had tried to mount the actress Janie Carson, who looks like and who attended school with Imogen. The Bangkok incident takes the incest motif back to the stage, where Oedipus first lived, as Janie hopes one day to play Cordelia to Basil's Lear.

Janie will never play opposite Basil, if he has any say in the matter. The futility of merging life and art recurs in *The Charterhouse of Parma*, the favorite novel of both Bill and Dorothy Hunter. Bill so admired Gina Pietranera, the subtle, vital, and beautiful Duchess of Sanseverina, that, in marrying Elizabeth, he felt he could become one with her real-life counterpart. The many years he lives apart from her and her inability to give him the love she knows he deserves both describe a failure as dismal as her son's stage-ridden behavior. Stendhal's 1839 novel sheds other revealing light on *Eye*. The total effect is one of depth, drive, and effortless flow. More inventive than managerial, *Eye* deals with profound, timeless emotions in a crafts-manlike way, and it gives them contemporary relevance. The ease with which the narrative elements join show in the book's undersea references. "Over there you look like something underwater" (p. 532), says Mrs. Hunter to Lal Wyburd; the idea of death by drowning comes to Flora; Edvard Pehl specializes in marine ecology; the skia-pod, that carnivore to which Mrs. Hunter likens herself, inhabits the sea. Besides evoking the mysterious unity that permeates all White's work, the ocean metaphor presents unevolved characters daunted by problems as ancient as the immortal, rolling sea.

The divisions in the book capture this rhythm. Like Part One of the bipartite *Happy Valley*, the first half of *Eye* covers one day. Repetitions both within and between its two time settings establish a flow that controls the later book. Some of the repetitions and variations count more than others. Mrs. Hunter married at age thirty-two, the same age as Mary De Santis's father; Mary, who has been a nurse for thirty-two years at the time of the novel, used to give pain-killing injections to her dying father, as did Mrs. Hunter to Bill in his decline. These repetitions reinforce existing patterns. All along the undersea logic of the novel has fused the husband with the father and has also raised ambiguities between the roles of healer, life-giver, and destroyer. Some of the repetitions gain more from accretion than from ambiguity. Basil gets his foot jammed inside one of his father's old boots while prowling around an old shed. Later he wears his father's boot in another sense by having sex in his parents' bed. Dorothy is again with him, rocking back and forth in the same anguished rhythm displayed in her attempt to remove the boot. Their sexuality will hobble both of them. They couldn't have hoped to destroy their mother without destroying something vital in themselves.

Moments like this make *Eye* one of the best novels of the 1970s. Brady's praise both typifies the reception the book received and explains the critical eminence it enjoys: "If the story of civilization is the story of the growth of consciousness, then White's achievement here is to make available areas of awareness hitherto out of range of all but the most ambitious artists."[7] White does display a heightened sense of artistic purpose in *Eye*, aiming for truths and effects beyond the grasp of realism. The already quoted description of Mrs. Hunter drinking water imparts a primitive dread and endows Mrs. Hunter with an ancient wisdom; it also makes us wonder if her children don't have more to fear from her than she does from them. And it comes at a good time, on page 22. The opening pages of *Eye* make the reader worry whether he can slog through the next 600. White has drawn the vastness of Australia tightly around himself by seating his opening scene in the cramped, static confines of a sickroom. The son and daughter of the patient create a symmetry that also bids to block outlets for the plot. Nor does the dying old patient promise to lighten the languor that looms ahead, judging from the adverbs in the book's brief opening paragraph: "The old woman's head was barely fretting against the pillow. She could have moaned slightly" (p. 9). Mrs. Hunter's head is so wasted that it hardly frets, or makes an impression on, the pillow supporting it. Yet this same head also heads a family, and it will vex and fret other heads as it comes to life in the course of the book. White has both direct knowledge and an intuitive grasp of the effects of Mrs. Hunter's resurrection. Observing the dramatic ideal of Mitty Jacka, he will not use plot or thesis to cage his characters. The people in *Eye* are seen from both inside and out, at the moment of dramatic enactment and in historical depth. Instead of becoming simple, the reality they portray grows complex. The technique of *The Eye of the Storm* imparts depth, grandeur, and mystery to the dark fire of its theme. Only a handful of English-language novels of the century can boast such a blend of form and content.

Notes

1. Elisabeth Riddell, "The Whites: Patrick, Pastoralists, and Polo Ponies," *Bulletin* 8 (January 1980): 44.

2. D. T. Suzuki, *Zen Buddhism*, ed. William Barrett (Garden City, N. Y.: Doubleday, 1956), 292.

3. Manfred Mackenzie, "Dark Birds of Light: *The Eye of the Storm* as Swansong," *Southern Review* 10 (November 1977): 276.

4. Veronica Brady, "The Eye of the Storm," *Westerly* 4 (December 1973): 60.

5. Ibid., 61.

6. Brian Kernan, "True Smell of Mortality in New White Novel," *Age* (Melbourne), 6 October 1973, 13.

7. Brady, "Eye of the Storm," 64.

A Properly Appointed Humanism: Australian Culture and the Aborigines in Patrick White's *A Fringe of Leaves*

Veronica Brady[*]

> Till well into my life, houses, places, landscape meant more to me than people. . . . It was landscape which made me long to return to Australia. . . . As a child at Mount Wilson or Rushcutters Bay, relationships with even cherished friends were inclined to come apart when I was faced with sharing surroundings associated with my own private mysteries, some corner where moss-upholstered steps swept down beside the monstera-deliciosa, a rich mattress of slater-infested humus under the custard apples, or gullies crackling with smoky silence, rocks threatening to explode, pools so cold that the breath was cut off inside your ribs as you hung suspended like the corpse of a pale frog.[1]

Patrick White's sense of himself is bound up with this sense of place, and of what might be seen as the savagery of nature. But it is also bound up with an awareness of the Aborigines, of the continuity between these feelings and the Aborigines. As a child on the mountain, he goes on:

> I often flung stones at human beings I felt were invading my spiritual territory. Once I set fire to a gunyah to show that it couldn't be shared with strangers. Years later I persuaded myself that I hadn't been acting merely as a selfish lad, but that an avatar of those from whom the land had been taken had invested one of the unwanted whites.[2]

This connection has not been much noticed and discussed. But it may well be crucial to his understanding of himself as an Australian and of Australian culture in general. As this passage from his autobiography suggests, it may also point to the positive side of his notorious fascination with the process of nature, especially the process of decay. In *Voss*, for instance, the Aborigines function as emissaries of the land itself, celebrants of the sacrifice Voss must pay to its mysterious powers. In *Riders in the Chariot*, the novel which follows, the Aborigine, Alf Dubbo, is the one of the four visionaries who manages to express as well as to live what he sees. His element is fire, the element of triumphant creativity, and his life is an indictment of the "Great Australian Emptiness" which surrounds him. But *A Fringe of Leaves* is the novel which shows most clearly what the Aborigines mean for White's imagination, showing on the one hand the impotence

[*] Reprinted from *Westerly* 28, no. 2 (June 1983): 61–68; courtesy Veronica Brady.

of white culture, and on the other the liberating effect of contact with the "savage" domain which they represent and inhabit.

His choice of incident and central character is significant. Set in the nineteenth century, the story, based on the experiences of Eliza Fraser, shipwrecked off the Queensland coast and taken captive by the blacks, stresses the insecurity and vulnerability of white settlement and the squalor and hunger of the Aborigines which followed the white invasion. White Australian culture tends to value aggression, energy and material possession, but in his choice of this story and this heroine White throws the emphasis on passivity, subjection and dispossession.

The changes he makes to the original story underline human vulnerability on the one hand and the savage power of nature on the other. The original Captain Fraser was a sea captain, not the delicate, bookish and ultimately ineffectual husband White gives his Ellen Roxburgh. True, Captain Fraser made the voyage to Australia for the sake of his health, but where Austin Roxburgh is more or less impotent Captain Fraser and his wife had three children. The changes to the story of Ellen's rescue are also significant. In the original story the rescuer, John Graham, was a far less disturbing figure than White's Jack Chance, convicted murderer and escaped convict. True, Graham also was a convict and an escapee but where he had returned to white "civilisation" and given himself up, White's Jack Chance cannot face the brutalities of the chain gang, finding life with the blacks less savage. For White there is little difference between "civilisation" and "savagery." The original John Graham, however, presented himself in the account he wrote as the champion of civilisation. Hearing news of a white woman made prisoner by the blacks, he says, he thought it his duty to "snatch a fellow Christian from a lingering state of brutality"[3]—in fact he may also have had his eye on the pardon and the £10 which was his reward and throughout he insists that he maintained the standards of propriety even "in the midst of the horror surrounding me, nothing but native savages, clubs and spears. . . . I had my clothes on,"[4] secure, he declares, in his trust in Providence who "alone strengthened and assisted me in this virtuous act of humanity."[5] Though in some other respects White plays down the violence of the original story—the mutterings of the crew became open mutiny in real life, for instance, and far from admiring Mrs. Fraser as his equivalent admires Ellen Roxburgh, the cabin boy actually snatched a cup of water from her—nonetheless in general his changes work to blur the distinctions between nature and culture. The glimpses of the convict system work to remind us that, as the second epigram from Ibsen suggests, there are "gnawing things" in the house of civilisation as well as in savage life. Even as a lady, Austin Roxburgh's wife, Ellen is aware of the chain gangs and floggings in Van Diemen's Land and shortly after her return to Moreton Bay and white civilisation, she meets a chain gang, to be "united in one terrible spasm with this rabble of men" (370). She may have suffered and been humiliated during her time with the Aborigines but "civilisation" has its sufferings as well.

White's view of human existence, then, is the disastrous one expressed in the scene shortly after the survivors of the shipwreck have managed to beach their boat on an island and the captain offers her a sip of rum which at first she refuses:

> . . . "Ellen" her husband chirruped, "you must take a sip at least, out of deference to the captain, and because," he thought to add, "the Almighty has brought us safely to land."
> For one blasphemous instant there arose in her mind the vision of a fish the Almighty was playing the distended lip in which the hook was caught, her own. (203)

The fascination with decay which might be seen as apparent in the passage from *Flaws in the Glass* points to this sense of the power of nature and to the reasons for the choice of this story. Here on the frontier the concept of civilisation has no corroborating power. Austin Roxburgh's death dramatises the futility of the merely decent and rational man. Facing a group of armed and hostile blacks, he feels that he must do something:

> [He] ran forward, to do what only God could know. Here he was, bestirring himself at least, in the manner expected of the male sex. Into action! He felt elated, as well as frightened, and full of disbelief in his undertaking. (It was not, however, an uncommon reaction to his own unlikelihood.) (239)

As a man of words and books, he is helpless in this savage world and as he falls with a spear in his neck his main reaction is surprise. However, as he dies White suggests that at least he catches a glimpse of what he has missed: "The light . . . or the brim of that . . . huge . . . country . . . *hat*. Raise it, please . . . so that I can see . . ." (240).

For White Australia seems to be the place in which the complacencies by which people like Austin live are no longer viable, "A country of thorns, whips, murderers, thieves, shipwrecks and adulteresses" (311–2) as it appears here, it is nevertheless the place for testing communal values and discovering the true lineaments of humanity. In this test and discovery the Aborigines play a crucial part.

It has not, I think, been remarked how closely the structuring of *A Fringe of Leaves* echoes the structure and method of Lévi-Strauss' anthropology. Ellen Roxburgh's story (in which she is successively a farm girl, the wife of the Gentleman, Austin Roxburgh, his brother's lover, slave of the Aborigines, mistress of her convict rescuer and, finally, is about to become the wife of the merchant, Mr. Jevons),[6] illustrates Lévi-Strauss' notion that the basis of society lies in the exchange of women which in turn becomes an exchange of services. The novel also makes great use of the homologies of food and clothing (which we will discuss later), attempting as the French anthropologist does to come at some basic understanding of common humanity by a comparative study of the underlying codes of social existence. Leading Ellen through a whole gamut of experiences and of different cultures and classes White is thus in search of that "properly appointed humanism" which Lévi-Strauss describes which "cannot begin of its own accord but must place the world before life, life before man, and the respect of others before self-interest."[7] Moreover it is clear that as he describes it, and for all its rigour Aboriginal culture is closer to this ideal than the white society represented by people like the Merivales, the Lovells and Austin Roxburgh. Ellen can only become

> The perfect Woman, nobly planned,
> To warn, to comfort, and command

when she has learned from her experience after the shipwreck and with the Aborigines that, as Lévi-Strauss has it, "man is not alone in the universe, any more than the individual is alone in the group, or any one society alone among other societies."[8]

To look, then, at White's picture of Aboriginal life. He has been criticised for perpetuating the racist stereotype that Aboriginal culture is both degraded and degrading, and it is certainly true that the life Ellen shares is a perpetual struggle with hunger and on one occasion she is even driven to cannibalism. But this picture needs to be set against the description of the cruelties of white society. The main difference between the two cultures, the comparison suggests, is that the Aborigines acknowledge their debts to nature whereas the white people do not. Even as the story concludes, Miss Scrimshaw, typically, still lives by the delusions of grandeur Ellen has learned to see through. She longs "to soar! . . . to reach the heights! . . . look down on everything that lies beneath [her]! Elevated, and at last free." But Ellen has learned that the true humanity comes from acceptance and thus remains "ineluctably earthbound."

> "I was slashed and gashed too often," she tried to explain. "Oh no, the crags are not for me. . . . A woman, as I see, is more like moss or lichen that takes to some tree or rock as she takes to her husband." (402)

Merely private and individual preoccupations are dangerous, part of the illusion with which in White's view Australian culture conceals its true situation from itself. What is necessary is to learn, as Ellen does, to acknowledge our vulnerability.

In this sense while the account he gives of their way of life may not be flattering, the book as a whole endorses the Aboriginal habit of mind, the "primitive" sense of the world as one great system of symbols. Moreover, although it could be argued that the squalor of Aboriginal society is the consequence of the white invasion and its disruption of traditional food supplies and ceremonial life, it is more to the point that what we see of this society is through Ellen's eyes and that her sojourn with them represents for her the return of the repressed self—always a painful and sometimes even a violent experience. It is only after her return to Moreton Bay that she is able to look back on this experience and claim it lovingly. Significantly, this occurs when she has taken off the clothes she has been given and stands naked before a mirror (mirrors associated symbolically with the dread of the sight):[9]

> She was at first too amazed to move, but then began to caress herself while uttering little, barely audible, cries of joy and sorrow, not for her own sinuous body, but for those whose embraces had been a shared and loving delight. (348–9)

Set in the pattern of scenes concerned with clothes and nakedness, this is a crucial occasion. It contrasts with the two scenes in which she appears as someone else's work of art, the one in which her husband contemplates her coming down the stairs elegantly dressed and adorned with jewels and the one in which the Aboriginal women strip her of her white woman's clothes, cut her hair and then adorn her head in their own way with feathers. Here she is her own creation, poised between the two extremes of the "raw" and the "cooked," nature and art, in possession of herself whether naked or clothed because she has taken possession of an essential humanity. For this reason while she may exist in society her centre of gravity now is to be found elsewhere, and this is why she is made to appear to Mr. Jevons in the last scene as if she were a kind of goddess, a "smouldering figure in garnet silk" (404) and is set beside the pregnant Mrs. Lovell "in her nest of drowsy roly-poly children." Ellen has paid her tribute to nature and to society and is now free.

But this freedom is only possible when she has come to terms with the dark side of herself and with the dangerousness of experience. The moment at sunset in the Aboriginal camp shows her coming to understand this, learning to let go the confidences in order and rationality by which her husband has taught her to live:

> Round her the blacks were proceeding with their various duties, beneath a splendid sky, beside a lake the colour of raw cobalt shot with bronze. . . . Evening light coaxed nobler forms out of black

bodies and introduced a visual design into what had been a dusty hugger-mugger camp. What she longed to sense in the behaviour of these human beings was evidence of a spiritual design, but that she could not, any more than she could believe in a merciful power shaping her own destiny. (247)

The structuring of the book as a whole, based as it is on an underlying pattern—the homologies of food, clothing and sexual relationships which Lévi-Strauss sees as basic codes of all human existence—also challenges the claims of rationality. In contrast with civilisation's preoccupation with explicit meaning and verbal precision White's style is highly metaphoric and works to give voice to the natural as well as the human world as the "primitive" consciousness does,[10] and the introductory chapter which features the Merivales and Miss Scrimshaw shows that he is aware of what he is doing. Their fear of the alien and the strange, their determination to order and explain the world and circumscribe their experience of it is set up as a clear contrast to Ellen, whose destiny it is to explore the "secret depths" (20) they shrink from.

To recur to our opening passage from *Flaws in the Glass*, White thus becomes in effect an avatar of Aboriginal culture and his preoccupation with decay reveals its source in the sense expressed here of the sheer power of nature and of the mysteriousness of existence. Ellen's story functions as a kind of ritual of initiation, involving first of all a separation from family, friends and all that is familiar, then a time of testing in the wilderness which leads to a crucial revelation and is then followed by a ritual of re-entry, ceremonies of clothing, eating and finally of the reconciliation promised in her meeting with Mr. Jevons and return to Sydney. In this way her life fulfils the mystery foreshadowed in Cornwall as a girl when she lets herself down into the dark waters of St. Hya's Well "crying for some predicament which probably no one, least of all Ellen Gluyas could have explained: no specific sin, only presentiment of an evil she would have to face sooner or later" (110)—an echo, perhaps, of White's own recollections of childhood initiation, of "hanging" suspended foetus-like in a cold pool,[11] which, connected with his sense of being somehow a reincarnation of the Aborigines and thus in possession of the mysteries of the land, points to the wider significance of this scene. In turn this scene points, as baptism does to the Eucharist, to the celebration of this communion, the moment in the forest when, driven by hunger, she shares the Aborigine's dreadful meal, picking up and eating a piece of cooked human flesh which has fallen from one of their overflowing dillies.

Here as elsewhere it is important not to be distracted by irrelevant concerns: by the question as to whether or not Aboriginal people ever practised cannibalism, or by the shock which follows the violation of taboo. White's concern is not with the facts but with what they signify. Our present culture with its fear of alien images, values and ideas demands the symmetry of rational meaning and thus tends to subjugate the powers of metaphor and symbol, the forces of ambiguity and multiplicity. But this novel works to release these powers, demanding that the reader lets them work, gives them mental and emotional force. In this scene especially it is necessary to cross the frontiers, leaving behind the anxieties of visualisation and moralising by "deepened and re-visionary strategies of the word as an innovative medium" and enter into the fullness of symbolic consciousness—as Ellen does after the event:

> She was less disgusted in retrospect by what she had done, than awed by the fact that she had been moved to do it. The exquisite innocence of this forest morning, its quiet broken by a single flute-note endlessly repeated, tempted her to believe she had partaken of a sacrament. But there remained what amounted to an abomination of human behaviour, a headache, and the first signs of indigestion. In the light of Christian morality she must never think of the incident again. (272)

On the frontier between her cultural inheritance and a savage and mysterious universe, she crosses over, dislodging the division between the tenderness and ferocity. Cannibalism becomes a kind of "transubstantiation in reverse"[12] as Ellen is taken up into the life according to nature, into the community of suffering, vulnerability and oppression represented by the Aborigines. The power of this incorporation is signalled by the "single flute note endlessly repeated"—an image, significantly, which recalls the story of the Carib devils who consumed a ritual morsel of the enemy god, the god of the conquistadors who had invaded their world, and fashioned a flute from his bones.[13] The pressure of this moment acts as a kind of alchemy to fuse the human and, indeed, conquistadorial sense of guilt Ellen feels here into genuine creative humility and compassion. Thus, paradoxically, what she experiences is not so much loss as gain, not so much exclusion as the reconciliation she had looked for as a girl in Cornwall. Moreover, this feeling grows. Her "civilised" self attempts to repress the memory of what she has done but in "not remembering" she continually recalls the event, finding that it makes her "tolerably happy," happier than her white conscience should have allowed:

> [In recollection her action] seemed less unnatural, more admissible if only to herself. Just as she would never have admitted to others how she had immersed herself in the saint's pool, or that its black waters had cleansed her of morbid thoughts and sensual longings,

so she could not have explained how tasting flesh from the human thigh bone in the stillness of a forest morning had nourished not only her animal body but some darker need of the hungry spirit. (273-4)

We are back here with Lévi-Strauss' notion of the "properly appointed humanism" in which human life is related to the whole range of existence. Acknowledging the "darker need of the hungry spirit," Ellen has become more, not less human, testing possibilities she has only been able to glimpse as a lady, as on the occasion when out walking in Van Diemen's Land she is overcome by the savage abundance of the bush and, sitting down on a compost of decaying leaves and bark, like the young Patrick White "celebrating [his] own private mysteries" becomes aware of "the being her glass could not reveal, nor her powers of perception grasp, but whom she suspected must exist none the less" (92).

What is revealed in these scenes is the possibility of worship, the possibility unsatisfied in white society, even on "religious" occasions like that in church on Christmas Day in Van Diemen's Land when all that Ellen feels she is celebrating is the "God of the winning side" who supports and justifies the system which sets her and the Roxburghs in the front pew and the wretched convicts in their misery behind them. Not that the possibility which "savage" life opens out is comfortable. Physically her time with the Aborigines reveals a life that is "nasty, brutish and short." Spiritually, however, it enables her to come at the truth of her humanity, her subjection to physical necessity, and above all to the ultimate necessity of death. Where society represented by people like the Roxburghs, the Merivales, the Lovells and Miss Scrimshaw wants to triumph over this subjection she finds happiness in acceptance, the acceptance she celebrates in the moment in the empty chapel, left unfinished by the only other survivor of the wreck, Pilcher. Here in this poor little church she sits weeping, "reliving the betrayal of her earthly loves." In contrast with the church dedicated to the "Lord God of Hosts" in which she worshipped on Christmas Day in Van Diemen's Land, above the altar here the legend, "God is Love," "in the wretchedest lettering, in dribbled ochre" reminds her of all that she has lost. But acceptance of this loss becomes something positive:

At last she must have cried herself out: she could not have seen more clearly, down to the cracks in the wooden bench, the bird-droppings on the rudimentary altar. She did not attempt to interpret a peace of mind which had descended on her (she would not have been able to attribute it to prayer or reason) but let the silence enclose her like a beatitude. (390-1)

She has learned humility as "primitive" people do, by acknowledging her limits and finding her place in the universe. Exile, physical exploitation and oppression have been positive, not merely negative in their effects, teaching her to live with uncertainty. As Wilson Harris has remarked, the relative self-sufficiency of the traditional "strong" character does not fit the experience of the new world, being unaware of the need for change and apt to consider as evil any alteration of his other accepted character.[14] But Ellen is ready to live in a state of flux, to confront the savage domain, finding it not so much a threat as a fructifying mystery[15] from which she returns with a new definition of good and evil: evil as the non-acceptance which excludes what is "other" from the dialogue with the self, good the universal reverence and acceptance she celebrates in Pilcher's shabby chapel.

White's view of Australia, then, is of a kind of frontier, a place of disorientation, a place of the mind for the testing of communal values which must there be confirmed or repudiated. What is in question in the crisis which occurs here is not just personal identity but the nature of humanity itself, and in the series of comparisons that *A Fringe of Leaves* sets up civilisation seems just as demeaning as Aboriginal life. Leaving the chapel after her moment of illumination Ellen has a sense of returning to imprisonment, a sense confirmed on the voyage to Sydney when she goes up on deck for a final glimpse of "a jewellery of stars such as [she] believed she might be seeing for the last time before a lid closed" (401–2). The cruelties of civilisation are psychic whereas primitive societies' are physical, but the "country of thorns, whips, murderers, thieves, shipwreck, and adulteresses" (311–2) is the product of civilisation and its discontents. With the Aborigines, however, Ellen returns to her childhood world where "rocks had been her altars and springwater her sacrament" (248), a world in which she acknowledges that primal "law that man does not invent" (Lévi-Strauss), the law of physical necessity. Else-where[16] I have discussed the importance of this law for White's work as a whole. Here, however, it is clear that he sees it as the law of life and judges societies according to their acceptance of it. So the Aboriginal culture which acknowledges its debt to nature is closer to the human truth than white colonial society which does not—the society represented by Mrs. Merivale, who is "an adept at closing her mind to awfulness" (11), or by Mr. Roxburgh for whom even death has become "a literary conceit" (76). They, not Ellen, are the ultimate prisoners in an illusion which must inevitably be shattered by the fact of their mortality.

What White has done in this novel, then, is to exploit the Janus-like possibilities of the frontier, suggesting that white Australian culture will be incomplete until it comes to terms with the full range of human possibility, above all with the claims of nature, honoured by Aboriginal culture and intensified by white society's rejection which has laid the whole burden of them on a people ill prepared to resist. Ultimately his Australia is not unlike Naipaul's Africa, a place where the task is to survive. But it is also more positive. *Flaws in the Glass* confirms what the rest of his work intimates, that White lives by the secular myth of the writer who looks to language to initiate different modes of existence, attempting to express "a grandeur too overwhelming to express."[17] And *A Fringe of Leaves* comes closest perhaps to being explicit about the nature of this grandeur. What emerges here from "the wrestling match with an opponent whose limbs never become material"[18] is a return to childhood, to the primitive perception, and the celebration of mysteries which are primarily mysteries of decay and therefore of liberation from the confines of the merely material and even of the merely rational. What Ellen discovers, White implies, is her proper place in the universe, and she discovers this amongst the Aborigines "in a country designed for human torment, where even beauty flaunted a hostile radiance, and the spirits of place were not hers to conjure up" (248). Her situation is only evil to those who live by the spirit of possession and desire for mastery. This experience helps her to unlearn the conceptions of the individual and society inculcated by the Roxburghs and to return again to the awareness of herself as part of the larger scheme she knew as a child and glimpses again for the first time one night in Van Diemen's Land. As she describes it in her journal:

> The moon was in its first quarter, the river a faint, silver coil in the distance. Often on such a night at Z., a country to which I *belonged* (more than I did to parents or family) I would find myself wishing to be united with my surroundings, not as the dead, but fully alive. Here too, . . . I begin to feel closer to the country than to any human being. Reason, and the little I learned from the books I was given . . . tells me I am wrong in thinking thus, but my instincts hanker after something deeper, which I may not experience this side of death. (104)

A Fringe of Leaves then, stands at the opposite end of the scale to *Happy Valley*, White's first novel. There Australia represented an ultimate alienation, the land and its white inhabitants cut off from one another, towns like Happy Valley being merely "a peculiarly tenacious scab on the skin of the brown earth." *A Fringe of Leaves*, however, celebrates a reconciliation between the two, a renunciation of the pretensions of the enlightenment that leave one grasping still "at any circumstantial straw which may indicate an ordered universe" (405), in favour of a more "properly appointed humanism" which takes account of the full range of existence.

Notes

1. Patrick White, *Flaws in the Glass*. London, Cape, 1981, p. 16.

2. Ibid.

3. Robert Gittings (editor), *John Graham (Convict), 1829: An Historical Narrative*. London, Faber, 1937, p. 90.

4. Ibid., p. 94.

5. Ibid., p. 81.

6. C. Lévi-Strauss, *Totemism*. Translated by R. Needham. London, St. Martin's Press, 1964.

7. Edmund Leach, *Lévi-Strauss*. London, Collins/Fontana, 1974, p. 36.

8. Ibid., p. 18.

9. Gilbert Durand, *Les Structures Anthropologiques des l'Imaginaire*. Paris, Bordes, 1969, p. 96.

10. C. Lévi-Strauss, *The Savage Mind*. London, Weidenfeld & Nicolson, 1966, p. 219.

11. *Flaws in the Glass*, p. 16.

12. Wilson Harrison, *Explorations*. Aarhus, Denmark, Dangaroo Press, 1981, p. 31.

13. Ibid., p. 37.

14. Wilson Harris, "Metaphor & Myth," in Robert Sellick (editor), *Myth & Metaphor*. Adelaide, Centre for Research in the New Literatures in English, 1982, p. 4.

15. Harold Beaver, "The Drama of Disorientation." *Times Literary Supplement*, 24 April 1981, p. 451.

16. Veronica Brady, "The Novelist and the Reign of Necessity: Patrick White & Simone Weil," in R. Shepherd & K. Singh (editors), *Patrick White, a Critical Symposium*. Adelaide, Centre for Research in the New Literatures in English, 1978, pp. 108–116.

17. *Flaws in the Glass*, p. 20.

18. Ibid.

Australian Contemporary Drama: Patrick White

Dennis Carroll*

In the early 1960's it seemed that a lively investigation of Australian life through realistic plays alone was at a standstill. No new important plays emerged. Lawler, Beynon and Seymour went to England for the productions of their plays and stayed there—at least for the time being. The first sign of some new development was the

* Reprinted by permission of the publisher from *Australian Contemporary Drama 1909–1982: A Critical Introduction* (New York: Peter Lang, 1985), 107–20; all rights reserved.

theatrical furore over, and then acceptance, of the plays of Patrick White from 1961 to 1964—and, significantly, this development marked a break with the major tradition of the 1950's in being primarily non-realist. It was sustained and advanced in the work of other playwrights, most of whom are now still active and collectively have brought Australian drama to its maturity. The work of Dorothy Hewett, especially, is the work which in tone and technique most closely approximates White's. The technique and style of many other playwrights whose work is also non-realist will be dealt with subsequently—they owe more to later developments, whereas those of Hewett and White hark back to the classic non-realist movements of Symbolism, Expressionism and Surrealism—the same movements which left their traces on Atkinson, Tomholt and McCrae.

White's plays were preceded in the 1950's by an "underground" non-realist movement of sorts. The playwrights worked in isolation and none of them quite managed to vindicate their chosen form and style with a play of the stature of White's *The Ham Funeral*. One of the most talented was Ray Mathew, whose *Sing for St. Ned* (1950–51) is partly a parody of Stewart's *Ned Kelly*, and includes group asides, soliloquies, and direct audience address which are also later used by White and Hewett, and others. In his later *A Spring Song*, produced in 1958, Mathew experiments with heightened dialogue. In his opening scene it takes the form of an Expressionist hymn to spring.[1] David Ireland, later to be famous as a novelist, wrote two non-realist plays around 1960, *That Freedom Gas* and *The Virgin of Treadmill Street*. The latter play has been praised by some academic critics,[2] but its Expressionist-inspired device of shrunken sets and furniture is not theatrically very practical. More important was the work of Ric Throssell, who ironically worked in Canberra—in the 1950's an artistic backwater, though it was the Federal capital of the nation. By profession a diplomat, Throssell had worked in Moscow in 1945–46 and had seen and been impressed by the muted legacy of the great Russian non-realist theatre of the 1920's.[3] *Valley of the Shadows*, written in 1948, already shows more theatrical know-how in making Expressionist conventions work in stage terms than any of its forebears, though the content is sometimes banal. *Devil Wear Black* (1955), a satire on the Australian garment industry, involves both Surreal and Expressionist techniques and literary parody. The later *Dr. Homer Speaks: "Oh, Ai-lar-tsua, Farewell!"* written in 1962 and thus coinciding with some of White's work, involves much the same techniques, but includes more Surrealism and a long, foreshortened "flashback" forms the major action. Two shorter plays, *Suburban Requiem* and *Epitaph for the Unborn*, use devices of distorted sound and area lighting and a play-within-a-play device. Unlike the other playwrights of this 1950's "movement," Throssell had a practical theatre workshop to try out his ideas: the amateur Canberra Repertory Society, in which the postage-stamp sized stage did not entirely preclude experimentation.[4] But very few of the other non-realist plays of the 1950's were staged by leading little theatres, let alone the emergent non-commercial professional theatre.[5]

As exemplified by White and Hewett and some of their precursors, the new non-realism moves beyond Symbolism and Expressionism into a kind of Surrealism sometimes "justified" by emanating from the perceptions of a leading character, but which can also independently infuse a play's whole form. Music was to be an important convention in these plays. So was "heightened language," as it had been in some of the pioneer non-realists and in the verse drama of Stewart. But critics at the time perhaps unduly stressed the importance of language. At the time of *The Ham Funeral's* Sydney premiere, for example, critic Roger Covell remarked that the play "demands to be listened to with a care almost unknown in Australian theatre until now," and Kippax declared that language had been restored to Australian drama.[6] But in these plays, the all-important poetic images are only sometimes conveyed through words. More important still is the playwrights' control of theatrical *mise en scène*—settings, lighting, props, costumes, and sometimes groupings of actors—and the way that this control can effect changes of gear between the different degrees of realism and non-realism.

Developments in Australian theatre during the 1960's had positive effects on the nurturing of the new development. The Elizabethan Theatre Trust abandoned its national touring with plans for a national theatre and instead became a largely entrepreneurial rather than a producing organization: it selected theatres in each state capital for subsidy, or even created new ones, so that there would be a "regional" network of fully professional repertory non-commercial theatres. (The days of the Trust's importance were numbered by the creation in 1968 of a new government subsidizing body, the Australian Council for the Arts, later the Australia Council.) The regional theatres were the already established Melbourne Union Theatre Repertory, which changed its name to the Melbourne Theatre Company in 1968; the Old Tote Theatre, founded at the University of New South Wales in 1962; the South Australian Theatre Company, 1965; the Queensland Theatre Company, 1969; and the Tasmanian Theatre Company, 1971. In addition the Perth Playhouse, which had earlier existed in a different form, was subsidized in 1962. The beginnings of the non-realist development were marked by philistine salvos from certain sections of the general public, notably over White's *The Ham Funeral* and *The Season at Sarsaparilla*,[7] but there can be little doubt that the development and existence of the new subsidized theatres smoothed the way for non-realism later. Also, as the theatres became better established, they often opened smaller auditoria or alternate programs where more "experimental" work could be tried out. The first of these was the Jane Street Theatre, which the Old Tote opened in 1965. It saw some important premieres of offbeat plays, including the East Coast premieres of some of Hewett's plays. The Melbourne Theatre Company had an Australian Workshop series of new plays by the late 1960's, but by that time several important alternative theatres were open, or about to open, for the nurturing of new unusual Australian work.[8]

But at the same time as the regional theatres slowly developed more sophistication in play choices, productions and audiences, many lacked the physical facilities the new non-realist plays, and especially those of White and Hewett, demanded. Even in the early 1970's many of these theatres and the newer alternative theatres had extremely makeshift lighting systems and facilities for developed physical staging. Of course some of the plays, for example White's *The Ham Funeral*, did not make for really extravagant visual and physical demands—but a play like the same author's *A Cheery Soul* (1963) did. John Sumner directed the premiere of that play in Melbourne at the old Union Theatre on a stage much too small and cramped to do it justice, and the lighting cues on opening night were a disaster.[9] On the other hand, the Perth and Adelaide University organizations which premiered several of the most scenically demanding White and Hewett plays did have large, modern and well-equipped theatre buildings, but could not muster completely professional casts. After large-scale government subsidy and the opening of several new buildings, the physical facilities situation changed somewhat for the better in the later 1970's, but not so completely that very visually demanding plays were always staged in an adequate space.

Patrick White's first four plays forever exploded the dominance of realism in Australian drama. The plays' first productions did not have large-scale commercial success. But White's provocative use of non-realist conventions reached sufficiently large audiences to constitute a major landmark in the coming of age of Australian drama.

Of course, White's major reputation is as a novelist, and it was chiefly for those that he received the Nobel Prize in 1973. But his playwriting spans the period from the early 1930's to the present. Two short plays were staged by Bryant's Playhouse in Sydney in 1933, and revue material by the Little and Gate theatres in London in 1935. White is apparently glad that all of this material has disappeared, along with his first full-length play *Return to Abyssinia*, performed in London in 1947.[10] Shortly afterwards, however, he wrote *The Ham Funeral*. Return to Australia, several major novels, and fourteen years elapsed before the furore of its Adelaide Festival rejection and first production. The next three plays were written in short order and partly in reaction: *The Season at Sarsaparilla* in 1961 and both *A Cheery Soul* and *Night on Bald Mountain* in 1962. All were produced by 1964. The disappointing reception to the last of these surely contributed to White's long theatrical silence afterwards. Certainly it was the success of Jim Sharman's Sydney revival of *The Season at Sarsaparilla* in 1976 that prompted the playwright's new work *Big Toys*, well received in 1977. His film adaptation of a short story, *The Night the Prowler*, as directed by Sharman, was a critical and box office disaster in 1978, but Sharman's revival of *A Cheery Soul* the following year at the Sydney Opera House Drama Theatre first revealed that play's true stature. This in turn spurred him to writing another play, *Signal Driver*, first performed at the 1982 Adelaide Festival—this time by invitation.[11] In spite of the interest of the newer plays, it is arguable that the first three are both the most significant and the most original. *The Season at Sarsaparilla* is closest to the Australianist mainstream tradition, but it is *A Cheery Soul* which is the most exciting foray into the furthest reaches of Surrealism.

White has been extraordinarily adept at allowing the organic demands of each play's material to determine the conventions which express it at any given point in the action. In doing so, he flouts the "last unacknowledged unity," that of style;[12] and it was this that bothered so many of White's critics.

The implications of *The Ham Funeral* for the Australian context are only indirect. It is set in London in 1914 and was partly suggested by the William Dobell painting, *The Dead Landlord*.[13]

The play deals with the progress towards deeper self-realization of not only the Young Man who is the protagonist, but the Landlady Alma Lusty. Although the play moves on a unit set, the space is fragmented by the Young Man's memory, and the structure takes on an Epic character, a Morality of maturation. The Young Man is an aspiring young writer in a London boarding house, closeted in an upper room. His Landlady invites him to the basement for sandwiches of bread and dripping. In Act I, she loses her husband, and the Young Man helps her by dashing across London to inform the Relatives. In Act II, after the ham funeral and their departure, she starts a hot pursuit of the Young Man and corners him on a table; though aroused, he rejects this initiation. He bids her farewell and walks out into the night, as the walls of the house dissolve around him. He has rejected two undesirable extremes: his earlier narcissistic introversion, and a total loss-of-self in extreme extroversion which has stunted others in the play. The Landlady, his antithesis, is a woman who has an all-consuming love of the flesh, who loves eating, who wants to eat even faces. But her "real" name, Alma Lusty, indicates the paradoxes of her identity and hints at her capacity to develop. She cannot understand the Young Man's introverted fantasies about the girl in the room next to him, but in the routine of her own life she feels that something is being denied her, and it is that which attracts her to the Young Man as well as her sexual appetite. In the end, his sensitivity has reactivated the latent sensitivity in her, while she has been the catalyst for his maturity.

White skillfully manipulates his conventions to alter the level of the play as needed—to indicate the Young Man's and finally the Landlady's oscillations between aesthetic self-absorption and earthy extroversion. For much of the time, the action proceeds on the level of realism foreshortened by memory, in a rather Symbolist manner; but White achieves theatrical richness at key moments by heightening the level to Expressionist nightmare, or lowering it to a more re-portorial naturalism. An example of the former process is the front cloth scene, Act I Scene vii. Here two old lady music hall performers who have become scavengers, crack jokes, rummage in garbage for food and clothing, eat imitation pearls, encounter the Young Man in his journey across London and finally flee from a foetus in a trash bin. Some critics objected to this scene as unnecessary and in ques-tionable taste, but the music hall conventions which White here uses are grafted onto subject matter which is basically horrific, and they are an excellent way to render the Young Man's fear of life outside the house. Such life, for him at this point, is a nightmare of raucous disorder and sinister absurdity. An example of the opposite process, White's lowering of the action, occurs in Act I Scene vi, where the body of the Landlord is laid out and White records every fluctuation of the grotesquerie of grief. Like the heightening, this lowering of style is also purposeful: to the Young Man, life in the basement seems overly "objective," exclusively earthy, physical, and practical.

The setting and the dialogue are root conventions for White's control of level. Superficially, the set might appear unduly semaphoric: two identical upstairs rooms of introverted aestheticism, the basement of practical "life," and the no-man's-land staircase between them. But lighting can erase certain areas from the consciousness of the audience when appropriate and thus underline changes in stylistic level. The front cloth scene reinforces the Expressionist and vaude-villian style of that episode in an effective way, while many of the props in the basement—the ham, table, bread and dripping—have realistic utility as objects and powerful import as symbols.[14] The dialogue is rooted in the idiom of London speech but can effect changes in levels as effectively as use of the space. Mrs. Lusty's early speeches are stuffed with food images, the Young Man's soliloquies perfumed with flowers and dreams and sometimes designated "arias" and underscored with music.[15] Then there are the telegraphic, Expres-sionist exchanges of the Relatives, the vaudevillian, knockabout lines of the scavengers. Towards the end, the Landlady's dialogue becomes more similar to the Young Man's, and it thus becomes a barometer to measure her alteration through the Young Man's influence.[16] White indicates that these main characters are to adopt a recitative-like delivery as they go through the near-seduction, and this suggests incantation over a life-restoring, near-ceremonial act.

The predominant allegorical and Symbolist tone of the play, as well as its form as "memory" play, is chiefly sustained by the characterization of the Young Man and two devices associated with him: his function as "engaged" Chorus, and his *anima*. The latter takes the imagined form of the girl boarder next door, whom the Young Man has never seen. The choral function of the Young Man sometimes has the effect of limiting empathy in certain scenes or larding it with irony; it is also a means whereby the inner searchings of the character can be directly expressed in soliloquy. Appropriately, the Young Man is most often Chorus when more detached from the action early on; later he becomes less so and his choral function decreases. The *anima* is derived of course from Jungian psychology and refers to the inner adjustment of the psyche, defined by various fantasies of the subconscious. Critics have suggested that the *anima* expresses the Young Man's virginal fear of the outside, his integrity, his immature desires for completeness, and his feminine sensibility.[17]

In White's hands, the *anima* becomes an excitingly effective theatrical device. Especially important are mirror movement, blocking and gesture—patterns which stand out all the more because the upstairs rooms are identical. The wrestlings of the Young Man with his *anima* proceed like a finicky, dated ballet. While he is standing spot-lit in his room, she is in a corresponding position; when he moves towards the dividing wall of the rooms, she does the same. The final explosion of this symmetry is extraordinarily powerful. The Young Man breaks into her room and she disappears. Just before she does so, she moves desperately around the room, *"almost like a bird in a cage, in search of a possible avenue of escape."*[18] The Young Man finds in the room only a spray of white lilac, and goes out. Immediately afterwards, White gives the audience a prosaic shock to emphasize the exorcism: the same actress who played the *anima* enters as the real and mousey next-door boarder. She goes through some commonplace "business" and is then faded out.

The Season at Sarsaparilla deals directly with Australian subject matter and is more hard-edged in outline than the earlier play, Expressionistic rather than Symbolist in overall effect. The unit set juxtaposes three neighboring kitchens and backyards in three look-alike houses in the fictional Sydney outer suburb of Sarsaparilla. The Stage Right house is occupied by a menswear salesman, his pregnant wife, and her brother Roy, a frustrated writer; the Center one by a business executive and his wife and daughters, Judy and Pippy; and the Stage Left one by a sanitary carter and his wife. An important subplot consists of a relationship between the latter character, Nola, and Pippy, and Pippy's curiosity about the dogs in "season" yapping and copulating brutally all over the neighborhood, and how Pippy observes and becomes reconciled to the existence of similar behavior in humans. But the main plot consists of the working out of two triangles. In the first, Judy is attracted to Roy, but his cruel irony repels her and she settles for a devoted postal worker instead. In the second, Nola has a one-night stand with "digger" Masson, her husband Ernie's World War II "mate" visiting from Brisbane. Ernie finds out and gives Masson an obligatory right-to-the-jaw when he leaves. Then Nola and Ernie manage to avoid past patterns of re-crimination and uneasily reconcile; and a wide, if possibly temporary rapport is established between all three houses with the imminent arrival of a baby in the menswear house. Roy decides to leave Sarsaparilla—"There's practically no end to the variations on monotony"[19]—but he knows that he will eventually be back. But in the play the splicing is everything: the way that the actions and suburban routines in the three houses are almost filmically cut and juxtaposed.

The play treats interestingly the old motif of the individual's relation to group stylization. The outsider Roy, unlike the Young Man of *The Ham Funeral*, does not become humanized, and gradually loses both the sympathy of the audience and his authority as "Chorus." Conversely, several characters who at first seem entirely in thrall to suburban conformity are shown to have more individuality than was apparent at first. In the beginning, the play is truly the "charade of suburbia" of the subtitle. Many of the characters are flattened into comic strip grotesques, and White's stage directions indicate his distaste for them. But then he penetrates the charade, investigates more deeply, and transforms his material. For example, the postal worker is shown to be more than the dull clod of the beginning, with aspirations to upward mobility—he is revealed as a young man of more than usual steadfastness, loyalty and devotion. And the business executive's absorption in the bourgeois stuffiness of his career gives way to certain unpretentious forthrightness which is likeable. It seems that White's interest in his characters triumphs over his original intentions, and the nearest he comes to spelling out the philosophy that finally informs the play is in Judy telling Roy that "kindness. Affection. That's all that really matters."[20] Ultimately the play is not an attack on suburbia, but a humanistic affirmation of individualism and diversity within its apparently limiting routines. The breakfast scene in which Ernie confronts Nola and Masson seems the pivot for this change in attitude and style. But even earlier, the Boyle household seems the heart of the play both structurally and emotionally, and it has been the main reason for the erosion of the satirical style. It is possible that White intended the comparatively realistic presentation of Nola and her two men to ironically contrast with the others in Act I, but he could hardly have foreseen them stealing focus and empathy to the extent they do—partly because these roles proved easier to energize in performance than others. (In the Adelaide premiere, Nola was played by Zoë Caldwell.) Thematically, too, the Boyle sections of the play plug in directly to old Australianist issues. Masson, from Brisbane, criticizes Ernie for falling victim to domesticity and modern conveniences such as mixmasters, and he revives memories of how close all the blokes were in the foxholes of the Western Desert. Ernie replies: "I reckon I was never closer to nobody, before or since, as I waited for the Jerries to blow me bloody 'ead off. *(Shouting)* But I'm 'APPY now!"[21] White suggests that Australianist models of masculinity may well attract Nola, but he lambasts the hypocritical kind of mateship that Masson professes.

This time the changes of stylistic level, from Expressionist satire to a greater realism, are not helped by all of the staging conventions. The set, for example, is really geared only for the beginning of the play: the identical comic strip kitchens with most props and furniture mimed, and a cyclorama at back, with some entrances down lanes to backyards made through the auditorium. But the space does make possible a battery of other conventions which are not so closely related to the psyches of characters as in the earlier play and thus work more independently to drive home thematic points and effect irony, parallelism, and counterpoint. Time and space are cleverly manipulated to bring off distancing effects. A striking instance occurs in Act I, where the salesman's wife is remonstrating with her brother Roy on the virtues of practical suburban life and criticizing his desire to quit teaching and write. In the business household, Judy's mother is criticizing her for wanting to become a concert violinist in almost the same terms. Conversational exchanges and simultaneous action in both households are spliced together, with the characters in the disengaged group either formally freezing, or, if the director chooses, busying themselves with breakfast business. A second convention is the more obviously Expressionist "razzle-dazzle of time."[22] This is a silent film effect of flickering light and stylized, speeded-up movement, and is especially related to rituals of arriving and leaving home sneered at by Roy, "Out and in! In and out! Direction is the least of it,"[23] but later affirmed by Nola: "My life's been set by you, Ern. By your comin' in and goin' out."[24]

One convention does reflect White's change in attitude to his material: the group soliloquies. These are interior monologues delivered often by several characters on stage at the same time, the words contrapuntally intertwining, sometimes setting up intricate patterns of resonances and ironies. The device is independent of any one set of characters. But it is especially valuable for digging under the more routine-bound bourgeois characters; it gives White a lever to expose aspects of their "withheld selves" which they would not express even to family members. For such group soliloquies, the characters speak in a heightened form of address still strongly based in Australian idiom.

Many of the techniques of this play are carried over to *Night on Bald Mountain*, though *A Cheery Soul* was written in between. *Bald Mountain* is a portrait of individualism gone destructive, as emotionally sterile and dominating Professor Sword works his influence on his alcoholic wife Miriam and a young nurse hired to care for her. The setting is an elaborate construction involving an exterior, the mountain path to the Sword house, and the many rooms of the house itself. It sets up the conditions for group soliloquies to work; and the spatial counterpoint, especially inside the house where there are no less than three upstairs bedrooms, a living room, a staircase, an entrance hall, and a study. The full and naturalistic furnishings reinforce integration of the soliloquies with the play's pervading realism. But often the scenic arrangement of the areas lends itself to the characters being alone in local light, and so drives home isolation and loneliness. The play as a whole, however, is probably White's least successful one, mainly because the realistic action is pushed out of kilter to fit the allegorical import White wants to give it. The way that White engineers the nurse's suicide or accidental death by Sword's planting in her head that she may be incestuously attracted to her father is especially difficult to swallow.[25]

White's two recent plays of the 1970's and 1980's are "chamber plays" for small casts but are very much related to *Night on Bald Mountain* in their greater reliance on realism. This is especially true of *Big Toys* (1977), for the action remains representational throughout. The plot deals with the corruption of a Union leader by a wealthy homosexual lawyer and his *arriviste*, ex-model wife. The Union man, Terry, compromised by an affair with the wife, is persuaded to be a friendly witness in the trial of a titled and powerful magnate who has turned his back on his class and has betrayed "mateship" with Terry. In the end, however, Terry refuses the thank you present of an expensive car and forces the couple to face the fact that their marriage is an empty charade—something that their affluence and "big toys" have helped them to avoid facing.

The play repeats the strategy of *The Season at Sarsaparilla* in that it moves from satirical point-scoring to a more serious examination of the limits of individual action in the net of a group consensus. As Katharine Brisbane has pointed out, White hooks the audience through apparent use of the genre of trivial domestic comedy, then twists the hook in their stomachs with a strongly critical, indeed political statement about the misuse of privilege in Australia.[26] There is a presentational touch which appears to signal the twist: a sudden appearance of a black hole in the back picture window of the set, where before the lights of Sydney Harbor had been twinkling. Unlike the earlier play, there is no affirmation of the "health" of any patterns of consensus presented. Terry is irredeemably compromised and has not been able to prevent the misuse of privilege, and the wife is a despairing victim of her husband's manipulations. The play is ultimately a powerful condemnation of moral delinquency in high places.

The characterization of the men—the vulnerable Union man with an Achilles heel, and the Establishment man who has adjusted his sexual inclinations to attain the benefits of playing a "straight" role in society—is more multi-faceted and particularized than in any other White play so far. The portrait of Terry, especially, confounds the old Australianist stereotype that some of the play's first critics seemed to expect—especially in his incipient responses to the lawyer's initial sexual interest in him, and his open vulnerability. Kippax thought that, in light of his reported status as a Union leader, his actions in the play are stupid, weak and "unconvincing."[27] Fitzpatrick has suggested that White's approval for his character seems excessive in terms of his actions in the play, and he suggests that this makes the overall stance of the play ambivalent.[28] Against this it can be said that the final frozen image of the wife's despair, and the implications of the play's action as a whole, sufficiently iron out this ambivalence to make White's stance clear.

Though *Signal Driver* has been described by White as a very "inward" play, the scope in time is much greater than it is in *Big Toys*, and the increased use of non-realism suggests a stronger affinity with the plays of the 1960's. The playwright has said that the theme is the "decay of Australian society as reflected in two characters— a man and woman, husband and wife from about 1920 to the present."[29] There are three acts, one set just after the Great War, the second after World War II, and the third in 1980. The nominal setting is a transport shelter shed. The lack of conventional dramatic action in the play suggests Beckettian allegory: In Act I Theo, trying to leave his young wife to fulfill his aspirations as artist-craftsman, signals a tram which fails to stop, and then is persuaded by Amy to return home. In Act II Theo is affluent as a result of Amy's relationship with a wealthy businessman. Again he tries to signal the driver to escape her and the shelter, and again he fails. In Act III it is the aged Amy who has the impulse to leave and signals the driver, once again with no result. Theo guides her home. By Act III, the solidarity of the relationship between Amy and Theo has strengthened, while the condition of the surrounding society has deteriorated; it is implied that individuation, and strength in human relationships, can best be achieved by a growing apart from society.

One critic of the Adelaide premiere commented that White never quite managed the "transition from the particular to the general."[30] The difficulty is rather that the play's allegorical shape and function is so clear that it makes seem awkward the naturalistic detritus which is also present in the play. *Signal Driver* has a simplicity of design and a clarity of formal outline much removed from the exciting sprawl of some earlier White plays. White chooses to limn the societal and metaphysical background to his human couple through a reduced, all-purpose chorus of two super-heros called First Being and Second Being who have supernatural prescience: they can interpret the past and foresee the future. Their lines sometimes link up with the human characters, in patterned solos, unison or harmony, though the two humans remain unaware of their presence. The speech ranges widely through Expressionist and music hall modes, parodies of television commentators, and references to the Great Snake and Great Computer; it is given further expressivity through Carl Vine's specially composed music.

A *Cheery Soul* very probably remains White's greatest claim to originality as a playwright and the most provocative example of his utilization of disparate non-realist conventions. The play goes further than any previous Australian one of stature in incorporating Surrealism. Conventions of setting, characterization and staging are once again utilized in tandem with the developing action.

According to Fitzpatrick, the "main business" of the play is the "knowing of Miss Docker," the main character, and that fascination with her is a "product of an achievement of form."[31] That's putting the cart before the horse—the course of Miss Docker's unbridled individualism, struggling to dominate and control a Sarsaparilla which thwarts her, determines the play's form, and this illustration of the destructiveness of her individualism is the play's business. Certainly the "scourge and victim"[32] of her society, certainly "splashed on with summer prints,"[33] she is at the same time shallow and complex, sympathetic and repellent. Her sentimental, aggressive temperament is characterized by a pragmatic literalness. This is epitomized in her hectoring addresses to the audience, in which she threatens to take over their space as well as the characters', and her snapshots, with which she tries to invade the specialness of others' memories with evidence of what the past was "really like." Her course of action and view of her world determine the choice and employment of the conventions, particularly the Surreal ones which are first associated with her developing paranoia and then take over the entire action and form of the play, as if independent of her perceptions.

The action consists of three stages, not quite coincident with the three acts, and the conventions are closely related to each stage. The first begins in near-realism in a neat suburban home in Sarsaparilla. Mrs. Custance, feeling guilty because of her comforts and happiness, proposes to her easygoing husband that they invite Miss Docker, an elderly spinster known for her good works in the neighborhood, to live with them. Custance reluctantly agrees. Until now the action has been realistic, but the setting contradicts this somewhat. Though the furniture looks pleasant, it is obviously painted and stylized, and many props are mimed. Everything is overshadowed by the huge tomato plants which can be seen outside the verandah. They prove a talisman to protect the Custances' world. Their size at first is grotesquely threatening, and so is Miss Docker's arrival. A car is heard approaching, *"very loud and menacing,"*[34] then a blast on the horn, and Miss Docker's voice. Her soliloquies, and the inimitable largeness of her expression, extend the threatening undertone to the basic realism of the act, as she gradually takes over the Custances' routine and adjusts it to hers, giving hints about the food, the lighting, and the use of first names, and finally, fatally, fiddles with the tomatoes. The realism is also threatened by six blackouts to indicate the passing of time. At the end of this first stage, Miss Docker is defeated. She is asked to leave. She turns her attentions elsewhere, and the Custances' world is still intact. They embrace in a tender, casual, very naturalistic little love scene.

At the beginning of the second stage, the setting immediately prepares us for the content and style of the new direction. It is the Chinese Room of the Sundown Home for old people at Sarsaparilla, with its impression of faded splendor, dusky dark, disintegrating hangings, and scrim walls behind which three *rostra* will be spotlit. The furnishings include lacquered consoles with cloisonné vases, upright chairs, armchairs, and standard lamps, some of which are painted to fade with the scrim walls. This, then, is the world of old age—exotic, grotesque and disintegrating, but surprisingly strong; and this second stage of the play, which lasts until Act III Scene i, presents Miss Docker's assault on it. Once again she is not successful.

There are two conventions prominent in this section. The first is the Chorus of old ladies who speak in part and in unison. The device has several functions: to comment on the flashbacks that occur, to narrate parts of the action, and to express a corporate sense of the terrors and loneliness of old age. The chorus is grouped, lighted and spatially divided in several ways. Sometimes it is fully lighted, at other times not. It receives its fullest expression in Act III Scene i where, against a scrim suggestive of spring blossoms and weathered brick, the chorus begins a cruelly counterpointing cantata on the effects of spring on the old. The second major device here is a series of acted-out evocations of the past, which take place on the three *rostra.* These flashbacks dramatize the way that Miss Docker was left accidentally on purpose by the roadside in the funeral cortege of a man she tried to appropriate in his final illness. As his widow reminisces about the past, handsome "figments" of the young couple act out the idealizations of her memory.

The chorus suggests the unanimity of old age and its various defences against death; the flashbacks suggest the sanctification of remembered experience. Together, the devices theatricalize the qualities of a world too strong for Miss Docker to subvert, stridently as she tries. But she is also viciously excluded by connivance of some of the old ladies from a Bible class conducted by the Reverend Wakeman. His is the next world she looks to conquer.

Like the Custances', this is a gentle world—a world protected not by giant tomatoes but tenuous religious faith. Miss Docker's mind and will quickly invade the stage. She goes to Wakeman's office and tells him that his sermons are inarticulate and devoid of inspiration. He is tortured by the validity of her criticism, and his wife fails to solace him. Now White employs Surreal devices which distort the present, not only the past. They give us an extraordinarily immediate sense of Miss Docker's view of the world. The setting, like the action, becomes broken down and disjointed. There are transparent scrims of garden, church, and street, and starkly lit neighbors appear and disappear on the *rostra.* There are more soliloquies than earlier; disembodied voices are heard. Characters talk to Miss Docker in the dark before light identifies them.

In the climactic Church scene, time seems suspended as Miss Docker's obsessions rush into the vacuum opened by Wakeman's doubts and his congregation's indifference. Surreal devices now seem to transform the action and invade it independently of her will. The absence of proper faith, a root condition for this to happen, is established by a light change to express interior action; there is a group soliloquy in which the suburbanites pray for the material goods they want most, in the parody of a litany, which culminates seriously when they express terrors of nuclear holocaust. Then all is jarred back to Miss Docker's hectoring insistence as she savages Wakeman in public, dominates the stage, takes over the sermon, and brings on his catatonic collapse, as his wife prays for protection against the powers of Darkness. But the powers do not abate. They now turn on Miss Docker herself. As she goes home on the road, treble and bass disembodied voices haunt her: "The wind, the wind . . . / . . . the wind is circular . . . / . . . and cuts . . ./ . . . with little invisible knives. / It slashes with razor blades!"[35] A dog (invisible), front of the apron, relieves himself on her. Children (visible) see this and laugh at her. She does a last "kindness" by giving an alcoholic tramp a shilling, and goes off towards the Old People's Home. This final

admixture of Surreal and realistic conventions at the very end reinforces the feeling that her world will remain fragmented and haunted
by the dark forces she has unleashed.

Notes

1. Mathew's *A Spring Song* was published by the University of Queensland Press in 1961.

2. See, for instance, Fitzpatrick's sympathetic analysis in "After The Doll", *Australian Drama Since 1955*, ed. John Colmer (Melbourne: Edward Arnold, 1969), 40–41.

3. Ric Throssell, personal interview, Canberra, April, 1976.

4. *Valley of the Shadows* was published in Perth by Paterson's Printing Press in 1950, *Devil Wear Black* in Melbourne by Coronation Press in 1955. *Dr. Homer Speaks* is in the Hanger Collection. *Epitaph for the Unborn*, written 1955, is in the Hanger Collection; *Suburban Requiem*, written in 1962, was published in *Australian One Act Plays*, Book I, ed. Eunice Hanger (Adelaide: Rigby, 1962).

5. For example, *Sing for St. Ned*, finished in 1952, had to wait until 1960 for its first performance by a Queensland University amateur drama society. Plays by David Ireland, John Naish and other "experimental" non-realists lay in typescript unproduced.

6. [Roger Covell,] "*The Ham Funeral* at Palace Theatre," *Sydney Morning Herald*, 12 July 1962:7; Brek [i.e., H. G. Kippax,] "The Fourth Chapter," *Nation*, 28 July 1962:18.

7. While the furore over *The Ham Funeral* was mainly over that play's form and style, that over *The Season at Sarsaparilla* was mainly over content. Many saw it as an attack on Australian suburban life. On May 23, 1963, on the occasion of the play's professional opening in Sydney, the tabloid *The Daily Mirror* ran a banner headline, NEW PLAY STINKS. For a full account of the early reception to White's plays, see H. G. Kippax's Introduction to the Australian Sun Books edition of *Four Plays* by Patrick White (Melbourne: Sun Books, 1967).

8. There was a certain reluctance on the part of the Australian Elizabethan Theatre Trust to wholeheartedly support White's plays in fully professional productions, though they helped subsidize the three White premieres by the Adelaide University Theatre Guild. There was a Trust season of *The Ham Funeral* in Sydney in 1962. The first professional stage production of *The Season at Sarsaparilla* was by J. C. Williamson's in Sydney in 1963.

9. John Sumner, "Note on the Play," Melbourne Union Repertory Company Program for *The Cheery Soul*, Nov. 1963, n.p.

10. "Patrick White—Playwright," A chronology published in *Theatre Australia* 6.6 (1982): 15. Dates for first four plays as given by Kippax, Introduction to *Four Plays* 2.

11. "*Signal Driver*—Patrick White and Director Neil Armfield discuss *Signal Driver* with Gus Worby," *Theatre Australia* 6.6 (1982): 12–15.

12. Michael Kirby, "On Style," *Drama Review* 15.3a (1971): 11.

13. Chronology, *Theatre Australia* 6.6 (1982): 15.

14. See R. F. Brissenden, "The Plays of Patrick White," *Meanjin* 23 (1964): 249; and Eunice Hanger, "Place in Australian Drama," *Australian Quarterly* 34.2 (1962): 72–73.

15. See Thelma Herring, "Maenads and Goat Song: The Plays of Patrick White," *Southerly* 25 (1965): 222; and John Tasker, "Notes on *The Ham Funeral*," *Meanjin* 23 (1964): 300.

16. Kippax, "The Fourth Chapter," *Nation*, 28 July 1962: 18–19.

17. See J. F. Burrows, "Patrick White's Four Plays," *Australian Literary Studies* 2 (1966): 157; and Elizabeth Loder, "*The Ham Funeral:* Its Place in the Development of Patrick White," *Southerly* 23 (1963): 90.

18. White, *The Ham Funeral*, in *Four Plays*, II, viii, 70.

19. White, *The Season at Sarsaparilla*, in *Four Plays*, II, 173.

20. White, *The Season at Sarsaparilla*, II, 162.

21. White, *The Season at Sarsaparilla*, I, 112.

22. White, *The Season at Sarsaparilla*, I, 99.

23. White, *The Season at Sarsaparilla*, I, 100.

24. White, *The Season at Sarsaparilla*, II, 167.

25. For instance, Herring, Kippax and Brissenden all feel that the characterization is forced and contrived. For a detailed discussion of the problems the play raises, see H. G. Kippax, "Patrick White's Mistake," *Nation*, 28 March 1964: 18–19.

26. See Brisbane's Preface to *Big Toys* by White (Sydney: Currency Press, 1978), xiii; and her review, "*Big Toys:* Patrick White's *Power Without Glory*," *National Times*, 1–6 August 1977: 26.

27. Kippax, "A Shaky Season," *Sydney Morning Herald*, 30 July 1977.

28. Fitzpatrick, 67.

29. *Signal Driver* discussion cited above, *Theatre Australia* 6.6 (1982): 13.

30. Leonard Radic, "The Theatre: Patrick White in Adelaide," *Age* (Melbourne) 8 March 1982.

31. Fitzpatrick, 62.

32. Terry Sturm, "Drama," in *The Oxford History of Australian Literature*, ed. Leonie Kramer, (Melbourne: Oxford University Press, 1981), 242.

33. James Merralls, "Patrick White's Charade," *Nation*, 25 January 1964: 19.

34. White, *A Cheery Soul*, in *Four Plays*, I, 188.

35. White, *A Cheery Soul*, III, viii, 263.

Epiphanies in Tables and Goats: *The Burnt Ones* and *The Cockatoos*

John A. Weigel[*]

Most of Patrick White's short stories have been collected and published in two volumes, *The Burnt Ones* (1964) and *The Cockatoos* (1975). Four of his early plays, originally produced in Australia, have been published in one volume in 1965. For many admirers of Patrick White, his shorter fiction and his plays are epiphenomena. That is,

[*] Reprinted from *Patrick White* (Boston: Twayne, 1983), 87–97; © 1983 and reprinted with the permission of G. K. Hall & Co.

although White's reputation as a significant writer may be reinforced by them, they are not essential. Like his novels, they do, however, bear witness to the author's cosmopolitanism and his ambivalence about Australia. The stories in particular, which vary in length from extended sketches to novellas, employ diverse techniques for a wide range of effects.

When White returned to Australia after years abroad as a student, a soldier, and a wanderer, he brought with him memories of his sojourns in exotic places, material which he used in his short fiction. He was unsympathetic with the Australian literary nationalism that had emerged during the 1930s.[1] The writings of Joseph Furphy and Henry Lawson were always cited as examples of what the home folks could do. Both Furphy and Lawson were masters of the anecdotal style and their stories are easy to understand. Their home-spun quality contrasts with the literary sophistication of White and Richardson, who could not conceal, even if they had chosen, their interest in the experiments of British and Continental dramatists and storytellers.

Patriots such as Nettie Palmer continued to prefer the home-made stories of Henry Lawson, for example, praising their "loose, easy look."[2] At the same time, others began to break away from the old ways. Hal Porter, for one, took a new look at familiar places and people. G. A. Wilkes was one of the critics who understood what Porter was trying to do, and he tried to explain it: "The world of Porter's stories is the familiar world seen as slightly askew, the personalities sometimes neurotic, the events sometimes macabre." Human beings are perceived as "enigmatic and astonishing."[3] Just as Virginia Woolf in England had rejected gig-lamps for the personal reality of luminous halos, Christina Stead and Randolph Stow in Australia—as well as White and Porter—began to express impressions rather than report. White's short stories, in particular, led the way.

THE BURNT ONES

Patrick White's first collection, which he called *The Burnt Ones*, contains eleven stories. Nine of them originally appeared in periodicals such as *Meanjin, Australian Letters*, and *London Magazine*.[4] Several of the stories are Greek in setting and characters. One mixes modalities by transporting an Australian woman to Greece for its moment of truth. One is set in the neutral city of Geneva, while others are highlighted by the plastic suburbia near Sydney which White calls Sarsaparilla. All of them, however, investigate concerns familiar to White's readers: suffering, loneliness, and frustration as constants in the human equation, an equation in which the variables may contain humor and irony but seldom high tragedy.

White found ideas and characters compatible with his themes—

unfortunates burned by life—while living in postwar Greece where he met and sympathized with the victims and exiles whose quest for salvation had been secularized by wartime hardships. God seemed remote and improbable, often even a mockery after the "Catastrophe" at Smyrna, where many Greeks were slaughtered by the Turks and others fled with their lives only. Also, severe shortages following World War II, particularly in Athens, where aristocrats were forced to forage for food, intensified passions and escalated issues.

In "The Woman who wasn't Allowed to Keep Cats" White contrasts two rich, Americanized Greeks, proud owners of a Cadillac, with a married couple struggling to adjust to life in Athens. The local Greeks seem eccentric. The man is a left-wing writer, the woman a cat-lover. The "authentic" Greek woman blames her compatriots for not loving cats. Greeks, she says, are "too egotistical, quarrelsome, lazy, and gluttonous to understand the force of love" (257). The visitors find the cat-lover mad, and when they return two years later to visit their friends again, they discover that the cat-lover has given up her cats because the formerly liberal husband has forbidden them now that he is a prosperous, right-wing writer. The Americanized Greeks get the impression that the cat-lover has been transformed into a cat. They are glad to return to New York. No one has escaped deterioration.

In another of the Greek stories, "The Evening at Sissy Kamara's," memories of Smyrna are the pedal point in a contrapuntal conversation between two couples. The hostess, Sissy, once had intellectual pretensions. She has published some poems, but "so privately nobody has read them." Once she declaimed an epic poem—"On a theme nobody can remember," says Basil Patzopoulos upon being informed by Poppy, his wife, that she has accepted an invitation to spend an evening at Sissy's. Of Sissy's declamation he adds: "On a mountain side. To a group of women, most of them by now dead" (128–29).

In the course of the evening the hosts and guests share a small balcony. As Sissy serves indifferent food, her husband breaks Sissy's last good dish from Smyrna. In a confusion of emotions Sissy laughs as she cries, then philosophizes: "Almost my last possession of importance . . . when one had hoped with age to grow less attached when age itself is the arch-disappointer a final orgy of possessiveness of of of [sic] a gathering of minor vanities" (139). Sissy also "explains" Greeks to her guests: "We are a brutal, detestable race," she pontificates. "If we care to admit, we are little better than Turks turned back to front" (136). Although Basil and Poppy Patzopoulos disagree with Sissy, they suppress possible rejoinders and depart with feelings of guilt. There is no resolution.

"Being Kind to Titina" begins in Alexandria where a "good" Greek family and a "bad" Greek family are neighbors; then the story moves on to Athens for an ironic conclusion. There the Greek boy-man from the good family has his first sexual experience with an amoral but happy whore. The woman turns out to be the formerly plain Titina from the bad Greek family, whom he had once been forced to treat politely when they were childhood neighbors. The upgrading of Titina is contrasted with the disillusionment of the good boy. Again, however, there is no resolution.

In "A Glass of Tea" White utilizes Geneva as a neutral setting for a conversation between two casual acquaintances, both Greeks of different histories and generations. Malliakas, a middle-aged bachelor, a writer manqué in search of a story and in Geneva on business, finally decides to present a letter of introduction to Philippides, an elderly Greek now living in Switzerland. During his short visit Malliakas finds his story. It is based on what the old man tells him of his first wife, Constantia, emended by what the old man's second wife, Aglaia, tells him about the first wife and a set of tea glasses. A gypsy had once prophesied that the old man would live until the last of the glasses was broken, but it was his first wife who broke instead. At the time of the visit there is just one glass left unbroken. It will not last long, however, Malliakas knows, as he sadly leaves.

In "Dead Roses" White combines the decadence of Greece with the sterility of respectable Australia. Anthea Scudmore, a forerunner of Theodora Goodman of *The Aunt's Story*, is a wealthy Australian widow traveling in Greece. There she is eventually rebuffed by a former admirer also visiting Greece. She is also insulted and threatened by a beautiful young Athenian. That night the Australian woman, who is so sterile that most flowers die on her, dreams neither of the young Greek nor of her former admirer but rather of the latter's wife, who had been wearing "stained leopard-skin matador pants" (66). The story is heavy with Freudian symbols and itself ends in a dying fall—as dead as the dead roses Anthea had found in the home of her impotent husband on her wedding night.

The Australian stories in the collection often satirize generalizations that begin "We Australians," but with a difference from the "We Greeks" philosophers. There is less poignancy in the Australians, with whom White is less patient than he is with babbling Greeks. In "Miss Slattery and her Demon Lover" an Australian lady objects strenuously when she hears her country reduced to "nossing" by her Hungarian lover. She counters at once with, "We Australians are not all that uncivilized. Not in 1961" (200). Miss Slattery, however, is not taken very seriously by Tibby Szabo, her masochistic, rich, and fat Hungarian lover, until she threatens to leave him. When Szabo asks her if she is "ze Defel perheps?" she answers: "We Australians are not all that unnatural" (215).

In "A Cheery Soul" a self-righteous husband and wife argue themselves into sharing their home with an unfortunate woman, a Miss Docker. When the arrangement soon turns into a domestic disaster, the "cheery soul" is transferred to a respectable institution for impecunious aged men and women. There her cheeriness moves from nuisance to menace when she challenges the minister in church, destroying his sermon and literally striking him down so that the minister's wife accuses her of having killed not only her husband but perhaps also her God. The effect of such blasphemy is devastating, as White well knew, and he later developed this story into a drama.

Reasonable people often insist on being considered both civilized and normal and are easily satirized because no one is ever quite reasonable except in his own opinion. When the hero of the story "Clay" asks his mother why she named him Clay, he receives a reasonable answer: his mother had been interested in making pottery. There is little else in the sketch, but it makes a sharp point economically. In another short piece, "The Letters," a mother-dominated son finally tries to make love to his mother. White suggests that the son's violent behavior was programmed by his mother's devotion to him. The incest episode yields to an anticlimax. Instructed as a child never to read other people's letters, the son finally stops reading even those addressed to him!

In the most ambitious story in the collection, "Down at the Dump," a boy-man and girl-woman meet at the line between the dump and the cemetery, having been brought to the dump and the cemetery respectively by their parents. The boy's family are "doing the dump"—which means scavenging. The girl's parents are burying a relative, Daise, a woman of easy virtue. It is clear that she is also one of the *illuminati* when at the cemetery her spirit speaks of love.

Although the meeting between the youths is contrived, the effect crescendoes before the quiet ending as the potential lovers return home with their respective parents, passing one another on the road: "They lowered their eyes, as if they had seen enough for the present, and wished to cherish what they knew" (308).

Big questions are asked of Destiny and Accident in the story called "Willy-Wagtails by Moonlight" via a slip in the making of a tape of the song of a bird. A respectable husband, while recording the Willy-Wagtail, also inadvertently records the sounds of his adultery with his secretary. Only a visiting couple, however, hear that part of the tape, the unfaithful husband and the betrayed wife being destined accidentally to be out of the room. This trivial and bitter story is characteristic of the "black in White." Accidents are the only miracles.

THE COCKATOOS

The Cockatoos, White's second collection of stories, appeared in 1975.[5] It contains six substantial pieces of short fiction which testify to the writer's growing maturity. Less gimmicky than several of the stories in *The Burnt Ones,* these later narratives reflect the author's concern for ways in which desperate human beings confront the odds against them. Here a few of them are allowed to find a kind of salvation outside churches, or even in the improper use of a church as a place of assignation. White's secular offerings include a cup of coffee, a handful of rice, a glimpse of cockatoos or peacocks, sunsets, and an old man's urine.

In "The Night the Prowler" an old man, far into his dying, explains to a young woman that there are only two goods: to piss easily and to shit smoothly. And so when he urinates over himself as the woman holds his hand, the woman feels a momentary grace as "she continued up the hill to report the death of an old man she had discovered a few moments before, but knew as intimately as she knew herself, in solitariness, in desolation, as well as in what would seem to be the dizzy course of perpetual becoming" (168).

Evelyn Bannister, the recipient of this unusual grace, is just nineteen years old on the eventful night in which she encounters a prowler in her home. The assumption that she is raped and otherwise mistreated by the prowler is the invention of her parents and neighbors, who need to be protected from the truth that Evelyn frightens the prowler more than he frightens her. After drinking and smoking in his presence, she sends him away, disgusted by his unimaginative timidity.

Soon thereafter, using her "rape" as an excuse, Evelyn cancels her engagement to a nice young man, who is relieved. Evelyn then begins to break into houses in the neighborhood herself, not to steal or rape but to extend her freedom. In the final, good-Samaritan scene she embraces a repulsive derelict. He dies in her arms while offering her his urine.

In "Sicilian Vespers" White again challenges convention and Christian morality. The piece is a carefully dramatized tale about a failure of faith between persons who rely too heavily on rationalism and humanism. Ivy and Charles Simpson represent those Australians who accept being Australian without either glorifying colonialism or hating other colonials, such as Americans. The Simpsons are genuinely kind, honest, intelligent, and well enough off to travel. Abroad, they tolerate foreign eccentricities they would not dream of accepting at home. In Sicily their planned itinerary becomes an empty time because of Charles's almost incapacitating toothache.

During the pause the Simpsons make friends with the Clark

Shacklocks, a rich American couple who seem a bit vulgar but kind. Clark *may* be Roman Catholic but the Simpsons are not sure. His wife Imelda certainly seems to be a Christian Scientist. As the relationship between the couples begins to get complicated, Ivy Simpson suddenly, against her better judgment, allows herself to be possessed one evening by Clark in the Duomo at San Fabrizio during vespers. Imelda and Charles, meanwhile, wait patiently for their respective spouses in the lobby of the hotel. Imelda is reading an ironically appropriate Italian novel: *I Promessi Sposi.*

Upon her return, Ivy Simpson remains cool and lies. She later realizes she is still hungry for a religious experience, or rather, she tells herself, at least for religious words. She had always respected the word "*Godhead:* as a mere word leaping at her from off the printed page, it made her turn over quickly, to escape something far beyond what Charles and she had agreed to find acceptable" (230).

In "A Woman's Hand" Clem Dowson tries to explain to his friend, Harold Fazackerly, why he and his wife have separated:

> "My God," Dowson was gasping and mouthing, "one day, Harold, when we meet—in different circumstances—I must try to tell you all I've experienced." He was speaking from behind closed eyes. "That was the trouble between us. Between myself and that woman. We had lived at the same level. It was too great a shock to discover there was someone who could read your thoughts." (76)

There is no chance, however, for the two men to meet "in different circumstances," for that night Clem is killed by a bus whose wheels he makes no attempt to avoid. Harold is left friendless and confused, realizing he has missed something. His need, however, has not been defined so there is no way of satisfying it. Also, Harold's wife, despite her good intentions, cannot understand either her husband's need or that of his friend. It was she who was originally responsible for adding "a woman's hand" to bachelor Clem's house overlooking the sea. The woman she paired with Clem, however, ends in a psychiatric hospital: she had heard the sunset shriek "with the throats of peacocks" (70). The moral is a bitter one: it is dangerous to hear the sunset shriek.

In the title story of the collection, "The Cockatoos," a Mrs. Davoren and her husband are as alienated from one another as possible until the cockatoos arrive. They have not exchanged spoken words for years. When necessary, they communicate via pencil and pad. But when they see the spectacular cockatoos, the Davorens begin to speak to one another again—about the birds, of course—and even celebrate their reunion in bed. Their joy is short-lived, however. One day a neighbor shoots two of the birds, and in the ensuing struggle for the gun Mr. Davoren is killed. But that is not all that happens.

When a neighbor boy, Tim Goodenough, finds the last of the cockatoos, a cripple, he kills it and cuts off the bird's crest as a trophy to mark his victory. Cockatoos can bring joy to those who love them but the price is high.

The two most ambitious stories in the collection are "Five-Twenty" and "The Full Belly," each of which celebrates a secular communion and its terrifying inadequacy: a cup of coffee that is never served and a handful of rice that degrades decent people. In the former story a childless, elderly couple spend their days sitting on a porch watching the traffic pass on the highway. Royal and Ellen Natwick are dependent on the regularity in the lives of others, particularly upon a man in a Holden who drives by at five-twenty every evening. He is a flat-headed, unusual looking fellow. They have found him memorable and essential. If he occasionally misses his "five-twenty" passing, the Natwicks are upset. Their clock has betrayed them: the universe is not orderly after all.

When Royal Natwick dies quietly, Ella is left "with his hand, already set, in her own. They hadn't spoken except about whether she had put out the garbage" (184). Ella accepts widowhood and takes the pills the doctor prescribes. As far as she can, she begins to relate to her "things," among which the man in the Holden is still real. Then one day he stops and asks to use the phone.

Excited, unable to speak clearly, she babbles in a "new language." He is not upset. He holds her in his arms. She responds, watching "the world of his mouth"—he has a hare lip—"struggling to open." At this moment of recognition Ella kisses him "as though she might never succeed in healing all the wounds they had ever suffered" (190). He promises to return the next day for a cup of coffee. In the meantime Ella learns how to make coffee, having had previous experience with tea only. This communion cup will contain a brew new to her.

When five-twenty comes and passes without him, Ella fears the worst. There is a bad wreck up the road. Has he perhaps been killed? He finally appears: he is late because he is ill. The symptoms indicate angina, with pains up and down his left arm. Ella vows to save him. In fact, however, in her eagerness she embraces him too forcefully and kills him "by loving too deep, and too adulterously" (196). The author's verdict is ruthless: Ella's worldly reward for all that patient watching was only a chance at adultery, no more and no less than a chance, and she lost. The coffee was never served.

The rice becomes moot in the story "The Full Belly," which returns to the Athenian scene. During the occupation of Greece, Athenians were severely tested not only by hunger but also by a patriotism that required strict resistance to collaboration. Two proud and elderly spinster sisters, Maro and Pronoë, have long ago bartered away all their valuable possessions for food but still refuse to collab-orate with the prosperous Germans who occupy the city. The older sister, Maro, begins to starve herself to death in order to save food for others in the family. Her nephew, Costa, who is a talented music student and the orphaned son of a former President of Greece, decides to sell himself for food.

Costa first refuses the advances of a neighbor woman who would pay him in eggs. He then encounters a German soldier in one of the side streets of Athens who offers him meat in exchange for what Costa knows he has already done but this time chooses to refuse. Not much later, driven by hunger for meat, he changes his mind and searches for the soldier, who, however, has disappeared. Rushing home because he remembers a dish of rice left next to dying Aunt Maro's bedside, he finds Aunt Pronoë already there and gorging herself on the few grains of rice. They struggle for the food, breaking the dish in the contest. After Pronoë leaves in disgust, Costa kneels and picks up bits of rice mixed with bits of carpet and stuffs them into his mouth. When his dying aunt sees him, she says: "Eat, poor souls. . . . Fill your stomachs, children." Then she adds, before she dies: "I only pray you'll know how to forgive each other" (118). After such knowledge, what forgiveness?

The extent to which one can accept White's specifications for and significance of the "course of perpetual becoming," which for him is obviously a good—if not the only good—in living, correlates with the degrees of praise allowed these stories. The alleged epi-phanies are often blurred. Grace is neither easily won nor freely bestowed by either writer or reader. Characters behaving decently in a godless universe are sometimes seen as foolish. What price courage if there is no reward here or in an afterlife? Certainly White allows little probability of judgment days that will rectify and punish fairly.

The Cockatoos is condemned as "a strong anti-marriage tract" by a woman obviously upset about the failure of marital bonds in the stories to restrain immorality. The same critic prefers White's novels, concluding that "the short story does not offer White the space he needs for his greatest strength, the portrayal of a character's fantasy."[6] Eudora Welty, however, praises White's stories, noting that "they go off like cannons fired over some popular, scenic river—depth charges to bring up the drowned bodies."[7] Brian Kiernan compares White's stories favorably with those of Hal Porter, finding that "White's style has become more muted over the years, more an instrument than a self-regarding end." Unlike Porter, however, "White is concerned to engage life, and in the better stories, this takes the form of his emphatically imagining how life might be experienced by others."[8]

Notes

1. See Vincent Buckley, "Towards an Australian Literature," in *Twentieth Century Australian Literary Criticism*, ed. Graham Johnston (Melbourne: Oxford University Press, 1962), pp. 75–85.

2. A. A. Phillips, *Henry Lawson* (New York: Twayne Publishers, 1970), p. 138.

3. G. A. Wilkes and J. C. Reid, *The Literatures of the British Commonwealth: Australia and New Zealand*, ed. A. L. McLeod (University Park, Penn.: Pennsylvania State University Press, 1970), p. 120.

4. All references here are to *The Burnt Ones* (New York: Viking, 1964); page references cited in the text in parentheses.

5. All references here are to *The Cockatoos* (New York: Viking, 1975); page references cited in the text in parentheses.

6. Rose Marie Beston, "More Burnt Ones: Patrick White's *The Cockatoos*," *World Literature Written in English* 14, no. 2 (1975): 520.

7. Eudora Welty, "Patrick White's *The Cockatoos*," in *The Eye of the Story* (New York: Random House, 1978), p. 264.

8. Brian Kiernan, "Short Story Chronicle," *Meanjin Quarterly* 34, no. 1 (1975): 37.

Patrick White's Style
Harry Heseltine*

The debate over the nature and worth of Patrick White's achievement has by now crystallized into a number of clear issues: foremost among these is the question of his style. Ever since Alec Hope's notorious dismissal of *The Tree of Man* as "illiterate verbal sludge" (*Sydney Morning Herald*, 16 June 1956), White's style has been one of the chief weapons in the armoury of his detractors. David Martin, for instance, is quite blunt in his assessment of its function:

> The whole trouble is that [White's] kind of novel demands too much intuition of readers, almost an act of faith. Why should they be asked to make it? . . . To get around the difficulty Mr. White has adopted a peculiar style. . . . It is, let us say it boldly, first and foremost an interest-whipping device. It covers a hole. . . . *Voss* does not create a new style, only a new muddle. (*Meanjin*, 1959, No. 1.)

In a more recent *Meanjin* (1962, No. 1) an Englishman, Peter Wood, has questioned whether White's style is the vehicle so much of moral complexity as of moral snobbery. Writing in the Autumn 1962 issue of *Overland*, David Bradley has voiced the opinion that "the further his search for a style goes, the more divided against themselves his novels seem to become."

Even critics favourable to White have exhibited some uneasiness

* Reprinted from *Quadrant* 7 (Winter 1963): 61–74; courtesy of H. P. Heseltine.

in dealing with his idiosyncracies of manner. H. J. Oliver concluded his more than sympathetic *Southerly* review of *Voss* with the remark that "it must be said again, therefore, that Mr. White does not give thought *enough* to his prose style" (*Southerly*, 1958, No. 1). Or R. F. Brissenden, noting White's curious dislocations of syntax, confesses that he "cannot suggest why he should choose to use words in this way" (*Meanjin*, 1959, No. 4). In general, those who discover greatness in White's fiction, discover it in spite of, rather than because of, his style. I would like to propose the view that, whether we like it or not, White's style is neither a cover over a hole nor an impediment in the way of the full display of his powers. It is in fact a direct function of his deepest response to life. Whoever would come to grips with the themes of White's fiction can do so only through the words in which they are embodied.

If the great writer is a man obsessed by the images which constitute his sensibility, then Patrick White can make a clear claim to being a great writer. He is also a lucky one. For the range of images to which he responds with depth and urgency seems to be rather wider than that granted to most novelists. From his very earliest work, there has been established in White's work a large fund of recurring interests which force their way into his prose as characters, situations, images. It is this fund of images, metaphors, verbal motifs, which is at the basis, not only of his sensibility, but of his style. White's whole career can be seen as the progressive explication of the materials of his sensibility into the patterned and evaluated elements of his mature style. In bringing the basic stimuli of his imagination more and more into the foreground of his judging mind, White has developed a rich vocabulary of feeling, emotion, and belief, an interlocking and consistent pattern of image and symbol.

Happy Valley, White's first novel, we can see with the wisdom of hindsight, laid out much of that store of situation and image which White has subsequently moulded into the substance of what he has to say. One of the early scenes of the novel involves Chuffy Chalmers, a simple-minded young man, driving the newcomer Clem Hagan into Happy Valley. Chuffy plays a small but significant role in the story, and White writes about him well. Apparently he likes to write about the simple-minded, for he has written about them frequently since *Happy Valley*: Bub Quigley in *The Tree of Man*, Harry Robarts in *Voss*, Mary Hare in *Riders in the Chariot*, whom her father "supposed to be simple" (p. 102). But as each figure has successively taken shape in White's imagination, he has sought more and more to know the meaning, the implications, of these images so native to his fiction. Chuffy Chalmers is just simple-minded; Bub Quigley is simple-minded, and somehow good, better than the average run of men; Harry Robarts is good, and faithful unto death; Mary Hare is privileged to see the chariot.

The feeble-minded is not the only kind of character first revealed in *Happy Valley* and examined in later books. Alys Browne, the lonely, sensitive music teacher, provided White with an image of personality which has fascinated him ever since. There is in his work a long line of isolated women, deprived for the most part of active participation in the physical world, but deriving interest in White's eyes from their pursuit of the inner life. Theodora Goodman of *The Aunt's Story* is the prototype. She is close kin to Mary Hare, more distantly related to Laura Trevelyan. In creating such characters, White has moved from direct delight in rendering this kind of feminine sensibility for its own sake to an inspection of its possibilities and values. In so doing he has arrived at one of his central themes—the infinite possibilities of the single personality. The process can be seen most clearly at work in *The Aunt's Story*, where image moves to abstraction in the repeated phrase, "our several lives."

Those who seek freedom of spirit through the cultivation of more than one of their several lives are likely to appear a little odd, to say the least, to outsiders. And insanity is a mode of behaviour which has always held interest for White. It is possible, for instance, to read *The Aunt's Story* as a straight-out account of the disintegration of the mind of Theodora Goodman, a brilliant virtuoso performance on the motif of madness. But *The Aunt's Story* is not only that. If one of its unifying images is that of the mirror (life seen from all angles and in all its fragmenting facets), one of its key abstractions is freedom. There can be no doubt that by the end of the novel White has made a connection between the image and the abstraction; the fragmentation of insanity leads to liberation of the personality. Some of the major images which thrust themselves out of White's sensibility have been converted into an enduring concept of the mind. It is not surprising, therefore, that the hero of *Voss* and all four main characters of *Riders in the Chariot*, although they seem mad to outsiders, are shown by their privileged interpreter to enjoy a special kind of freedom and wisdom. The sanity of madness, the reasonableness of unreason, have come to be among the central concerns of White's later novels. "The purposes of God," he wrote in *The Tree of Man*, "are made clear to some old women, and nuns, and idiots."

The inner life, pushed beyond the borders of commonsense, will yield, if nothing else, intensity of experience. Yet there are other images of intense living which have always fascinated Patrick White, even if he has found them sometimes uninviting. From the outset of his career he has been drawn to the depiction of certain family relationships—notably between mother and son, or father and daughter. The father-daughter relation is often tentative, incomplete, but potentially good. There is Theodora Goodman, for instance, and her failure of a father; or Mary Hare and the fantastic Norbert. Even one thinks of the fumbling attempts at warmth between Mr. Furlow and his daughter Sidney in *Happy Valley*. Mothers, though quite as numerous in White's pages as fathers, come off much less happily. From Mrs. Furlow, through Mrs. Goodman and the widows Mrs. Flack and Mrs. Jolley, to the fiendish Mrs. Polkinghorne of "The Letters," middle-aged matrons are perhaps the most savagely portrayed class in the whole range of White's characters.

But whether they be simpleton or saint, fiend or fool, White early developed a quite personal technique for dealing with the characters who people his books. Once their physical appearance is set, he tends to render their states of mind, their relations with others, through a very specialized set of images. We come to the inner lives of his characters as much through their hands, their skin, their breathing, as through anything else. In White's novels, the image of a pair of hands (and the image occurs with extraordinary frequency) is never just that; it is always some kind of comment on their owner. In *The Aunt's Story*, for instance, during Theodora's crucial conversation with the Greek musician, Moraïtis, White records that "Theodora looked at his thinking hands." There could be no more certain indication of the musician's importance or of the reality of his rapport with Theodora. Later, at the critical moment in Part II when the nautilus shell is dropped and broken, there is definitive evidence of crisis in the image which is introduced into the prose: "And the nautilus became a desperate thing of hands. Theodora heard the crack of bones. Hands were knotting the air. Then, hands were hands."

The same pattern of imagery is continued in all of White's other books. Early in *The Tree of Man*, what is apparently a description of Stan Parker's hands becomes in fact a precise indication of his community status: "His hands, with scabs on the knuckles, were respected as they received change." Nor is it any accident that Bub Quigley has "innocent hands," or that late in his life Stan's become "bony." Or, at a meeting with some aborigines in *Voss*, the German makes one of his rare attractive gestures—attractive not only by virtue of its traditional significance but because it has all the force of White's accumulated imagery behind it:

> . . . Now he approached the black whose instincts had rejected
> Turner's offer, and, holding out his hand, said stiffly:
> "Here is my hand in friendship."

Characteristically, then, the image of human hands in White's work offers a clue to the human being. Equally, images of skin (which also abound in White's prose) provide the medium by which he discusses a man's capacity for personal relationships. The quality of an individual's skin is a fair sign of his capacity to make contact with others. The close companionship of Stan Parker with his mates, as they row over the waters of the flood, is indicated in a sentence like this: "As they rowed under the liquid trees the sound of leaves, swishing, dipping into his wet skin, was closer to him." Or any experienced reader of Patrick White should be able immediately to predict Blue as the chief danger in *Riders in the Chariot* from a single item in the very first description of him: "skin—dry and scabby, wherever it was not drawn too tight and shiny, giving an impression of postage stamps." It is quite literally through the touch of skin that a man makes contact with others. But when White's characters seek to withdraw into their essential selves, he abandons images of hands, or skin, or flesh, in favour of the sparer images of bones and skull. When the essential self seeks communion with another, there must be more than a touch of flesh, there must be a mingling of breath. Whenever White draws attention to the act of breathing, his characters are close to revealing the inmost quality of their souls. Hence the apparently ludicrous opening of *Voss:* " 'There is a man here, miss, asking for your uncle,' said Rose. And stood breathing." What the second sentence in fact conveys is that with the arrival of Voss something important has been set in motion, that Rose Portion has an inner self of some importance, and that she is prepared to reveal it to Laura.

Through a set of physical images, then, White has developed a very precise means of dealing with the intangibles of human behaviour. But these by no means exhaust his stylistic apparatus. He has also explicated from the basic elements of his sensibility a whole range of natural, non-human images. *Happy Valley* opens with a hawk swinging high over the landscape—a hawk which is an important structural device in the novel. It will reappear as the red-eyed hawk shot down by Theodora in *The Aunt's Story,* converted into a means of conveying theme. And the number of birds (of many kinds) which sweep through the pages of White's books is quite remarkable. It is not often that they are there for their own sake. The advent of wings almost invariably coincides with scenes in which human beings aspire to a state of existence beyond the normal; or the death of a bird may be the emotional accompaniment to a scene which witnesses the defeat or constriction of an individual soul. Thus magpies carol joyfully in the full summertime of the Parkers' lives. "The passionate cries of birds exploded wonderfully overhead" during one of the brief harmonious episodes of Voss's expedition. But quite as important as real birds are the images of flying, of feathers, of soft down, or of beaks, which are diffused through nearly all White's major scenes of human aspiration: a use of imagery at its most intense in *Riders in the Chariot,* where it evokes the concept of the birds of the spirit, of the flight of the human being towards spiritual illumination.

At a lower level, White is just as attracted to the beasts of the field. He discovered the humble cow as early as *Happy Valley.* A moment of peace is recorded in what may have been a chance image: "Down the slope Schmidt's cows were arriving to be milked, walking heavy with shadow into the curve of the hill." Ever since, cows have been for White the emotional correlative of the slow-moving peace his characters can sometimes attain. Indeed, they are elevated into a major thematic symbol in *The Tree of Man.* At their most endearing moments, Stan and Amy Parker are likely to be found, if not walking through their cabbage patch, then down at the bails milking their cows. But towards the end of his life Stan seeks to move beyond his inarticulate communion with Amy. His spiritual quest is ushered in by a further image from the animal kingdom which White had established for this purpose as early as *The Aunt's Story.* Stan "was sitting in the meantime. . . . And ants came out across the ground." The appearance of those ants is a precise indication that Stan is about to be vouchsafed some perception beyond the ordinary. The ant image is introduced into *The Aunt's Story* through the cruel figure of Lieselotte: " 'At your age you should take care,' said Lieselotte, quietly squeezing the head off an ant." Later, as Theodora moves towards her final madness, she replies to Mrs. Johnson's suggestion that there will be a war: "Probably, unless God is kinder to the ants." The connection between these tiny insects and divine knowledge, so obscurely suggested in this remark, is made explicit in *The Tree of Man:* not, at first, through Stan Parker, but through Mr. Gage, the postmistress's retiring husband, who is later discovered to have been a genius. Mr. Gage's first significant appearance in the novel is when he is discovered by Amy Parker staring at an ant, as though in its small body he would find the answer to the whole of life. It should have been easy to foresee Mary Hare's concern for beetles, her tunnelling affinity with the natural world.

It is not even in animals that Stan Parker finds his God: it is in a gob of spittle. In making such a discovery he is merely acting out the belief that White has expressed earlier in *The Tree of Man,* that "there is a mysticism of objects." That statement of belief simply made explicit the value he had already sensed in another set of images. In the opening of *The Living and the Dead,* Elyot Standish returns to the loneliness of his empty house and finds comfort in contemplating some bread and cheese. "There was something solid, soothing about the yellow wedge. Only to look at this. He was not hungry." By the time he came to write *The Aunt's Story,* White had become so imbued with the intense actuality (or, he might say, the essential honesty) of objects that he could write "There is perhaps no more complete a reality than a chair and a table,'' and make of these humble articles of kitchen furniture two of the major unifying symbols of the entire novel. In all his works, simple things of this order have provided a large part of his vocabulary for dealing with moral virtue and a sense of actuality. One thinks of Rose Portion in *Voss,* whose solid presence derives from her association with the humble accoutrements of the kitchen; or of the simple beauty of Himmelfarb's seder table. Conversely, there can be no greater condemnation of Mrs. Jolley and Mrs. Flack than their irreparably bad taste in interior decoration, or the phrase by which they are repeatedly described: they are the "plastic ladies"—and the phrase condemns them out of hand.

Inanimate objects may console and soothe by the solidity of their presence, but White is much more likely to see the large processes of life in terms of images drawn from the natural world. A country-bred Australian, he might have been expected to evince a continuing interest in landscape—from the harsh portrait of the Snowy country in *Happy Valley* to the searing interior depicted in *Voss.* It would have been less easy to predict the specific uses to which White would put some of the images yielded up by the land. An interest in trees, for instance, seems to be a native element in White's sensibility. And that element has developed in the regular pattern of his imagery. It has remained at one level simply a part of the mechanism of creation, evoking some of his richest prose. At another level, it has been brought into the foreground of the style and becomes available as a vehicle for some of White's important thinking and imagining. Thus, there does not appear to be any necessary structural or thematic reason why, in *The Living and the Dead,* one of Elyot Standish's formative experiences should have taken place in a mulberry tree. But the success of the scene provided White with a stylistic device which he was to exploit most notably in *The Tree of Man,* wherein trees become a symbol for life itself. Subsequently, the varying fortunes of Voss and his party can almost be measured in terms of the descriptions of the trees that they pass. Or a willow tree provides a bower of quietness within the seclusion of which Himmelfarb can reveal to Miss Hare all the horrors of his past life. More often, perhaps, the most intense revelations of soul to soul take place within the context of a more formalized nature—a garden. The clearest example of this conjunction of major experience and specific location is the crucial scene between Laura and the German in Chapter 4 of *Voss.* And it is generally true of White's fiction that any scene set in a garden is likely to be of especial importance. The implications of the image are most thoroughly worked out in Part II of *The Aunt's Story,* which is, in fact, entitled *Jardin Exotique.*

Before Voss's departure from Sydney, he has two significant

encounters with Laura—one in the garden of the Bonner home, the other by the water, during the picnic at Potts Point. In neither case is the setting accidental. If White tends to situate his major dramatic encounters in gardens, water is usually the concomitant of life moving successfully along its natural paths. There is peace for Himmelfarb in the green waters of the river flowing alongside the Brighta Bicycle Lamp factory. The Parkers find the fullness of their ordinary lives in the time of the floods. Voss undergoes a kind of spiritual baptism in the river crossing of Chapter 10 of *Voss*. Just as important as scenes like these is the pervasive water imagery through which White so often renders the successful moments of his characters' lives. "Lives," Amy Parker realizes at one point in *The Tree of Man*, "can only touch, they do not join." But there are at least moments when two lives seem to flow together into a single stream of being. And Patrick White frequently indicates such moments by the kind of imagery I have had to resort to myself. As Theodora Goodman spoke to Moraïtis at Huntly Clarkson's dinner table, "she swam through the sea of roses towards that other Ithaca." Later, as she concludes a chance meeting with Pearl, once her servant, now a prostitute, "her veins ebbed, which had flowed before."

Water imagery points to the successful moments of human life within the dimension of time. It is fire which burns through the flesh to the enduring spirit; and images of fire nearly always accompany the most intense ordeals in the lives of White's characters. In many instances, the images are realized as literal flames; houses burn down with remarkable regularity in White's fiction (in *The Aunt's Story*, *The Tree of Man*, and *Riders in the Chariot*), and the conflagrations always are intimately associated with some crisis of soul. But even when White's men and women are not subjected to the ordeal of fire, their inmost selves sometimes stand revealed. Then they are seen as statuary, as sculptured stone. Nearly all of White's characters are, at some stage or other, revealed for what they are in terms of shaped stone or bronze.

Nor is sculpture the only art that White has plundered to bring back riches to his own. From the creation of Alys Browne in *Happy Valley* he has repeatedly introduced music as a significant element in his work. It sometimes serves, for instance, as a means of evaluating character: nearly all his important figures are tested by their attendance at a concert or response to a piece of music or performance on an instrument. It may be diffused into a pervasive pattern of metaphor. It may be projected into the social world. Some of White's most joyful social gatherings are dances. Dances, too, are events when personal encounters of some moment may take place. There is, for instance, the scene between Sidney Furlow and Clem Hagan at the Race Week Ball in *Happy Valley*. There is the ball in *Voss* to celebrate

Belle Bonner's wedding—one of the very few social occasions when Laura can be both happy and true to herself. There is the dance at Meroë in Part I of *The Aunt's Story* when Theodora finds a similar moment of inner release. It is at a dance that Stan meets Amy, his future wife. As usual, the possibilities of the images are made more and more explicit as White advances in his art. So that in *Riders in the Chariot* dancing had become more than a verbal or actual accompaniment to momentary joy; it is a special technique for achieving ecstasy or some awful state outside the bounds of normal experience. There is the ghastly parody of a dance as Miss Hare and Mrs. Jolley pivot through the halls of Xanadu and towards Miss Hare's realization of the evil in Mrs. Jolley, the widow's perception that she is employed by a mystic. One of the very last glimpses of Xanadu reveals a young labourer dancing on its ruins, dancing himself briefly into a new plane of existence.

Music and dancing, then, have provided White with some significant items in the furniture of his imagination. But painting plays a more important role than either. The serious desire to paint is the unfailing mark of the sensitive man. Talent in the art can be an indication of genius: Mr. Gage and Alf Dubbo are both shown as artistic geniuses by virtue of their ability to capture their vision in paint. And those visions, in themselves, are exceptional. Painting, like dancing and music, can open up a path to the infinite. White's affinity with the painter is not exhausted by the creation of a number of artists within the pages of his novels. His prose has no more prevailing set of images than those of colour. White is dominant in *Happy Valley;* yellow in *The Aunt's Story;* green in much of *The Tree of Man;* red and black in *Riders in the Chariot.* Generally speaking, grey is the colour of listlessness and mediocrity. Yellow occurs when life is stripped down to its essentials. In *Riders in the Chariot* mauve is peculiarly the colour of the nasty bourgeoisie; red, black, and gold the colours which flash before those privileged to see, by glimpses, a vision of the chariot. Of all the painter's attributes that White displays in his prose, the most constant is his awareness of the various qualities of light. It would be possible to construct from within the canon of his novels a whole anthology of the changing light of day from dawn to dusk, in all seasons, and in all circumstances. All of his major scenes are bathed in a light which, like all his other images, is a perfectly calculated emotional accompaniment to, and comment on, the action which is being played out.

It is possible, thus, to advance the proposition that by the time he wrote *The Aunt's Story* White had pretty thoroughly developed those elements of his style which give it its characteristic emotional attitudes, tone, and texture. From an uncommonly fecund sensibility he had extrapolated certain interlocking images, metaphors, and symbols, which provided him with a vocabulary capable of great subtlety in dealing with personal relationships and inner states of mind. Further, in transforming the raw materials of his imagination into the images of his art he had subjected them to sufficient scrutiny to enable them to become, on occasion, tools of judgment as well as vehicles of feeling. If we combined the elements of this preparation with the notion of a syntax calculated to render, before all else, streams of individual consciousness, we might arrive at a fairly accurate account of White's style up to this point in his career. White's early novels, in other words, are in the main uncommitted novels of sensibility. Dr. Brissenden makes the point, perhaps over-forcibly, with respect to *The Living and the Dead.* He describes that novel as "so close to Virginia Woolf in theme, structure and style that in places it reads almost like a parody" (*Meanjin,* 1959, No. 4).

He goes on to add, however, that "*The Aunt's Story* is a most unusual novel," that it "would be enough to establish Patrick White as a distinctive and more than merely competent writer." Indeed, *The Aunt's Story* does represent a turning point in White's career as a novelist. It is not really until the novel after *The Aunt's Story,* until *The Tree of Man,* that there emerges what has since established itself as White's characteristic, mature style. That style has been exhibited consistently ever since. The new features of the style of *The Tree of Man* were developed in response to some significant new attitudes which were becoming apparent in *The Aunt's Story.* Instead of saying that *The Aunt's Story* stands between the early and the late work, it might equally well be said that it stands between the novels of noncommitment and the novels of commitment. *Happy Valley* and *The Living and the Dead* had rendered the interweaving patterns of the lives of a number of characters in two widely disparate communities— Happy Valley and London. But they had rendered, largely without judging. White had given his account of the several lives of his several characters, without necessarily finding much to choose between them. Indeed, the milieu of *The Living and the Dead* is one of nihilism and intellectual despair, a world devoid of value. To be sure, both books had been prefaced with epigraphs which indicate a certain moral worth in pain and suffering. But their worth seems to lie chiefly in inculcating a stoic fortitude in the face of a meaningless world. Such at least is the impression conveyed by Oliver Halliday, the principal character of *Happy Valley,* in his letter to Alys Browne near the close of the book: "Man hasn't much say in the matter, I know. He's a feeble creature dictated to by whatever you like, we'll call it an irrational force. But he must offer some opposition to this if he's to keep his own respect."

This is scarcely a hopeful view of the human condition, nor perhaps one that might have been expected in Patrick White from a reading of his later work. Nevertheless, the attitudes embodied in *Riders in the Chariot* do, I believe, develop directly out of those in *Happy Valley* and *The Living and the Dead,* and in large measure because of White's continuing preoccupation with the implications of his imagery. Starting out from a concern with individual states of mind and the multiplex possibilities of the individual life, White was led to a belief in the superiority of the inner life of sensibility, particularly that kind of inner life which makes actual our fragmented potentialities, i.e., madness. By the time he came to *The Aunt's Story,* White pretty clearly had more than an interest in Theodora's insanity; he assigned to it a special kind of value. Theodora had wisdom and knowledge unavailable to those who limit themselves to common sense. The next step is to seek for the source of the superior knowledge of madness. White's answer is "intuition," or even "illumination." For such a view to make any kind of sense, it requires that man have a soul and that there be a God, or at least some kind of divine force, to make the intuition and illumination possible. I do not know what, as a man, Patrick White now believes, or what he believed before he wrote *The Tree of Man;* but that is his first novel to accept, as an axiom, the duality of man's nature and the existence of a divine spirit. Such a belief, it seems to me, is the only possible next step after *The Aunt's Story;* while *The Aunt's Story* was the only possible result of White's initial explication of his sensibility into image, metaphor, and situation.

The interplay of style and theme since *The Aunt's Story* has been no less intimate than before. Nothing of what had already been gained has been abandoned. A literal belief in the soul can make the inner life only more, not less, important to the novelist. The developments in White's style since *The Aunt's Story,* that is to say, have been designed not to countermand what had already been achieved but to add to it, to incorporate the new items of White's belief into the basic structure and texture of his writing.

Characteristic of this further refinement of his style has been the exploitation of a device which Marjorie Barnard noted in her article, "The Four Novels of Patrick White" (*Meanjin,* 1956, No. 2). "*The Living and the Dead,*" she wrote, "is drenched in the pathetic fallacy." In the later books this has ceased to be merely a special technique for instilling feeling into a situation; it has become almost a staple of White's style. When a literary procedure passes from the status of a device to that of a constant and definitive element of a style, it can only be considered as an article of faith. When, in *The Tree of Man* and *Voss,* White speaks constantly of "suave flesh"; when Stan Parker fills his mouth with "righteous potatoes"; when Amy sees that "peace fell into her bucket"; when Voss and Laura walk "over grass that was still kindly to their feet": when such statements occur over and over again in a novelist's work, they cannot be dismissed as rather coy attempts to create emotion. They are the linguistic embodiment of a belief that the world is dual, that it is composed of both spirit and matter, which, though separate, are capable of being fused the one into the other.

The same point can be made with equal justice of a construction which occurs with increasing frequency in *The Tree of Man* and after. Characteristic is the description of Himmelfarb's ruined house as "stripped by bombs and human resentment." Bombs are put in the same grammatical category as human resentment; the very syntax is put to the service of White's belief in the interplay of matter and spirit. It is constructions such as this and other idiosyncracies of White's syntax which have more than anything else caused uneasiness, even among White's admirers. Certainly, some of his sentences do exhibit an odd structure, at times even violate the canons of accepted grammar. But the violations are not haphazard; there is a pattern to the oddity of structure, and the pattern is directly germane to White's meaning. Thus, White's punctuation has always been eccentric. In the earlier books its purpose was that of any stream-of-consciousness writer—to indicate the continuity of our experience and the limitation of our perception. But at least since *The Tree of Man* its purpose seems to me to have been somewhat different. The punctuation now functions to enforce attention on the individual moment, to insist on its metaphysical significance; in short, to suggest that while experience may be continuous, some parts of it are more important than others. The punctuation, further, indicates that experience is not merely continuous but that it has causes and consequences. One of the most frequently recurring of White's incomplete sentences is the result-clause introduced by the conjunction "so"; as in *The Tree of Man:* "So that in the end there were the trees. The boy walking through them with his head drooping as he increased in stature. Putting out shoots of green thought. So that, in the end, there was no end."

It is worth noting that not only are there consequences in White's world, but that as often as not they are less logical than emotional; reason is not of prime value in these later works. It is worth noting, too, that White's syntax stresses possibilities as well as consequences. Himmelfarb and his young friend Jurgen Stauffer "could not wrestle enough on the beds of leaves" (*Riders,* p. 116). The syntax as well as the sentiment is typical—the spirit striving beyond the limits of flesh. Or one of White's most common syntactic patterns must be the conditional construction, real or hypothetical, as in *Voss:* "If the others barely listened, or were only mildly disgusted by his outburst, it was because each man was obsessed by the same prospect." Or in *The Tree of Man:* "If Amy Parker continued to sit, it is because the rose is rooted and impervious." Or in *Riders:* "If it had been evening, she might have done something with a fan—if she had had one." Even in recording particular situations or events, White's prose habitually indicates possibilities beyond the present moment.

White's later syntax imposes on events the relationships that his metaphysics requires. But nothing is more characteristic of his mature style than the projection of his themes beyond significant scenes and images into a number of deliberately abstracting words. The technique first appears in *The Aunt's Story*. That novel certainly has some important unifying images—mirrors, the hawk, ducks, the nautilus shell. But another of its key words is *freedom*. In the same way, the words *body* and *soul* first start to play a significant role in White's vocabulary in *The Tree of Man*. In *Voss* the key word is *suffering*. In *Riders in the Chariot*, the words *good* and *evil* make their first explicit appearance. This increasing explicitness has probably contributed to Patrick White's curious reception in Australia. *The Tree of Man* tells us that the man next door has a soul, and that is what makes him important. *Voss* tells us that arrogant maniacs are far more important than the man next door. *Riders in the Chariot* tells us that probably the only people who really count are those who see God in this life. These are hard things for Australians to accept. They are even harder when they are based on a religious sense which is neither softly pious nor necessarily Christian. John Douglas Pringle, writing in the *London Magazine* of November 1961, made a most perceptive comment when he said that "A hundred years ago he would have written great, long Shelleian poems." Today Patrick White has to write novels like *Riders in the Chariot*. We may in the long run reject them, but we cannot ignore them. And we cannot ignore them because White has so completely transformed his beliefs into the structure of art. It is my contention that that transformation is in large measure made possible by White's developed style. Gifted with an unusually rich sensibility, he has explicated its materials, stage by stage and through a responsive syntax, into a powerful set of images, a vocabulary of judging metaphor, a range of abstractions articulating belief. Every element of White's style works to explore and elucidate his themes. Like it or lump it, his style is the very linchpin of what he has to say.

From *The Articles and the Novelist*

Hilary Heltay°

[Editor's note: Until the point at which this extract of Heltay's essay begins, the author has been showing how White's use of articles (that is, *a* and *the*) and other frequently overlooked function words have thematic import in the fiction.]

. . . The next example again features an enumeration with variation of determiners, but is principally interesting for the change in "camera position" which is involved.

> Mrs. Godbold coughed, because she did not know what to answer, and followed the slippers of her new acquaintance, slit slat slit slat, down *a* passage, into *a* yellow light and *some* confusion. (*RC* 274)

Whereas in the previous examples the scene has been viewed from outside with the camera as it were scanning it from a fixed position beyond the frame of the set, here the camera is suddenly between the viewer and the objects, moving with the character Mrs. Godbold and creating the scene as it opens up in successive stages before her eyes. The process starts already with "the slippers of her new acquaintance," which itself represents a kind of segmentation of perception or division of the material into bands or shots. The syntax is largely responsible for this effect, the *of*-genitive allowing for a more sequential coming-into-view than the alternative "her new acquaintance's slippers," and allowing also for the part or the detail to precede the whole. And then the enumeration that follows features not objects as such, but rather successively registered sense perceptions as new aspects come into view. Thus a scene whose total communicative content might have been conveyed in the narrative statement that the two women suffered excruciating embarrassment when Mrs. Godbold fetched her husband from Mrs. Khalil's (" 'No one,' said the woman, 'never came for their husband. Never.' ") is given a highly visual (and aural) treatment such as could be translated directly into a film sequence.

It is this segmentation of perception and the dynamic filmic quality that it gives to a description that is illustrated in the next example. Amy Parker visits the O'Dowds after a long period without any contact. She registers various details of the farm-yard scene, familiar and at the same time newly unfamiliar because of the time that has passed, until her eye comes to rest on an activity that begins to

° Reprinted from *The Articles and the Novelist: Reference Conventions and Reader Manipulation in Patrick White's Creation of Fictional Worlds* (Tübingen, Germany: Gunter Narr, 1983), 74–78, 89–93; courtesy Gunter Narr Verlag.

compel her attention in the foreground: a fire is burning there and giving off unpleasant fumes. As a piece of information, this could no doubt be conveyed in any number of ways. The German translator goes for basic content and renders: "Das Feuer verbreitete einen schrecklichen Gestank" (*Baum von Mann*, 317). This is straightforward, flat narrative, with no contours, no dynamics. And now the actual English original:

> Now, in fact, there was *a* fire in the middle of the yard, or a sulky black heap of ash with smoke upon it, just rising and coiling, dirtily. There was *the* fire, and there was *a* stink. This reached out, and down the nostrils—there was no mistaking they were two pipes in the skull, exposed to unreasonable torture. (*TM* 285)

The difference between the flat wash of plain narrative statement and the dynamic, plastically contoured three-dimensionality of the English realization is almost entirely a matter of reference. What White has done, using the simplest means imaginable, has been to make a montage, to segment the information he wants to convey and deliver it as a sequence, of which each element develops logically from the previous one. The basic formal element is, with minimal narrative modification, an introducing speech act. The joints that articulate the elements of the sequence are the articles, whose camera-eye properties are demonstrated almost schematically here as they initiate a movement of attention *to* the new object (*a* fire), a holding of the focus *on* the object (*the* fire), then a move to the next, logically consequent perception (*a* stink).

We have a further example of how syntax can be manipulated to add an extra dimension to content in the next extract. The scene is from *The Tree of Man;* Amy Parker's first infidelity with the travelling salesman Leo is about to take place. I quote at length in order to establish the point of view:

> It was exciting and disturbing for her to reveal the intimacies of her house, but all the time she was remembering that he was repellent to her, with his reddish skin and red hair. The obscenity of his fingers too, with those brown stains.
> Then they were in the kitchen, which did have *an* amplitude, of *a* comparatively big old kitchen. The common but living furniture was pleasant to the hands. So the man rested his knuckles as a matter of course on the surface of the big worn table. . . . (*TM* 301)

White is using a favourite device here: an *of*-genitive construction introduced not with cataphoric *the*, which might be expected, but with an indefinite article. The effect of this is that the freshness, the immediacy of registered impressions is directly conveyed, resisting the distancing tendency of narrative. Looking for a linguistic explanation for this effect, we discover it in the presence of an underlying introducing speech act. In other words, what Leo thinks to himself ("It's quite *a* big kitchen!" or "What *an* unexpectedly big kitchen!") retains its directness in narrative through the agency of the unmodified indefinite article. At the same time, by foregrounding the indefinite article, the construction naturally segments perception, into first the registering of a sound, sight or smell, then the pin-pointing of its source. This effect is compounded in our example here by the punctuation, which suggests that a deletion might have been made: "an amplitude [the amplitude], of a comparatively big old kitchen." So what is conveyed is Leo's first impression, of amplitude, followed by his second, the comparability with other old kitchens once he has registered that this is indeed the kitchen. This dimension of successiveness, of different visual aspects of a scene making their impact in sequence, is lost in the German because it ignores the foregrounded indefinite article: "Dann standen sie in der Küche, die *die* Geräumigkeit *der* Küchen in alten Häusern hatte" (*BM* 335). What is also lost in the German, through the substitution of the two cataphoric determiners, is the clear shift in narrative point of view that is marked by the indefinite article, namely from Amy's to Leo's point of view exclusively, since he alone could register the *new* impression of "*an* amplitude" and "*a* comparatively big old kitchen." The question of narrative shifts effected by particular article choices will be dealt with in detail at a later stage of the discussion.

The final example in this section is taken from a scene in *Happy Valley*. On a night full of happenings, with a murder being committed, and a dead body found in the road preventing an elopement, Sidney Furlow, in the middle of a sleepless night, sets off to seduce Hagan the overseer, whom she will later blackmail into marriage by means of the alibi she perjuriously sets up for him. It is a night which comes to life less through visual images than in sounds and impressions registered in the darkness by taut nerves. I quote at some length to capture the atmosphere of the scene:

> She walked and felt the grass sharp against her legs, *twigs* pause in her hair, slip, she was walking beyond *trees*, would walk up and down till light, she knew where it came beyond that hill, where you looked for light when you could not sleep. In the stable something stirred *chaff*, a cat perhaps, or mice. The sleepy sound of chaff that fell beneath rafters. She was very remote from this, and *horse's* feet mounting out of a well, up and up, they came up the hill with no body, she looked out to attach some form to *a* sound.
>
> Getting off *a* horse was the chime of steel, *a* voice. He was getting *a* horse. Hagan stood on the gravel. She knew. She held herself against *a* door, very flat, heard *the* horse shake itself free of the bit. (*HV* 281f)

Just as the sentence syntax in general is manipulated here to allow "stream of consciousness" elements to weave themselves into the narrative (there is a great deal of this in this first published novel), so also the articles contribute in their own wise to giving a highly personalized, even a dream-like surrealistic emphasis to the scene, with the choice of preponderantly indefinite reference establishing very powerful perception-reaction signals between the phenomena in the landscape and the viewer or re-creator (Sidney/reader), whose perceptions are reaching out in the darkness towards them. Thus for instance "and *horse's* feet mounting," with its oddly insistent zero article (deleted indefinite), conveys more vividly the impact of a sound suddenly reaching the alert ear out of the dark and being identified than would a version more smoothly and unobtrusively adjusted to narrative, for instance: "She was very remote from this and *from the* horse's feet *that she heard* mounting." The same is true of "she looked out to attach some form to *a* sound." "To *the* sound" would have been a mere syntactic slot-filler, an anaphoric reference identifying the "horse's feet" as the actual indirect object of the verb "attach." The indefinite article has in contrast a vivid foregrounding effect, which is reflected also in the different intonation it generates. Whereas the identifying anaphoric *the* referring back to "horse's feet" ("to *the* sound") generates a falling intonation, the actual version with the indefinite, insisting on the new introduction "of *a* sound" despite the earlier identification of its source, generates a rising intonation. The sound thus emphatically foregrounded hangs there expectantly, palpably in the darkness, waiting to materialize and be more precisely identified with the next moment or the next camera shot. And indeed *a* horse duly materializes, then remains steadily perceived as *a* horse while the materialization of its rider proceeds along a different focus-seeking sequence: *a* voice > he > Hagan. Finally, "she held herself against *a* door." Why not *the* door, since Sidney presumably knows intimately the landscape in which she is standing, and the reader too must have figured out that the scene is taking place near *the* stable? The answer would seem to be that the indefinite article is more compatible with the fragmented, alienated quality of the whole scene, which in the dark offers only the vaguest orientation aids: "beyond trees," "that hill," "the stable." "A door" contributes to the impression of fragmentation by alienating, by disputing acquaintance, by throwing all the weight of awareness (Sidney's and the reader's also) onto the central focus of her momentary recognition processes ("Hagan stood on the gravel") and away from her habitual, daytime-influenced ones. "*The* door," on the other hand, by inappropriately claiming recognition as a familiar landmark in the night-alienated landscape, a landscape of emotional rather than actual reality, would split the focus of recognizing attention between the horse in front of her and the stable behind her, and thus dilute and detract from the intense concentration on sounds, out of which the figure of Hagan materializes into the centre of the picture. "A door," in short, with its, on first reading, rather strange indefinite article, contributes significantly to the organization of the picture by marking a clear separation of peripheral from central, or observer from observed, of the already recognized (by Sidney) from the still unnoticed (by Hagan), of temporarily emotionally alienated background from illuminated foreground.

The next example, from *Riders in the Chariot*, is something of an exception in this group, since an alternative definite article choice is hardly possible. Still, it does have something to add to the argument for a connexion between the use of the indefinite article and the immediacy of impressions impinging on the awareness of a character. Himmelfarb has miraculously escaped, after a fire and an explosion, from a Nazi concentration camp, but he has lost his glasses. The series of indefinite articles in the extract that follows helps to convey an exact impression of his half-blind, stumbling progress, forced as he is to employ senses other than sight to establish his whereabouts:

> *Shapes* welcomed, whether of *men* or *trees*, he had not the strength to wonder, but did at last touch *bark*. . . . . He wandered through a forest, from trunk to kindly trunk. (*RC* 186)

It is not a question here of a shift in orientation centre from outside to inside, but of a concentration on inward impressions in the absence of the faculty that normally receives the stimuli of the outside world. It is interesting, though, from the point of view of the grouping of receivers of information, that the reader is not allowed any prior or privileged knowledge of what is going on here, but must wait for information to be filtered through Himmelfarb's impeded senses. Thus, in "he wandered through *a* forest," the reader has to wait for Himmelfarb's deductions from his identification, by touch, of "bark." Once again, therefore, article usage is seen to exercise a rigorous control over point of view.

> Then Mrs. O'Dowd, who had been asleep, or withdrawn by some other tongs of mercy, opened her eyes with the wideness of pain and said, "Now that there is too many ladies there is no more mulberry jam."
> "That is so, Mrs. Parker," she said to her friend, who was sitting there at the bedside, on *a* chair, in *a* hat. "You was always a one for mulberry jam." (*TM* 455)

Amy Parker has come to sit at Mrs. O'Dowd's deathbed, around which a macabre and scurrilous Irish "wake" is in progress. Mrs. Parker, a stranger to the circle, is ignored by the other guests, and we lose sight of her in the goings on, until she re-appears, or rather one might say, interpreting the syntax, she re-surfaces in Mrs. O'-Dowd's returning consciousness, as the dying woman opens her eyes and focuses with recognition at last on the figure by the bed. The lifelong relationship between the two women has been one of casual encounters and shared adventures, devoid of formalities apart from the stiff mode of address. So it is natural for Mrs. O'Dowd, caught up in this strangest of all situations, to fasten her attention on the two unwonted details of Mrs. Parker's appearance that comment so eloquently on the state of her own affairs. The translator sacrifices in his version not only the indefinite article with its focusing effect but also the attention-compelling double occurrence of it:

> "So ist das, Mrs. Parker," sagte sie zu ihrer Freundin, die mit *dem* Hut auf *dem* Kopf neben ihrem Bett sass. . . . (*BM* 508)

An egg is the object, in the next example, which contributes, through the strategic placing of an indefinite article, to the emotional dimension of a scene—to the suggestion, that is, of distraughtness and controlled desperation in a character, which is nowhere identified as such, explicitly, by a commenting narrator. Ailing, asthmatic Ernest Moriarty, in *Happy Valley*, hopelessly in love with his vulgar, unsuitable and unfaithful wife Vic, has just received an anonymous letter informing him of the affair she is having with Clem Hagan. The scene, which starts with Vic at the races with Clem, looking back on an incomprehensibly "cranky" Ernest at breakfast earlier that morning, is put together with jumbled time levels and stream-of-consciousness elements, and the egg, occurring in Vic's recollections before we meet it in fact, is one of the structural elements that hold it together. So the egg is thoroughly familiar to us through innumerable references before the striking indefinite occurs. This is the moment where it does:

> Gertie Ansell brought him an egg, sulking, she had not washed her eyes, and stove-black on her hands.
> No, he said. No. I don't want the egg.
> She looked at him in surprise. Then she went out of the room leaving the egg behind.
> Ernest Moriarty sat staring at *an* egg. The letter said, forgive me Hagan for wishing you well said take your pyjamas said just another case of anonymous adultery tapping her knee and laughing at a joke. (*HV* 244)

Thus Ernest Moriarty's apparent lack of recognition of "*the* egg" underlines the discrepancy between the outward scene and what is going on under the surface, a touch that gains in poignance from the fact that Vic has already *mis*interpreted the scene for us before it is played before our eyes: ". . . and Ernest cranky at breakfast about that egg, as if you could know the history of an egg right the way from the hen, you said, or get inside and look, I like that, but nobody's going to spoil my day not about a bloody egg" (HV 242). The striking and unexpected reference to "*an* egg" at the climax of the scene some pages later adds an extra little touch to the suggestion of Ernest Moriarty's private agony and isolation from what is going on around him.

It is the same sort of inner agony, otherwise uncommunicated either to another character or by a commenting narrator to the reader, that is suggested again by an unexpected indefinite reference in the next example. Amy Parker receives a letter from her no-good son Ray, asking her to meet him secretly and bring some money. The scene starts with Amy escaping from her family commitments: "Then Amy went quickly and got *the* chicken she had roasted that day, and of which the smell was still hanging in the house. She took the long loaf, a bit floury, and made the basket ready" (TM 347). After the unsatisfactory and, for her at least, heart-wringing meeting is over and her son has gone, we read:

> Then Amy Parker, who had been rolling her handkerchief into a ball, before realizing it was not something to throw away, took the basket up. There was *a* cloth too, with which she had hidden *a* chicken from sight, and which she would wash on Monday. (TM 355)

This odd re-introduction of the chicken—in the meantime we have seen Ray consuming it with gusto—has the effect of isolating Amy momentarily from the rest of us, as she deals wordlessly with her private grief. The indefinites seem to convey her struggle to return anew, though with difficulty, to those objects that maintain the continuity of her life before and after the great hiatus of her devastating interview with her son. Indeed the next sentence confirms this reading exactly: "She looked at the crumbs on the floor, wondering whether she should resume her life to the extent of sweeping them up." The German, by choosing an anaphoric definite determiner which links up the various mentions of "the chicken," loses the powerful effect achieved by the unexpected choice in the original: "Es lag ein Tuch darin, mit dem sie *das* Hühnchen zugedeckt hatte; sie würde es am Montag waschen" (BM 396).

The need to interpret this feature not only as a choice of one *and* simultaneously a rejection of the other available alternative, but also as a choice that has been made for deliberate effect against the background or environment of the surrounding text, is made very clear in the next example from The Twyborn Affair, Patrick White's latest novel to date. Eddie Twyborn is on a ship bound for Australia after being decorated for bravery in the trenches. We have got to know him, at the beginning of the novel, in his female persona as Eudoxia, the beautiful Byzantine empress hetaera, concubine of homosexual Greek Angelos Vatatzes. But on Angelos' death, he reverts to his male self and sublimates his grief by going to war. On board ship, the beauty of the young lieutenant, much to his own disgust, excites the lust of both male and female passengers, who struggle for possession of him at a fancy-dress ball on deck:

> Margs was determined to prove a point. She had thrust a campaigning vulva as deep as possible into his crotch; her rather flat little breasts were bumping and grinding against his chest. . . .
>
> He was saved by the ginger baby.
>
> Brandishing its rattle at the end of a hairy arm, it screamed, "You're hogging the lieutenant, Mummy! Poor Baby, must have a turn."
>
> The colonel's crotch was almost as possessive as Margie Gilchrist's, and certainly more developed than her breasts.
>
> "Eddie," the sultana called across the deck, "save me the waltz. A waltz is what I'm dying for. . . ."
>
> At that moment the music stopped and Eddie Twyborn escaped from the muscular embrace of ginger arms.
>
> While they were all laughing, stamping, shouting, clapping, he scuttled down the companionway into the smelly-clean bowels of *a* ship and the asylum of his cabin. (*TA* 140f)

The deviant re-introduction of "a ship" is a clear signal that something is to be interpreted here, to be read between the lines, and our theory would suggest that the interpretation is to be sought in a sudden and private insight exclusive to Eddie alone. The rising intonation generated by the choice of the indefinite article (cf. the extract above from *HV*, 281f) suggests an unspoken alternative: the bowels of a *ship* are infinitely preferable to the bowels of . . . . . . , whereby for scatological read sexual, in other words the "campaigning vulva" and the "possessive crotch" of the alternative environment.

The final example is taken from a scene in *The Tree of Man* where Stan and Amy Parker arrive home by cart from the floods in Wullunya, bringing with them various objects salvaged from the water, and a child. The last few miles before they reach home see a heightening of the emotions—Stan's troubled acquiescence in the adoption plans of his wife, the child's doubting resentment, childless Amy's nervously apprehensive possessiveness.

> "Anyway," said the woman, her voice exhausted by the weight of possessions, "we're home."
>
> "Give us your hand," she said to the boy in a revived but dangerously personal tone. "You can jump down, can't you? You're quite big, you know."

"Of course he can," said the man, who was shifting about, and stamping and avoiding the bath, "he's a sollicker."

So the child jumped towards them, as he was told, and they were calling goodbye, and bundling through the darkness, past the twigs of *a* rosebush, into *a* house. (*TM* 92)

It is clear that what is being expressed through these two un-expected indefinites is an inner state of uncertainty and alienation. Not only is Amy returning to the house that she has left for the first time in her life for any considerable period, but she is returning to it in a new status, as the hopeful mother of a foundling child. Maybe, in her fierce hope that the child will accept her and be content to live in a strange house, she even momentarily identifies with him as the only viewer on scene who is really seeing house and rosebush for the first time. The reader at any rate is already well acquainted with the rosebush and the house, as are Stan and the departing Ossie Peabody in the cart. All of these are excluded, therefore, from this highly personal, emotionally angled perspective, in which we see, momentarily illuminated, not the real scene but the projection of an emotionally coloured inner landscape.

Patrick White and Lawrence: A Contrast
Rodney Mather°

Clearly, the prose styles of Lawrence and White, though both shaped by a commitment to the tracing out of the lineaments of lived meaning, exhibit striking differences even on the surface. We might well begin by acknowledging these, for they are indicative of, and lead naturally on to, a fundamental contrast.

While the narrative of both writers is shaped very largely by actual situations, Lawrence's is clearly the more expansive, openly germinal treatment; his language is more plastic, unself-conscious, and indeed insouciant: it traces in a more sustained way the instinctual life-flicker in individuals. White's prose is relatively brittle; it jumps from object to gesture to observation and then back to object. The (idiosyncratically) personal or individual viewpoint, whether of char-acter or narrator (these sometimes merge sloppily), is always present. All experience is filtered through the framework of personality—we might say, through ego. Lawrence, by contrast, unmistakably yearns to leave this ego, or self, behind, to escape to the "beyond," various though its agencies of release are. White's wry overt comments and

° Reprinted from *Critical Review* (Melbourne) 13 (1970): 34–50.

objectified disclosure of motives can be rapier-like, as can Lawrence's, but they are presented abruptly—often, it seems, for effect. For, though intricate, White's prose is, in its disconcertingly singleminded way, stilted, mannered, over-punctilious, a little frigid, perhaps imaginatively anaemic, while sometimes at the same time garish, over-romantic in seeking effects. Structurally, White's prose is more composite, fragmented, a matter of interlacing or juxtaposing jerkily disparate details, outlines and epigrammatic statements. These are held together by a tonal deftness, a voice, a personal stance, or at least presence. However, with his prismatic opulence of differing, patchwork-quilted effects, his rococo ornamentation and recurrent tendency to the gargoyle-like, the distended, we often have to suspect White of dilettantism, flirting with life. His control, too, is not evenly maintained. However, his ability to fuse comic and pathetic, grotesque and tragic, clearly signals a complex and compassionate personality. Unfortunately, he is also given to meaningless flourishes and by turns can be fanciful, wry, florid, and self-indulgently "experimental."

Lawrence, not intent on playing out on a slender thread such a commixture of images ritually wrought, is nevertheless the more swayed and beset by his material, which he sometimes, in revenge, belabors with doctrine. This proclivity is part of his ability to follow issues through in a more genuinely engaged, exploratory, less brittle and sportively exhibitionistic way; but the cost of his capacity for heedless absorption in a sort of diagnostic impressionism is an artless, and sometimes gauche tastelessness, dropping even at times to oversimplified and disgusted effigy-making in the name of diagnosis. White's diagnosis is certainly more readily comprehensible; but its bases are vaguer and relatively ill-informed—less positive, perhaps more of a mere reflex.

But out of these surface impressions, I want to select and highlight several further differentia. Quite simply, how does each come at experience? What is the quality of the grasp he maintains on reality?

For the first point of difference, we might consider the areas of experience treated by each. Lawrence, characteristically "seeing" in terms of a heightened, instinctual-intuitive probing, aims at participation in new or hitherto untried states of being, spiritual states. Modes of being are the stuff of personal relationships, the "meaning" with which landscape, animals, nature generally, communities, and individuals are seen as impregnated, and the matrix of Lawrence's wisdom. He therefore characteristically dwells on states, usually semiconscious, often occasioned in personal relationships or as a response to environments whether of nature and animals or "civilization." One has only to recall some of the states he dramatizes: "tremulations on the ether," swoonings, passing into darker states, the blood beating up in waves, the farmers at the beginning of *The Rainbow*, or the response to civilization implicit in *Kangaroo*, when the freedom of Australia is felt as partly liberating, partly a loss of meaningfulness, after the "old closing-in" of Europe. There is again the contact with Victoria Calcott, like a "sacred prostitute," and the similar rendering of people in *Women in Love* (e.g., Hermione), and *The Plumed Serpent* (Don Ramon and Don Cipriano). In all of these, the characteristic stress never varies.

White, on the other hand, typically dramatizes the existence of isolated, sensitive individuals who are very often out of contact with others and with communities except through telepathic communi-cation or reminiscence or self-projection or through symbolic vision. Nor, at their most colorful, are they very truly in contact with "nature." Nevertheless, one has only to contemplate *The Tree of Man* to realize that the grasp on life available through White's type of commitment can be wide-ranging and solid. Thus, if Lawrence de-pends more directly on actual experience than White does, White, perhaps because more removed from it, is freer from it, and can range widely over it, exhibiting great variety, not only, of course, in *The Tree of Man*, but from novel to novel. Moreover, he is, quite clearly, happier with ordinary experience than Lawrence. He is more willing to face the barren, intractable areas of life; and his experience is, characteristically, less heightened purely as actual experience than Lawrence's. (The heightening comes very largely from its artistic treatment—the two are not identified, as in Lawrence.) And being at home with ordinary experience, White knows all too well those who are confined to it. Whereas in *Women in Love* Birkin's experience is more real than, and dwarfs, Gerald's, White's endorsed, wisdom-embodying characters don't really supersede the others imaginatively; they are no more or less real. White's attachment to a wide range of ordinary experience gives him a kind of "negative capability"— an ability to face *un*meaning or semi-meaning in life; and, as any Australian knows, there is plenty of this around.

But to substantiate this point: is Theodora *(The Aunt's Story)* any more real than Frank and Fanny? She should be (she of course *looms* much larger spatially), but, though of course their comfort is dev-astatingly shown up, they remain solid, almost more convincing than Theodora, precisely because White knows the texture of their ex-perience so well and presents it in such an unforced way—in contrast to the strain with which Theodora's is presented, especially in "Jardin Exotique." For this strain there is a reason of course—Theodora's progress to alienation must be seen for what it is, while remaining real. In this second part, it has to be both madness and reality— hence the strain. In the third part, it no longer has to be real. We can share all of Theodora's experience in "Jardin Exotique," which is no more and no less than a sustained thrumming of object-interaction, the purest manifestation of it in all White. But it is a rarefied order of experience, and her excursions, a one-way telepathy, into the pasts and beings of the people she meets, amount to little more than a random and questionable bravura. It may be because they are given nothing against which to prove their reality, no challenge, that one always has the sense that at any moment they may be, almost should be, punctured—a strain quite apart from their not being very feasible. Even more to the point is the enormous range of typical experience in *The Tree of Man,* a range both fertile and copious. Such small, yet typical, sketches as the account of Lola's life, or of Mrs. Fisher's, can easily be overlooked, because overshadowed. But even the highlights, such as the flood, demonstrate a surety of touch with regard to the situation as felt by all those implicated in it which is astonishing—and unique.

Even so, when all is said and done, apart from the recurrence of experience of isolated sensibilities, which are the preoccupation of White, we are hard put to it to find an *experiential centre* to his novels. Instead, we are driven to invoke other terms: the centre of the *reading experience,* i.e., the core, the imaginative centre of the *art*—this we could talk about; or the *range* of experience, the projection, possible through such an accomplished art; or, again, we might, very tentatively, and with the isolated experience in mind, suggest that White's interest in "experience out there" is confined to a sort of aesthetic, imaginative, arty meaning in terms of surface impressions, which tends strongly to self-projection, *enlisting* details, and to a sense of ritual cohesion in situations, together with a rich (if perhaps superadded) aphoristic wisdom. Even so, the states focused by or located in situations, objects, etc. are in one sense more profound than those in Lawrence. Essential longings, such as for permanence, the need for something to have faith in, inarticulateness in the face of the ceaselessly flowing dreamlike present (as in *The Tree of Man*), are very often not just more typical but more universal, more immediately recognizable, more neatly identifiable than in Lawrence, whose preoccupations are more provisional, more formed by their circumstantial context (e.g., the marriage relations of Harriet and Somers in *Kangaroo*), more involved, carrying the sense, confirmed by our knowledge of Lawrence's life, of Lawrence's own heated implication in them. White's mode of encounter permits of greater imaginative freedom, in that there is less involvement. But the preservation of the ego and its freedom to project involves a loss in outgoingness and maybe a fundamentally more static position on the part of the artist.

In his article "The Novels of Patrick White" in the Pelican *The Literature of Australia,* Vincent Buckley speaks of the "labour of objectification" accomplished in the writing of *The Tree of Man.* This, it seems to me, is the core of the matter: we have to accept that White's is a relatively detached art, even at its best. Its language is cool, hard, brittle, noticeably (from even a mere glance at the printed page) more aloof and collected than Lawrence's. And surely the time of life at which he came to artistic maturity as compared with Lawrence prompts us to expect just this. White's freedom, in relative detachment, to range widely, to display, to fondle and thrum the textures of experience, to create an embroidery as it were, finds its finest expression in dealing, as in *The Tree of Man*, with universals, with generic experience. White is, we sense, relatively uneasy in handling individuals; a personal animus or anxiety makes him defensive, resulting in the bifurcations of characters discernible in all of his novels (faintly even in *The Tree of Man*). But that "labour of objectification" saves White there from the over-involvement that vitiates *Riders in the Chariot*.

We may, I believe, discern in this situation two differing means of release of the imaginative energies. Lawrence's very involvement releases him; the converse is true for White. White is characteristically much tighter, more self-conscious, and his prose lacks Lawrence's plastic, insouciant flow. Lawrence craves waylessness, is ever reaching into the outer darkness. White, on the other hand, maintains a stiff poise and a cold, sometimes near-hysterical impersonality—with, as the gain, an exquisite sharpness and variety of tone and sense of form beside which Lawrence can seem simple-minded. With White, whether he is tracing Theodora's progress to madness, life at Durilgai, the megalomanical musings, mysticism and moods of Voss, the outrageous self-projections of Miss Hare, the quietly recounted goodness and hell of Himmelfarb's existence, Arthur's fearful fumbling with the "unlived life," or whatever, there is always—and added to the face of the breadth of experience, it means much—the sense of lived meaning, of the mystery and poetry of life. But, unlike Lawrence, he has no innate, or at least pre-existing, spiritual focus that he must lose. He compensates for his lack of spiritual direction by artistic deliberation and venturesomeness in his themes and locally by the pointedness of the prose, which Lawrence can safely do away with, as with self-consciousness, through the need to quest which dogs him at every turn—to search for wholeness of being. Hence, too, White's dependence on society, his use of scandal effects (implying a society and its values) and his "poise." These Lawrence can disdain. But hence White's ability to project himself, luxuriantly to encircle other people, to be preoccupied with the typical. Lawrence can't do that; his focus won't let him abandon his quest.

Their characteristic attitudes to the world—or rather, their ways of experiencing and conceiving it—are neatly epitomized in a couple of passages, from *Kangaroo* and *The Tree of Man*. In them Lawrence and White are explicitly confronted by reality. In each case, it is an enigma. Lawrence's response is to dwell on it, acknowledging its mystery—for him, it is fascinating, beyond, a release. White's response is to see it as a taut, poignant, while grotesquely arty, bundle of details; to acknowledge that he has no hope of understanding it; and in doing so to reveal that at the moment he is strong. The latter stress is revealing indeed: here we have the saving presence of the artistic self, the deliberating, venturing self-conscious ego. Here, in miniature, we have Theodora, Voss and the other elect, standing out from the flux. The solitary performance of withdrawal suggested by the last sentence of the White is highly suggestive:

> "Como," said the station sign. And they ran on bridges over two arms of water from the sea, and they saw what looked like a long lake with wooded shores and bungalows: a bit like Lake Como, but oh, so unlike. That curious sombreness of Australia, the sense of oldness, with the forms all worn down low and blunt, squat. The squat-seeming earth. And then they ran at last into real country, rather rocky, dark old rocks, and sombre bush with its different pale-stemmed dull-leaved gum-trees standing graceful, and various healthy-looking under-growth, and great spiky things like yuccas. As they turned south they saw tree-ferns standing on one knobbly leg among the gums, and among the rocks ordinary ferns and small bushes spreading in glades and up sharp hill-slopes. It was virgin bush, and as if unvisited, lost, sombre, with plenty of space, yet spreading grey for miles and miles, in a hollow towards the west. (*Kangaroo*, ch. 5)

> The postmistress removed the string from the bundle with great skill. When she licked her yellow thumb it was more than an official act, a ritual rather, to soothe the humble suppliant, who would stand snuffing the scent of melted sealing-wax as it mounted in the sanctuary behind. It was improbable that any of those letters, elevated like a host to the level of the postmistress's eyes, could belong in substance to anyone. Many of them never did. But Amy Parker continued to attend this ritual, because it came at the top of the hill, and sometimes there was a catalogue, with pictures of things, and once there had been a letter from her Aunt Fibbens, dictated to a lady who could write, about some unpleasantness.
> "No, dear," said Mrs. Gage, "it's as I thought. People are not writing in the heat. There was a storm, though, on the North Coast, and a young fellow struck by lightning on his horse. It ran up the stirrup irons. Had a baby, it said, only six months. He was a timber cutter. Can you understand?"
> "How should I understand, Mrs. Gage?" said Mrs. Parker, who at this moment was strong.
> She began decently to walk away. (*The Tree of Man*, ch. 8)

Another clear point of contrast, to which the above two attitudes towards reality bring us, is to be found in the relations between actual and aesthetic experience. The elements that give imaginative life to the scene of Norbert Hare firing at the chandelier, for instance (*Riders in the Chariot*, ch. 2)—the grotesquerie of the gesture, the boiled fowl, the cry "munching!", the taking-over of silence, the sensations—are ordered from within the narrative activity; they are a set of effects whose focus is not the people concerned (who, as in the case of Norbert, are to some extent themselves "effects") but *we*, as readers. Exemplified here is the pervasive, recurrent orientation of White's prose—to the reader. When O'Dowd chases the women around the house in chapter 10 of *The Tree of Man*, for example, it is we not the women who experience the main impacts of the situation. With all its lineaments, it is more meaningful as a reading experience than as actual experience. By contrast, when Ursula in *The Rainbow* laughs at Skrebensky's singing in church, it is the character to whom the experience is meaningful and to whom the meaning is addressed. This is entirely characteristic of Lawrence. In his writing we witness someone experiencing meaning; in White we receive "meaning" (aesthetic meaning) by witnessing experience in a detached, spectatorly way. In White, laughter would be reserved for the reader.

> To stay put was, in fact, just what the young man Stanley Parker himself desired; but where, and how? In the streets of towns the open windows, on the dusty roads the rooted trees, filled him with the melancholy longing for permanence. But not yet. It was a struggle between two desires. As the little boy, holding the musical horseshoes for his father, blowing the bellows, or scraping up the grey pairings of hoof and the shapely yellow mounds of manure, he had already experienced the unhappiness of these desires. Ah, here, the sun said, and the persistent flies, is the peace of permanence; all these shapes are known, act opens out of act, the days are continuous. It was hard certainly in the light of that steady fire not to interpret all fire. Besides, he had an affection for his belching and hairy father, and quite sincerely cried when the blacksmith finally died of the rum bottle and a stroke. (*The Tree of Man*, ch. 1)

The reader's experience is not identical with the boy's. Part of the meaning, the wit, of the writing resides in that rum-bottle, which isn't detachingly grotesque for the boy, who "quite sincerely cried," but for the reader. (To retort that the boy may have seen it as grotesque is beside the point, of course: his function in the writing as it stands is not to do so, as it would be were he a Lawrentian protagonist.)

Throughout White's prose, the terse, pointed clarity, the often over-elaborate images, the aloof comments, all provide coherence for the actual, talked-about experience which is itself often brittle, shifting, a matter of one striking sensation after another without *intrinsic* unity *as* experience. Thus, the reading experience (the aesthetic order) and the actual, talked-about experience in White are at a remove from each other. It is not a great remove, because to keep them together White tries as far as possible to make actual experience itself aesthetic—sometimes, however, with a sense of strain. Nevertheless, it is a completely different relationship from that typical of Lawrence, who doesn't recognize aesthetic experience in its own right at all, but instead tries to find his order, or unifying principle, in life, in the "perfectly good form" of following the tender life-flicker of impulses, instincts, intuitions. Experience is used always as an exploratory medium, whereas White's stance over experience tends to make him lose serious contact with the world, to create a salvific artifact, a chariot. That is what happens in the following passage. What is interesting here is that the golden sphere is interposed by White's artistic act between us and the experience talked about. It is not seen by the Jew and Mrs. Godbold, and only "glimpsed" (metaphorically) by Mrs. Flack and Mrs. Jolley. It is an imported, factitious metaphor, essentially part of the *reading* experience. The vantage-point it creates supports that "quick as snakes," which is emphatically *not* experienced by Mrs. Flack and Mrs. Jolley:

> Then, as people will toss up the ball of friendship, into the last light, at the moment of departure, and it will hang there briefly, lovely and luminous to see, so did the Jew and Mrs. Godbold. There hung the golden sphere. The laughter climbed up quickly, out of their exposed throats, and clashed together by consent; the light splintered against their teeth. How private, and mysterious, and beautiful it was, even the intruders suspected, and were deterred momentarily from hating.
>
> When they were again fully clothed in their right minds, Mrs. Jolley said to her companion:
>
> "Do you suppose she comes to him often?"
>
> "I would not know," replied Mrs. Flack, though it was obvious she did.
>
> "Tsst!" she added, quick as snakes.
>
> Mrs. Godbold had begun to turn.
>
> "See you at church!" hissed Mrs. Jolley.
>
> "See you at church!" repeated Mrs. Flack.
>
> Their eyes flickered for a moment over the Christ who would rise to the surface of Sunday morning.
>
> Then they drew apart. (*Riders in the Chariot*, ch. 8)

The point here is that writing that seeks to render the texture of experience can, by generating image-structures, become a *way out*, a solution to the ravages wrought by life, life for art's sake.

Our first impression might be, indeed, that both White's and

Lawrence's approaches can lead to evasion. In Lawrence's case, while it is true that he tackles the Geralds and Hermiones head-on, it is also true that, to do so, he has to make them as narrow, intense and singleminded as he himself is, has to drive them, with some falsification, to their ultimate implications, whereas in actual life not everyone has this singlemindedness. Hermione, by virtue of her very lack of real focus, would in real life have an inclusiveness, something of a negative capability—or at least, a receptivity—that Lawrence never shows as a positive. Her very delight in simple things is always (falsifyingly) presented as an over-intense, wilful vampirishness, e.g., in the chapter "Sketch-Book." But, apart from this, the sheer full-blown qualities of Lawrence's textures of experience at their worst become a mark of Lawrence's being too close to the experience, desperately wanting to lose himself in it.

White's characteristic evasion is exactly the opposite. At his most evasive, the shifting rhythm, the jump from detail to detail, provide a film of motion that substitutes for intrinsic interest in the experience talked about, i.e., substitutes for a highly focused, singleminded dedication to life—and does so very effectively because of the surface sharpness. Neither Lawrence nor White is at his best handling descriptions of love-making and the retreat in each case is characteristic. For example, in a scene such as that between Birkin and Ursula at the inn (*Women in Love*, ch. 25), a phrase like "Something was tight and unfree within him . . ." doesn't much help the haziness of the language or the inanity of the tone; and the unintentionally bathetic effects of the experience are disconcerting. All of this is the cost of Lawrence's commitment to the textures of the experience, which requires an abandonment of bearings. It is just this simplistic quality of the handling that, by jettisoning bearings, results in an unreal language: "He looked down at her with a rich bright brow like a diadem above his eyes" indeed! Even Shelley's "cheeks and eyelids pale" were more "in touch" than this.

If Lawrence is *in* the situation to such a degree that he can't see beyond it, and so loses perspective and therefore taste, White by contrast doesn't seem happy about getting into it at all. Ostensibly, his grasp is strong, incisive:

> Then, suddenly, Tom was down upon his knees. He had put his arms around her thighs. For the first time, against her body, she experienced the desperate bobbing of a human being who had abandoned himself to the current. If she herself had not been pitching in the darkness, his usually masterful head might have appeared less a cork. But in the circumstances, she would not have presumed to look for rescue to what her weight might have dragged under, just as she resisted the desire to touch that wiry hair, in case it would wind about her fingers and assist in her destruction.

Instead, she began to cry out softly in protest. Her mouth had grown distorted and fleshy. She was bearing the weight of them both on her revived legs. But for how much longer, she did not like to think.

"Ah, no! Tom! Tom!" she breathed; her voice could have been coming from a shell.

As the mouths of darkness sucked her down, some other strangled throat in the distance laughed out from its game of lust. In the spirals of her ears, she heard the waves folding and unfolding on their bed.

Then the sand dealt her a blow in the back. It, too, was engaged apparently, beneath her, but with the passive indifference of thick sand. As the two people struggled and fought, the sand only shifted its surface, grating coldly. The girl was holding the man's head away from her with all her strength, when she would have buried it, rather, in her breast. In the grip of her distress, she cried out with the vehemence of soft, flung sand.

"I would marry you, Tom!" she panted.

"That is news to me!" Tom Godbold grunted, rather angry.

He had known it, though; he had known many women.

But her announcement gave him an excuse to pause, without having to admit his lack of success. (*Riders in the Chariot*, ch. 9)

White clearly isn't interested in the experience as experience—only in the accidentals of it, which he continually resorts to (in their own way they are real enough), like the sand; and then he treats it in a withdrawn, abstract way. This is characteristic, too: White's thinking, we continually feel as we read, is decidedly not the straightforward, direct process that Lawrence's is. While it is all too true that Lawrence's thinking hardens into high-and-dry doctrine, at least it proceeds visibly from the over-all sweep, the structure, of the situation, i.e., we are very well prepared indeed for Anna—and Lawrence— to conclude that the cathedral leaves too much of life out, or for Ursula to reject Skrebensky's ideals and mode of existence. The argumentative movement is simple, slow and richly and amply embodied. With White, however, the movement of the prose (and, with it, the argumentative process) is more often than not staccato and jerky; his pointed economy has as its obverse a hobbling of outgoing response. For some reason, we have the impression that he won't let himself go, that he has the habit of emaciating his life-sources, that somehow he is offering a brilliant substitute for holding the situation steadily in front of him. Thus it is that his eminently quotable aphoristic observations, brilliant and brittle as they are, seem wilfully inserted into the prose; his thought-structures are like arabesques, in which features or items are juxtaposed but not fused.

At best, White's brittle prose gains a hold on absurdly disparate aspects of life, of which the accommodation is *not* facile; their reality is allowed to come through by the dry tone:

> Because now they were on the outskirts of the town. They stumbled past the hulks of cows. There was a smell of sheep, and of water drying in a mud hole. And soon the yellow Fibbens's doorway, leaning outwards, and the yellow straws of light that fell from the cracks in walls into darkness.
>
> "Well," she said, "this is where I take off the shoes."
>
> "It looks like it," he said.
>
> He wondered if, after all, this girl might not be a box of tricks. She was a skinny one, and sharp.
>
> The whimpering of a waking child was not contained by walls.
>
> "A-myyyy?"
>
> "Yes, Aunt," called the girl.
>
> The shadow of Mrs. Fibbens heaved into fresh shapes on its frail bed. Her belly was fretful with her seventh.
>
> "Anyway," said Amy Fibbens, "we have had a talk. About a lot of things."
>
> It was quite right. They had talked about almost everything, because words occasionally will rise to the occasion and disgorge whole worlds.
>
> Just as the darkness will disgorge a white face under a dusty tree.
>
> "Will you be coming to this place again at all, perhaps?" asked the girl.
>
> "On Saturday week," said the usually slow man.
>
> And again he was surprised.
>
> Under the sad tree, more frond than bark, beside the girl's blurred face, less shape than longing, in an amorphous landscape of cows' breath and flannelly sheeps' cud, his intention was absolute.
>
> "Oh," she said, "In that case."
>
> "A-myyyyyy!" called Aunt Fibbens, the shadows knotting on her dreadful bed. "Stop maggin, An come inside."
>
> "Yes, Aunt," said the girl.
>
> "A person could be dead," complained the shadow, "an only the flies would cotton on. Here am I, reaching, ever since I swallowed me tea."
>
> There were people in that place who said that Mrs. Fibbens was as rough as bags. (*The Tree of Man*, ch. 2)

Here the brittleness is positive. It is remarkable, surely, that the strength of the prevailing grotesquerie doesn't by any means swamp out the physical "feel" ("hulks" of cows and so on) of the situation, his wondering about the girl, the child, the feel of being under the tree. The interspersed abstraction is there; but with their dry clarity and the dexterity of selection, the minutiae work positively. The humanity evinced in the depiction of the young man's situation is notable, and its reality is intrinsically interesting. And yet all too often White's inventiveness allows him to *exploit* experience, that is, cash in on its impacts without following up its implications except in pretentious gestures which are themselves an exploitation of image-meaning. At worst, the encountering can be minimal. The brilliance of the clarity actually limits, *reduces*, what is seen—as with the description of Norm Fussell's party (*Riders in the Chariot*, ch. 11).

"Mobility" in White's theatre of consciousness is just what he describes it as being to the inhabitants of Sarsaparilla, release, "freedom"—through an art with its unity over and above experience. And this suggests something basic about those energies he is prepared to invest in life: that they are not active, dynamic, aggressive energies, as Lawrence's clearly are, but instead are inert, static—the energies of withdrawal, the energies of hypnosis and ritual. Again and again we note in White's prose that the energies informing life make of its contours a series of static arrestments of motion, arrested gestures ("the pen appeared to be resisting," *Riders in the Chariot*, ch. 1), or posed rituals, a continual shift from detail to detail, intercalation of overt comments. The "wisdom" does not grow out of the imaginative life of the prose; White must hold on to the self, or ego, or personality, in order to control tone, form, since the energies drawn on are not vital enough to do all the work themselves.

Thus we find ourselves invoking terms like "projection." That suggests irresponsibility, however, and by itself it is too damning a term. After all, what about White's ability to discover fundamental spiritual longings and urges in situations? And yet these spiritual energies don't quite provide the novel's argumentative fibre, which they do in Lawrence. Rather, they are sketched in impressionistically in a more illustrative, less exploratory way: where, for example, in chapter 1 of *The Tree of Man* we are told of Stan's struggle between two desires (quoted above), in Lawrence this description would serve to raise an issue that would pervade the novel. In White, it is artistic opportunism; the other few references to permanence can (only just) be related to it; there is some slight echoic contribution from one reference to the other—for the reader with an exceptionally good memory; but the general effect is of a plethora of deft, minute brush-strokes whose total argumentative effectiveness is slight indeed. Less implicated than Lawrence, he can afford to endow (a word more appropriate to him than to Lawrence) his experiences with a greater mature collectedness. We must not underestimate White's sheer knowingness, the unremitting accuracy of his acquaintance with many forms of human life, and it is his more withdrawn stance that enables this—enables, in fact, greater self-determination. But should we not rather say: a greater *sense* of self-determination—by which we mean a lesser self-transcendence?

If the colorful variety of White's subjects and themes can be said to exhibit more artistic freedom than it can spiritual or imaginative development, it is no less true that the ostensibly varied existence of White's characters have a certain sameness. I do not mean just that the existence of Theodora Goodman has similarities with that of Laura Trevelyan and Miss Hare. More significantly, although the meaningful experiences of Stan Parker (unevenly presented), Voss (to some extent), Himmelfarb, Mrs. Godbold, Alf Dubbo, and Waldo Brown are quite distinct, the separate identities shaping in varying degrees the films of consciousness of each, there is still a certain sameness in the imaginative life that gives texture to the experience. Lawrence's consciousnesses, by contrast, are somewhat more deeply differentiated—or, rather, the difference is recognized for what it is, and Lawrence doesn't presume to enact it to the same extent, knowing that he can't in fact get "outside" himself. But to the extent that he does, the difference is deep—Gerald Crich, for example. Real values are at stake. White's is a more brilliant and a more bored art; his theatre of consciousness is a collapsible tent. Thus from novel to novel, Lawrence's is (in the main) a spiritual and imaginative progress; White's development from *The Tree of Man* onwards is rather a spiritual regress. From that novel onwards, we have a narrowing, a contraction, an increasing militance (indeed, hysteria)—and, finally, in *The Solid Mandala*, a greyness—of soul. White is still Theodora Goodman at heart, having been first subdued and chastened by his return to a gritty, recalcitrant environment—an environment at which *Voss* fortunately just misses being a pathological protest, and before whose post-war chromium White is helpless. (Consider the periods of all his mature novels; in only one, the shrillest, does he attempt to face it.) Underlying the surface "mobility" we have spiritual immobility—perhaps the paralysis of fear. The progress is all "artistic." Moreover, the conceptions of the novels, their dominating images, are bizarrely and unpredictably varied in the same time-span. The very subjects of the novels have a game-like, capricious quality, which the tone often, betrayingly, works *against*.

A phrase from *The Living and the Dead*, the "abstract nobility" of the mass, suggests White's sense of belonging to society, being an insider looking *out*, rather than an outsider, for the outside is desert. For Lawrence the outside, the unknown, is anything but desert. White seems to need society's abstract clichés, i.e., generic, aphoristic, predefined ideas, which he illustrates; and he writes at his best with a communal sense *(The Tree of Man)* which does not attain to radical challenge (unlike *The Rainbow*).

If White is the artist *par excellence*—art, pure and simple, forms the imaginative core of his work, though seemingly motivated in part by an anxiety which forces the lifebelt of diagnosis on it—Lawrence is, antithetically, a "philosopher of being," a diagnostician or prophet.

This is his core of integrity—and his *art* is suspect. It is suspect, not (as White's diagnosis is) because it is a camouflage, but because of its radical blindness, its sometimes curious, eccentric qualities: of melodrama (e.g., the paperweight scene in *Women in Love*), of formless, clumsy repetition (the laughing-in-church scene in *The Rainbow*), of inhuman revulsion (the beating scene in *The Rainbow*), of hypersensitivity (the bullfight in *The Plumed Serpent*, and the rabbit scenes in both *The White Peacock* and *Women in Love*), and of, again, hypersensitive hysteria (the wartime scenes in *Kangaroo*). But Lawrence was quite right to describe himself as a "passionately religious man," and so was Murry (*pace* Leavis) when he said: "Art was not his aim." "Art for *my* sake!" said Lawrence, and could well have added, "and me for *Life's* sake." His novels are not "art." He is uninterested in "beauty," in the aesthetic, in form in the autotelic sense, in imagination in the stricter sense. Modes of being are his preoccupation. The following passage, "almost his last words," Hough tells us, is one of his most central and characteristic utterances and—for me, at least—one of his very finest:

> For man, the vast marvel is to be alive. For man, as for flower beast and bird, the supreme triumph is to be most vividly, most perfectly alive. Whatever the unborn and the dead may know, they cannot know the beauty, the marvel of being alive in the flesh. The dead may look after the afterwards. But the magnificent here and now of life in the flesh is ours, and ours alone, and ours only for a time. We ought to dance with rapture that we should be alive and in the flesh, and part of the living, incarnate cosmos. I am part of the sun as my eye is part of me. That I am part of the earth my feet know perfectly, and my blood is part of the sea. My soul knows that I am part of the human race, my soul is an organic part of the great human soul, as my spirit is part of my nation. In my own very self I am part of my family. There is nothing of me that is alone and absolute except my mind, and we shall find that the mind has no existence by itself, it is only the glitter of the sun on the surface of the waters. (*Apocalypse*, 1932, pp. 222–3)

"My soul knows. . . ." Lawrence traces spiritual states, though the spirit has an unorthodox allegiance—to instincts and intuitions, which is what is meant by "blood." He is, adopting his own terms, at worst a Sunday-school preacher, a priest. He does, quoting Birkin, have "all the soul in the world." His venture in search of wholeness of being and spiritual, emotional and physical vibrating relatedness to the universe, partly through relatedness to a woman, is a search for a body. Hence the assertions of maleness (e.g., Ursula doing homage to Birkin's thighs, the vicarious maleness achieved through beating Gerald in wrestling, and much overwriting elsewhere); but the venture is clearly more than this. Above all, it is a venture in diagnosis, in search of wholeness, a pursuit (to invoke Birkin again) of "serious living." Lawrence has no poise, no stance, faced with life—life, or his style of commitment to it, provides all the stance he needs. This is seen when we put Lawrence's plunging, forward-gazing prose beside White's. It is surely significant that in Part Three of *The Aunt's Story* White has Mrs. Johnson confront Theodora in the following terms:

> ". . . I suggest you come on down to our place. It's brighter there. And comfortable. I'll fix some dinner for you. We got steak for dinner," she said.
>
> All this was said and said, Theodora realized, because Mrs. Johnson dared not stop. Mrs. Johnson would not know the great superiority of stationary objects.

The point here is that White has earlier had Theodora explicitly claim to be a seer: "I don't want to marry . . . I want to see" (ch. 3)—which statement links her with the creative types, Wetherby and Lieselotte, who, like her, both gaze at "objects" as no one else in the novel does. Since White recognizes that the seer and the things seen are interdependent, White is here endorsing the static stance towards life. This might seem a tenuous assertion. But it is substantiated consistently in the quality of his imaginative life. In fact, to make the point is surely to point up the central limitation of White's prose: the absence of a sense of the free, forward movement of the spirit, the leap that says "yes" to life, the spiritual *élan vital*, the sense of adventure that issues in acts of faith (faith in life)—this dimension is denied him. Instead, we feel a recoil; White is even committed to a state of being driven in upon himself—up to a certain, pretty clearly defined point, at any rate. Life is by no means absent; but neither is it the final arbiter; it subserves art. Putting it another way: it can be said that when we look for an ontological dimension in each, White suddenly seems to lack stature—indeed, seems stillborn, sterile. The laborious, flat consistency of the psychic flow of his language somehow precludes complete openness of being. It precludes a certain sense of adventure, of the fresh air of renewal. All that satiric edge of his comes to seem something of a fake, a dodge, since it springs more from revulsions than from any maturely worked out viewpoint wherein he knows his own being to centre. It seems deadeningly self-contained, and it is linked with an elaborate deflection of his own contact with the "other." Lawrence, in fact, is far clearer about his points of contact with the "other," i.e., he is far more sharply focused. In White's case, this focus is so elaborately modified or contorted or blurred as to become less than an open inquiry. This leads to a fundamental boredom, speciously enlivened by White's systematic determination to cull some of life's decorative potentials.

To claim that White is only a pseudo-outsider, seeing salvation, finally, in society, may seem incongruous with his attitude both to individuals and to society. But let us look more closely. Voss is "so vast and ugly," because he is ego, or will, personified. The Bonners of the world are every bit as real, convincing, and "there" as the outcasts, i.e., White is attracted equally strongly to them and to society in general. Moreover, the outsiders aren't just usually seen from within society, or surrounded by society and its expectancies, reticences, etc., which are done in the finest detail, but they are at their *best* seen thus. Like his novels, White's short stories are socially oriented through and through, employing (i.e., believing in the vindicability of using for art) shock and scandal effects. The situation is epitomized by Norbert Hare firing at the chandelier. This scene is a set piece; the chandelier (i.e., nostalgia for a past age of elegance in Australia) signifies; Norbert is a freak, a misfit; and the scene is one of socially unacceptable, and *therefore* horrifying, spectacle. White stands in utter contrast to Lawrence, who wants to make a new society; to imagine White doing so is impossible. In *Voss*, the undercutting effect of Sanderson on the whole Voss-Laura system confirms White's suspected attachment to the society that Voss rejects. But not only do we sense that, in terms of sheer imaginative reality (the only ultimate test), the Chalmers-Robinsons of the world are at least as truly "there" as the Miss Hares, and handled with decidedly less strain; but the solipsism of a Miss Hare reads at times—disconcertingly and, indeed, embarrassingly—like a parody of her, which suggests an underlying, unconscious cynicism about her and the "chariot," the erected salvific artifact she is supposed to embody. But even more clinching is the evidence of the prose itself: mannered, very firmly poised (i.e., not *submitting*, losing its bearings, and its "ego," in experience). With wryness, aloof comment and irony, it implies an audience, a "civilized" audience. But considering that audience, we might well ask why does White hearken back again and again to an earlier age, favoring especially the late nineteenth century? This was a society whose attitudes, values, ironies, tones were somewhat more stable, agreed-on. And White's prose, in celebrating and partaking of such a society, using for "effects" its scandals and shocks, clearly underwrites it, while also chafing against it, looking outside to the deserts of mortification and reward, to the crag-like Voss. Note: *not* looking at society from the deserts—Laura's worthiness, after all, is proposed in terms of her (interestingly protracted) "return" to society. For White, the actual in his prose subserves the artistic act; the writing brilliantly articulates pre-defined, readily identifiable states of being, unlike Lawrence's brilliance, which comes nakedly through from the actual. In short, the scope of White's prose in evolving values, its spiritual focus, is limited; society provides values. Its exploratory capacity, then, is limited. Hence, our age being what it is, White's relevance is, in this sense at least, limited.

The Novelist and the Reign of Necessity: Patrick White and Simone Weil

Veronica Brady[*]

I start with a remark of White's, that Simone Weil has been a considerable influence on him. True, hunt-the-influence can be a sterile and boring critical exercise. But in this case some understanding of the thought of a philosopher whose work the novelist has long reflected on not only illuminates the sense of life which inspires his work, but also helps to rescue him from the charge of eccentricity. For if it has long been clear to some of us that his work has never been an art which expresses "self-division and separateness" but rather a sense of responsibility for his fellows and brotherhood,[1] the problem has been first, to define the order he has been endeavouring to create, then to find common ground with it, and finally to be convinced that it is capable of generating a new, more coherent way of life than the one which prevails around us. Simone Weil's thought, I believe, helps to identify this order and to suggest that indeed it may be a viable one.

White's whole *oeuvre* depends upon a peculiar sense of the structure of fate. This is expressed in the epigram from Gandhi prefixed to *Happy Valley*, his first published novel, and the sense of life it expresses pervades every subsequent novel, namely, that everyone is doomed to suffer and that greatness is measured by the capacity to do so. This sense owes much no doubt to personal and temperamental factors and even more to the fact that White reached artistic puberty in England in the 1930s, personally aware what was going on in Germany and, in particular, of the plight of the Jews.[2] But Simone Weil's thought arises from a similar intuition which is the result of prolonged reflection upon the history of our time. Beginning with the proposition that ours is an age of "malheur"—best translated perhaps as the "evil hour"—she goes on to question the basic premise upon which Western culture has been based since the Enlightenment, the Cartesian premise that mind is the dominant factor not only in the individual life but in the universe as a whole. Against this Weil

* Reprinted from *Patrick White: A Critical Symposium*, edited by Ron Shepherd and Kirpal Singh [Bedford Park, South Australia: Flinders University Press (Centre for Research in the New Literatures in English), 1978]: 108–16; courtesy Veronica Brady.

asserts the primacy of physical necessity. For her, as for Wittgenstein, the world is all that is the case: impersonal, with nothing to do with human feelings or intentions, governed by inexorable rules which determine the behaviour of all that is physical and material, including the human body. Far from being master of the Universe, man is essentially its victim, to the extent that he depends upon his body— and that is a very large extent—and is thus subject to physical necessity. Flesh is fragile, but matter is strong, can pierce, crush and destroy the body, prey upon the emotions and humiliate the spirit.

A similar sense of life underlies White's novels and helps to account for the duality, the tension between body and mind so evident in his work, in his insistence upon physical weakness, in particular upon an "excremental vision" which many find so distasteful. Even his language insists upon paradox as it reminds us of the bodily origins of experience, contesting the mind's longing for permanence and illusions of mastery, and showing how these origins precede the claims of grammatical propriety. At the level of structure, too, White's distrust is evident of the individual's power to choose, the power on which all claims to autonomy rest. His people do not make their lives, they live them out according to a pattern determined for them, mostly according to the logic of the myth which underpins their story—the myth of Ulysses in *The Aunt's Story*, *Hamlet* in *The Tree of Man* and so on. Where the classical novel, based on the premises of the Enlightenment, moved to glorify the individual's ambition to master the elements and make his world and his destiny, White's novels work towards that wisdom Simone Weil speaks of, "becoming master of myself and knowing that I am not God."[3] This is the central theme of *Voss*, of course, as Voss learns the truth Laura insists upon and which Le Mesurier's poem expresses: "Then I am not God, but man, I am God with a spear in his side."[4] But to a greater or lesser extent, every one of his protagonists is in search of a similar under- standing, characterised by Laura at the end of *Voss* as the "true knowledge which only comes of death by torture in the country of the mind" (p. 446).

In effect, then, White is writing a kind of Wisdom literature, seeking to demonstrate the rule of powers beyond human compre- hension and to lead the individual to worshipful submission to them. Where the traditional novel, the "novel which raises no questions" as Butor has called it, seeks to endorse the power of social convention, White, following Simone Weil, tends to suspect all human artifice and to distrust all intentions that are socially conditioned, "civiliza- tion" being all too often, in his view, a conspiracy to conceal the way things really are. So, the crucial point in Laura's development in *Voss* comes at Rose Portion's funeral when, faced with the fact of death, Laura realises that "the clouds were loading lead to aim at men . . . that terrestrial safety is not assured and that solid earth does eventually swirl beneath the feet" (p. 235). In similar vein, after Munich Simone Weil welcomes the fact that the general "sense of security had been profoundly undermined." "There can be no security for man on this earth, [she wrote] and beyond a certain measure, the feeling of security is a dangerous illusion."[5] In *Voss* people like the Bonners demonstrate just how dangerous this longing for security can be. "The shell-less oyster is not more vulnerable than man" (p. 349), as the expedition's fate shows, and it becomes clear that the only way to survive is to be like Laura, ready to pursue that "true knowledge [which] only comes of death by torture in the country of the mind" (p. 446).

True, the moral passion which underlies this intuition, particularly strong in *Voss* and *Riders in the Chariot* but evident in all his novels, makes them somewhat melodramatic in their structure, dividing people, places and events into good and evil. Nevertheless, far from being an expression of arrogance and of an ideology divorced from reality, it represents an attempt to transpose art into terms which the realities, political, psychological, economic and social, around us insist upon and which form the centre of the understanding of Man in Marx, Nietzsche and Freud. Hence the pressure upon language in his work, for in effect White is attempting to dramatise something like the "transvaluation of value" Nietzsche speaks of, a transvaluation which shatters our present sense of what is humane and even of what is human but which arises not from mere wilfulness but from an intense moral passion. No doubt, to some tastes this moral passion will smack of fanaticism, especially in *Riders in the Chariot* and at times in *The Vivisector*. Even a work as humane as *The Tree of Man* shows little faith in human relationships, the stuff of the traditional novel. "Two lives can only touch, they cannot join,"[6] the novelist declares, as Stan and Amy Parker move apart, each into his or her own solitude. However, despite the assertions of some critics, this does not mean that White's novels lack tenderness, though it is true that this tenderness arises more from relationships between the novelist and reader and the characters in the novel rather than between the characters themselves. Nevertheless, this intensifies rather than diminishes the respect for humanity the novels generate since it is based upon the understanding Simone Weil writes about in her essay on *The Iliad*, the understanding that every human being must acknowledge, the universal subjection of the human spirit to force in the fact that bodies die, can be hurt and grow old.

"This subjection is the common lot, although each spirit will bear it differently. . . . No one who succumbs to it is by virtue of this fact regarded with contempt. Whoever, within his own soul and in human relations, escapes the domination of force, is loved but loved sorrowfully because of the threat of destruction that constantly hangs over him."[7]

A sorrowful love of this kind informs White's most recent novels, *The Eye of the Storm* and *A Fringe of Leaves* in particular, and gives them their peculiar quality. But even in an earlier work like *Voss* it accounts for the otherwise unaccountable affection apparent for people like Belle Bonner, particularly on her wedding day,[8] and for the new feeling of sympathy Laura discovers for her uncle and aunt as she contemplates their bewilderment during her illness, seeing them from "her tragic distance" as "two children" (p. 335). Yet in his work love has little to do with the personal relationships which exist in the novels. On the contrary, far from being a refuge, these relationships, dependent as they are on bodily and social interaction, only multiply the possibilities of suffering, making the characters more than ever subject to necessity, and it is this insight which sets White's attitude at odds with current pieties. Nevertheless, as Hurtle Duffield's career suggests, the sufferings others occasion are not to be seen negatively. Rather they serve as a form of purification, an intensification of that awareness of self as vulnerable which lies at the heart of his vision.

Here again, of course, White's work differs from most other novels with their respect for what Henry James called the "surrounding envelope" of manners, customs and social relationships. For White, solitude, not society, is the true human milieu, and passivity, not action, the proper mode of being. Hence the city in general and social gatherings in particular are contrasted with the state of "silence, simplicity and humility"[9] which is usually achieved in some kind of communion with the natural world. True, he also has a tendency to bring his characters back to civilisation from the wilderness when they have experienced this state, Laura Trevelyan, Elizabeth Hunter and Ellen Roxburgh being paradigmatic in this respect. Yet, even while they pay tribute to the obligations of civilised life, these characters primarily inhabit their own inner space and draw their strength from it. Nevertheless, they are not Romantics opposing their desires to the world and living within them, exempt from the claims of matter-of-fact. White has no great confidence in the subjective life in itself. What matters for him is the dialectic, the tension between body and spirit. Thus, preoccupied with ecstatic states he also insists on the sheer intractable givenness of objective reality—hence his fascination with rocks, glittering mineral forms and with the Australian landscape generally. For him its harshness, its power to humble man's aspirations and pride, points to the paradoxical nature of existence, the reign of necessity Simone Weil speaks of which co-exists also with the longing for infinity and, by definition, for freedom. So, in *Voss* the desert becomes the place of salvation precisely because it defeats Voss's claim to be God, subjecting him to necessity but awakening in him a knowledge of the true God who is not merely a projection of Voss's image of himself but something totally other from this world, cruel to the extent that he is absent from the world, leaving it instead to the rule of necessity but kind in that he thus releases Voss at last from self-seeking.

Evidently, in proposing such a vision White has had to reinvent not only the environment he describes but also the expectations of his readers since in his work the interplay between the self and the world becomes a process not of accretion but of diminution—Simone Weil's word for it is "decreation"—and the self-humiliation, even vulgarity, of the novelist appears as a form of asceticism and a part of his vision. Similarly, the rewards to be achieved are unfamiliar; not power, position or even love but that attitude of waiting which Simone Weil also admires, a patient, expectant emptiness which is open to the influence of what she calls "grace," the power located out of this world which she opposes to the gravity of material concerns pulling away from this centre of stillness.

Here, with this word "grace," we reach the crux of the critical debate touched off by Leonie Kramer some years ago.[10] Just what does it mean? What exactly is this "power beyond this world" which obsesses White? When he dedicates a character like Hurtle Duffield to the pursuit of the "vertiginous blue," the "otherwise unnameable I-N-D-I-G-O," the symbol for God in the alchemical spectrum, characterising it as "not so much . . . a colour as a long standing secret relationship" (p. 641),[11] is this not mere sentimentality, "working off in words of feelings you haven't got" (Lawrence) and which no one else could be expected to have either? At best when White makes the vision of God—whatever that may be—the reward to be worked for he may seem to be more of a hagiographer than a novelist, and even then, as it has often been observed, though his heroes and heroines may be "saints" they are often also unpleasant people, so that asking the reader to admire them entails a kind of perversion of thought and feeling.

Simone Weil's sense of God raises similar problems. In her case, however, the intellectual and personal integrity through which she reaches her position makes her right to it incontestable. Starting with her own version of Descartes' *cogito*, "I can, therefore I am," she continues: "I do not exist except in so far as I create myself. I am God. But this is not true. I am not God. I must recognise the limits of this power; my sovereignty ends where I must give myself something to think about."[12]

This passage might serve as a gloss on the development of the action of many of White's novels, notably *The Vivisector, Voss* and *A Fringe of Leaves*, and on the paradox John Colmer has referred to within them of the interplay between glad tidings and grim truth. But it also indicates what it is which enables Laura's passivity to triumph over the imperious energies of Voss's will, an existential honesty, and thus suggests that what White calls "God," the reward she and other such protagonists achieve, is also the product of this honesty, not of illusion or wish fulfilment. For him, as for Weil, it appears that the first step is to acknowledge the absence rather than the presence of God since by definition he is a reality alien to the world, "located . . . outside space and time, outside man's mental universe, outside the entire domain that human faculties can reach."[13] Thus he has nothing but scorn for those like Mr. Bonner, for example, whose God is nothing but the projection of his own desires—the position Feuerbach attacked, of course. On the contrary, knowledge of the true God begins with the experience of physical exigency, with knowing oneself alone and powerless and subject to the determinisms at work in history and in an unfeeling universe. Corresponding to this sense of exigency, however, "at the centre of the human heart, [there] is a longing for an absolute good," and this absolute good it is which is God. Yet the longing for him "can never be satisfied by any object in this world,"[14] so that it exists as a kind of torment. So too with White's characters. The "torment of exhilaration" Laura is feeling that Sunday morning she first meets Voss, Ellen Roxburgh's "instinct for mysteries which did not concern her,"[15] Hurtle Duffield's response when he first sees the chandelier in the Courtneys' house, "looking up through the glass fruit and flickering of broken rainbow . . . [when] he knew all about [it], from perhaps dreaming of it, and only now recognizing his dream" (p. 24), all of these intuitions make them uncomfortable in this world, impel them out of it since nothing here and now can satisfy them.

This impulsion is the equivalent in White's novels to the social ambition and erotic desire which motivate characters in other novels and, since it is heroic longing, calling them to contest the normal conditions of existence, it gives his protagonists an epic stature—they are destined to fight the demons which seem to be destroying society and reconstitute human existence on a new level. Reversing the conventional order, it is thus the visionaries who appear as those most in touch with reality and those who cling to current common sense, people like Hero Pavloussi, Mrs. Jolley and Mrs. Flack, Frank Parrott, who appear as cowards, clinging to a state of illusion which is destructive to themselves and others. Following on from this reversal, the novelist's concern with suffering thus reflects a concern for truth, the truth of our subjection to necessity and separation from the God who appears as the "Divine Vivisector," as Hurtle Duffield sees him, the power beyond this world who is ultimately responsible for a universe in which human beings exist as vulnerable and mortal.

No doubt this is an austere vision but, to repeat, it is not necessarily inhumane since it tends to enlarge the scope of responsibility and, by implication, of moral choice. "I would agree to call God my freedom,"[16] Simone Weil wrote. Acknowledging the limits of human power her thought focuses responsibility where it really counts, on taking up the full burden of one's own life, in particular, of living out one's awareness of truth. In Weil's case this meant that she shared the lot of the oppressed people she spoke for. In White's work Ellen Roxburgh also learns to live with those who are humiliated, though Voss also moves into freedom by learning a similar mystery of humility. Shipwrecked, having lost her husband and her child, made captive by savages,[17] Ellen makes what is destructive and degrading count for truth, demonstrating the inner freedom which allows nothing to appal her.

In this perspective the moral scheme of the novels no longer seems perverse though it may seem boring to some tastes. Most clearly in *A Fringe of Leaves* but in other novels also, error and passion are not so much glorified as the material from which the protagonists are able to fashion their freedom, learning to live as they must and coming to realise that it is possible to redeem a tyrannous situation by enduring it with composure. Just as importantly, far from destroying humanity, the preoccupation with the antithetical God guarantees its dignity, making for composed acceptance of the self and its situation. Accepting that the scope of human action and choice may be limited by determinisms of all kind, historical and psychological—of all our writers White has perhaps most fully absorbed the implications of Marx, Nietzsche and Freud for the sense of possibility—White would have it that it is still possible to achieve integrity and that, precisely where these determinisms challenge the individual will. So it is that Stan Parker affirms the longings within him most intensely when, old and decrepit, he is about to die. The God he sees in the gob of spittle, "glittering intensely and personally," is the reward of a lifetime of fidelity to intuition. He has been true to the conviction that, as Weil argues, life has no meaning except as an expectation of the revelation of the truth, the truth which is not necessarily in conformity with human intentions and desires and figured by Mrs. Volkov as the sting of a wasp:

> I got stung not by putting up my hand my hand was put. I was shocked white, it felt. . . . It was like red hot needles entering at first very painful then I did not notice any more, only sea and sky as one, and me like a rinsed plate. (p. 637)

For her, fidelity has turned into a kind of laceration which is the consequence of attempting to "think with truth at the same time about the afflictions of men, the perfection of God, and the bond between the two."[18]

In effect, then, reference to Simone Weil leads to the conclusion that, far from being sentimental, the vision of God which White proposes as the reward of his characters rests on an insight into what may be a central dilemma of our times, the split between what is objectively given and subjective desire, which may be heightened in Australia by the sheer force of the environment which haunts White, as he said, "by reason of generations of my ancestors."[19] Far from being the product of fanaticism or wish fulfilment, this vision of the intense otherness of God exists alongside, indeed arises from, the kind of scepticism Laura expresses at the end of *Voss:* a readiness to live in doubts and uncertainties, and to let "the air tell us" whatever the truth may be. Indeed, this truth depends upon the fact that human beings are limited and governed by necessities of all kinds, above all that of death, because it is a paradoxical truth, that man is not God but drawn irresistibly to the impossible prospect of knowing Him.

But what are the literary effects of this world view? Let us admit that it has its dangers. It tends to generate authoritarian habits of heart and mind which make for a machine-like efficiency in the structure of the novel, leaves little time for what is not relevant to the grand design and often leads to a cavalier attitude to people in general, especially those unable to measure up to the rigours entailed by such a bleak vision of the universe. Nevertheless, White's sense of reality protects him from the sloppiness and projective enthusiasm responsible for what Doris Lessing once called "this monstrously isolated, monstrously narcissistic, pedestalled paragon; the contemporary writer."[20] Beginning not with sensation but rather with sensation elaborated by thought, White finds his support not in himself but in an order of clear ideas. Moreover, this order makes sense not so much to those of us who belong to the privileged minority but to the majority oppressed by necessities of all kind and profoundly aware of it. To us who still cling to the illusion that we are not, his moral passion may often be distasteful, even disturbing. But, as Simone Weil insisted, "nothing concerns human life so essentially, for every man at every moment, as good and evil."[21] That means that it is not questions of social position or even of personal relationship which are central, but what Solzhenitsin (another such writer) called attention to the division which runs through every human heart between good and evil, truth and falsehood. As a novelist, White wants to drag us, even critics and dilettantes, from the level of existence Kierkegaard characterises as the aesthetic, to the moral and even to the religious level. This may not be to our taste, but it may be helpful, even necessary. "If our present suffering is ever to lead to a revival [Simone Weil reflects, commenting on the claims the moral life makes upon literature], this will not be brought about through slogans but in silence and moral loneliness, through pain, misery and terror in the profoundest depths of each man's spirit."[22] That sentence may sum up the significance—is it literary? is it human?—of Patrick White's visions.

Notes

1. Doris Lessing, *The Golden Notebook* (London: Panther, 1976), p. 13.

2. One thinks in particular of the "little Jew" seen by Elyot Standish in *The Living and the Dead* on the London station waiting to go back to Germany.

3. Simone Pétrement, *Simone Weil* (Oxford: Mowbray, 1977), p. 65. (Hereafter referred to as Pétrement.)

4. *Voss* (Melbourne: Penguin, 1963), p. 297. (Hereafter references to this book will be given in the text.)

5. Pétrement, p. 337.

6. *The Tree of Man* (Melbourne: Penguin, 1963).

7. Pétrement, p. 317.

8. *Voss*, p. 310.

9. In "The Prodigal Son," *Australian Letters*, Vol. 1, No. 3, April 1958, p. 38.

10. Leonie Kramer, "Patrick White's Götterdämmerung," *Quadrant*, Vol. 17, No. 3, May/June 1973, pp. 8–19.

11. *The Vivisector* (London: Cape, 1970). (Hereafter references to this book will be given in the text.)

12. Pétrement, p. 64.

13. Ibid., p. 493.

14. Ibid., p. 493.

15. *A Fringe of Leaves* (London: Jonathan Cape, 1976), p. 46.

16. Pétrement, p. 41.

17. White's picture of the aborigines here emphasises their savagery not out of prejudice—he treats aborigines with great sympathy elsewhere—but to underline the hostility of the natural world.

18. Pétrement, p. 516.

19. To John Hetherington in *Forty-Two Faces* (Melbourne: Cheshire, 1962), p. 142.

20. Lessing, *The Golden Notebook*, p. 12.

21. Pétrement, p. 408.

22. Ibid., p. 408.

A Severed Leg:
Anthropophagy and Communion
in Patrick White's Fiction
Don Anderson°

> When Emerson decided, in 1832, that he could no longer celebrate
> the Lord's Supper unless the bread and wine were removed, an
> important step in the vaporization of religion in America was taken,
> and the spirit of that step has continued apace. When the physical
> fact is separated from the spiritual reality, the dissolution of belief
> is eventually inevitable.
>
> —Flannery O'Connor[1]

PROLOGUE

I have indicated elsewhere[2] my interest in the topic of dinner-
parties and eating as a significant structural pattern in fiction. There
are two paradigmatic "dinner-parties" in the written mythologies of
the West. The Gospels record Christ's Last Supper, the essence of
which is the meal as symbolic ritual, with its promise of a new
covenant and of a greater meal "in my Father's kingdom," yet
containing the necessity of its own secular disruption through betrayal
("He that dippeth his hand in the dish with me, the same shall betray
me" *Matthew*, 26:23). This archetype is institutionalized in the celebration of communion in the Canon of the Mass. *The Symposium*
provides the second paradigm of the drinking-party that follows upon
the dinner-party that Socrates misses. Here, the topic of discussion
is Love, a quality or condition which one might, in either the Christian
or the Platonic tradition, expect all dinner-parties to aspire to through
communitas.

No less significant in our mythologies than the sense of communion generated by suppers or symposia is the dark image that
those feasts beget. Socrates is alone both before and after the symposium. Judas Iscariot may dip his hand in the communal dish, but
his heart is elsewhere; his great betrayal is a renunciation of the
community that the Last Supper celebrates. Indeed, the refusers of
the feast are crucial imaginative projections in our literature. It is
notable that two of the great "nay"-sayers of American fiction, Melville's Ahab and Faulkner's Thomas Sutpen, resolutely refuse to sit
down at a meal with their fellow men. Of course, it is that very
"fellowness" that they would repudiate, thus generating their tragic
ends.

Patrick White's fiction participates in these structures which I

° This article, from a paper delivered at the 1980 conference of the Association for
the Study of Australian Literature, first appeared in *Southerly* 40 (1980): 399–417;
courtesy Department of English, University of Sydney.

have outlined. Given that the meal is a symbol of communion, it is important that the more prominent among his central figures, who might be designated "artists" (after Hurtle Duffield) or "Nietzschean heroes" (after Voss), are, at crucial stages of their careers, refusers of the feast. It is no less important that Ellen Roxburgh, in *A Fringe of Leaves*, is a communicant at the end of a cannibalistic feast.

Given that the sacrament that Ellen Roxburgh feels herself to have participated in is neither Western nor Christian, it might be appropriate here, before undertaking my examination of Patrick White's fiction, to outline some paradigms of the communal and sacramental functions of feasting other than those two with which I began. In *The Origin of Table Manners*, Lévi-Strauss, for whom "cooking is a language through which [a] society unconsciously reveals its structure,"[3] points out that in some cultures cannibalism is an index of *virtù*: "I am brave, I can eat anything."[4] Cooking, which is a "semantic field,"[5] has a mediatory function between nature and culture.[6] Again, in *The Raw and the Cooked*, Lévi-Strauss suggests that in certain cultures, "cooked" is homologous with "socialized."[7] Let me try to integrate Lévi-Strauss's fecund suggestions with my reading of White's fiction by anticipating my later argument. The particular object that is cooked (a thigh, or "severed leg"), as well as the manner in which it is cooked (roasted), will have a significant structural function in the "semantic field" of *A Fringe of Leaves*, and will help "unconsciously" to "reveal its structure." Ellen Roxburgh will nourish not only her flesh but her spirit through anthropophagy, and will ingest *virtù* as well as flesh. The roast thigh may serve as an emblem of the narrative transmissions from culture to nature and back to culture that mark the plot of *A Fringe of Leaves*. The eating of "cooked" human flesh will play its symbolic role in Mrs. Roxburgh's "socialization," her communion, her sense of having partaken of a sacrament.

Before quitting Lévi-Strauss, I want to offer one quotation which may suggest how his books have contributed to the *methodology* that underscores "A Severed Leg." In *The Origin of Table Manners* he asserts that he has "simply been putting into practice one of Ferdinand de Saussure's teachings: 'As one probes more and more deeply into the subject-matter of linguistic study, one becomes increasingly aware of a truth which—it would be useless to deny—offers remarkable food for thought: namely, that, in this field, the link which one establishes between things exists *before the things themselves*, and helps to determine them.' "[8] With regard to *A Fringe of Leaves*, the crucial links which exist before the text itself are, for my purposes, anthropophagy and eating as sacramental communion. These crucial links not only provide the climax of the text's narrative, but suffuse it, even at the level of what might appear to be accidental minutiae, at the level of imagery, verbal detail, and apparent ambiguity. To be bold: the structures of anthropophagy and communion, which precede White's text, may write it through him, to no less an extent that he, by acts of artistic will, shapes such structures to his ends. Just as Lévi-Strauss defended structuralism against historicism by asserting that myths contain no gratuitous themes,[9] so might one urge that works of the imagination contain no accidental or gratuitous elements, irrespective of authorial intention. It is a wise author who knows who is writing him, and his text. And, before leaving the topic of *writing*, let me suggest parenthetically that *A Fringe of Leaves* shows a seemingly modern (well, it is as "modern" as Roland Barthes on *écriture*, but as "classical" as Defoe's Robinson Crusoe recording himself and our being offered three different versions of his landing on his island!) and definitely pervasive concern with writing. With writing one's journal, with writing one's self, with resisting being written by others, with writing as an index of culture.

My researches into the sacramental and communal role of eating of course led me to W. Robertson Smith's *Lectures on the Religion of the Semites* and to Freud's *Totem and Taboo*, which is a psychoanalytic commentary upon Robertson Smith's work. Here, then, is Robertson Smith on the original significance of animal sacrifice: "The sacrificial meal was an appropriate expression of the antique ideal of religious life, not merely because it was a social act and an act in which the god and his worshippers were conceived as partaking together, but because, as has already been said, the very act of eating and drinking with a man was a symbol of and a confirmation of fellowship and mutual social obligations."[10] One might mention that this was most literally interpreted by certain Arab tribes, who held that eating begat communion, but only until the food had been expelled from the body—fellowship had to be continually renewed. Here is Robertson Smith on piacular sacrifices: "The fundamental idea of ancient sacrifice is sacramental communion, and . . . all atoning rites are ultimately to be regarded as owing their efficacy to a communication of divine life to the worshippers, and to the establishment or confirmation of a living bond between them and their god."[11] We may see, then, that for the ancient Semites, sacrifice and the meal as sacramental communion were functions both of a divine and a social structuring. Doubtless the Christian and Platonic paradigms cited earlier participate, knowingly or not, regardless of causal patterns, in this antique structure.

Freud extends Robertson Smith's researches to provide himself with a base from which to articulate his psychoanalytic thesis that the *primal* sacrificial meal was that in which a band of brothers killed and ate the potent father in order to possess power and the mother. "Psychoanalysis has revealed to us that the totem animal is really a substitute for the father, and this really explains the contradiction that it is usually forbidden to kill the totem animal, that the killing of it results in a holiday and that the animal is killed and yet mourned."[12] Freud's reading of the true nature of the primal meal feeds into his assertions that "society is now based on complicity in the common crime," religion on guilt and remorse, and morality partly on the necessities of society and partly on the expiation of guilt.[13] While these notions are now recognized as commonplaces of Freudian theory, they are worth repeating here as *A Fringe of Leaves* offers itself as a narrative of social complicities opposed to an act of individual assertion (by which I refer *both* to Ellen Roxburgh's cannibalistic communion *and* to her "communion" with the escaped convict, Jack Chance). Whether Mrs. Roxburgh is also killing the "father" in eating of a severed leg will be worth consideration. Freud stresses that "the thoroughly realistic conception of consanguinity as an identity of substance makes comprehensible the necessity of renewing it from time to time through the physical process of the sacrificial repast."[14] Flannery O'Connor would have given assent. And, while Ellen Roxburgh only once literally partakes of consanguinity, the text which contains her will, through its details of narrative and image, stress the "necessity of renewing it from time to time."

WHITE'S REFUSERS OF THE FEAST

If the meal is a communal sacrament, then a recurring significant action in White's fiction is the refusal of the feast, the abjuration of communion. White has his Ahabs and Sutpens, and not surprisingly, they are among his most commanding characters. Indeed, if it did not seem wilfully paradoxical, one might be tempted to say that the importance of dinner-parties and meals as emblems of communion is attested to by their considerable absence in the fiction of Patrick White. Recent theorists such as Pierre Macherey[15] have drawn our attention to the significance of absences in texts, to the often crucial nature of what the text does not, or cannot, speak.

There are just sufficient dinner-parties in White's *oeuvre* to suggest, by their scarcity, that he has made choices to direct his, and our, attentions elsewhere. He is certainly aware of the conventional functions and implications of such events. Thus, towards the end of her pilgrimage, Theodora Goodman "breaks bread" with the Johnson family in California.[16] A dinner-party is used as a dramatic setting in "Willy-Wagtails by Moonlight."[17] The possibilities of the dinner-party for social documentation are exploited in *The Twyborn Affair*, for example, when Eddie dines with the Lushingtons, and, "In the mock-Tudor dining room, mint sauce took over from Chanel. Greg Lushington stood at the sideboard carving the leg like a surgeon under hypnosis."[18] There is no doubt about the documentary character of that sideboard, whatever we may think of the surgeon. Or, for social documentation, one might turn to *Riders in the Chariot*. "It was the period when hostesses were discovering *cuisine*, and introducing to their tables *vol-au-vent, sole Véronique, beignets au fromage* and *tournedos Lulu Wattier*, forcing their husbands into clubs, hotels, even railway stations, in their longing for the stench of corned beef."[19] Again, social documentation may combine with satiric intention and obsessive textual detail, and we will find, in *The Eye of the Storm*, the Princesse de Lascabanes at her Ladies' club, surrounded by her peers who are daintily demolishing a "forkful of breast, with the merest smear of bread sauce," herself terrifying the waitress by ordering "a nice, thick, mutton chop . . . rather pink."[20] Significantly, Dorothy is unable to eat it; the social *frisson* has, however, been produced—as has a deeper, mythic one, which Dorothy herself is unaware of. The dinner-party which Olivia Davenport gives for Hurtle Duffield and the Pavloussis will bear comparison with the celebrated "Stuffed Carp" chapter of Christina Stead's *House of All Nations*, sharing Stead's interest in the cash/sex nexus.[21] In *The Eye of the Storm*, the fish which Elizabeth Hunter prepares for Professor Pehl is a work of art, though Dorothy suspects it may be serving "immoral purposes."[22] Again, the meal as dramatic focus for eating and sexual possession is exploited. *The Solid Mandala* gives sufficient overt evidence of the author's awareness of the sacramental significance of feasting. One example must suffice: "All the bread and milk in the world flowed out of Arthur's mouth on to Waldo's lips. He felt vaguely he should resist such stale, ineffectual pap. But Arthur was determined Waldo should receive. By this stage their smeary faces were melted together."[23] That is a literal communion indeed! A final example of overt reference to the meal as sacrament may be found in *The Twyborn Affair* when Lord Gravenor, still wearing his waterproof apron (a priestly vestment? if so, a most domestic one), serves Eadith a "wartime dinner [which] would have encouraged cynicism if it hadn't been for the air of last supper about it."[24] But we must note that "last" and "supper" have lower case initial letters, and that they are not preceded by a definite article. If this is an analogue of "the Last Supper," it is considerably displaced and secularized, if not ironized.

But these instances have been itemized rather to indicate White's awareness of structures upon which he chooses not to concentrate, than to show his concern with them. It is significant that, on occasion, he raises the spectre of a dinner-party which might be exploited as a dramatic focus, merely to use it as a narrative convenience and not to develop it as, say, Christina Stead might. (Sunday lunch at the Standishes in *The Living and the Dead*[25] and the Cheesemans' dinner-party for Dorothy de Lascabanes[26] may serve as examples.) His attention is elsewhere.

Before turning to that world elsewhere, it will be pertinent to consider instances where communion and sacrament are deployed conventionally. It is necessary for Rhoda Courtney to instruct Hurtle Duffield on the functions of eating. " 'Aren't you coming, Hurtle? I've made us a nice fricasse of rabbit. People eat to live you know. And they eat together because it's sociable.' When he didn't answer, she shouted: 'Then you *are* mad.' "[27] For Elizabeth Hunter, a chip of a tree on Brumby Island is a "transmuted wafer"; while, in the same novel when the Macrorys make up after a fight, "Dorothy saw that Anne must have laid the wafer on his tongue: they both looked so meek, as though returning from communion."[28] If Voss strives continually for "a world elsewhere," others in his narrative see the necessity for communion. Laura "sees" Judd's Christmas feast as a communal "act of praise"; Harry accepts Judd's witchetty-grub, and "they were both to some extent soothed and united by its substance and their act," but Harry is "aware of some disloyalty to his leader"; in his last days with the blacks, Voss eventually swallows the witchetty-grub proffered him, which reminds him of the rejected, "struggling wafer of his boyhood"; and, in Voss's final "hallucinations," he and Laura eat lilies, "But of greater importance were his own words of love that he was able at last to put into her mouth. So great was her faith, she received these white wafers without surprise."[29] Thus does the Nietzschean hero submit to the necessity of communion. It is a submission undergone by a very different figure in *Riders in the Chariot*, when Himmelfarb suffers that parody of the Crucifixion which is a crucifixion, in the presence of what White precisely designates "the *mass* of the spectators."[30] The genuine communions in White's work may be thrown into relief by the description of Mrs. Flack and Mrs. Jolley "rumbling liquidly" over tea: "This could have been the perfect communion of souls, if, at the same time, it had not suggested perfect collusion."[31]

But White's artists and Nietzschean heroes strive against any need for communion, however unsuccessfully; and this striving frequently finds expression in the manner in which they take their meals. There is something touching and symptomatic about the fate of that cheery soul, the awful Miss Docker.

> All along the empty street, behind the shops, and in the homes, the members of the congregation who had accepted the crisis in the church as an excuse to clean that carburettor, clip the hedges, or baste the joint extra good, were by now sitting down to family dinners.
> Miss Docker was all alone.[32]

It is hard to accept that even Miss Docker deserves that extremity of isolation; she is indeed a "burnt one." But she is no nearer a sense of communion at her story's end. Hurtle Duffield, created with considerably more sympathy, eats thus: "He would hurry back with food, anything that could be quickly and easily eaten, and after stuffing his mouth with handfuls of torn-out bread, 'salmon' straight from the tin, or chunks of marbled bully, he continued working. Sometimes he cut his hands on the tins and the blood worked in with the paint." So anti-social is Hurtle that, when Rhoda uncharacteristically if not miraculously cooks him a soufflé, he does not even come down to eat it. "It was the most unorthodox hour: she should have been chopping up the horse for her surviving cats."[33]

Even White's artists-manqués participate in this pattern. Thus we find Waldo Brown, after his music lesson, "gnawing at a trotter on the journey home."[34] The situation is even invoked comically. In *Riders in the Chariot*, Norbert Hare, the artist of Xanadu, "took the fowl by its surviving drumstick, and flung it through the open window, where it fell into a display of perennial phlox."[35] A loaf of bread, a carving knife, and a decanter of port wine follow, and Norbert declaims, " 'It is never possible to free oneself. Not entirely.' " Then he produces the pistols.

But it is in the pages of *Voss* that the most fully developed display of the Nietzschean hero as refuser of the feast is found; the refusals which give way to an eventual acceptance of communion and concomitant submission of will on the part of the hero help to structure the narrative. In the opening chapter of the novel, Voss demonstrates his willed isolation and pride by declining to dine with the Bonners. This contrasts with Lieutenant Radclyffe, "who would cheerfully have abandoned this unnecessary acquaintance, to rush in himself, slash with a sword at the sirloin, and watch the red juices run." Voss has thus distinguished himself from the herd ("A rude man, saw Mrs. Bonner. / A foreigner, saw the P.s.") But his pattern of great refusals is more forcibly figured only two pages on. Voss has walked back to the town, where he

> . . . went and sat in the Gardens beneath a dark tree, hoping soon to enter his own world, of desert and dreams. But he was rest-less. . . .
>
> An old, grey-headed fellow who happened to approach, in fustian and battered beaver, chewing slowly from a small, stale loaf, looked at the stranger, and held out a handful of bread.
>
> "Here," invited the oldish man, himself chewing and quite contented, "stick this inside of you; then you will feel better."
>
> "But I have eaten," said the German, turning on the man his interrupted eyes. "Only recently I have eaten. . . ."

> At once the German, beneath his tree, was racked by the fresh mortification to which he had submitted himself.

Thus, *Übermensch* refuses the Samaritan. Soon, he expresses his rejection of all communion. "The German began to think of the material world which his egoism had made him reject. In that world men and women sat at a round table and broke bread together. At times, he admitted, his hunger was almost unbearable." When, later in the second chapter, Voss does eat a "nice sweetbread" in company, "there was no question of his offering anything to his two dependants." At Jildra, he will decline "the inevitable leg of charred mutton"; nor will he participate in Judd's Christmas feast. "He could not. The liver stank."[36] As has been indicated earlier, this Luciferan *non serviam* will produce its own reversal. Pride comes before a Fall, and Voss will eat the blacks' "wafer" of witchetty-grub, and will "take communion" with Laura.

One can at times sympathize with those White characters who refuse the feast, who would repudiate the flesh and aspire to a world of pure will and spirit, especially when one contemplates some of the more solid incarnations of the Flesh in White's work. Mutton chops, mutton fat, and boiled mutton abound. There is no space here adequately to document the insistent presence of these images in White's work. Let me acknowledge that they are pervasive, and as undeniable as a blocked drain. Some examples must serve. In *The Eye of the Storm*, Dorothy prowls through her mother's vast house. She does not, however, find a skeleton in the cupboard; rather, "in the scullery, a bowl with a growth of green-to-bluish fur. The princess slammed the door on an obscenity; before it struck her that probably everybody has their basin of fur." Or, take her brother, Sir Basil: he "found himself instead, still running his tongue around the structure the mutton fat had emphasized, in the belly of a spiritual whale: unlike Jonah's, his would not spew him out till she died, and perhaps not even then." And when distinguished brother and distinguished sister commit inevitable incest, their companion is no less inevitable: "She was deafening him; and smelt—they both probably did—of mutton fat." Not Flora Manhood or even Nietzsche can escape the inevitability of the flesh. "Among the dishes on the table, bacon rind set in waves of fat, lettuce leaves wilted by vinegar dregs, one of Col's books was lying: *Thus Spake Zarathustra*, whoever he was to sound so certain."[37] Topp, the music master in *Voss*, deplores "the stupor of mutton."[38] Even the aesthete and eccentric Norbert Hare cannot escape: while working on a long poem, in Florence, on Fra Angelico, he lives in hope of discovering "some respectable woman who will know how to prepare him his mutton chop."[39] At times it seems that the "solid mandala" might only be discovered in a setting of mutton-fat.

> All this while the mutton fat was curdling round them in skeins, clogging corners, filling bowls with verdigris tints and soft white to greyish fur. You couldn't be bothered to empty the mutton fat out. Like a family, it was always with you. Set.

Is it any wonder that Mrs. Brown laments her lost youth in these terms?

> "But if you could have seen us *dancing!* . . . That," she said, sinking her mouth in the glass, "was before I married your father. It was all utterly rotten. But how deliciously memorable"—working her mouth around it—"after the mutton fat has dragged one down."[40]

Not even in his transvestism can Eddie Twyborn escape this insistent reminder of the shackles of the flesh. He treats his "coarse, labourer's boots" with rendered-down mutton fat. And when, alone in Marcia Lushington's bedroom, lusting to deck himself in her finery, he struggles to shed his old self, "the laces of his wrinkled boots, stinking of rancid mutton fat, lashed at him as he got them off."[41] It is, then, little wonder that White attached an epigraph from Paul Eluard to *The Solid Mandala*—"There is another world, but it is in this one." Set!

ELLEN ROXBURGH: CANNIBAL / COMMUNICANT

At the risk of being bold once again, I would suggest that, within the terms of White's *oeuvre*, the drama of *A Fringe of Leaves* might be represented as—Laura: becomes Voss: becomes Laura once again. In the first chapter, the choric Miss Scrimshaw offers a Sybilline divination of Ellen's fate: " 'I only had the impression that Mrs. Roxburgh could feel life has cheated her out of some ultimate in experience. For which she would be prepared to suffer, if need be!' "[42] And Ellen Roxburgh's narrative will represent that pursuit of "some ultimate," though it is an ultimate that escapes her conscious artic- ulation; again, "suffer" is an appropriate word, as Ellen is a curiously passive heroine. Similarly, the Captain of the *Bristol Maid* has inti- mations of Mrs. Roxburgh's difference: "he sensed that his passenger had an instinct for mysteries which did not concern her" (p. 46). They may not concern her because, unlike Voss, she is a woman; but the Captain suspects that there is more to it than that. Garnet Roxburgh, her brother-in-law and lover-beyond-the-law is seen by Mrs. Roxburgh as "less her seducer than the instrument *she had chosen* for measuring depths she was tempted to explore" (p. 117, my emphasis). And those depths are not only of sensuality, but also of the spirit. Much later, when the black women approach her, prophecy is fulfilled: "This, Ellen Roxburgh sensed, was the beginning of her martyrdom" (p. 243).

A martyrdom of sorts it will be; but, as Ellen Roxburgh is a woman, it will be the "martyrdom" of a barren *mater dolorosa* rather than of a suffering Christ. Images of the Virgin enthroned, the Virgin adored, the sustaining Virgin, and *pietàs* recur throughout the text. Thus, on board the *Bristol Maid*, Austin Roxburgh sleeps against her breast.

> The breast had escaped from its covering, at its centre the teat on which his struggling mouth once or twice threatened to fasten.
> She lay awhile longer, at peace. Then, ashamed of her opulence, she covered herself, and climbed to her own berth. (p. 161)

The boy, Oswald Dignam, adores her. He has one end in mind in the cutter: "to seat himself at the knees of one who was not so much the lady as a Divine Presence. Thus crouched, he would concentrate on the pair of hands lying in a lap" (p. 195). During the rum-communion in the same vessel, Ellen, after protest (the cup will not "pass from" her), accepts "the tin cup as though it had been a silver chalice, and despite her nausea, sank her face" (p. 203). Among the blacks, Ellen becomes a surrogate Virgin Mother as she is made to carry the sick, pustular aboriginal child. When the black women transform her, "planting feathers in her wax helmet," they make her no less qualified and ambivalent an object of adoration than White's prose has made her in the instances already cited: "If they had made her the object of ritual attentions, they had not forgotten her practical uses. Again pulled to her feet, the slave was loaded with paraphernalia, and last of all, the loathsome child" (p. 252). "When released from their worldly preoccupations," the women of the tribe "treated her with almost pious respect." They "anoint" her body, they "enthrone" her, and "their faces were her glass, in which she and they were temporarily united, either in mooning fantasy or mystical relationship" (p. 266). Note, yet again, how the physical or worldly possibilities qualify the spiritual, and *vice versa*. Mrs. Roxburgh will again be briefly enthroned at the Oakes': "They had sat her to wait upon what her fingers slowly discovered in the dark to be a leather throne, its woodwork carved, but very roughly, with a leaf-pattern" (p. 335). And, in the final paragraphs of the novel, Mrs. Roxburgh is yet again, perhaps, adored, when the substantial Mr. Jevons, who has spilled the tea and cake, falls to his knees in front of her. "He could not give over contemplating the smouldering figure in garnet silk beside the pregnant mother in her nest of roly-poly children, a breathing statuary contained within the same elipse of light" (pp. 404–405). It is a secular enthronement; "Garnet" does pursue her; she is *beside* the Madonna; indeed, if she is decked in the shades of conventional iconology, she is now the Magdalene rather than the Virgin. But surely she was the Virgin when Jack Chance confessed to the murder of Mab:

> She succeeded in forcing him round until he faced her. She was holding him close, against the wet flaps of her withered breasts: her little boy whom she so much pitied in his hopeless distress.
> He did in fact nuzzle a moment at a breast, not like an actual child sucking, more like a lamb bunting at the ewe. (p. 323)

But that was in the bush, in the world of nature, before she returned to culture and the roles it dictates. Indeed, Ellen Roxburgh declines the roles that Miss Scrimshaw, the Captain, the blacks, and Jack Chance might try to impose upon her. In terms suggestive of an anti-Voss, she responds to Miss Scrimshaw's "flight of eagles" speech, uttered, significantly, on shipboard on the way *back* to Sydney, in the following terms: "Somewhat to her own surprise, Mrs. Roxburgh remained ineluctably earth-bound. 'I was gashed and slashed too often,' she tried to explain. 'Oh no, the crags are not for me!' " (p. 402). And, despite the Captain's intimation at the beginning of the journey of the *Bristol Maid*, Ellen chooses to associate her earth-boundness with her sex. Thus, Mrs. Roxburgh declines to be Voss; she declines to break out of the roles that culture dictated for an Englishwoman in the 1830s; and it is, perhaps, to be regretted that it would be futile to speculate whether she will reject Mr. Jevons. But, at the end of the penultimate chapter, she has already declined something no less significant—interpretation, and, even, interpretation of self. "Mrs. Roxburgh could not have explained the reason for her being there, or whether she had served a purpose, ever" (p. 333). She is not even allowed a choric interpretation of the kind that Voss was permitted. Indeed, she defies her choric commentators. The text remains curiously enigmatic. Where has Ellen Roxburgh's narrative led her? For what have her several transformations prepared her? For further transformations yet? The text will not abide our question. But we may speculate.

Mrs. Roxburgh's history is a narrative that proceeds from culture to nature and back to culture; from the world of her pretty, green, fringed shawl to that of her "fringe of leaves" back to that where she wears borrowed clothes. It is a series of transformations: from the Cornish Ellen Gluyas to the English Mrs. Roxburgh (who speak, it might be noted, different "languages") to the "black" goddess/slave (where language is of no avail) to Jack Chance's mistress/mother to being, in delirium, Jack's Mab (who is dead) to being "reborn" as the enigmatic Ellen Roxburgh and perhaps, future Mrs. Jevons. It is essentially a picaresque narrative: Ellen Roxburgh is one to whom things happen, rather than one who wills them to happen. In its dramatic structure, the novel is classically simple (it even has a Prologue and an Epilogue). It has a rising action to the climax of its heroine's act of anthropophagy, then falling action, dénouement, and enigmatic resolution. But everything—transformations, picaresque narrative, and dramatic structure—points to that climax.

I feel that I must cast myself as a critical Odysseus in order prudently to sail between the Scylla of eccentricity and the Charybdis of obsession in insisting upon and articulating the detail with which *A Fringe of Leaves* substantiates the significance of its climax. I would say, in my defence, that I am dealing with an obsessive text within an insistent *oeuvre*. So, at the "valedictory meal" on shipboard in Sydney, "Mr. Roxburgh noticed his wife's ear-rings. 'I believe you would dress yourself up, Ellen, for a breakfast of yams and opossum with savages in the bush' " (p. 40). The prolepsis is, of course, fulfilled; but who, in the light of the details I will produce, will be bold enough to say that "dress" is *not* ambiguous? As the ship leaves Sydney, the sails' "bellies were filled," like those of the passengers. In her recollections of Van Diemen's Land, Ellen is aware of her yearning for communion of speech with the brutalized convicts, and observes that the Catholics among them are denied the communion of the wafer (p. 106). Garnet Roxburgh's sexual presence is insistent even in church, where Mrs. Roxburgh is aware of the pressure of his *thigh* (p. 108). When they have intercourse, Ellen thinks of the late Mrs. Garnet Roxburgh: "She could imagine the body of a murdered woman lying thus, a bundle of disarranged clothing, the flesh of a *thigh* half buried in leaves, the gaping corsage. But in this case the victim was a man, whose dead weight she was supporting" (p. 116, my emphasis).

After the shipwreck, even the refined and valetudinarian Austin Roxburgh contemplates cannibalism, and is disgusted with himself, even though he recognizes "his thoughts were only cut to a traditional pattern," and he dreams (for *his* cannibalism is displaced), *"This is the body of Spurgeon which I have reserved for thee, take eat, and give thanks for a boil which was spiritual matter"* (p. 231). After the feast of roasted, putrefying kangaroo, all of the party, except Ellen, is racked by diarrhoea. Like vomiting, diarrhoea signifies an untimely rejection of sustenance. According to Lévi-Strauss,[43] anthropological evidence about vomiting is contradictory, in some cultures suggesting a regression from culture to nature, in others a means of transcending culture. Mr. Roxburgh chooses to attribute their indisposition not to the gamey flesh, but to the minerals in the water (p. 235). This may well be a subconscious rejection of the cannibalism of which he has dreamed.

At her first meal after her capture by the blacks, Mrs. Roxburgh sees a brace of small, furred animals, which she could eat raw. But she is not invited to the feast. She is flung scraps, a fish-tail, and a dorsal fin, which taste "glutinous" (p. 248). It may be significant that the only time this term has been used previously in the text was by the late Mr. Roxburgh, who employed it to describe a kiss. But, from now on, for Mrs. Roxburgh and the blacks, "the whole of life revolved round the search for food" (p. 253). Mrs. Roxburgh's crucial meal is prepared for gradually; so she comes upon the charred remains of the first officer, and "one of the legs had been hacked away where the thigh is joined to the hip." The skin of what remains has been roasted (p. 256). Mrs. Roxburgh has yet to encounter that "severed leg."

When she comes upon the blacks after the rite at which they have eaten the slain girl, she finds that their faces are "curiously mystical," and that they look like "forgiven" "communicants." Their response to her is no less insistently signalled: "After *swallowing* their surprise at the intrusion on their privacy, the initiates *regurgitated;* it came spluttering back as rude and guttural sounds of anger" (p. 271, my emphasis). Mrs. Roxburgh follows at a distance from these communicants, and then the long-awaited climax occurs. She picks up a thigh bone that they have dropped. She tears at it, swallows it by great gulps, and flings it away only after it is cleaned. "She was less disgusted in retrospect by what she had done, than awed by the fact that she had been moved to do it. The exquisite innocence of this forest morning, its quiet broken by a single flute-note endlessly repeated, tempted her to believe that she had partaken of a sacrament" (p. 272); yet, "she could not have explained how tasting flesh from the human thigh-bone in the stillness of a forest morning had nourished not only her animal body but some darker need of the human spirit" (p. 274).

Ellen Roxburgh is a singular communicant, but no less a communicant for that. Her cannibalism may be taken (by the cultured?) as an index of her regression from culture to nature; but surely the text does not offer it that way. But she *is* a singularly isolated communicant, separated not only from her fellow whites but from her black captors who also, at times, worship her. Perhaps, if we recall Robertson Smith's account of the twofold function of animal sacrifice, we may read Ellen's partaking of a sacrament not as "a confirmation of fellowship and mutual social obligations" but as "a communication of divine life." Though Mrs. Roxburgh's very isolation may stress that the divine life is *within* the individual. "There is another world, but it is in this one."

I must reassert, before proceeding, that the text has been insistent, and often subtly and curiously so, about the specificity of the limb with which it is concerned. Consider an early sequence: on page 17, with respect to the choric ladies' speculations upon Mrs. Roxburgh, Mr. Merivale is of the honest opinion that " 'the ladies haven't left her a leg to stand on' "; three paragraphs later, Mr. Merivale announces his intention of driving round by the brickfields to collect a leg of pork; and on page 23, the emancipist Delaney, who has provided the leg of pork, also provides the information that two men had just been found with their guts laid open. " 'Stone cold, they were, an' the leg missin' off one of 'em.' " Again, in the opening paragraph of Chapter 3, Ellen Roxburgh allows "wakefulness to seep back into *filleted limbs* and a stuffy mind" (p. 43, my emphasis). While the primary meaning of "filleted" here is probably one which is used to refer to something being bound up with a narrow band of linen or silk, who is bold enough to deny the possibility of an insistent "secondary" meaning, in which the "fillet" is the fleshy part of the *thigh?* As I quoted from Lévi-Strauss previously, myths contain no gratuitous themes. And if themes are gratuitous, what are we to make of this?—None but Austin Roxburgh's wife "ever guessed that he must have reacted to his brother's departure as though he had suffered the *amputation of a limb*" (pp. 148–149, my emphasis). These examples are symptomatic of this insistent and obsessive text.

But now it is time to ask: *why* the insistence on the *thigh?* and *why* the insistence on "roasting"? In *The Origin of Table Manners,* Lévi-Strauss has much to say about the role of roasting within the "semantic field of recipes"; far more, I regret, than can be integrated here. Let me merely cite that he insists that, on the axes of his "culinary triangle," roasting is always on the side of Nature while boiling, which necessitates a man-made artifact, is on the side of Culture.[44] The roast limb that Mrs. Roxburgh partakes of may, then, symbolize, in its being roasted, a regression to nature. (We might note that while Mrs. Roxburgh will long for tea in a porcelain cup on her return to civilization, Jack Chance dreams of *boiled* beef. But he is a plebeian.)

Which brings us to that insistent limb, the thigh. In *The Raw and the Cooked,* we will find evidence that a "severed leg" may symbolize the phallus.[45] I am not sure that we need South American evidence to support this obvious "Freudian" symbology, but need not reject it, once found. I want to be bold once more: in her sylvan sacrament, in her isolated, momentary, soon to be lost and never to be understood, anthropophagous communion, Ellen Roxburgh, swallowing the literal flesh of an aboriginal girl, is, metaphorically, *eating the patriarchy.* "I am brave, I can eat anything." She is partaking of their *virtù.* In eating the phallus, in partaking of the insistent thigh that men in her culture have been constantly pressing against her and that the text has been consistently displaying to the reader, Mrs. Roxburgh "kills" the father-totem within her (to take up Freud's suggestions) by literally consuming its metaphor. It is indeed *her* spirit that is nourished, her essential "she-ness," momentarily free of the roles that a patriarchal society would write for it. Eddie Twyborn/Eadith Trist/Eudoxia Vatatzes would approve. Such a sacrament, such a communion with self, can only be momentary but its having transpired, even though *she* could not have explained it, accounts, I would suggest, as much as her "communion" with Jack Chance, for her initial enigmatic silence and passivity on her return to the world of "European" culture.

Every climax must be followed by a catastrophe. The insistent details that prepared us for Ellen Roxburgh's "sacrament" are no less there as her tale moves towards its end. When she rejoins the tribe, she feels that she "could have eaten" the black children (p. 276). At the corroboree, her lips part to receive, what?—"the burnt sacrifice? the bread and wine?" (p. 284). When Jack Chance first kisses her, it is her *thigh* that he kisses through her fringe of leaves; and their first sexual communion is described thus: "It became a shared hunger. She would have swallowed him had she been capable of it" (pp. 298, 299). The text moves away from its cannibalistic climax by way of displacement. Ellen and Jack eat an emu, and she "thought she could detect moral censure directed by the convict at himself for having murdered *the human bird*" (p. 314, my emphasis). This reminds her of her literally human meal: "with the passing of time she would not have known how to exculpate herself, or convey to the convict the sacramental aspect of what could only appear a repellent and inhuman act" (p. 315). For she is already moving back into the codes of the patriarchy. Thus it is impossible for her to explain to the Commandant at Moreton Bay what transpired in the bush. How could *he* understand? " 'It was too private. For me too, I realized later. A kind of communion' " (p. 364). As she also tells him of the fate of the men of the expedition: " 'Some of them probably eaten. Only the condemned survive' " (p. 343). Ellen Roxburgh is condemned to the world of the 1830s where men write women's roles; she is condemned to have undergone her sacramental communion with self, not to have understood it, not to be able to explain it, and possibly, not to have been transformed by it, except for being "condemned" to that curious terminal passivity. How else explain her final exchange with the once-Sybilline Miss Scrimshaw, who longs to be an eagle, and is prepared to reveal still more?

> "Have you ever noticed that I am a woman only in my form, not in the essential part of me?'
> Somewhat to her own surprise, Mrs. Roxburgh remained ineluctably earthbound. "I was slashed and gashed too often," she tried to explain. "Oh no, the crags are not for me!" She might have been at a loss had not the words of her humbler friend Mrs. Oakes found

their way into her mouth. "A woman, as I see, is more like moss or lichen that takes to some tree or rock as she takes to her husband." (p. 402)

Must we not say that Ellen Roxburgh is "condemned" to and by her culture with a vengeance?

Notes

1. *Mystery and Manners: Occasional Prose*, ed. Sally and Robert Fitzgerald, New York, Farrar, Straus, & Giroux, 1977, pp. 161–2.

2. "Christina Stead's Unforgettable Dinner Parties," *Southerly* XXXIX (1979), 28–45.

3. *The Origin of Table Manners*, New York: Harper & Row, 1978, p. 495.

4. *Ibid.*, p. 428.

5. *Ibid.*, p. 484.

6. *Ibid.*, p. 489.

7. *The Raw and the Cooked*, London, Cape, 1969, p. 336.

8. *The Origin of Table Manners*, p. 264.

9. *Ibid.*, p. 396.

10. W. Robertson Smith, *Lectures on the Religion of the Semites*, New edn. revised, London, A. & C. Black, 1914, p. 269 [New York, Schocken, 1972].

11. *Ibid.*, p. 439.

12. Sigmund Freud, *Totem and Taboo*, New York, Norton, 1946, p. 182.

13. *Ibid.*, p. 188.

14. *Ibid.*, p. 178.

15. *A Theory of Literary Production*, London, Routledge and Kegan Paul, 1978.

16. *The Aunt's Story*, Harmondsworth, Penguin, 1977, p. 270.

17. *The Burnt Ones*, London, Eyre & Spottiswoode, 1964.

18. *The Twyborn Affair*, London, Cape, 1979, p. 216.

19. *Riders in the Chariot*, London, Eyre & Spottiswoode, 1961, p. 275.

20. *The Eye of the Storm*, New York, Viking, 1974, p. 213.

21. *The Vivisector*, London, Cape, 1973, pp. 317–44.

22. *The Eye of the Storm*, pp. 398–406.

23. *The Solid Mandala*, London, Eyre & Spottiswoode, 1966, p. 209.

24. *The Twyborn Affair*, p. 412.

25. *The Living and the Dead*, Harmondsworth, Penguin, 1977, pp. 173–90.

26. *The Eye of the Storm*, pp. 286–96.

27. *The Vivisector*, p. 588.

28. *The Eye of the Storm*, pp. 418, 515.

29. *Voss*, London, Eyre and Spottiswoode, 1959, pp. 212, 262–3, 413, 418.

30. *Riders in the Chariot*, p. 460 (my emphasis).

31. *Ibid.*, p. 82.

32. *The Burnt Ones*, p. 185.

33. *The Vivisector*, pp. 344, 639–40.

34. *The Solid Mandala*, p. 91.

35. *Riders in the Chariot*, pp. 36–7.

36. *Voss*, pp. 27–8, 30, 39, 43, 192, 213.

37. *The Eye of the Storm*, pp. 227, 519, 526, 572.

38. *Voss*, p. 44.

39. *Riders in the Chariot*, p. 522.

40. *The Solid Mandala*, pp. 203, 272.

41. *The Twyborn Affair*, pp. 281, 282.

42. *A Fringe of Leaves*, London, Cape, 1976, p. 21. Further page references in body of text.

43. *The Raw and the Cooked*, p. 135.

44. *The Origin of Table Manners*, p. 49. On the cultural functions of roasting, see also pp. 484–90.

45. *The Raw and the Cooked*, pp. 266–7.

The Psychic Mandala   Peter Beatson°

THE SOUL AND THE SELF

In this Part we turn from the principles that run through the groundswell of Being to the human personality through which these principles express themselves. This Part is organized like a mandala of which the core is the soul and the outer circumference is society. In the discussion, certain concepts will be employed to indicate different zones of the temperament. These concepts are all components of that one mysterious entity "I." At certain points they merge into one another in such a way that it is not always easy or even desirable to make rigid distinctions between them. But if we are to grasp the metaphysical basis of White's characterization, it is a necessary preliminary to disentangle and express as clearly and simply as possible the different meanings that the word "I" may contain. Three basic distinctions will be made, of which each but the first is capable of further subdivision.

The ineffable core of the mandala-personal is the spark of divinity that is planted as potential in everyone at birth. This will be referred to as "the higher soul," "the hidden soul" or simply "the soul." This is the indwelling Christ of Christian mysticism or the *shecchinah* of

° Reprinted from *The Eye in the Mandala: Patrick White: A Vision of Man and God* (London: Elek, 1976), 81–110; courtesy Grafton Books, a division of the Collins Publishing Group.

Jewish mysticism. Surrounding this like a womb or alchemist's retort is a lower, or working soul. This will be called "the self" or "the core of being" and is similar to the Jungian Self that is the end-product of the individuation process. The division or rupture that occurs in this core of being is between the principles of Nous and Physis. Finally, there is the existential or phenomenological self—the subject of orthodox psychiatry and psychology—of which the potential divisions are manifold. The "I" can be experienced as identical with any one of these three selves or with any subdivision within them. I can identify with my having self, my erotic self, my cogitating self, my social self, my core of being or with the soul. A quotation from Gabriel Marcel may help pinpoint the area of religious philosophy in which Patrick White is working:

> We can find no salvation for mind or soul unless we see the difference between our being and our life. The distinction may be in some ways a mysterious one, but the mystery itself is a source of light. To say "my being is not identical with my life" is to say two different things. First, that since *I am* not my life, my life must have been given to me; in a sense unfathomable to man, I am previous to it; *I am* comes before *I live*. Second, my being is something which is in jeopardy from the moment my life begins, and must be saved; my being is at stake, and therein perhaps lies the whole meaning of life. And from this second point of view, I am not *before* but *beyond* my life. This is the only possible way to explain the ordeal of human life (and if it is not an ordeal, I do not see what else it can be). And here again, I hope very much that these words will not stir up in our minds memories of stereotyped phrases drowsily heard in the torpor too often induced by a Sunday sermon. When Keats—certainly not a Christian in the strict meaning of the word—spoke of the world as a "vale of soul-making," and declared in the same letter of April 28th, 1819, that "as various as the Lives of men are—so various become their souls, and thus does God make individual beings, Souls, Identical Souls, of the sparks of his own essence," he had the same idea as mine, . . .[1]

The relationships between the hidden soul, the self and the temperament are analogous to the relationships between the Hidden God, the paired principles and the phenomenal world. The soul emanates outwards through, and in turn is nourished by, the external aspects of personality. Like the Hidden God, it must express or even find itself through cleavage and pain, but although psychological and physical existence—the vehicles of the divided soul—are "real" they exist on a lower ontological plane than the soul, and their dissolution is not necessarily the dissolution of spirit. The hidden soul is faceless, nameless and unknowable. Like the Hidden God its presence can only be surmised, but without this supposition no other psychic event in Patrick White's novels is fully explicable. There are enough hints in White's writing to make this act of faith justifiable:

> . . . this ruin of an over-indulged and beautiful youth, . . . was also a soul about to leave the body it had worn, and already able to emancipate itself so completely from human emotions, it became at times as redemptive as water, as clear as morning light. (*ES* p. 12)

> All of which has only indirect bearing on your significant life, revealed nightly in the presence of this precious wafer of flesh from which earthly beauty has withdrawn, but whose spirit will rise from the bed and stand at the open window, rustling with the light of its own reflections, till finally disintegrating into the white strands strung between the araucarias and oaks of the emergent park, yourself kneeling in spirit to kiss the pearl-embroidered hem, its cold weave the heavier for dew or tears. (*ES* p. 335)

The most numerous references to the soul are found in *Voss*. As the explorers move into the desert, some of them develop hallucinated or visionary awareness of the animistic desert religion of the aborigines. The soul, as it is encountered in the interior, is an almost corporeal entity—a bird, a spirit or a ghost, rather than the incorporeal, almost abstract soul of Christian theology. The visions or dreams of spirits point towards the existence of the higher soul, but their very concreteness hides as much as it reveals of its true nature:

> "These dead men" the native boy explained, and it was gathered that his people lay their dead upon such platforms, and would leave them there for the spirits to depart.
> "All go," said the blackfellow, "All."
> As he placed his hands together, in the shape of a pointed seed, against his own breast, and opened them skyward with a great whooshing of explanation, so that the silky, white soul did actually escape, and lose itself in the whirling circles of the blue sky, his smile was radiant. (*V* p. 260)

"The shape of a pointed seed," or of the almond, appears frequently in *Voss*, suggesting the almost biological link between generation and regeneration of the soul.

In the bird and ghost souls of *Voss*, we have already moved away from the hidden soul towards spiritism. At a slightly lower level again, there are various forms of uncanny psychic occurrences in the novels, which are, strictly speaking, parapsychological rather than religious. In *The Aunt's Story*, Theodora has the prophetic dream mentioned in the last chapter. In *The Tree of Man*, Thelma Forsdyke becomes aware through some extra-sensory intuition that her father has died. In *Riders in the Chariot*, Reha appears in dreams and visions to direct her husband. Above all, there is the strange link between Voss and Laura, which may, for much of the novel, be explained naturalistically, but, at least in the climactic chapter, must be accepted at its face value as a "real" abnormal psychic event. Like so much else in the book, this telepathic relationship shows the blend of European and aboriginal beliefs that White creates. The German romantics, whose influences can be felt strongly in *Voss*, were fascinated by such parapsychological occurrences, while anthropologists have observed telepathic powers among the inhabitants of the Australian interior:

> The Aborigine has, in fact, developed the art of contemplation to a much greater degree than most of us. He may be taking part in general conversation . . . when . . . he drops into a state of recollection and receptivity, lasting minutes, until he has realized who will be "coming along" in the near future. . . .
>
> Many white folk who have known their native employees well, give remarkable examples of the Aborigine's power for knowing what is happening at a distance, even hundreds of miles away . . . how he could have known, they do not understand, for there was no means of communication whatever and he had been away from his own people for weeks and even months. . . . In any case, granted their animistic and "dreaming" philosophy, they are quite logical, and what is more, they act on their logic and apparently seldom find it wanting.[2]

Although the relationship between Voss and Laura serves a religious end, it is in itself not religious—it demonstrates the power of the mind to transcend normally accepted physical limitations, but it does not really illuminate the nature of the soul. ESP has the same tangential connection with the hidden soul as miracles have with the Hidden God.

For a novelist, there is a more important aspect of the soul than its hidden, theological nature, ghost appearances or psychic occurrences. For existential purposes, for the business of living in the flesh and in the world, these are crucial but latent concerns. The centre of the psychic mandala as it is actually experienced in life is a core of being which has a more personal and fleshly reality than its ghostly twin. This core of being is the centre of the temperament, and is fed by the total personality, including sense impressions, fears, instincts, dreams, conscious thought and memory. It has the capacity to blaze up in response to the poetry of life, or to undergo the torments of personal suffering. It relates outwardly to the entire temperament and inwardly to the higher soul. The latter, whose mission it is to achieve unity with the Hidden God, can only fulfil its destiny by living out the implications of existence. It must emanate through the phenomenological self and enter into dialogue with the external world in both its social and its natural aspects. The core of being is the first stage in this emanation. Whereas the higher soul is faceless and, in a sense, anonymous, the working soul is tied more closely to the individuality of its possessor. It does not have a single essence but expresses itself in various vocations. Its vocation may be love of nature or love of humanity, an obsession with exploration or a gift for painting. It can inform the life of a *zaddik* or a handmaid, a simpleton or a genius. It seeks to express itself in action, but it can exist (as with Rhoda Courtney or Theodora Goodman) even when its only vocation is to be itself. What is essential is that this centre should be open, accepting completely the conditions of existence; if it is closed, as it seems to be in most people, it will fail in its first function, which is to nourish the higher soul within.

Those who possess this core, genius or daemon are marked off by the intensity and genuineness of their responses to joy and to suffering. Its existence is hinted at in *The Aunt's Story* by the image of the Indian filigree ball:

> So they took the filigree ball and rolled it over the carpet . . . And although its hollow sphere was now distorted and its metal green, when rolled across the drawing-room carpet the filigree ball still filled with a subtle fire.
> "It's silly," said George.
> Suddenly he wanted to kick it.
> "It's not," said Lou.
> Her hands protected not only the Indian ball, but many secret moments of reflected fire. (AS pp. 14–15)

> There were the people as empty as a filigree ball, though even these would fill at times with a fire. (AS p. 136)

In *The Tree of Man,* Stan Parker experiences his true self as a powerful but inexpressible surge of inner poetry:

> "The Gold Coast, eh," said the young man.
> As if the permanence of furniture was a myth. As if other glittering images that he had sensed inside him without yet discovering, stirred, heaved, almost to the surface. . . .
> . . . It was as if the beauty of the world had risen in a sleep, in the crowded wooden room, and he could almost take it in his hands. All words that he had never expressed might suddenly be spoken. He had in him great words of love and beauty, below the surface, if they could be found. (TM pp. 34–5)

Intuitive knowledge of the existence of the core of being may lead White's characters into wrong paths. One such false belief is that the true self can be totally identified with the gift, vocation, genius or daemon through which it expresses itself. The "gift" or obsession can take a character a long way in his discovery of the self, but it cannot take him all the way and if it is allowed to flourish unchecked and untempered by spiritual wisdom it may pervert the soul's destiny. This can be dramatically highlighted by contrasting the two following quotations from *The Eye of the Storm:* "my gift, which is myself" (p. 241); "myself is this endlessness" (*ES* p. 551).

Another misconception is that the true self can be reached by subtraction. Several of White's characters attempt to realize themselves by amputation, trying to slice away the external, existential aspects of their lives, in order to release the core of reality. As was pointed out in Part One, this effort is self-defeating—the centre of the mandala is finally released only by first embracing existence. In *The Aunt's Story,* Theodora commits several acts of symbolic suicide in an attempt to reach a state of pure being. Holstius saves her by pointing out that reality lies not in subtraction but in the organic processes of multiplication and division. Voss, too, attempts to find himself by self-destruction. He mistakenly identifies the self with the Nous principle in his nature and is only saved when, with the assistance of Laura, Nous is married to Physis to make him a whole man. Mary Hare also toys with this heresy of reduction: "Eventually I shall discover what is at the centre, if enough of me is peeled away" (*RC* p. 57).

The production of the self, which Jung sees as analogous to the philosopher's stone, can only be achieved if the raw material of life is fed into it. The elixir can only be created if the womb of the self is fertilized, the furnace fed; there must be complete openness to the outside world. In *The Solid Mandala,* Waldo Brown—in spite of his obsession with his "crystal core"—is a false alchemist who lets the stone slip through his fingers by keeping the core of being shut off from life. Like Voss, Waldo makes the mistake of confusing a limited aspect of the self—the Nous aspect—with the whole self. The more he nurtures his fantasy of genius, the less capable he is of realizing it:

> To submit himself to the ephemeral, the superficial relationships might damage the crystal core holding itself in reserve for some imminent moment of higher idealism. Just as he had avoided fleshly love—while understanding its algebra, of course—the better to convey eventually its essence. (*SM* p. 183)

> More than anything else these dubious overtures, such an assault on his privacy, made Waldo realize the need to protect that part of him where nobody had ever been, the most secret, virgin heart of all the labyrinth. (*SM* p. 191)

The self can be either developed or destroyed according to the

temperament and life style of the individual. The spirals of degeneration and regeneration mentioned in Part One relate directly to
the core of being. The misuse of a lifetime will corrupt and destroy
it by an almost organic process, and this corruption will, in turn,
destroy the potential higher soul. On the other hand, if the separate
elements of the personality can be wedded one with another within
the core of being, so that the word "I" is spoken from the centre
of the mandala, then this personal "I" will itself dissolve and be
transcended as the hidden soul returns to the Hidden God.

Chance has endowed the English language with the possibility
of symbolizing the "I" by the "eye." Most clear-sighted, reasonable
people, who believe that if I think therefore I am, see only as through
a glass darkly. The blind eyes of Elizabeth Hunter, through which a
mineral blue will flash from time to time, are the most fitting emblem
for the condition of the soul impeded in its attempts to see clearly.
Its sight is obscured by a film of matter, just as the Eye is obscured
by the Storm. Only when the Eye is focused on her for the last time
is it implied that the scales will fall, and she will see face-to-face on
a level where blindness and illumination are one.

We have now established the heart of the psychic mandala. From
this point, the discussion will flow out through more external aspects
of the temperament and beyond this to the relations between the
individual and the external world. It will emphasize the divisions and
obstacles that the soul encounters as it pulses outwards, and the
nourishment it acquires as it flows back to the central organ.

THE TRAGIC CLOWN

Fundamental to White's characterization is a sense of discrepancy
between the core of being and the temperament through which it
must express itself. The goblet is seldom adequate for the elixir that
it contains. As the soul moves out from the centre it is impeded and
distorted by limitations and imperfections of mind, emotion or body.
Existence is never adequate to express the pure poetry of essence.

Unlike the Greek sculptors, who attempted to create a perfect
harmony of idea and form, White emphasizes the pathetic incongruity
of inner and outer. This accounts for the constant sense of the
ludicrous, the ironic and the grotesque which surrounds his characters
even when they are at an extreme point of suffering or ecstasy. In
pure tragedy, as with Sophocles, and pure comedy, as in Dante's
Paradiso, irony is discarded to be replaced by complete congruity of
spirit, emotion and style. There is no such unmediated flow in White.
His style is at its most wry and bathetic as the zenith or nadir is
reached. It is important to realize that this irony is not directed at
the spirit, nor is it intended to undercut or pervert the meaning and

importance of the events. It is a reflection of his constant and inescapable sense of the imperfection and limitation of the human vessel, the inherent inadequacy of form to convey the full implications of idea.

The impediments that the temperament opposes to the core can be seen in the case of Theodora Goodman, incapable of expressing the "flaming moments," and in Stan Parker who never succeeds in writing down the poetry that swells inside him. In *Voss*, the Faustian or Luciferian resonances of the German are undercut by an essentially limited and nasty temperament; Voss is ludicrous rather than terrible. Mary Hare has visions of God, but her frame is so frail that, like some little wood sprite driven mad by the presence of Pan, she is bludgeoned and terrified, rather than uplifted, by her experience. Arthur Brown's mission of responsibility and love is turned aside and frustrated by the lumbering mind and clumsy frame which have been tied to his dedicated soul.

This aspect of characterization is expressed through images of clowns, harlequins, dolls and pierrots. It lies behind the references to circuses, vaudeville, pantomime and farce. These sum up the sense that man, in his highest aspirations to love or lowest depths of suffering, is still inescapably encumbered by the inadequacy of personality. This image pattern is found in its relation to love in *The Solid Mandala*:

> The *pierrot d'amour* on the cover certainly conveyed less expectancy, less of the slightly scented breathlessness of the afternoon when Dulcie had explained about the *pierrot* on Mrs. Musto's bottle.
>
> So Arthur sat, and as the clanking tram flung the passengers together, composed his own version of a song. (*SM* p. 248)

"Who am Ieeehhh?
Guess! Guess! *Guesss!*"
"*Peerrot d'amor*
At half-past four,
That's what I am!
How the leaves twitter—
And titter!
No one is all that dry,
But Ieeehhh!" (*SM* p. 134)

In its relationship to suffering, the clown image appears in *Riders in the Chariot*, in a vignette that pointedly precedes the crucifixion of Himmelfarb:

> "Oh, I say, a circus!"
> Most comical was one of the clowns who pretended to enact a public hanging on the platform of a lorry . . .

"They will kill the silly bugger yet!" screamed one of the grannies. . . .

It did seem as though the clown's act had been played out at last, for a second procession . . . had united precipitately with the first . . . the second procession was seen to be that of an actual funeral. . . .

As the clown spun at the end of his rope, and the little property coffin hesitated on the brink of the lorry . . . a woman rose in the first funeral car, or stuffed herself, rather, in the window; a large, white woman—could have been the widow—pointing, as if she had recognized at last in the effigy of the clown the depth, and duration, and truth of grief. . . .

It had not been established whether the clown was dead, or again shamming, when the interlocked processions dragged each other round the corner and out of sight. (*RC* pp. 453–5)

After a brief and ribald expression of this motif in *The Vivisector*, where Hurtle Duffield paints "The Old Fool Having Bladder Trouble," it is developed at length in *The Eye of the Storm*. The sad, masochistical little Jewess Lotte Lippmann expresses it in all its twentieth century hopelessness and desolation during her vaudeville song-and-dance routines for Mrs. Hunter and also in her own pathetic life and death:

> "*Wenn Mutter in die Menage ritt,*
> *Wie jauchzt' mein Herz auf Schritt und Tritt*
> *Hoppla, hoppla, tripp, trapp, trapp. . . .*"
> "*Es ist'ne Welt für leere Laffen,*
> *Ein Zirkus mit dressierten Affen*
> *Die Löwen und die Löwenkätzchen*
> *Die Dame ohne Unterleib,*
> *Die Hohe Schul' mit allen Mätzchen,*
> *Was ist es schon? Ein Zeitvertreib!*" (*ES* p. 444)

For Lotte there appears to be no escape from the masquerade of life. The case of Sir Basil Hunter, however, suggests that there may be a resolution to the pantomime. To himself—and often to others—Basil is not so much the Great Man as the Eternal Fool. Basil's foolishness constantly flickers around him, undercutting his pretensions: " '. . . I'm the one who's the fool!' " (*ES* p. 509); ". . . still the FOOL." (*ES* p. 595). The identification becomes complete in the dream sequence quoted in Chapter Three and in the realization that follows the dream: "Compose a wire, then, to the Jacka, if he could get his tongue round the significant word. (FOOL. . .)" (*ES* p. 595). The Fool, in fact, has a crucial role to play in Basil's quest to create the unplayable Lear: ". . . this is why He is unplayable by actors anyway at those moments when the veins are filled with lightning the Fool flickering in counterpoint like conscience . . . (*ES* pp. 272–3). Lear, as well as being the most powerful figure in tragedy, is also a foolish old man, and if Basil is to achieve him it is necessary that the fool as well as the lightning should expose him for what he is. Basil's confrontation with the fool and the panto suggests that Lotte Lippmann's travesty world need not be a cul de sac. The black comedy of human folly and inadequacy can be transcended by the very act of acceptance, as long as this acceptance is coupled with a vision or dream of a possibly attainable higher peak. It is those who have never accepted the motley who are truly ludicrous.

This section has tried to bring out an area of White's artistic temperament, an area which he has in common with such twentieth century household names as Picasso, Kafka and Schönberg. It is important to stress that White's sense of the ludicrous elements in the human situation is not generated by his consciousness of the Void. It is not the meaninglessness of the universe and the futility of all human enterprise that makes man absurd. On the contrary, man's absurdity exists in the face of a fullness of Being so vast that his pretensions can only be seen as comic. The clown's mask in White does not conceal a void. It is stretched over a plenitude so rich and charged with meaning that no human face is adequate to express it.

THE GREAT SPLINTERING

Outside the core of being, the inner lives of Patrick White's characters exist in a state of considerable fragmentation and disorder. People are divided within and often against themselves, dominated by one function and repressing others. The will, the conscience, the instincts, the social facade or the unconscious assert themselves, suppressing or ignoring other faculties or entering into conflict with them. The discussion that begins in this section will continue in various forms throughout the rest of Part Two. Even so, it is impossible to explore all the complexities of White's psychology. The analysis will concentrate mainly on the area where psychology and metaphysics join hands. The emphasis will mainly be on the spiritual functions and disfunctions of the process of psychic splintering as it is suggested by the following quotation: "Only de Santis realizes that the splinters of a mind make a whole piece. Sometimes at night your thoughts glitter; even de Santis can't see that, only yourself: not see, but know yourself to be a detail of the greater splintering" (ES p. 93).

The various components of the fragmented personality are almost always personified as some significant figure in the environment, so that personalities are intimately locked together. Characters project their inner life onto others, or have fragments of another's personality lodged in theirs. This process can take place at any level of personality, from superficial imitation of another's manners and tones of voice, to discovery of the Christ within in the form of a friend. The progressively deeper possibilities of this mode of psychic symbolism are suggested briefly in the following examples. Rhoda Courtney infuriates her brother by borrowing from time to time the inflections of their mother's voice, while Hurtle himself carries all his family in his memory, from which they rise on occasions to haunt him. Reha accompanies Mordecai Himmelfarb in dreams, while Amy Parker projects her wish-fulfilment fantasies on Madeleine. Theodora Goodman discovers many aspects of her own nature in the occupants of the Hôtel du Midi (the "many lives of Theodora Goodman") and later projects a personification of her own *animus* onto the figment of Holstius. Doll Quigley is possessed, like an unhappy and unwilling medium, by the ghost of her brother, as is Jackie by Voss's spirit. Mrs. Poulter discovers the Word in the flesh of Arthur Brown, as Mrs. Godbold, Mary Hare and Alf Dubbo have Christ made real for them by their relationships with the crucified Jew.

Many of White's novels, at least at one level, can be read almost as psychic allegories. The works can be thought of as taking place within the being of macrocosmic Man—the Author Himself. The interactions of the characters can thus be seen as the interplay between the different faculties of this larger, unspoken character. In *The Ham Funeral*, the stage is set out like an exposed soul, of which the four characters are the four dominant functions; the nascent "I" is the Young Man, who is finally born into true existential selfhood through interacting with the three other sides of himself. The action of *The Living and the Dead* all takes place within the mind of Elyot Standish, aspects of which are exposed and explored in the lives of the other characters. At the end, all these lives fold back again into the central consciousness which has finally been germinated by their fruitful conjunction. Theodora's "I" divides into a multiple existence in Part Two of *The Aunt's Story* and through the interaction of the parts comes to a deeper understanding of the experiences of her earlier life. The four Riders in *Riders in the Chariot*, like Blake's four Zoas, may be regarded as four aspects of one Cosmic Man—the Jewish Man Kadmon or the Christian Christ Pantocrator. Among many other things, the twin brothers in *The Solid Mandala* represent in almost Taoist terms the higher and lower souls of the same body, the one rising to become a kind of god, the other sinking down into the soil:

> The body is activated by the interplay of two psychic structures: first, *hun*, which, because it belongs to the yang principle, I have translated as animus, and secondly, *p'o*, which belongs to the yin principle, and is rendered by me as anima. Both ideas come from observation of what takes place at death. . . . The anima was thought of as especially linked with the bodily processes; at death it sinks to the earth and decays. The animus, on the other hand, is the higher soul; after death it rises in the air, where at first it is still

active for a time and then evaporates in ethereal space, or flows
back into the common reservoir of life. . . . The animus is bright
and active, the anima is dark and earth-bound.[3]

Once we have pointed out this possible level of interpretation,
it is immediately necessary to qualify it. The novels are not just
psychomachia, with each character representing merely one aspect
of the soul. It is perhaps better to say that the characters themselves
see things in these terms, and that their perceptions, while being
true up to a point, may, in fact, falsify the full complexity of the
emotional lives of others. The characters, rather than the author,
allegorize those around them in order to give body to a portion of
their own nature. Returning to *The Living and the Dead*, for instance,
the Standishes' servant Julia Fallon plays an important symbolic role
for both Eden and Elyot, restoring them to the innocence and simplicity with which they had lost contact. What is hidden from them,
however, is the other side of Julia's nature. They do not see the
perplexity and frustration which her very simplicity forces upon her.
Elyot is cursed with literacy and "knowingness"; Julia is trapped
within the limitations that her "admirable" illiteracy imposes on her.
She experiences, and is tormented by, the full reality of the condition
which others, more sophisticated than she, sentimentalize. By the
end of the book, she is so tormented by frustration, confusion and
jealousy that she has become almost evil, while remaining a touchstone
of primitive goodness for the oblivious Elyot.

This point is made because some readers seem confused in the
later novels, particularly in *Voss*, about the Christian symbolism; being
unable to resolve the question: "Who is the Christ-figure?" they
accuse White himself of confusion. In fact, nobody is precisely a
"Christ-figure," while everyone contains a little bit of the divine
archetype. In situations where a parallel is set up between the particular events of the novel and the legend of Christ, this divine spark
is stirred, brought to consciousness, and projected by the characters
themselves onto those involved. This is made quite clear, for instance,
in the death of Palfreyman. Palfreyman is no more (and no less)
"Christ" than anyone else in the book, but in his manner of dying
he arouses the divine image that has been latent in the memories of
the onlookers and makes it potent and unforgettable:

> . . . the members of the expedition were so contorted by appre-
> hension, longing, love or disgust, they had become human again. All
> remembered the face of Christ that they had seen at some point in
> their lives, either in churches or visions, before retreating from what
> they had not understood, the paradox of man in Christ, and Christ
> in man. (V p. 364)

In *Riders in the Chariot,* Himmelfarb becomes the chief activator of the Christ principle in those around him. Those who crucify and those who testify are projecting latent psychic content on him. It is the characters themselves who create the allegory, attempting to reject or release, to deface or beautify the most important part of their own souls. The miracle play that they enact at Easter does not violate the conventions of literary realism as all involved have been acquainted, through their culture, with the parts they are compelled to play; their self-identifications flow naturally from the nature of the event as it unfolds.

The splitting of the personality into different components, and the personification of those components, immediately suggests a certain schizoid tendency in White's writings. *The Aunt's Story* makes controlled literary use of schizophrenia in both the phantasmagoria of Part Two and the appearance of Holstius in Part Three, while the novel as a whole is an astonishingly vivid and accurate study of the schizoid disintegration that can result from ontological insecurity. In his short stories *The Burnt Ones,* White once more investigates the problem of the psychotic personality, particularly as it is generated by the relationship between a dominant mother and a recessive child. These sketches are developed into the full-length portrait of Waldo Brown. But personality splitting in White's novels is not purely or necessarily a matter of schizophrenia; it can be pathological or therapeutic according to the end it serves. The appearance of another person within may be obsessional and disruptive, as it is in the case of Jackie, but it can also be redemptive if the figure gives life to a necessary but hitherto dormant part of the psyche.

Four examples will be given of how splitting and personification can work for either redemption or damnation, two from *Riders in the Chariot* and two from *The Solid Mandala.* In the former novel, Harry Rosetree is divided against his own nature, repressing the Jewish element in his personality, which is not only his past and his race but is also the spiritual component of his own psyche. Roused at Passover by the smell of cinnamon and the presence of Himmelfarb, the ghost of his father emerges from Harry's unconscious, tormenting him by pointing out that he was the one who should have been the first to greet the Messiah. The resident father-figure in Rosetree's soul torments the conscience-stricken apostate to the point where, after a belated attempt to remedy his betrayal by giving Himmelfarb a Jewish burial, he commits suicide. Alf Dubbo, on the other hand, who is also divided against himself, manages to resolve the schism and achieve spiritual fulfilment. Alf is torn between his instinctual, chthonic nature and a higher consciousness which for much of the book remains inaccessible to him: "His mind was another matter, because even he could not calculate how it might behave, or what it might become once it was set free. In the meantime, it would keep jumping and struggling, like a fish left behind in a pool—or two fish, since the white people his guardians had dropped another in" (*RC* p. 393). Although both the teachings and the temperament of Timothy Calderon and Mrs. Pask are of dubious spiritual integrity, they create an awareness in Alf of the possibility of that "ambitious abstraction"—Christ—which once acknowledged never leaves him in peace. Through his own limitations and the inadequacies of others, he cannot reconcile his instinctual nature with his "pastor conscience," until his silent dialogues with Ruth Godbold, Mary Hare and Himmelfarb, and his participation in the Crucifixion and Deposition, allow him to realize that love and goodness can really exist in the flesh and not just in theory.

Although he still cannot act to save the Jew and has a bitter sense of betrayal that links him with Peter, he can bear witness through paint and achieve the same true self or Christhood that is granted to the other three Riders. It is significant that the "Christ" he paints is not only Himmelfarb; it is also Alf Dubbo: "If Dubbo portrayed the Christ darker than convention would have approved, it was because he could not resist the impulse. Much was omitted, which, in its absence, conveyed. It could have been that the observer himself contributed the hieroglyphs of his own fears to the flat, almost skimped figure, with the elliptical mouth, and divided, canvas face, of the Jew-Christ" (*RC* p. 511).

An important aspect of personality division, that has already been touched on several times, is the split within the self of Nous and Physis. The idea of androgyny appears repeatedly in the novels. One thinks of Theodora Goodman and her many masculine attributes, of Voss and his struggle against the woman inside, of Himmelfarb who carries Reha under his left breast, of Hurtle Duffield who plays the female role in many of his sexual relationships and "gives birth" in old age to Kathy Volkov. The concept of the hermaphroditic self receives its most complete expression in *The Solid Mandala*. In Waldo Brown, the division between the masculine and feminine is never healed; throughout his life he remains a victim of his bi-sexuality. Waldo obstinately and neurotically asserts his masculinity, despising Arthur for being a "fat, helpless female." His very denial of the female component in his nature, however, makes him most vulnerable to its assaults. As he grows older, denied more and denying more, he increasingly falls prey to the autonomous assertions of his own *anima*. This reaches its climax in the transvestite scene quoted in an earlier chapter. Waldo identifies himself from time to time with Tiresias, but unlike Tiresias, he never learns wisdom from his encounter with the female principle. Arthur's poem, which forces Waldo to face Physis directly, destroys him.

Arthur is also interested in Tiresias, but unlike Waldo he never experiences his hermaphroditic condition as a lethal schism. Instead, he uses it to explore the true nature of both his own self and that of other people. He is excited and fascinated whenever he comes across the phenomenon of bi-sexuality, accepts it without reservation or shame, and through this very acceptance achieves a unity of personality unknown to his schizoid twin. His interest in Tiresias begins in childhood: "Then there was that other bit, about being changed into a woman, if only for a short time. Time enough, though, to know he wasn't all that different" (*SM* p. 224).

The idea of the spiritual hermaphrodite is presented to him in later life when he is reading in the library:

> On one occasion, in some book, he came across a message. . . .
> "As the shadow continually follows the body of one who walks in the sun, so our hermaphroditic Adam, though he appears in the form of a male, nevertheless always carries about with him Eve, or his wife, hidden in his body."
> He warmed to that repeatedly after he had recovered from the shock. (*SM* pp. 281–2)

The difference between the attitudes of Arthur and Waldo to this potentially dangerous subject is highlighted by this interchange between the brothers:

> "If you want to know, I was thinking about Tiresias," Arthur said to interest him. "How he was changed into a woman for a short time. That sort of thing would be different, wouldn't it, from the hermaphroditic Adam who carries his wife about with him inside?"
> Then Waldo took him by the wrists.
> "Shut up!" he ordered. "Do you understand? If you think thoughts like these, keep them to yourself, Arthur. I don't want to hear. Any such filth. Or madness." (*SM* p. 283)

The final resolution of the problem of the spiritual hermaphrodite is suggested in this last quotation, in which male and female are united at the heart of the mandala: ". . . for a moment she was pretty certain she saw their two faces becoming one, at the centre of that glass eye, which Arthur sat holding in his hand" (*SM* p. 313).

At every level of personality we find the occurrence of splitting, in which fragments of others are embedded in the temperament, or psychic content is projected onto another. Where these different components cannot be reconciled, the personality eventually disintegrates or collapses into chaos, which may end in schizophrenia or even daemonic possession. When they can be made conscious and reconciled, however, they may finally harmonize and consolidate in the core of being, from which the higher soul will finally be born.

IDENTITY

All of White's characters, explicitly or implicitly, are groping to find some satisfactory answer to the existential or ontological question: "Who am I?" Threatened by chaos within and without, they must find some mode of "being there" in the world that will allow them to say with confidence "I am I." "I am" is not the simple assertion it appears on the surface. It can torment a person to the point of madness, and it is amenable to a variety of false applications.

The problem of finding and maintaining a stable identity in the face of a hostile environment is at its most acute in the early works when, presumably, the theme was most personal to the young artist himself. It reaches its climax in *The Aunt's Story*—a novel that was written by an expatriate wrestling with the problem of returning for good to Australia. Although the writing of this book precedes the work of R. D. Laing by over a decade, it may be useful to begin a discussion of Theodora Goodman's predicament with two brief quotations from *The Divided Self*, since they illuminate so vividly the source of her madness:

> A man may have a sense of his presence in the world as a real, alive, whole, and in a temporal sense, a continuous person. As such, he can live out into the world and meet others: a world and others experienced as equally real, alive, whole and continuous.[4]

> The term schizoid refers to an individual the totality of whose experience is split in two main ways: in the first place, there is a rent in his relation with his world and, in the second, there is a disruption of his relation with himself. Such a person is not able to experience himself "together with" others or "at home in" the world, but, on the contrary, he experiences himself in despairing aloneness and isolation; moreover, he does not experience himself as a complete person but rather as "split" in various ways, perhaps as a mind more or less tenuously linked to a body, as two or more selves, and so on.[5]

(The application of these remarks to the problems touched on in the preceding section is too evident to need further amplification. Indeed, there is no better gloss on all of White's early writings up to and including *The Ham Funeral* than *The Divided Self* and its central theory of "ontological insecurity.")

Theodora's sense of identity is sustained by a few brief positive moments or relationships. In Part One, we find such reality-giving moments in her early awareness of the beauty of roses, and in her relationships with Father, the Man who was Given his Dinner, Moraïtis and, above all, the "spirit child" she bears Moraïtis—her niece Lou. Around the precarious core that these create, vast areas of personality are eroded, either by the negative attitudes of others—particularly her mother—or else by her own attempts at self-annihilation. A poignant and possibly crucial early trauma is recorded in the following quotation:

> Once there were the new dresses that were put on for Mother's sake.
>
> "Oh," she cried, "Fanny, my roses, my roses, you are very pretty."
>
> Because Fanny was as pink and white as roses in the new dress.
>
> "And Theo," she said, "All dressed up. Well, well. But I don't think we'll let you wear yellow again, because it doesn't suit, even in a sash. It turns you sallow." Mother said.
>
> So that the mirrors began to throw up the sallow Theodora Goodman, which meant who was too yellow. Like her own sash. She went and stood in the mirror at the end of the passage, near the sewing room which was full of threads, and the old mirror was like a green sea in which she swam, patched and spotted with gold light. Light and the ghostly water in the old glass dissolved her bones. The big straw hat with the little yellow buds and the trailing ribbons floated. But the face was the long, thin yellow face of Theodora Goodman, who they said was sallow. She turned and destroyed the reflection, more especially the reflection of the eyes by walking away. They sank into the green water and were lost. (AS pp. 26–7)

Theodora learns that she is worthless in the eyes of "normal," successful people, and that the few positive people in her life are also undervalued. As already hinted by the end of the above quotation, she is forced in paradoxical self-defence to commit acts of "suicide"; negating her own existence so that it might not be hurt or destroyed from without. She begins a quest to destroy "the monster Self." This is seen in the following passage in which she shoots a little hawk with which she had identified, and, in doing so, wounds the vanity of Frank Parrott (who missed it) and thereby loses the small possibility she might have had of marrying him:

> Now she took her gun. She took aim, and it was like aiming at her own red eye. . . . And she fired. And it fell.
>
> "There," laughed Theodora, "it is done."
>
> . . . She felt exhausted, but there was no longer any pain. She was as negative as air.
>
> . . . I was wrong, she said, but I shall continue to destroy myself, right down to the last of my several lives. (AS pp. 73–4)

The death of Theodora's mother grants her the "freedom" for which, during her years of spinster bondage, she had craved, but it is a strange and disembodied freedom which solves nothing. It is to Lou that Theo turns, for it is above all Lou who confers identity on her. Lou gives her a role in the external world, making her an Aunt, and also, through the similarity of their features and their mutual dissimilarity from others, ratifies her existence. The relationship with Lou, with its shared affection and physical intimacy, also allows Theodora to feel the reality and meaningfulness of her own body:

> It was Lou, whose eyes could read a silence, and whose thin yellow face was sometimes quick as conscience, and as clear as mirrors. Theodora loved Lou. *My niece.* It was too intimate, physical, to express. Lou had no obvious connection either with Frank or Fanny. She was like some dark and secret place in one's own body. And quite suddenly Theodora longed for them to bring the children, but more especially Lou, when they came to town for the funeral. Since her mother's death, she could not say with conviction: I am I. But the touch of hands restores the lost identity. The children would ratify her freedom. (AS p. 11)

But the presence of death in the house frightens her niece and creates a barrier between them that cannot be passed. Theodora realizes, as Part One ends, that there is no real connection between herself and the lives of others, and her sense of total loneliness begins to blossom imperceptibly into madness:

> The child shivered for the forgotten box, which she had not seen, but knew.
> "If I do not die," she said.
> Theodora looked down through the distances that separate, even in love. If I could put out my hand, she said, but I cannot. . . . There is no lifeline to other lives, I shall go, said Theodora, I have already gone. The simplicity of what ultimately happens hollowed her out. She was part of a surprising world in which hands, for reasons no longer obvious, had put tables and chairs. (AS p. 137)

Part Two of *The Aunt's Story* is one of the most delightful and also one of the most puzzling passages that White has written. On a commonsense reading, we find Theodora arriving at a hotel in the south of France and participating in the lives of the other lodgers through a mixture of imagination, intuition, telepathy and, perhaps, a little lunacy. She has already shown her powers of empathy in Part One, when she participates in other lives, like those of the little hawk or Moraïtis, and what happens in Part Two is a simple, if startling, extension of this capacity. But there is another current of evidence in the book that suggests that the unreality of events in Part Two is not limited to Theodora's vicarious experience of the lives of others but extends to all of this section of the novel; it is possible that all the incidents, characters and even the Hôtel du Midi itself are no more than the creations of Theodora's ebullient but untrustworthy mind. This latter interpretation raises a vexing question: if the hotel and its inhabitants do not exist, then where exactly is the corporeal Theodora while they are being dreamed? The arguments for and against these two possible readings cannot be entered into here. But one can say that neither is true, neither is false, and that they are mutually incompatible. For that reason we must accept.

Theodora's experiences in the Hôtel du Midi, like those of Elyot in the deserted house in Ebury Street, are psychotherapeutic. This psychotherapy is not directional, does not reveal one psychological truth. It is simply a vivid re-enactment of all the experiences in the first part. During this re-enactment all the latent emotional content of the events of her earlier life is laid bare. In Part One, she tended to anaesthetize her full emotional responses in order to avoid suffering. In Part Two, the vivisector is at work without the anaesthetic. We find her, for example, re-living the loss of Frank Parrott through the experiences of Sokolnikov, experiencing the ferocious knot of love-hate with Lieselotte and Wetherby, or sharing the spurious delights of having a fantasy child with Mrs. Rapallo. But underlying all these relationships there lies one nagging dread—the dread of non-existence, of having no identity:

> She . . . took out objects of her own, to give the room her identity and justify her large talk of independence. . . . All these acts, combined, gave to her some feeling of permanence. . . . Lying . . . in sleeping cars . . . she had recalled the features of relations. These did give some indication of continuity of being. But even though more voluble, they were hardly more explanatory than the darning egg or moist sponge with which she invested each new room . . . she could not escape too soon from the closed room . . . avoiding the brown door, of which the brass teeth bristled to consume the last shreds of personality, when already she was stripped enough. (AS pp. 114–15)

> I am preparing for bed, she saw. But in performing this act for the first time, she knew she did not really control her bones, and that the curtain of her flesh must blow, like walls which are no longer walls . . . her identity became uncertain. She looked with sadness at the little hitherto safe microcosm of the darning egg. . . . (AS p. 206)

The most important figure in Part Two is Katina Pavlou, as Lou Parrott had been the most important in Part One. Katina is, in fact, Lou's *avatar*. The events of Part Two mirror, in an amplified and distorted form, the rhythm of Part One. It begins with hope and ends with desolation; the hope that begins it is born of the desolation that ended Part One. Theodora's first fantasy involvement is her experience of the moment of death in close, almost erotic intimacy with Katina. The fear of death that had created the barrier between Theodora and Lou now becomes the bond that unites her with Katina. But as the section moves towards its nadir, Theodora "loses" Katina just as inevitably as she had lost Lou, though this time it is not the fear of death but Katina's sexual initiation (another form of death) that separates them. The close link between the Theodora-Lou and the Theodora-Katina relationships is shown by the fact that it was the following unspectacular, earth-shaking letter from Lou that began the unrolling of events that led to Theodora's estrangement from Katina: ". . . But I cannot see, from experience, that there is anything wrong with nuns. In fact, I love Sister Mary Perpetua. She has the loveliest, the saddest face. On my birthday she gave me a bag of aniseed balls and a little wooden cross. Sometimes in the afternoon we sit together, and watch the boats, and then I feel that I shall *never ever* have such a friendship ever again" (AS p. 228).

Lou, who confers identity, who creates that institution—an Aunt— could never, ever have another friend like Sister Mary Perpetua. It is after this blow that Theodora "destroys" the Hôtel du Midi and begins her return journey to Australia which for her has now become Abyssinia, the land of the dead.

In Part Three, where the seeds of madness finally blossom into the full flower, Theodora realizes hopelessly that there is no place for her in her native land, or anywhere: "Although she was insured against several acts of violence, there was ultimately no safeguard against the violence of personality. This was less controllable than fire. In the bland corn song, in the theme of days, Theodora Goodman was a discord. Those mouths which attempted her black note rejected it wryly" (AS p. 274).

Leaving her train at some anonymous spot in the USA, she once more applies herself to the destruction of the monster Self. Suicide is the last creative act of the threatened soul. She throws away her handbag, her tickets, and even adopts a false name. She is accepted by the Johnsons on her own terms, but the "violence of personality" of even these simple, honest folk drives Theodora out to the lonely shack where she makes pathetic efforts to parody the activities of normal, sane housewives. But she is hounded from this refuge by the well-meaning Johnsons, and flees like a hunted animal down to the spring. Here, if her unconscious had allowed, she would have dissolved the last remnants of identity and sanity in the eternal water. But her unconscious does not allow. The same fantasy power that earlier had led her along the paths of madness now comes to the rescue and, at the last minute, works to cure her. Holstius, a familiar compound ghost of all the meaningful men and incidents of her early life, intervenes. First in the cabin and then in the woods, the combination of his abstract words of wisdom and his warm, physical presence restores Theodora to a continuity of being that she thought was lost for ever. He does not lead her into new realms of madness or vision, but gives her the courage to return to humanity. His appearance allows Theodora to say "I am I" with confidence from a deeper level of personality than she had ever known. The last glimpse we have of Theodora is of her once more wearing her hat, upon which flourishes a now confident black rose—confident even of its right to doubt.

After *The Aunt's Story,* with its existential problems and its existential solution, there is a marked change in the tone of Patrick White's novels. This change may tentatively be linked with two important biographical developments. Between *The Aunt's Story* and *The Tree of Man,* White finally returned to Australia for good, and established an organic bond with his country by setting up a farm at Castle Hill ("Sarsaparilla"). Also during this period, the latent religious content of the early works came to the surface and infused into *The Tree of Man* and all succeeding novels a spiritual certainty that was lacking before. The return to Australia and the intensification of the religious factor greatly decrease the sense of existential uncertainty, and give new confidence in the strength of the core of being. The "I" that is the subject of all the books after *The Aunt's Story* is an ontological, not a phenomenological, entity. The quest for identity is no longer the major theme of any of the novels. In spite of the flickerings, uncertainties, doubts, divisions and sufferings of the external temperament, characters like Stan Parker, Voss, Laura, Himmelfarb, Arthur, Hurtle and Elizabeth Hunter have a sense of certainty and purpose that protects them from the inroads of doubt that torment Theodora Goodman. The quest for identity remains an important preoccupation for some minor characters all of the time and for some major characters for a little of the time, but it is not the central dynamic of the writing. White always uses his profound understanding of and sympathy with identity problems to create such characters as Harry Robarts and Basil Hunter, but this awareness is now woven in as one strand of characterization among many. Even Hurtle Duffield, whose defensive cry: "I am an artist!" sounds hollow in his own ears at those points where his deficiencies as a human being in every other way have been exposed, has a certainty about his gift and, finally, a conviction about God that renders him immune from existential assaults. Patrick White's major characters have two important experiences to live out, neither of which is, strictly speaking, a quest for identity. The first is the need to discover and to unfold their destiny as they understand it. The second, which is intimately linked with the first but not identical, is the need to achieve salvation. Thus, for example, Voss is not "looking for himself" in the desert. He knows who he is (Gott!) and is simply confirming his destiny. His journey may provide others like Judd, Harry or Frank with an opportunity to find themselves, but for Voss it is a voyage of ratification, not of discovery. Needless to say, his premises are faulty, but this is irrelevant to his confidence in them. The second crucial life experience for Voss—that of finding Grace—is also not the object of a quest. On the contrary, it is thrust upon his obstinate and unwilling soul by Laura. Whatever quests there are in White, the quest for identity is, for the major characters, the least relevant. Pursuit of the secular vocation and thirst for God are their main preoccupations.

The important division in the novels is between a small group of characters who have a sense of selfhood that is generated by a belief in their core of being and those who speak the "I" from one limited aspect of their external personalities. Most of White's characters outside the inner circle tend to identify the "I" with their thinking, their doing, or their having. They fortify themselves in the rational, social ego, and from this citadel they try to construct a sense of reality of both the nature and possibilities of the external world and the meaning and processes of their own psyches. Secular humanism, based on the Cartesian formula "I think therefore I am," is, for White, one of Australia's worst spiritual sicknesses. The conscious, rational mind and the reality it attempts to structure and define are epiphenomena, and to identify the self with them is to ignore nine-tenths of experience. There are many portraits in White of the plight of the rationalist—whose rationalism may appear as commonsense "reasonableness" or the clever "knowingness" of the socialite. There are the two rationalists Mr. Brown and Mr. Feinstein of *The Solid Mandala,* desperately trying to avert their gaze from the lethal numinous world that floats around them. There is Boo Davenport who uses her lively intellect to keep life at arm's length, and the clock-obsessed Wyburd and Alfred Hunter whose passion for chronological time suggests a spiritual incapacity to cope with more fluid forms of duration. In Judd, we find a very interesting, and also very sympathetic, picture of the limitations of the rationally defined self. Like the others, Judd is a quester, but his questing is limited by the limitations of navigational equipment. He is almost obsessed with his compasses, and when the last is broken so that distance can no longer be controlled or space charted, he turns back, leaving the three extremely unreasonable visionaries to explore areas that the intellect cannot reach. In all of the novels between *The Living and the Dead* and *The Vivisector,* White chooses characters who either cannot or will not mediate their experience through the rational intellect. Even Hurtle Duffield and Elizabeth Hunter, complex, cultivated and intelligent as they are, operate from a much wider range of the mind than just the cogitating component; their agile but not always trustworthy minds sport and flicker across domains that the intellect eschews.

To complete the identification of the self in terms of the limited ego, people add what they have and what they do to what they think. The "I" can then be reckoned up as the sum of social roles, possessions (amongst which are counted the possession of other human beings), achievements and activities. Having completed the reckoning, people then become frozen into their roles: Mr. Bonner *is* his material prosperity, Amy is her family and lover, Basil Hunter is his acting, Boo is her parties. The stereotype may prove limiting, the character may long to repossess tracts of himself that have been amputated or buried, as Basil Hunter longs to become a whole human being and discover the as yet "unplayed I" (*ES* p. 321), but often nothing short of an explosive and possibly mortal trauma will suffice to break the ice. In *The Cockatoos,* White shows several cases of good, honest, rational Australian couples, who are briefly and terrifyingly brought in contact with the voltage of the irrational which, because of their benumbed condition, they can only experience as diabolic or negative epiphanies. For others the "cure" may be a self-conscious and painful struggle, as it is for Basil Hunter, while others again may have the curse gently removed, as Mr. Feinstein is "saved" by his moments of silent communion with Arthur Brown.

Although the central characters do, of course, tend to identify themselves partly in terms of thinking, doing or having, they all, in the end, have a strength at the centre which permits them to surrender these external adjuncts without being destroyed in their being. They can, finally, render up their personal identity for the sake of being identical with God. The self becomes the Self, atman becomes Atman, the Christ within is merged with Christ Pantocrator. Those who cannot render themselves up in this way prove the shallowness of the "I" in which they believe.

The order that must be achieved within the psychic mandala cannot be imposed by external facets of the personality. The ego can never reach down into the centre, and its attempts to organize and dominate the personality frustrate the growth of the true self. It is by an open flow to and from the core of being that the divergent phenomena of mental life are ultimately given coherence. The potential self must emanate outward, for it is only by passing through a stage of fragmentation, confusion and multiplicity (the "great splintering") that it can achieve its final unity. This end will be thwarted if, in the process of diversification, the "I" chooses to believe in one of its external divisions at the expense of the totality.

One last quotation will highlight the significance of the discussion in this section:

> . . . there is something I must find out about, which is neither marriage, nor position, nor the procedures of formal religion, nor

possessions, nor love in *that* sense. If I could only ask Mother. . . .
(*ES* p. 271)

THE BODY

The body, or outer circle of the mandala, has a very solid presence
in White's novels. One of the most striking qualities of his books is
the vivid, sometimes almost obsessive or hallucinated, concentration
on the corporeal aspects of personality. He views human beings with
an openness of vision, a freedom from conventional modes of perception, that often results in a concentration on details that are usually
politely ignored. He sees gristle and sinews, veins in the eyeballs,
tufts of hair, the texture and pores of skin, nostrils, knuckles and
goitres. His subject is the Word made Flesh, and he creates a very
vivid sense of the implications of "being in the flesh."

This very insistence on the body suggests, however, a profound
ambivalence, both temperamental and metaphysical, in his attitude
towards the flesh. There seems to be a fascinated revulsion in the
books. Characters are drawn compulsively towards the flesh and at
the same time desperately try to reject it. At a metaphysical level,
this becomes the paradox that while the body is essential to the soul
it is of less ultimate value; it is simultaneously the most and the least
important of the soul's possessions.

The concentration on the uglier aspects of the body, and the
choice of misshapen or ugly characters, may stem, at least at one
level, from the belief that it is this aspect of the flesh, and not its
perfection, that is the most apt emblem for the condition of the
"descended" soul. The body is not necessarily degraded, but involvement with it does make the soul vulnerable. That this vulnerability
is feared, and that it must, at the same time, be accepted, is the root
of the emotional ambiguity towards the body. White's attitude is
encapsulated in a sequence from *The Living and the Dead,* in which
Joe Barnett wills himself to look at a dead dog: "The festoon of
helpless guts torn out like the last existing privacy. . . . He made
himself look. . . . Man was born to this, no other dignity. . . . But
there was a dignity he was jealous of, his own body, his privacy of
thought. . . ." (*LD* p. 257).

This same fascinated disgust for the more afflicted aspects of the
body, coupled with a sense that there is a personal, an ethical and
a spiritual duty to accept and embrace it, is found in many places
in White. *Voss* opens with Laura Trevelyan caught in the dilemma,
disgusted by the bodies of those around her (particularly the deformed
Rose Portion) and aware that this disgust is a moral weakness:

> But Rose remained, her breasts moving in her brown dress.
> Laura Trevelyan had continued to feel repelled. It was the source

of great unhappiness, because frequently she was also touched. She would try to keep her eyes averted, as she had from Jack Slipper. It is the bodies of these servants, she told herself in some hopelessness and disgust . . . am I a prig? So she wondered unhappily, and how she might correct her nature. (V p. 58)

The same temperamental ambivalence is felt in *The Vivisector*, in which Hurtle Duffield, through some necessity that he can scarcely articulate himself, is drawn time and again to create epiphanies of degradation. He is forced to paint Cutbush masturbating, Hero stabbing herself with a penis, the deformed Rhoda standing at a bidet or Nance spreadeagled on the floor. He seems determined to force into consciousness—his own and that of others—areas of bodily existence, or modes of incarnation, from which eyes are usually averted. Whether this is honesty or obsession is a question the novel leaves open.

This is not to say that White does not respond to physical beauty when it appears. He delights in creating portraits of beautiful women in gorgeous dresses, which he does with an evocative power equal to that of Lawrence or Proust. Limited as the temperaments of these women usually are, their beauty is a "contribution to truth," and White does full justice to the poetry they create. This is particularly evident with Elizabeth Hunter, whose past beauty had something almost sacramental about it, even for the ascetic Mary de Santis. But physical beauty, in the last analysis, must be a spiritual limitation. If too much attention is concentrated on the outside of the mandala the inner circles will be ignored. Ugliness is not in itself a virtue, but those who possess it cannot take refuge on the surface, and must look for truth at deeper levels. From that truth, a new and more significant type of beauty will be radiated, as in the case of the conventionally "plain" Laura Trevelyan, which supersedes the usual categories of beauty and ugliness. It is the beauty of Grace, not of form:

> Other individuals, of great longing but little daring, suspecting that the knowledge and strength of the headmistress might be accessible to them, began to approach by degrees. Even her beauty was translated for them into terms they could understand. As the night poured in through the windows and the open doors, her eyes were overflowing with a love that might have appeared supernatural, if it had not been for the evidence of her earthly body: the slightly chapped skin of her neck, and the small hole in the finger of one glove, which, in her distraction and haste, she had forgotten to mend. (V p. 474)

The intimacy between the soul and the body, however, should not be underrated. It is not irrelevant to the self what kind of a body it is tied to. Except for the very deepest layer of personality, the characters' mode of "being there" in the world will be determined by the form they assume, and the reactions of others to that form. None of White's characters are so intransigently strong or honest that they can withstand the conditioning effects of "being" their bodies. Theodora is driven mad partly by the alienation from herself that occurs when she discovers how ugly she is. Rhoda Courtney has not only the body but also the personality of a hunchback. Everything about Mary Hare except her core of reality is shaped or misshaped by the destructive reactions of those around her, particularly her father, to her stunted body. Although being trapped in a plain, or even repellent, body may, as was suggested above, almost accidentally serve a higher spiritual end, White in no way romanticizes the existential suffering that it inflicts on the self, nor the degree to which the identification of the self is governed by it. He has a profound and sympathetic understanding of the subjectivity of his deformed or afflicted characters, and does not sentimentalize them from the outside.

As well as feeding into, and to a large extent shaping, the "I," the body is also the medium through which this "I" flows out into the world. Not only does it express the innate capacity for love or cruelty, for action or art, but also every part of the human body becomes a speaking symbol for emotional, moral or spiritual states. The body is the most important of the various language systems through which White gives expression to the flickerings of the inner life. Crotches tighten as emotions grow congested, hair evokes latent sexuality, heads shrink down to the bone in states of spiritual deprivation, lips swell or parch as emotions wax and wane, spiritual tension is expressed through a physical limp, breasts sidle, spectacles flash and teeth gnash and worry. To the same end—the expression of the inner life—the body is also coerced into taking on the nature of other forms of existence. There are as many metamorphoses in White as there are in Ovid. Bodies are frozen into the forms of architecture, sculpture, icons or wood-carving, then flow like water, music or fire. They take on the qualities of trees, flowers, scrub, sticks, stones, potatoes, birds, dogs or cows. They are like rock, wood, ash or air. On the purely descriptive level this constant flow of form and substance helps create that rich, bewildering density of texture that typifies White's writing. On the level of "meaning," each change of state releases or identifies some condition of the soul.

The intimate, almost biological, link between the soul and the body, which has been stressed so often in this book, is expressed through many apparently obscene images in *The Vivisector* and *The Eye of the Storm*. These connect the physical processes of excretion or constipation, ejaculation or childbirth with central emotional, artistic or spiritual experiences. Even a cursory reading of *The Vivisector* reveals the more than metaphorical association of masturbation-fertilization and constipation-defecation with the different modes in which Hurtle Duffield experiences art. The same connection is revealed through the meanderings of the senile mind of the omnivorous Elizabeth Hunter, whose career in the "hard, commodious world" comes to an end on her swan-bedecked commode, her soul being expelled like a last gaseous offering. This line of imagery culminates in the remarkable observation that "souls have an anus" (*ES* p. 194). The import of this stream of cloacal symbolism is clear, if theologically unorthodox. The Word must, in every sense, be absorbed into and express itself through the flesh. Biology cannot be shirked.

At another extreme, the flesh and blood with which the Word is consubstantial can be seen as the bread and wine of Holy Communion. The mystery of man in Christ and Christ in man is brought home most fully in the symbolism of the Host. For White, the giving and receiving of Communion means always the generosity and acceptance of the questionable gift of carnality. To give of oneself without reservation, to be able to accept the passion and compassion— these are the marks of the true communicant. Mass may be celebrated in unexpected, even diabolical forms. The "high old Mass" that Boyle of Jildra had predicted for Voss is celebrated by the reluctant communicant as a white grub is thrust into his mouth by his aboriginal captors. In the short story "Sicilian Vespers," Ivy Simpson, rejecting her husband (the "temporary host"), celebrates a Dionysiac communion with the flesh and blood of a chance American acquaintance. In *The Eye of the Storm,* Elizabeth Hunter's "precious wafer of flesh" (*ES* p. 335) has always been denied to her children, her husband and even her lovers. At the moment of Grace in the centre of the cyclone, she is allowed—as she never has allowed herself—to offer the Host to the black, accepting swans. This symbolic act is followed through and consummated fifteen years later when, sensing that the only thing she now has to offer her children is her death, she voluntarily renders them this service. It is, perhaps, this last and first gift of herself, that requires the destruction of herself, which hallows Mrs. Hunter. That her children are unworthy is irrelevant. If Christ had considered only the cannibalistic greed of His followers he might never have consented to be sundered and ingested. Mrs. Hunter, who herself possesses a capacious maw, is no Christ, but the direction of this and the previous paragraph suggests how, in the depths and the heights, the destiny of the Word is bound up with the processes and the symbolism of the flesh.

I am not only my body, but only through my body can I know what I am. Yet having stressed this intimate link between soul and body, it is necessary to turn and point out that it is not complete identification. White, were we to give him a philosophic label, is an ontological, not a phenomenological existentialist. Although existence in the body predominates for much of the time, the core of being has a higher ontological reality. All things are real, but some are more real than others. This brings us to the metaphysical ambivalence which underlies the temperamental difficulties felt by so many of White's characters. The body is the only vehicle for, but the greatest burden to, the soul. The soul only takes on existence by wearing the clothes of flesh, yet as the core of being is raised to a higher level its bodily encumbrance becomes increasingly anachronistic. During the first phases of its cycle, the "I" feels no disparity between itself and the body. But towards the end this congruity falls apart. One cannot say "I am my body" but only, with decreasing relevance, "I have a body." As time goes on, the once organic relationship of body and soul turns into a rather uneasy coalition of core and carapace.

As the soul approaches its zenith, the body is seen at its most clumsy, afflicted or dilapidated. Stan Parker is last seen externally as a grouchy old man with a stick, Laura Trevelyan as a plain headmistress with a chapped neck and a cough, Mary Hare as a singed and repulsive animal and, of course, Elizabeth Hunter's already repulsive frame is tortured into ultimate monstrosity by the fiend's mask that Flora paints on her.

White's style, as well as his situations, emphasizes the dichotomy of aspiring soul and earth-bound body. Not less but more emphasis is placed on the incongruity of the flesh as the soul swims closest to the surface. White holds the husk in his tenderly ironic hands as the spark darts free. This concentration on the mundane, which occurs in every book as the soul is about to "doff the outgrown garment of the body" (RC p. 480), creates a tension which prepares the reader for the final division. Any irony involved is intended for the flesh, not the soul; the more the grotesqueness of the body is emphasized, the less important it is felt to be. Every book ends with the implication that the shell has, or will, split apart, having outlived its protective and gestative functions.

Notes

1. Gabriel Marcel, *Being and Having*, trans. A. and C. Black (London: Collins, 1965), pp. 213–14.

2. A. P. Elkin, *The Australian Aborigines* (Sydney: Angus and Robertson, 1938), pp. 240–41.

3. Richard Wilhelm, *The Secret of the Golden Flower*, trans. Cary F. Baynes; foreword and commentary, C. G. Jung (London: Routledge & Kegan Paul, 1962), p. 14.

4. R. D. Laing, *The Divided Self* (Harmondsworth: Pelican Books, 1965), p. 39.

5. *Ibid.*, p. 17.

Duality in Patrick White   John Colmer°

"I expect we shall make our blunders," Miss Scrimshaw predicted, "but would you not say that life is a series of blunders rather than any clear design, from which we may come out whole if we are lucky?"[1]

My epigraph from *A Fringe of Leaves* can act as a signpost to my sceptical approach towards White's grand unifying designs. It is a truism to say that Patrick White is centrally concerned with "the mystery of unity." And, not surprisingly, Patricia Morley uses this phrase from White's first novel, *Happy Valley*, as the title of her monograph on the novelist.[2] Like most of White's critics, she concentrates on the archetypal patterns and symbolic structures, offering enthusiastic expositions of the meaning and significance of these, without enquiring too deeply into the kinds of duality White seeks to reconcile and without asking how successfully he embodies his vision of unity through character, episode, ritualistic action, and symbol. It is to these two questions that I wish to turn in this paper.

Since Patricia Morley's work first appeared, Peter Beatson[3] has usefully drawn attention to the various kinds of duality that we meet in White's fiction, but for the common reader one of the disadvantages of his patient analysis is its Jungian terminology. There are of course striking parallels between Jung's ideas on individuation and those of White, especially in *The Solid Mandala* (1966), and the two writers share a common interest in the mandala as a traditional symbol of unity; but it should be possible to examine the ideas of duality and unity in White without continuous recourse to either Jungian or theological terms. After all, he is a writer of fiction not of technical psychology or Christian apologetics, an explorer of reality, not a psychologist or priest. Granted that in Romantic and post-Romantic literature such distinctions are difficult to sustain, since roles tend to overlap to a surprising degree as Keats' poem *Hyperion* shows where the poet is seen as a "Physician to all men"; yet, in the case of the modern novelist, certain expectations about his role in reflecting reality, telling stories, creating credible characters persist. As common readers we are therefore justified in resisting works that have what Keats called too "palpable a design" upon us, whether that design is political or theological. The most damaging criticism that can be made of Patrick White's fiction is that in its symbolic configurations and apocalyptic climaxes its design is too palpable. Moreover, it is

° Reprinted from *Patrick White: A Critical Symposium*, edited by Ron Shepherd and Kirpal Singh (Bedford Park, South Australia: Centre for Research in the New Literatures in English, Flinders University Press 1978), 70–76.

often at odds with the authentically complex rendering of reality in the main body of the work, a rendering that forbids any final resolution of the duality that exists everywhere in the smallest detail of the fiction.

All the main dualities are reflected in White's fictional world, those between mind and body, matter and spirit, male and female, the individual and society, time and eternity, the Word and the Flesh, the wisdom of silence and the folly of speech. In addition, there is a striking sense of duality between the sophisticated European consciousness of the novelist and the crudeness and repellent ugliness of much of his Australian material. In this radical disjunction, which is a typical product of a colonial frontier experience, may be seen the characteristic feature of White's world-view. His vision is remarkably comprehensive; the duality is multilayered and multifaceted. It is deeply felt and expressed with intense dramatic power. This may be seen in a passage from *The Vivisector* that describes the anguish of the artist Hurtle Duffield as he struggles to unite the fragmentary and contrary ideas in his preliminary studies of Nance.

> He either saw in colours, and the architecture eluded him, or else he was obsessed by forms: Nance's yellow cheeses; suddenly out of the past Rhoda's Cranach figure standing beside the iron-legged bidet. In desperation he was almost settled for the self-portrait he had been for some time considering. But did he, any more than the others, see himself truly as he was? His doubts drove him to scramble down to the bottom of the gorge, slashed by swords, whipped by wires, trampling on the board-walk of fallen wood, sinking in the mattresses of rotting leaves. Reaching his nadir he lay full length and buried his face in brown water, gulping at it, watching it lap round the picture of his distorted features.
> Obviously he didn't know himself. (p. 242)

This passage, entirely characteristic of White in its violent imagery and antithetical structures, conveys an authentic impression of what it is like for an artist to be haunted by ideals of harmony and yet be imprisoned within a dualistic world. Such passages, I would suggest, carry altogether more fictional weight than the willed gestures towards a reconciling harmony that occur at strategically important places in his narratives: the apotheosis of Ruth, "touched by the wings of love and charity," at the end of *Riders in the Chariot,* for example; or Duffield's final vision of God in *The Vivisector,* which depends on an elaborate combination of letters, a telegram, a chorus of idle chatter at the art gallery, and the verbal miming of the effects of a paralytic stroke. It is surely only a trivial mind that can find deep meaning in the two senses of "stroke" in this context. And, as if half aware of the fundamental triviality of his cosmic pun, White releases it through two protective veils of irony. First, it is expressed in Mrs. Volkov's "laboured" and "anguished" handwriting, and second it is attributed to the pathetic Mr. Cutbush. "As Mr. Cutbush remarked who has more Education, we was all perhaps *stroked by God*" (p. 637). The pretentious artifice here, as so frequently in White's fiction, is self-defeating. It calls attention to the means, to the strenuous effort of the fancy and the will. Whether the passage is a piece of strained religiosity, as it is at the end of *Riders in the Chariot*, or a knowing piece of symbolism, as at the end of *The Aunt's Story*, when the black rose of Theodora's hat "trembled and glittered, leading a life of its own," or the calculated virtuosity of broken sense at the end of *The Vivisector*, where the colour indigo and the word *god* coalesce in the final word of the novel, whatever the ingenious device may be, the reader becomes uncomfortably aware of the author's fingers on the scales, tipping one pan in favour of the consolations of divine harmony, when the fictional weight of the whole novel falls heavily on the actual pain of duality.

Having said that, I must admit that throughout his career White has shown unfailing resourcefulness in creating the characters, incidents and dramatic scenes to communicate a sense of harmony reconciling the divisions in man and nature. He has never simply repeated himself, although indeed all the novels bear a close family relationship one to another, both in theme and style. His inventiveness, his capacity for experiment is particularly evident in the different types of characters he has created to embody his visions of duality and harmony: divine fool in *The Aunt's Story*, the uneducated pioneer in *The Tree of Man*, the singleminded explorer in *Voss*, a quarternity of visionaries in *Riders in the Chariot*, the imperfect but complementary twins in *The Solid Mandala*, the Accursed Artist in *The Vivisector*, a dying woman in *The Eye of the Storm*, a Wordsworthian "perfect Woman, nobly planned / To warn, to comfort, and command" in *A Fringe of Leaves*. He has also shown a comparable inventiveness in creating the great organising metaphors that bestow shape and significance on the rich diversity of material he habitually handles. And closely related to this is his gift for inventing ritualistic incidents that affirm the existence of an underlying order uniting man and nature, incidents grounded in the daily habits of a secular society but raised to sacramental and mythic stature by image and rhythmic prose. Of these ritualistic episodes the most persistent is the dance, a traditional symbol of harmony that appears in many guises in White's fiction. It appears in parodic form in Mrs. Jolley's obscene caperings in *Riders in the Chariot*, it becomes ecstatically affirmatory in Arthur Brown's carefully patterned mandalic steps and in Lottie's dance in *The Eye of the Storm*. It is linked in a number of novels, including *Riders in the Chariot* and *A Fringe of Leaves*, with what White calls the rite of the birds, so that the impression created is not only of harmony but of a gentle creativity.

A certain perversity, however, accompanies this abundant inventiveness of character, metaphor, and ritualistic scene. In all things White is attracted to the extreme case, the impossible choice. For his elect he chooses the most unlikely characters and then places them in situations that heighten the inherent improbability of their final salvation. While the obvious intention is to demonstrate that, by a certain mysterious grace, good can be wrested from evil, beauty from ugliness, salvation from apparent damnation, sanity from supposed madness; yet the preoccupation with the dark extremes of man's nature and the intense relish with which these paradoxes are explored combine to create a striking sense of unresolved conflict and duality. There is throughout White's fiction a deep discrepancy between the glad tidings announced by the grand archetypal structures and the grim truths communicated through the texture of his contorted, anxious prose. Nowhere is this seen more clearly than in *Riders in the Chariot*, White's most comprehensive but also his most programmatic novel.[4] Each of the four main characters is raised to mythic level; but it is one thing to give modern characters a mythic dimension and quite another to convince readers that they can sustain their archetypal roles. In this respect, White is only an extreme example of the modern writer who aspires to achieve the universal and the sublime through an artful overlay of myth. But unless the myths are relived and grow organically out of the characters and situations, as to some extent they do in *The Solid Mandala* and even more so in *A Fringe of Leaves*, they cannot exercise their ancient power. The interlocking profusion of mythic detail in *Riders in the Chariot* is more reminiscent of an unfinished jigsaw puzzle than the mystic unity of a sacred mosaic. As soon as we inspect the details more closely, especially if we concentrate on the texture of the prose, what we find is a recurrent falsity of tone in the affirmatory apocalyptic passages, a falsity rarely felt in the detailed recording of conflict and duality.

White's vision, like that of traditional Christianity, turns on the paradox that the spirit is incarnate in the flesh. It is necessary therefore for those who take the inward path not to forsake the world altogether, but to return to it with new insight into the hidden divinity; yet, as Peter Beatson has pointed out, there is a "profound metaphysical and temperamental ambivalence running through White's novels. The necessity of embracing the body is coupled, from his earliest books, with a deep aversion to it."[5] And, to this I would add, fascinated disgust is one of the strongest and most authentic elements in his fiction. It affects his response to Australian society as well as to the body. "Life in Australia," White has remarked, "seems to be for many people pretty deadly dull. I have tried to convey a splendour, a transcendence, which is also there, above human realities."[6] To communicate this sense of splendour and transcendence he creates his symbolic structures, with their carefully staged climaxes and characteristic elevations of tone.

One of the questions I set myself to answer in my monograph on *Riders in the Chariot* was whether White's prose was always adequate to his ambitious archetypal structure. To this I was regretfully forced to answer, no. To say this is not to point to a minor stylistic infelicity but to a radical difference between willed affirmation and achieved vision, evident in many of the climactic passages. Yet this sense of strain and contrivance is to some extent counterbalanced by the unforced vitality of the comic scenes and those passages in which White, like Wordsworth before him, makes us feel nature as a living force: in the sensitive descriptions of Miss Hare's response, "whose eyes were always probing, fingers trying," who would "achieve the ecstasy of complete annihilating liberation," and in those passages that suggest the instinctive ties that bind all four major characters to the earth. It is the deadness and sterility bred by convention that prompts the novelist's bitterest rage, whether it appears in the hesitant, suspicious rituals performed by Mrs. Flack and Mrs. Jolley, threading the labyrinth of evil together, as certainly damned as Milton's fallen angels, or in the class-conscious gestures and routines of the apostate Rosetrees. Implicitly the texture of the writing often calls in question conventional distinctions between good and evil, by revealing that love and good nature *can* lie behind the promiscuous squalour of Mrs. Khalil's brothel and the transvestite exhibitions at Hannah's place. Even in these unlikely places, the novel seems to say, the spirit may redeem the flesh. Spontaneity and instinct can transcend the tasteless materialism of Australian suburbia. Its mean vulgarity is not intrinsically and irredeemably evil: it only becomes so when it is accepted as a whole way of life, as it is by Mrs. Flack and Mrs. Jolley, and by the Rosetrees. Yet, one must add that the author's own distaste is so strong that it escapes his control and damages the otherwise delicate balance between life-giving spontaneity and life-destroying convention. Aesthetic revulsion distorts the moral vision. The structure of the novel affirms salvation through the senses, the texture shudders and vibrates with physical loathing.

Such a radical disjunction of structure and texture is most easily explained by reference to the dualities within the writer's temperament and sensibility; yet when full allowance has been made for the play of personal temperament, this disjunction can be seen to typify the world-view of the upper-class expatriate artist with a refined cosmopolitan sensibility who returns to encounter the intractable material offered by a society that is repellent to him and with which he has no significant relationship, economic, cultural or political. This is partly what George Steiner has in mind when he speaks of "the play of European densities against the gross vacancy of the Australian setting,"[7] but he does not develop this insight very fully. For White the Australian landscape becomes a source of potent myth, its people the object of harsh satire. As Jack Lindsay has shrewdly observed, there is a distressing lack of compassion for the denizens of Australian suburbia, a lack of faith in the forces of social renewal.[8] The inflated archetypal symbols that climax the novel offer no real solution to the social malaise mirrored in the texture of the agonised prose. They represent the expatriate artist's escape into European aestheticism. A symbolist form is presented as a solution to a humanist dilemma. The symbols operate within a purely literary context; they are not based on an ideological commitment to either Jungian psychology or Christian doctrine, although they are drawn freely from each system of thought. Consequently all attempts to translate the grand symbolic climaxes into humanistic terms fail. The inflated tone cannot disguise the emptiness of substance, the absence of social context, the arrogant irresponsibility of White's extreme solipsism.

Is man a solitary or a social animal? The appearance of *A Fringe of Leaves* invites us to see the whole of White's fiction in a fresh perspective. In the latest novel, as in the two immature early novels, *Happy Valley* and *The Living and the Dead*, White recognises the positive values of community, the benefits of social order. In *A Fringe of Leaves*, White finally abandons the negative and basically anti-humanist view of society that prevails in *The Aunt's Story* and succeeding novels. The heroine, Ellen Roxburgh, after passing through her period of compulsory initiation into primitive needs and rites, returns to society with a new understanding of herself and the value of civilised order. Unlike the heroes of White's middle period, she does not assert her spiritual supremacy by cherishing her condition as lonely outcast; she incorporates herself anew into the social fabric, imperfect as it is, bringing to her task the knowledge of hunger, fear, crime, and remorse that she has gained as an outcast. At the end there are no ecstatic affirmations, no lonely apocalyptic visions, only a few hallucinatory moments when, through identification with the slain harlot Mab, her slayer Jack Chance, and the instruments of primitive justice in a penal colony, she achieves her insight into the unity of man. For the first time in White's fiction there is a wholly authentic and deeply moving resolution of the dualities that lie at the heart of our existence, as solitaries and social animals.

Notes

1. *A Fringe of Leaves* (London: Jonathan Cape, 1976), p. 392. Note that page references in the text are to the original hardback editions of the novels.

2. Patricia Morley, *The Mystery of Unity: Theme and Technique in the Novels of Patrick White* (St. Lucia: Univ. of Queensland Press, 1972); for more extensive discussion see my review in *Australian Literary Studies*, Vol. 6, No. 1, pp. 95–99.

3. Peter Beatson, *The Eye in the Mandala, Patrick White: A Vision of Man and God* (London: Paul Elek, 1976).

4. In the ensuing discussion I draw from time to time from my *Patrick White: Riders in the Chariot* (Melbourne: Arnold, 1978).

5. Beatson, p. 47.

6. Patrick White, "A Conversation with Patrick White," *Southerly*, No. 2, 1973, p. 132.

7. Quoted by William Walsh, *Patrick White's Fiction* (London: Allen & Unwin, 1977), p. 127.

8. Jack Lindsay, *Decay and Renewal: Cultural Essays on Twentieth Century Writing* (Sydney: Wild and Woolly; London: Laurence & Wishart, 1976), p. 244.

Meaning and Experience: A Review-Essay on Some Recurrent Problems in Patrick White Criticism

Alan Lawson*

In 1973 I concluded a review article[1] of the then-recent books on White with the hope that we had graduated beyond the need for any more general introductory books and with the prediction that the most profitable task in White studies would be to examine in considerable detail the constantly fluctuating point of view and the carefully modulated imagery in his work. There seemed to me, then, to be two main flaws in the existing body of criticism of White's fiction: an obsession with categorizing characters, their experiences, and White's responses; and an excessive (and misguided) interpretative reliance on the oracular statements with which White so liberally endows each of his novels. Ron Shepherd, summing up his report[2] of the first conference of White scholars in February 1978, suggested that the most interesting directions revealed by a consideration of the papers delivered were those which point to "the literary implications of [White's] language and style." His conclusion is one with

* Reprinted from *Texas Studies in Literature and Language* 21, no. 2 (Summer 1979): pp. 280–95; by permission of the author and publisher; Copyright © 1979 by the University of Texas Press.

which I wholeheartedly concur: the fact that it is very similar to the one I reached five years earlier gives rise to no particular satisfaction, for it was a proposition made ten years earlier still, by H. P. Heseltine in his seminal article on White's style.[3] In fact, what has been written alters little the impression that the terms of White criticism were established at least fifteen years ago. There has certainly been progress, but little in the way of a radical departure from those early lines. The concern with language, with the quality of White's sociomoral discriminations, with the religious and philosophical contexts of his thoughts, and the skepticism about the achievement in relation to the intention have been familiar elements since the early 1960s (and before). How far, then, have continued debate of these attitudes and additional contributions to knowledge of the context and content contributed to a widespread understanding of White's particularly demanding and puzzling fiction? How far have the four or five major strands reached? What is the balance of judgment? Are there any new approaches? What is the achievement of the most substantial works? I want to discuss general approaches to White's fiction and the terms of the critical debate, and I want to examine some of the particular responses to *Voss,* the novel which has for a number of reasons evoked the most considerable critical advances.

One might well have expected that an examination of the books written on White in the past five years would provide an index of the state of White criticism and scholarship. That index though would be a depressing but fortunately unrepresentative one. The hope that was expressed in 1973 that we had had enough general introductory books on White was ill-founded, partly no doubt because of the award of the Nobel Prize to White weeks after I wrote that earlier article, partly (I imagine) because publishers can generally be persuaded to add yet another "valuable introduction for the general reader" to an already satisfied market much more easily than they can see their way clear to publish a genuine contribution to knowledge. Who could blame them: most libraries and too many students will buy the former product; very few will buy the latter. Since 1973 there have been three general introductions and one book which attempts to make a contribution to existing knowledge.[4]

Critics still claim that Patrick White is loved, read, and understood only outside his own country. I have argued elsewhere[5] that this view is not only false but culturally pernicious as well, and events since that important year of 1973 have not altered the argument. In fact, the announcement of White's Nobel Prize provided startling proof, not so much of his international recognition but of an extraordinary degree of international ignorance of him and his work. The international press, from tabloids to the cultural monthlies and scholarly quarterlies, produced a plethora of predictable, derivative, superficial, and frequently inaccurate and misguided introductions best characterized by the title of one of them, "Qui est Patrick White?" It was clearly necessary to answer that question, and within a couple of months there was already one book offering to do it for Scandinavian and then German readers, Ingmar Björkstén's *Patrick White: Epikern fran Australien*. Several of White's novels had been translated into Swedish, Norwegian, and Finnish, but although they were widely reviewed, sales figures would suggest that they were not widely read. An introduction to White and his work for Scandinavians may have been appropriate, though one regrets that they were not better informed at that first meeting.

Björkstén's book is characterized by factual error, careless argument, and misreading, and it is informed by an antipathy towards Australia and Australians that is compounded by an inability to comprehend the complexity of White's social vision or to appreciate the humorous and ironic resources of his language. It repeats the false cliché that White has only been appreciated outside Australia, though the *only* facts given in support of this tiresome old piece of humbug— the Swedish sales figures—clearly contradict it. Those figures indicate that White's readership in Björkstén's homeland was miniscule before the award of the Nobel Prize and that the Nobel-induced boom was rather brief. Apart from a very small number of academic articles, this special issue of *Texas Studies in Literature and Language* is the first solid indication of substantial interest in White outside Australia. On another level, the sales figures of his books would confirm this view.

Björkstén's book is a mélange of erroneous biographical assertion, the cultural impressionism of an unsympathetic tourist, and almost meaningless "critical" journalese. What is described as "an interview with Patrick White" is a rough repetition of information from much earlier Australian biographical articles, a goodly portion of it from the 1956 *Meanjin* feature at which he sneers and much from the 1958 "Prodigal Son" autobiographical essay White published in *Australian Letters*. Most of it is familiar enough for the errors and contradictions to announce themselves stridently to readers who know anything about Patrick White. The book's blurb claims: "it provides at long last a valuable introduction for the general reader to Australia's most celebrated novelist." This is mischievously wrong on two counts. The proposition that it is a valuable introduction is misleading; the "at long last" is unforgivable. This book has more accessible and far more valuable predecessors; by 1976 Geoffrey Dutton's *Patrick White* had gone into its fourth edition, and R. F. Brissenden's *Patrick White* had seen a second edition. The general reader would be far more reliably informed, far better critically guided, by either of those than by Björkstén's anachronism. There had also been Barry Argyle's

Patrick White (1967), another introduction, and the more ambitious critical introduction by Patricia Morley in her *The Mystery of Unity* (1972). By 1976 the "general reader" had had a surfeit of introductions.

The blurb is misleading, of course, but it is characteristic of an attitude of willful ignorance which pervades the book and which is an all too common feature of White criticism. The self-contained isolation, the lack of critical debate, and the patronizing assumption that the writer is the first to understand White genuinely are themes to which I shall return. Like many other critics, Björkstén is fascinated by White's intense social vision and seems incapable of reading it with critical discernment. The quality of White's social vision and its relation to his spiritual themes has long been one of the major problems in White criticism, but it is not examined by Björkstén: tone, irony, authorial point of view, and structural development are all ignored, and the resulting account is a simplistic one indeed. Anxious at every turn lest he miss an opportunity for describing the vacuity, hostility, or boorishness of Australians, Björkstén commits such elementary errors in reading as the following: "the powerful criticism that Patrick White makes of Australian society in *Voss*— where he speaks of 'our inherent mediocrity as people'" (p. 65). First, it is not White who so speaks; it is Willie Pringle. Second, he actually says "our inherent mediocrity as *a* people" (my italics); the difference in meaning is crucial. (This error may of course be a misprint—the book is peppered with them.) Third, it quotes out of context: the continuation of Pringle's speech is, "I am confident that the mediocrity of which he speaks is not a final and irrevocable state; rather it is a creative source of endless variety and subtlety." The extent of the distortion is staggering. Indeed, this passage from the final episode in *Voss* is one which several other critics have felt to be an embarrassingly optimistic view of Australia and the Australian artist.

This misreading is set alongside some introductory generalizations which are as ludicrous as those of any nineteenth-century "new-chum" or greenhorn. One wonders whether Mr. Björkstén, like Mr. Ludlow on the last page of *Voss*, also missed out on the baked Irish. Like the participants in the nineteenth-century debate about the nature of the Australian landscape, Björkstén holds a monistic conception of it. He writes:

> Nature here is more remorseless than in any other place. The Australian countryside does not welcome those who come to cultivate its soil. The sun shines harshly and unceasingly. Equally pitiless to man as it is to mother earth, it blazes down through the accompanying stillness, for in the Australian daytime nature is silent. For a long-awaited second of apparent coolness a stray wind stirs in the bush,

> through the hard, obliquely hanging leaves of the eucalyptus. Lack
> of water means disaster. (p. 15)

Charles Harpur, in "A Midsummer Noon in the Australian Forest,"
one hundred twenty years earlier did it so much better. That Australia
is a barren desert from coast to coast, silent throughout the day, and
plagued by incessant sunshine is preposterous. A reading of any of
White's novels ought to be enough to dispel this, but it is nonetheless
adduced as the context of his novels. The Australian literary context
fares no better. "The acknowledgement that wives of Australian
workmen and women in the bush have souls and feelings of their
own may be regarded as one of the contributions White has made
to the literature of his country." White is misrepresented as being
praised for the wrong things, and the misrepresentation does him no
service. Anyone who had read any of the work of Barbara Baynton,
Henry Lawson, Ada Cambridge, "Henry Handel Richardson," or
Katharine Susannah Prichard would immediately recognize the fat-
uousness of such a claim. White's Australian literary context has not
been extensively considered; it deserves to be. Some of the most
impressive recent work on White has attempted to come to terms
with this question.

In matters of interpretation, too, Björkstén epitomizes some of
the most damaging flaws in White criticism by expressing in extreme
forms several of the fallacies bedeviling the approach to White's
fiction. "For [White] sexual intercourse is no more than self-indulg-
ence, self-sacrifice, fertilization" (p. 35). What sexual intercourse is
for White is hardly the critic's business; as a comment about his
novels it is very familiar, but not very accurate. The lovemaking of
Alys and Oliver in *Happy Valley* and of Eden and Joe in *The Living
and the Dead,* the erotic dreams in *Voss,* and the varied sexual
experience of Ellen in *A Fringe of Leaves* and of Hurtle in *The
Vivisector* all suggest a far more generous and certainly more comprehensive view of sex than is sometimes critically suggested. Like
the common premise that White is a humorless writer and "not at
all given to the inflections of irony," it is one of the most pressing
areas for serious reexamination in White. "Sex and Humor in Patrick
White's Novels" is a valuable article that is yet to be written. The
title is not intended to be facetious. It would highlight the range and
the kind of responses of which White is manifestly capable. His
comprehensive concern with humanity, his compassion, would undoubtedly emerge.

The most recent general book on White is William Walsh's *Patrick
White's Fiction.* Professor Walsh has written on White many times in
articles, reviews, and his books on Commonwealth literature, so his
approach and his views are widely known. Walsh's critical method

is to write an illuminating synopsis, a lucid description of style and narrative. He exhibits, perhaps too prodigally, the gift (which he praises White for possessing) of "luminous generalization." If his own critical style seems excessively adjectival, it nevertheless gives a good, though imprecise, impression of the experience of reading Patrick White. One reviewer remarked of Peter Beatson's book, *The Eye in the Mandala*, that "we have the meaning but not the experience"; in the case of Walsh's work, the opposite danger is courted. The adjectives of approbation accrete fulsomely to describe the "qualities of largeness, uninhibited confidence, and potent creative energy" (pp. 41, 127) which Walsh repeatedly stresses as the most remarkable features of White's novels. They may not get us much closer to a detailed understanding of the meaning of the works, but they will undoubtedly invite the general reader to approach the novels with enthusiasm and with the right sort of expectations. In discussing the less successful elements of White's work, Walsh perceptively and usefully draws attention to the most difficult of all problems facing White studies. Here, as in his earlier essays, he remarks: "It is somewhere between imaginative power, and authenticity and crispness of detail that Patrick White's work is imperfect, in the area where architectural capacity and taste are required. The failure is not in the generating concept nor in the worked-out detail—neither in the idea nor in the vocabulary, that is—but somewhere between in what one might call the syntactical structure" (p. 63). Unfortunately, Walsh has never gone on to analyze the problem he describes in such an intriguing way.

Dorothy Green has described another aspect of the same problem as a constant war between White's gift for analysis and his dramatic gift.[6] Margaret Walters, in an important early article which set the terms for the long line of skeptical reactions to White, drew attention to "a general failure to distinguish between his intention and achievement."[7] However this gap is defined—and I suggest that while these definitions are not synonymous they are nevertheless responses to different aspects of the same problem—it clearly represents the gulf into which most conflicting opinions and interpretations, most critical debates, fall. Those who are attracted by what I earlier called the "oracular statements" and those who respond to the carefully modulated imagery and point of view derive divergent and often incompatible views of the novel. As Walsh says, between the multiplicity of observed detail and the grand conception (each easy to respond to) is a gap that seems to accommodate a bewildering array of interpretations.

The relationship between the multiplicity of detail and the archetypal pattern was seen by R. P. Laidlaw in a carefully argued and detailed paper[8] to place *Voss* both thematically and formally in the mode of the Romance. Thematically this was a very useful argument, for it enabled the clear interpretation of a particular form of dualism in Voss's quest. The nature of Voss's progress—and in this interpretation it can be seen as progress and not defeat—fuses the symbolic and the real, a fusion which is embodied in White's style. It is a convincing and particularly useful method, compatible with the other four most plausible interpretations of the novel by Peter Beatson, Brian Kiernan, Dorothy Green, and Michael Cotter.[9] But its most far-reaching contribution is the way it analyzes the problem of form, the mode, of White's novels, a problem first raised by the late Professor James McAuley in two articles on *Voss* in 1958 and 1965,[10] and returned to most recently by Veronica Brady.[11] As Brady has written, "the novels of Patrick White . . . have been consistently misunderstood and devalued by critics applying to them criteria appropriate to novels of the Great Tradition, novels which are based on premises White sets out to question" (p. 63). The "tradition" into which McAuley, Laidlaw, and Brady seek to place White includes (significantly) the great Americans Hawthorne and Melville, and the Indian Raja Rao, a tradition tangential to that of the great nineteenth-century novel in English and one in which the works are concerned with other matters besides psychological realism and the relationships of human beings in society. Although he does not address the generic question directly, Brian Kiernan explains the nature of White's concern in an interesting way. The predominant concern of all of White's central characters, he argues, is the attempt to find some correspondence between the inner and outer worlds.[12] This describes the area of operation of White's novels much more effectively and thus raises a more reasonable set of criteria, expectations, and reading strategies. Certainly the feeling arises that some readers' irritation with White is often a result of asking the wrong questions, of demanding that inappropriate criteria be satisfied. In such circumstances critical response and debate are impossible, for different critics do not share the same reading experience; the head-shaking, exasperated response, "but it isn't like that at all," is about all that is possible. However, since Laidlaw, Kiernan, and the other critics I have named have developed a line of inquiry in a particularly profitable direction, critical debate on this issue itself at least ought to be possible.

Although White is so often said to be a dogmatic, intrusive, too-knowing author, there are grounds, I think, for affirming the opposite or at least for insisting that the effect is the opposite to authorial certitude and interpretative limitation. At the very core of the experience of reading White's work is a puzzlement, an uncertainty which results not only from the continually diverse wry interplay of irony but from something which derives perhaps from what Walsh calls the "syntactical structure." In one of the most revealing of the interviews he has given, White said that "all the characters in my books are myself, but they are a kind of disguise."[13] This remark ought to alert us to the fact that White's sympathies are widely engaged but always qualified: he absolutely endorses none, is totally detached from none. White is not an autobiographical writer, but he is a very personal one. The kind of "biographical" material to be found in the fiction seems to be of two kinds. On the first level, which roughly corresponds to Professor Walsh's "generating idea," there is the broad correspondence of his family structure with what has been called the fictional "White family,"[14] the generalized experience of living in the Snowy Mountains *(Happy Valley)*, of being a "London intellectual" *(The Living and the Dead)*, of small-farming on the outskirts of Sydney *(The Tree of Man)*, or the concern with being an artist, and so on. On the level of the "multiplicity of detail," there is also much from his experience and background—names, places, and minor characters. What seems to be missing is the direct autobiographical presence, the level in between.

White's particular form of personal investment takes the form of frequent authorial manipulation and intrusion, but it is so often characterized by what Wayne Booth called "conjectural description" (the use of "as is," "perhaps," or "it seemed"), not only in the rhetoric but in the structure as well. These phrases offer interpretation but withhold from it authorial endorsement. All of White's novels have an exploratory structure; that is, they approach definition by progressive approximation, and the tentativeness and prevarication are a function of this. The novels evolve through the *developing* perception of *fallible* central characters in whom much of the novelist's viewpoint is only apparently invested. This, of course, leaves readers uneasy and uncertain; the cryptic, enigmatic, ironic, and satiric elements, instead of limiting interpretation, usually demand interpretative pluralism. Brian Kiernan has, for instance, argued (in my view quite correctly) that the three "conclusive" interpretations of *Voss* are merely the provisional viewpoints of particular characters who are themselves subjected to a range of (frequently ironic) points of view.[15] John Burrows long ago showed that the same was true for *Riders in the Chariot*. White is clearly less interested in absolutes than many of his critics have been.

But set against those critics who have sought to extend the appreciation and understanding of White's peculiar fictional manner is another group of critics who have expressed skepticism. Margaret Walters, Peter Wood, and Leonie Kramer[16] have each argued that there is a different kind of gap, a kind of credibility gap, inherent in White's method. The gap which they see between intention and achievement does not merely (or even principally) concern them for the way in which it can affect their evaluation of the works but for the way in which it affects their interpretation of the works. The range of uncertainty at the very core of the books which I have already mentioned is, for them, irresoluble. Between the grand design and the multiplicity of detail lies not a shadow but a change of direction. In both *Riders in the Chariot* and *The Tree of Man,* says Professor Kramer, the effect of this uncertainty is not an endorsement of transcendence or the immanence of the spiritual order but a critique of these orthodoxies. Each novel asserts a secular humanism. Stan Parker's famous expectoration is, she claims, a rejection of God; White's aphorism, "One, and no other figure, is the answer to all sums," is an assertion of human independence. In this interpretation, then, the novel's circular structure confirms the reacknowledgement of the centrality of the natural and the human. *Riders in the Chariot* discloses that White is intellectually committed to humanism and emotionally drawn to mysticism. This is her diagnosis of the "signs of irresolution and imbalance." But of the achievement of *Riders in the Chariot* she is pretty skeptical, too, asserting that "the prose itself seems constantly to suggest more than it states," the chariot "remains stubbornly unconvincing," and the novel as a whole suffers from "aggrandisement of its theme."

Professor Kramer's interpretation of *Riders* drew a rigorous response from Dorothy Green,[17] but, the merits of that particular debate aside for a moment, two general points emerge. The first arises from the earlier discussion about the generic expectations proper to White's fiction. Though Professor Kramer's interpretations run counter to almost all received versions of those two novels (and are notable phenomena for that very reason, too, in terms of my point about the lack of interpretative limits), they are cogently stimulating accounts of them. The essay on *The Tree of Man,* in particular, deals with some of the most difficult questions which that work poses, and its interpretation cannot be overlooked by anyone seriously concerned with that novel. What is at first puzzling, however, is that having presented such an interpretation of the novel, she finds it necessary to devote a large portion of her essays to deploring or at least regretting various features of the novel. Is this in itself a signal that the description of the novel is *not* the most appropriate one? All of the skeptical writers on White have proceeded in this way, blaming the novelist for not measuring up to the critic's hypothesis. There is, though, a consistency (not just a repetitiveness) about the charges laid against White, and those three which I have quoted at the end of the last paragraph are typical. No amount of insistence that White is concerned with the ineffable, the incommunicable, the "extraordinary behind the ordinary," can dislodge the feeling, shared by many of White's admirers, that White cannot always enact what his rhetoric seems to insist, that "too often what sounds profound turns out to be an effect of sonorous tone rather than intellectual substance";[18] and, above all, that failure in what is felt to be an *a priori* symbolic design is sometimes masked by a portentousness. These charges still have to be answered in terms of critical methodology. They are met, implicitly, in the five articles on *Voss* that I mentioned earlier, in which detailed, careful readings of the novel reveal a saving complexity of moral response through a proper alertness to the relationships between the symbolism, the point of view, the dramatic and structural functions of the imagery, and the interplay of irony and humor.

While the skeptical critics evince an unwillingness to accept too readily White's "own conception of his work,"[19] there is another small class of critics in whom that unwillingness becomes a radical refusal. There is a species of criticism still encountered in Australia which insists on conveying the critic's rejection of the basic premises or the mode of the work in question as though, in so doing, a valuable act of discrimination were being performed. Brian McFarlane's recent denunciation of *Riders in the Chariot*[20] is one of the more strident examples. He begins with the ostensibly disarming (but surely disqualifying) admission that "a distaste for the novel of mystical experience no doubt accounts for a good deal of my antipathy towards this novel," but goes on to claim that "I want to take issue with it on grounds more objective than this." McFarlane sees White's novel as an extreme but characteristic example of "the Australian novel's extraordinary concern with what is dehumanising and inhumane," and of that genre's constriction and impoverishment. The extent of his objective grounds is shown by the following phrases: "the aggressively inhuman stance," "his is a detestable vision," "a work of hysterical misanthropy," "extraordinary animus," "appalling," "alarming." It culminates in "the non-elect are exposed with a rawness that bespeaks so anti-human a bias as to render much of the book almost obscene." The article is remarkable for a vehemence never approached before by any critic of White, but I think it does indirectly illuminate some features central to the recurring problems in White criticism.

Does McFarlane's essay invite, or even admit the possibility of, an answer? In its form and vocabulary it manifests a mind so antagonistic to White's that no rational answer is possible. Why do people write like this? There are three possible answers to that question. The first lies firmly in the province of individual psychology and is plainly inadmissible here. The second is avowedly speculative, but it does seem that some critics who would otherwise ignore White (in the way that they would leave untouched a bowl of shrimp if they were allergic to seafood) feel that they must express the grounds for their dislike because he *is* such an important writer (and therefore demands an opinion), because he is *regarded* as such an important writer (and therefore standards must be upheld and restored), or because he is an important *Australian* writer (and some feel embarrassed by the shared national identity or by the suspicion of chauvinism). But the last can hardly be adduced to explain some hostile reviews that have appeared in America, in England, and in Finland. The third, and most pertinent, answer to the question, though, must lie somewhere in the work itself, for Mr. McFarlane quotes frequently from the novel and produces, if one holds one's own impression of the novel in abeyance, a considerable amount of circumstantial evidence to support his view. There must also—and this point takes us further into the emotional texture of the novel—be something there that has evoked the vehemence. White's own response to the world evinces an intensity which evokes a concomitant response from some readers, a response registering itself as complaint, occasionally distaste, but not usually disgust. But is it merely the quality (or the kind) of White's moral response to the world that causes such a reaction, or is there another issue, an aesthetic one, at stake here? What follows the candid admission at the beginning of McFarlane's essay is an oblique demand that novels should "dramatize the resilience of the human spirit"; he does not, that is, accept a novel which will not wholeheartedly confirm his view of human goodness and the appropriate forms of its manifestation. Professor Kramer's case against the same novel was quite a different one, although it also began from a dispute with the novel's metaphysical presuppositions. But she is not vindictive towards the novel; she does not find its vision of humanity repulsive, though she does find it to be confused. One might sweep aside as irrelevant McFarlane's objections on the grounds of his antipathy and his bias; some might even dismiss Professor Kramer's objections because they begin from the wrong premises. One might—no doubt some already have—but that would not get us any closer to understanding the basis of the objections, and at the basis of those objections lies a fundamental feature of White's kind of writing. As I suggested earlier, it is less a question of moral vision or metaphysics (though this is always the ostensible crux of the discussion) than a question of aesthetics.

The important point is that most other critics have seen in the novels a different moral vision from the one which Mr. McFarlane finds so detestable (for example, George Core speaks of love providing "the only basis for a genuinely self-affirming and self-fulfilling life"[21]) and a different metaphysical theme from the one which Professor Kramer controverts. There is clearly a hermeneutic problem, and it is one which White's work has consistently thrown up. One is seldom surprised by opposing judgments of a novel's quality, but one might be surprised when a novelist's work so frequently evokes such radically contradictory interpretations. The history of White criticism is full of utterly opposite, mutually exclusive thematic readings. Critics of White's second novel, *The Living and the Dead* (1941), have consistently been seduced by its title into compiling their lists of those characters who are living and those who are dead. The discrepancies are startling. One would have thought that a writer who was concerned with such dichotomies would have settled the issue incontrovertibly. The title seems to encourage such a view, and so do other aspects of his work.

An obsession with opposites, dualities, and dichotomies is endemic to White's work, and it manifests itself in many different ways on many different levels. In its stylistic manifestation of synesthesia it probably derives from his interest in the French Symbolistes, and his desire to transcend the boundaries of time, space, touch, and thought is also a strong continuing element. It is analogous to his well-known ambition (described in "The Prodigal Son") to combine the perceptions of "Blake and Delacroix," "Mahler and Liszt"; to combine the resources of Symbolism and Naturalism. One is reminded of Laidlaw's argument about the fusion of the archetypal and the immediate. White's characteristic forms of humor are also fundamentally dichotomous. His use of syllepsis is widespread and usually involves a yoking of a mental, emotional, or spiritual quality with a physical one (a crude example of Kiernan's argument about inner and outer worlds)—"Mrs. Moriarty molten with self-pity and sweat," "He groaned with compassion and a tight crutch." His fascination with puns is a further example of interest in the dual nature of reality. But it must be acknowledged that none of these, in fact, asserts dichotomy: they are all ways of expressing a desire to bring together, to combine the opposites, to transcend the distinctions. "There is sometimes little to choose between the reality of illusion and the illusion of reality," Holstius tells Theodora Goodman near the end of *The Aunt's Story;* or, as in terms of one of Alf Dubbo's last paintings (the one of the river), there is an attempt to present simultaneously illusion and reality. White is *not* concerned with crass, simplistic divisions: as Laura Trevelyan says, "all truths are particoloured." He is concerned with resolving the dualities of life into harmonies. His vision, as I hope to show elsewhere, is fundamentally comic.

One dichotomy, however, survives in his work to enter the structure in a most difficult way, and it is, I think, the root cause of much of the divergence in critical readings. Technically, despite the thematic and stylistic concern with yoking, the novels are written in two opposed modes. On the one hand, they attempt to reflect White's conviction that life is lived as flux or, in Frank Le Mesurier's words, in "a state of perpetual becoming." On the other hand, they clearly embody the belief, provisionally expressed by Eden Standish, that "perhaps the most important things only happened in a flash"; their structures are generally episodic and fragmented, they contain epiphanies, and the style is often gnomic, the grammar disjunctive. Perhaps in this distinction lies the beginning of an explanation of the divergence in meaning which, it seems, must derive from some aspect of the works.

Because White is nevertheless concerned with harmonies, and is in the broadest and highest sense a comic writer, he is characteristically involved with matters of redemption and grace. From the time of John Cowburn's elucidation of "The Metaphysics of *Voss*,"[22] many critics have contributed to our knowledge of the religious and philosophical context of White's *Weltanschauung*. Most recently these aspects of White have been discussed by Peter Beatson in *The Eye of the Mandala*, a work tracing correspondences and affinities rather than influences and so providing a framework for understanding White's text rather than an argument to explain its genesis. The book is to be praised for that. Yet, because it brings a series of extrinsic systems to bear on the works, it is, like Morley's *Mystery of Unity*, a curiously wooden and unengaged discussion. Beatson "extrapolate[s] from White's work a religious pattern that underlies his artistic universe," and to that end he suppresses any evaluation, any regard for "developments, changes in emphasis and alterations in style and form," in short, anything that makes them individual works of literature. His view of White's characters and plots is distinctly static; quotations are made without regard to their dramatic function. The sensitivity to narrative development which characterized his earlier excellent article on *Voss*[23] is seldom displayed here. Indeed, this book nowhere refers to the article, nor does it refer to any other critic or reviewer of White. Chris Wallace-Crabbe once referred to earlier Australian writers as standing "in a line, solemn effigies, staring straight towards us, but without so much as a sidelong glance at one another."[24] Far too many critics of Patrick White adopt the same posture. Substantial critical articles on White have been appearing since 1951, and a failure to take account of the ground already covered, the arguments already canvassed, and the facts already unearthed is clearly wasteful of critical time and energy.

In the face of such widespread unwillingness to be involved in a continuing critical endeavor, one would be foolish to hazard any predictions about where White criticism is headed. I will, however, briefly note those recent approaches which seem to me to offer the most profitable lines of development. There has been an interest in plotting the changes of direction which White's recent fiction seems to suggest. For some critics these changes began with *The Vivisector*, for others with *The Eye of the Storm* with its extended charity, its compassionate concern with a mind "so sensual, mendacious, materialistic, superficial"; for even more critics the changes began with *A Fringe of Leaves* with its concern with beatitude rather than apocalypse, with a return to ordinary life. The alertness to the individuality of each of White's books is a welcome change from the depressing vision of them all as versions of one compound book. The idea of progression, too, suggests an enthusiastic engagement with the creative process, but it manifests itself most interestingly in Kiernan's suggestion that White's recurrent themes and images undergo "a protean creative redevelopment . . . in each succeeding novel."[25] The observation has been made before, but it has never been extended or its implications explored. White characteristically develops in one novel an idea hesitantly or peripherally briefly introduced in its predecessor. For example, the notion of Elyot Standish "uniting . . . the themes of so many other lives" is transformed into the "several lives of Theodora Goodman"; Alys Browne's conclusion that California was not necessary leads to Elyot's bus journey to "nowhere in particular" and Theodora's "return to Meroë"—this notion of the relationship of the human soul to geography is further transformed in *The Tree of Man* and in *Voss;* the "vivisekshunist" is briefly mentioned in Arthur Brown's poem; Mrs. Hunter's time on Brumby Island is one germ of Ellen Roxburgh/Gluyas' time on Fraser Island.

The formal structures of White's fictions have not yet been studied thoroughly; the full implications of the vexed relationship between style and vision are yet to be plumbed. The awareness of irony and of the shifting authorial stance has led to some profitable interpretations of *Voss*, but the only "new" approach discernible in published criticism of White is the one which (at last) begins to examine the local habitation and historical context of White's fiction. John Docker, in a study of "Patrick White's Australian Literary Context,"[26] shows White to be representative of a "specific Sydney post-Romantic tradition of thought" and counters the conventional view of White (expressed by admirers and detractors alike) as being unrelated to any aspects of Australian literary development. The argument advanced by Michael Cotter[27] is that White's novels reflect a set of problems and concerns which are specifically part of the Australian colonial and postcolonial situations and that *Voss, Riders in the Chariot*, and *A Fringe of Leaves* each blend "the respective mythic wisdoms of the two cultures as a unified whole." Satendra Nandan's paper,[28] printed with Cotter's in a volume that encouraged an awareness of defining national images, takes as its text V. S. Naipaul's aphorism that "living in a borrowed culture, the West Indian more than most, needs writers to tell him who he is and where he stands." Nandan explores White's interest in the artistic possibilities of the colonial situation and finds the appropriate analogues in the colonial consciousness of writers like Naipaul and Soyinka. Keith Garebian, in an article on *Voss*,[29] passingly referred to some possible American analogues; these too are clearly worth pursuing. Until recently, few articles on White were concerned with developing an approach, a critical methodology, appropriate to the form and content of his fiction. For this reason alone, it is not surprising that the hermeneutic problems attendant upon the fundamental questions of appropriate mode and the discussion of the "gap" embodied somewhere in the work were not addressed rigorously and progressively. The many unambitious readings of particular novels that have characterized most of the history of White studies are more like random, isolated raids, so that in many areas little progress has been made beyond the substantial pioneering works of the early 1960s.

Notes

1. Alan Lawson, "White for White's Sake: Studies of Patrick White's Novels," *Meanjin*, 32 (1973), 343–49.

2. Ron Shepherd, "CRNLE Patrick White Seminar," *SPAN* (Queensland), No. 6 (1978), 9–14.

3. H. P. Heseltine, "Patrick White's Style," *Quadrant*, 7, No. 3 (1963), 61–74.

4. Ingmar Björkstén, *Patrick White: A General Introduction*, trans. Stanley Gerson (St. Lucia: Univ. of Queensland Press, 1976); William Walsh, *Patrick White: Voss*, Studies in English Literature No. 62 (London: Edward Arnold, 1976); William Walsh, *Patrick White's Fiction* (Sydney: George Allen and Unwin, 1977); and, in the second category, Peter Beatson, *The Eye in the Mandala: Patrick White: A Vision of Man and God* (London: Paul Elek, 1976). I know of two other books scheduled for 1978 publication—one by John Colmer on *Riders in the Chariot* and *Patrick White: A Critical Symposium*, ed. R. Shepherd and K. Singh (Adelaide: CRNLE, 1978)—but at the time of writing I had not been able to see either of them.

5. Alan Lawson, "Unmerciful Dingoes? The Critical Reception of Patrick White," *Meanjin*, 32 (1973), 379–92.

6. Dorothy Green, "*Voss*: Stubborn Music," in *The Australian Experience: Critical Essays on Australian Novels*, ed. W. S. Ramson (Canberra: Australian National Univ. Press, 1974), p. 309.

7. Margaret Walters, "Patrick White," *New Left Review*, No. 18 (1963), 37.

8. R. P. Laidlaw, "The Complexity of *Voss*," *Southern Review* (Adelaide), 4 (1970), 3–14.

9. Peter Beatson, "The Three Stages: Mysticism in Patrick White's *Voss*," *Southerly*, 30 (1970), 111–21; Brian Kiernan, "Patrick White," in his *Images of Society and Nature: Seven Essays on Australian Novels* (Melbourne: Oxford Univ. Press, 1971), pp. 95–147; Green, "*Voss*: Stubborn Music"; Michael Cotter, "Fragmentation, Reconstitution and the Colonial Experience: The Aborigine in White's Fiction," in *South Pacific Images*, ed. Chris Tiffin (St. Lucia: S.P.A.C.L.A.L.S., 1978), pp. 173–85.

10. James McAuley, "Comment: *Voss* and the Novel," *Quadrant*, 2, No. 4 (1958), 4–5; and McAuley, "The Gothic Splendours: Patrick White's *Voss*," *Southerly*, 25 (1965), 34–44.

11. Veronica Brady, "Why Myth Matters," *Westerly*, No. 2 (1973), 59–63.

12. Brian Kiernan, "Patrick White: The Novelist and the Modern World," in

Cunning Exiles, ed. Don Anderson and Stephen Knight (London: Angus and Robertson, 1974), p. 102.

13. In *In the Making,* ed. Craig McGregor (Melbourne: Nelson, 1969), p. 221.

14. Beatson, *The Eye in the Mandala,* p. 113.

15. Kiernan, *Images of Society and Nature,* pp. 116 ff.

16. Walters, "Patrick White"; Peter Wood, "Moral Complexity in Patrick White's Novels," *Meanjin,* 21 (1962), 21–28; Leonie Kramer, "Patrick White's Götterdämmerung," *Quadrant,* 17, No. 3 (1973), 8–19; and Kramer, "*The Tree of Man:* An Essay in Scepticism," in *The Australian Experience: Critical Essays on Australian Novels,* ed. W. S. Ramson (Canberra: Australian National Univ. Press, 1974), pp. 269–83.

17. Dorothy Green, "The Edge of Error," *Quadrant,* 17, No. 5/6 (1973), 36–47.

18. Green, "*Voss:* Stubborn Music."

19. Margaret Walters, "Patrick White," 38.

20. Brian McFarlane, "Inhumanity in the Australian Novel: *Riders in the Chariot,*" *The Critical Review* (Melbourne), No. 19 (1977), 24–41.

21. George Core, "A Terrible Majesty: The Novels of Patrick White," *The Hollins Critic,* 11 (1974), 3.

22. John Cowburn, "The Metaphysics of *Voss,*" *Twentieth Century* (Melbourne), 18 (1964), 352–61.

23. Beatson, "The Three Stages: Mysticism in Patrick White's *Voss.*"

24. Chris Wallace-Crabbe, "The Solitary Shapers," in his *Melbourne or the Bush* (Sydney: Angus and Robertson, 1974), p. 3.

25. Kiernan, "Patrick White: The Novelist and the Modern World."

26. John Docker, "Patrick White's Australian Literary Context," in his *Australian Cultural Elites* (Sydney: Angus and Robertson, 1974), pp. 59–76.

27. Cotter, "Fragmentation, Reconstitution and the Colonial Experience. . . ."

28. Satendra Nandan, "Beyond Colonialism: The Artist as Healer," in Tiffin, ed., *South Pacific Images,* 11–25.

29. Keith Garebian, "The Desert and the Garden: The Theme of Completeness in *Voss,*" *Modern Fiction Studies,* 22 (1976–77), 557-69.

BIBLIOGRAPHY

PRIMARY SOURCES

The Aunt's Story. New York: Viking Press, 1948.

Big Toys. Sydney: Currency, 1977.

The Burnt Ones. New York: Viking Press, 1964.

The Cockatoos. New York: Viking Press, 1975.

The Eye of the Storm. 1973. New York: Viking Press, 1974.

Flaws in the Glass. New York: Viking Press, 1982.

A Fringe of Leaves. 1976. New York: Viking Press, 1977.

Four Plays. 1965. New York: Viking Press, 1966.

Happy Valley. London: Harrap, 1939.

The Living and the Dead. 1941. Reprint. Middlesex: Penguin, 1967.

Memoirs of Many in One by Alex Xenophon Demirjian Gray. New York: Viking Press, 1986.

Netherwood. Paddington, Australia: Currency, 1983.

Riders in the Chariot. New York: Viking Press, 1961.

Signal Driver. Sydney: Currency, 1982.

The Solid Mandala. New York: Viking Press, 1966.

Three Uneasy Pieces. Melbourne: Pascoe Publishing, 1987.

The Tree of Man. New York: Viking Press, 1955.

The Twyborn Affair. 1979. New York: Viking Press, 1980.

The Vivisector. New York: Viking Press, 1970.

Voss. New York: Viking Press, 1957.

SECONDARY SOURCES

Anderson, Don. "A Severed Leg: Anthropophagy and Communion in Patrick White's Fiction." *Southerly* 40 (1980): 399–417.

Beatson, Peter. *The Eye in the Mandala: Patrick White: A Vision of Man and God.* London: Elek, 1976.

Berg, Mari-Ann. *Aspects of Time, Ageing and Old Age in the Novels of Patrick*

White. Göthenberg Studies in English 53. Göteborg, Sweden: Gothenberg University Press, 1983.

Beston, John B. "Voss's Proposal and Laura's Acceptance Letter: The Struggle for Dominance in *Voss.*" *Quadrant* 16 (July-August 1972): 24–30.

Bliss, Carolyn. *Patrick White's Fiction: The Paradox of Fortunate Failure.* New York: St. Martin's Press, 1986.

Brady, Veronica. "*A Fringe of Leaves:* Civilization by the Skin of Our Teeth," *Southerly* 37 (1977): 123–40.

———. "The Novelist and the Reign of Necessity: Patrick White and Simone Weil." In *Patrick White: A Critical Symposium,* edited by Ron. Shepherd and Kirpal. Singh, 108–16. Bedford Park, South Australia: Flinders University Press (Centre for Research in the New Literatures in English), 1978.

———. " 'A Single Bone-Clean Button': The Achievement of Patrick White." *Literary Criterion* (Mysore, India) 15 (1980): 35–47.

———. "Patrick White and the Question of Woman." In *Who Is She?,* edited by Shirley Walker, 178–90. St. Lucia, Queensland: University of Queensland Press, 1983.

———. "A Properly Appointed Humanism: Australian Culture and the Aborigines in Patrick White's *A Fringe of Leaves.*" *Westerly* 28, no. 2 (June 1983):61–68.

Buckley, Vincent. "The Novels of Patrick White." In *The Literature of Australia,* edited by Geoffrey Dalton, 413–26. Ringwood, Victoria (Australia): Penguin, 1964.

Campbell, Ross. "Foggy Weather Over Leichhardt." *Sydney Daily Telegraph,* 15 February 1958, 18.

Carroll, Dennis. *Australian Contemporary Drama 1909–1982: A Critical Introduction.* New York: Peter Lang, 1985, esp. 107–20.

Colmer, John. "Duality in Patrick White." In Shepherd and Singh, *A Critical Symposium,* 70–76.

———. *Patrick White's "Riders in the Chariot."* London: Edward Arnold, 1978.

Docker, John. "Patrick White and Romanticism: *The Vivisector.*" *Southerly* 33 (January 1973): 44–61.

Edgecombe, Rodney S. *Vision and Style in Patrick White: A Study of Five Novels.* Tuscaloosa: Alabama University Press, 1989.

Green, Dorothy. "*Voss:* Stubborn Music." In *The Australian Experience: Critical Essays on Australian Novels,* edited by W. S. Ramson, 284–310. Canberra: Australian National University Press, 1974.

Hansson, Karin. *The Warped Universe: A Study of Imagery and Structure in Seven Novels by Patrick White.* Lund, Sweden: GWK Gleerup, 1984.

Harries, Lyndon. "The Peculiar Gifts of Patrick White." *Contemporary Literature* 19 (Autumn 1978): 459–71.

Heltay, Hilary. *The Articles and the Novelist: Reference Conventions and Reader*

Manipulation in Patrick White's Creation of Fictional Worlds. Tübingen, Germany: Gunter Narr, 1983.

Herring, Thelma. "Odyssey of a Spinster: A Study of *The Aunt's Story.*" *Southerly* 25 (1965): 6–22. Reprinted in *Ten Essays on Patrick White Selected from Southerly,* edited by G. A. Wilkes, 3–20. Sydney: Angus and Robertson, 1970.

Herring, Thelma, and G. A. Wilkes. "A Conversation with Patrick White." *Southerly* 33 (June 1973): 132–43.

Heseltine, Harry [H. P.]. "Patrick White's Style." *Quadrant* 7 (Winter 1963): 61–74.

Hope, A. D. "The Bunyip Stages a Comeback." *Sydney Morning Herald,* 16 June 1956, 15.

Kramer, Leonie. "Patrick White's Götterdämmerung." *Quadrant* 17 (May/June 1973): 8–19.

―――. "*The Tree of Man:* An Essay in Skepticism." In Ramson, *The Australian Experience,* 269–83.

Lawson, Alan. "Unmerciful Dingoes? The Critical Reception of Patrick White." *Meanjin* 32 (December 1973): 379–92.

―――. *Patrick White.* Melbourne: Oxford University Press, 1974.

―――. "Meaning and Experience: A Review-Essay on Some Recurrent Problems in Patrick White Criticism." *Texas Studies in Literature and Language* 21, no. 2 (Summer 1979): 280–95.

Le Moignan, Michael. "Novels? Patrick White Wants the Machine Gun Burst of Plays." *Sydney Morning Herald,* 23 July 1983, 33.

Mackenzie, Manfred. "Patrick White's Later Novels: A Generic Reading." *Southern Review* 1 (1965): 5–18.

Mather, Rodney. "Patrick White and Lawrence: A Contrast." *Critical Review* (Melbourne) 13 (1970): 34–50.

McCulloch, A. M. *A Tragic Vision: The Novels of Patrick White.* St. Lucia, Queensland: University of Queensland Press, 1983.

McGregor, Ian, ed. "Patrick White." In *In the Making.* 218–221. Melbourne: Thomas Nelson, 1969.

Mitchell, Adrian. "Eventually White's Language: Words and More Than Words." In Shepherd and Singh, *A Critical Symposium,* 5–16.

Morley, Patricia A. *The Mystery of Unity: Theme and Technique in the Novels of Patrick White.* Montreal: McGill-Queens University Press, 1972; St. Lucia, Queensland: University of Queensland Press, 1972.

Porter, Hal. "Patrick White." In *Contemporary Novelists,* edited by James Vinson, 1345–8. London and Chicago: St. James, 1972.

Ramson, W. S., ed. *The Australian Experience: Critical Essays on Australian Novels.* Canberra: Australian National University Press, 1974.

Scheick, William J. "The Gothic Grace and Rainbow Aesthetic of Patrick White's Fiction: An Introduction." *Texas Studies in Literature and Language* 21, no. 2 (Summer 1979): 131–46.

Shepherd, Ron. "An Indian Story: 'The Twitching Colonel.' " In Shepherd and Singh, *A Critical Symposium.* 28–33.

Shepherd, Ron, and Kirpal Singh, eds. *Patrick White: A Critical Symposium.* Bedford Park, South Australia: Flinders University Press (Centre for Research in the New Literatures in English), 1978.

Tacey, David J. "Patrick White: The End of Genius." *Meridian* (La Trobe University English Review) 5 (May 1986): 89–91.

———. *Patrick White: Fiction and the Unconscious.* Melbourne: Oxford University Press, 1988.

———. "Patrick White: The Great Mother and Her Son." *Journal of Analytical Psychology* 28 (1983): 165–83.

Walsh, William. *A Manifold Voice: Studies in Commonwealth Literature.* London: Chatto and Windus, 1970.

———. *Patrick White: "Voss."* Studies in English Literature 62. London: Edward Arnold, 1977.

———. *Patrick White's Fiction.* Totowa, N. J.: Rowman and Littlefield, 1977.

White, Patrick, "On Factual Writing and Fiction. *Australian Literary Studies* 10 (1981), 99–101.

———. "The Prodigal Son." *Australian Letters* 1 (April 1958): 37–40.

Weigel, John A. *Patrick White.* Boston: Twayne, 1983.

Wilkes, G. A. *Australian Literature: A Conspectus.* Sydney: Angus and Robertson, 1969.

Wolfe, Peter. *Laden Choirs: The Fiction of Patrick White.* Lexington: University Press of Kentucky, 1983.

INDEX